Dana Facaros and
Michael Pauls

CRETE

'A place where the colours are richer, the
peaks and mountains taller, the sun bigger,
the drink stronger, the music and dances
faster, tempers quicker, laughter easier,
perfumes more intense.'

D0599875

CADOGANguides

Contents

Reference

About the authors

Dana Facaros and **Michael Pauls** have written over 30 books for Cadogan Guides, and have been visiting, and writing about, Crete since 1977. They have lived all over Europe, and are currently installed in a venerable farmhouse in southwestern France.

About the updaters

When not updating guidebooks, **Lily Pauls** and **Jerry Hatt** live in Swansea with their pet monkeys. They are currently working on the world's first cat rap song.

Acknowledgements

A big thank-you to Andrew Bampfield and Jeremy Masters for their Latin translations, and to Nick Rider for his editing prowess. The **updaters** would like to thank Peggy Sue for not breaking down, and all the Cretans who helped along the way, especially the old man with the watermelon, Efi at Taverna Anisara in Gouvés, Stavroula and Michelis at the Venus hotel in Sitía, and Mike and Brian and their associates – Lola, Tasha, Simon, Toby, Dusty, Buster, Bonnie, Seamus and Dougal.

Cadogan Guides
Highlands House, 165 The Broadway,
London SW19 1NE
info.cadogan@virgin.net
www.cadoganguides.com

The Globe Pequot Press
246 Goose Lane, PO Box 480, Guilford,
Connecticut 06437–0480

Copyright © Dana Facaros and Michael Pauls
    1996, 2003

Cover and photo essay design by Kicca Tommasi
Book design by Andrew Barker
Cover photographs: © jon arnold/jonarnold
    images.com and ©Tim Mitchell
Maps © Cadogan Guides,
    drawn by Map Creation Ltd
Managing Editor: Christine Stroyan
Editor: Nick Rider
Art direction: Sarah Rianhard-Gardner
Proofreading: Catherine Bradley
Indexing: Isobel McLean
Production: Navigator Guides Ltd

Printed in Italy by Legoprint
A catalogue record for this book is available
    from the British Library
ISBN 1-86011-106-8

The authors and publishers have made every effort to ensure the accuracy of the information in this book at the time of going to press. However, they cannot accept any responsibility for any loss, injury or inconvenience resulting from the use of information contained in this guide.

Please help us to keep this guide up to date. We have done our best to ensure that the information in this guide is correct at the time of going to press, but places and facilities are constantly changing, and standards and prices in hotels and restaurants fluctuate. We would be delighted to receive any comments concerning existing entries or omissions. Authors of the best letters will receive a copy of the Cadogan Guide of their choice.

harbour, Móchlos

14th-century Venetian castle, Frangokástello

Ag. Triáda

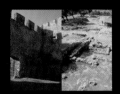

Sitía

harbour, Réthymnon

the island fortress of Gramvousa

painted pillars, Knossos

roadside shrine, Nomós Heraklion

boatmaker's workshop, Chaniá

Zambeliou street, Chaniá

Basilica of Ag. Títos, Gortyn

'Iron Gates', in the Gorge of Samariá

honey, olives and peppers, Saturday market, Heráklion

olive trees and ore-rich soil, southern Crete

freshly picked grapes, Archánes

farmhouse near Vaï

About the photographer
Tim Mitchell loves taking pictures. Based in London, he works as a travel and editorial photographer.
all pictures © Tim Mitchell   timwmitchell@yahoo.co.uk

Introduction

Chapter Divisions

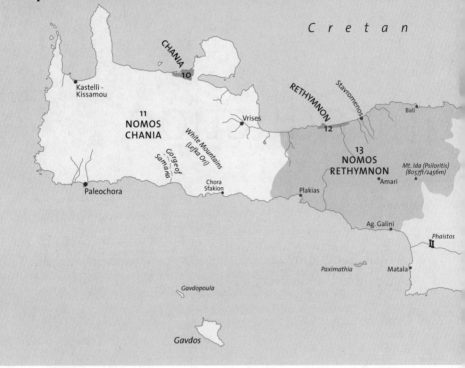

Column of the Levant,
My Crete, beautiful island,
Your soil is made of gold,
Your each stone a diamond.
                    traditional Cretan *mantináde*

Golden, diamond Crete is an enchanted isle. Other Greeks, with a mixture of envy and awe, call it the *Megalonisos*, the 'big island', a place apart, remote and often mysterious: the home of King Minos, Pasiphaë and the Minotaur, of towering snow-capped mountains that are blinding in the sun and of memory older than history, of bulls and double axes and indomitable resistance fighters against Turkish or German occupiers who believed in Freedom or Death; of yellow clouds of butterflies in jagged ravines and El Greco and shepherds improvising verses and Zeus of the thunderbolts and bare-breasted goddesses wearing scarlet lipstick, lemon groves and Zorba and Kazantzákis and wild thyme honey and Ariadne spinning on her dancing floor made by Daedalus: Crete is anything but ordinary.

Back in 1942, Henry Miller wrote, 'Crete is a cradle, an instrument, a vibrating test tube in which a volcanic experiment has been performed.' The result of the greatest of these volcanic experiments was ancient Greek culture. Many of its gods and oldest myths were born here with the Minoans, the first literate civilization on European soil, which burst into bloom like the first rapture of spring and created art

shot through with an ecstatic beauty that still thrills even after 3,500 years. Minoan Crete ruled the Aegean while the rest of Greece was just learning to speak Greek, yet up until Arthur Evans' excavations of Knossos in 1900 the sea-girt kingdom of Minos was considered only a myth. The discovery of its reality goes a long way in explaining the essential Cretan difference, the independent, freedom-loving spirit that flows in the marrow of the island's bones. Even when the Minoans declined, the Greek world still looked to Crete for religious beliefs and cults sanctified by time, and for its first laws – another former 'legend' that was confirmed in the 20th century when the oldest recorded laws in Greek were discovered in ancient Dreros, which also has the oldest known *agora*, the market and public forum that would be key to the Greek city-state ideal and the 'Greek miracle' that burst forth in the 5th century BC.

Then, having created so much, so early, the big island withdrew into its own world: familiar yet different, Greece in a magnifying glass, a disproportionate enchantment, a special world in which expectations are challenged and human limitations are constantly tested – true Cretans, *'kouzouloi'*, strive for the impossible, and will sacrifice everything to attain it. Extremes, in fact, almost come natural in a place where the colours are richer, the peaks and mountains taller, the sun bigger, the drink stronger, the music and dances faster, tempers quicker, laughter easier, perfumes more intense. Imagination is clothed in tangible, sensuous form, then melts into myths and archetypes that tease our deepest dreams.

A Little Geography

Crete (Κρήτη) on the map is an odd, horned, wasp-waisted creature that seems to scoot along the 35th parallel, midway between Europe, Africa and Asia: its south coast is only 198 miles (320km) from Egypt and further south than the Mediterranean coasts of Morocco and Algeria. It is Greece's largest island, and the fifth largest in the Mediterranean after Sicily, Sardinia, Cyprus and Corsica, roughly 160 miles long and an average of 30 miles wide (260 by 50 km). These rather limp numbers are ground into nonsense, however, by Crete's tremendous mountain ranges, especially the White Mountains (Lefká Óri) and the Idaean Mountains, centred on legendary Mount Ida or Psilorítis, both topping 8,000ft (2,400m), covered with snow each year until June and enough to make any journey from A to B an adventure. Crete simply wouldn't be Crete without this great spine: the mountains are responsible for its extraordinary beauty, its diverse climates, its independent spirit and resistance to heavy-handed invaders, be they Dorian, Roman, Venetian, Turkish or Nazi, and its tendency towards mysticism (peaks and caves – 3,000 of them – were the first shrines, even before the Minoans). Many of the same peaks and caves have churches on or in them to this day, giving perhaps a European record for continuity of worship in the same places.

Just under half a million people call Crete home, and they speak with distinct accents and dialects. There are enough local ones that a shepherd from Sfakiá in the west often cannot understand his counterpart from Sitía in the east; across Crete, linguists have found four different pronunciations of the sound *sti*, perhaps a last echo of the Achaeans, Dorians, Pelasgians and Eteocretans described by Homer in the *Odyssey*. This localism is also a matter of pride: not only do Cretans like to emphasize the things that set them apart from other Greeks, but they also like to mark out what sets them apart from other Cretans.

Unlike most Greek islands Crete rarely looks to the sea, but turns inward, self-absorbed and self-sufficient in many things. It has, in effect, only three seasons: the grey, rainy one, from November to the end of February; an exuberant spring, when nearly all its 1,500 kinds of flowers seem to bloom at once; and a dry hot summer of harvests – the Mediterranean winter, if you will. Vineyards, olive and citrus groves cover the coastal plains and hillside terraces of the north. Cereals, potatoes, pears, apples, walnuts and chestnuts come from well-watered mountain plains, especially in Lassíthi. Acres of plastic greenhouses blanket the south coast, adding no attractions to the landscape but gorging out bushels of winter vegetables and fruit for the rest of Greece, including bananas, avocados and pineapples. Sheep, goats and cattle provide protein and a variety of cheeses. Aromatic and medicinal plants are an important source of income, and in the past so much honey was exported from Crete that the island's Venetian name, Candy (from *Candia*), became synonymous with sweet things.

Crete's hot climate and bountiful beaches make it a major package holiday destination, from early spring right through to the end of October; some three million visitors arrive annually (over 40 per cent of them coming for a second time or more), adding hundreds of millions of euros to the local economy. After the Acropolis, Knossos receives more visitors than any other site in Greece, and Heráklion's

Archaeological Museum, with its wonderful Minoan collection, rivals the National Museum in Athens in admissions. Much of Crete's high-intensity tourist business, though, is concentrated on the northeast coast, with its epicentres in the holiday reservations east of Heráklion such as Chersónisos and Mália, and the rather more discreet and more upmarket resort towns around the corner near Ag. Nikólaos and the Gulf of Mirabéllo. To an extent that never fails to surprise and delight, and no matter where you stay on Crete, it's still remarkably easy to escape the crowds, just by heading a mile or two inland or down the coast – or by coming out of season.

A Guide to the Guide

The three mountain ranges of Crete neatly divide the island into four sections. These also divide modern Crete politically into its prefectures (*nomós* in Greek), which are used as convenient demarcations in this book. The first three, going from the west, are all named after their main towns – Chaniá, Réthymnon and Heráklion. Contrary to the style followed in most Crete guides, which start off in Heráklion and bounce around, the descriptions in this book run from west to east, not only for consistency's sake but also because the west really is the best introduction to Crete.

The natural point of entry into western Crete is **Chaniá**, with its airport and ferry port. Sometime capital of the island under Turkish rule, Chaniá is – despite Second World War bombing – the most elegant and attractive of all the Cretan cities, with its Venetian, Turkish and neoclassical architecture, charming hotels and buzzing café- and streetlife around its Venetian harbour. Outside the city, the prefecture of **Nomós Chaniá** is defined in dramatic strokes by the White Mountains, a string of sandy beaches and a series of spectacular keen-edged gorges that cut their way through the mountain fastness to the Libyan Sea; the Gorge of Samariá, the longest in Europe, is only the most famous. Overall, Nomós Chaniá is *the* place to go for walking, wild-flowers, wildlife and traditional mountain villages, as well as sumptuous beaches in intimate coves (especially along the west coast) and placid beachside villages such as

A Note on Transliteration and Place Names

In Greece, expect to see slight variations in the spellings of Greek place names in Roman letters. We've tried to use the forms you're most likely to see: a D when transcribing the Greek *delta* (Δ), which you may see as DH or TH to account for its soft *th* sound; a CH when transcribing *chi* (X), which is pronounced like the CH in loch, but is sometimes written as an H; and G for the Greek *gamma* (Γ), which sounds like a guttural GH verging on a Y, and is often transcribed as a Y or a GH, as in 'saint' (*ágios/áyios/ághios*). Also note that placing the stress on the right syllable (marked with an acute (´) accent) is essential to the pronunciation of Greek.

In the text, you'll find the **Greek letters for place names** which you may need to recognize when travelling, in lower case for signs that you're likely to see on back roads (to match the road signs, for those driving) and in capital letters when chances are that you'll be taking a boat or a bus.

Loutró that are ideal for travellers put off by mass tourism – even the larger 'resorts' like Chóra Sfakión or Paleochóra are laidback, mellow and never overwhelming.

East of Chaniá along the north coast lies **Réthymnon**, Crete's third city, a delightful, minaret-studded town, with as much Venetian and Turkish character as Chaniá, but which had the good fortune to suffer less bomb damage in the Second World War. It's the capital of **Nomós Réthymnon**, a smallish prefecture that forms a rugged bridge between the White Mountains and Psilorítis (Mount Ida). Its long north coast beaches contain a scattering of quite well-trodden resorts, like Pánormos or Balí; behind them, inland and to the south, there are celebrated monasteries and caves, the Amári valley and other traditional villages on the slopes of Mount Ida – many of them with exquisitely frescoed Byzantine churches – stretching down to the laid-back resort town of Ag. Galíni and the palmy beaches near Prevéli, facing the Libyan Sea.

From Réthymnon Crete's one main highway (the north coast E75) leads eastwards in about 80km to **Heráklion**, the grey, sprawling, unavoidable modern capital of Crete and fourth-largest city in Greece. Noisy, disorderly and often unloved, Heráklion is nevertheless a lively place and, more importantly for many, has within its limits a superb archaeological museum containing the great masterpieces of the Minoans, and the unmissable ruins of Knossos. Heráklion also has Crete's main airport, and is the island's often-unavoidable transport hub. **Nomós Heráklion**, between Psilorítis and the Lassíthi Mountains, contains an extraordinary range of Cretan treasures, with the biggest concentration of Minoan sites at Mália, Phaistos, Ag. Triáda, Týlisos and Archánes, together with the ruins of Crete's Dorian-Roman capital of Górtyn and the cave-lined beach of Mátala. There's also more superb scenery, especially around the Diktean mountain villages and Zarós. East of Heráklion you can find miles of excellent sandy beaches and the towns that are the prime destinations for most of Crete's package holidaymakers, all great if you want to meet lots of other foreigners and bop the night away in clubs with guest DJs. Mália and Chersónisos are big and brash, but also have a smattering of upmarket hotels, and the latter even has a new golf course. Meanwhile, though, down on the south coast anyone prepared to walk or take a boat can still find empty and often lovely beaches for themselves in lonely, rocky inlets.

East of the Lassíthi (or Diktean) Mountains is **Nomós Lassíthi**, Crete's hottest and driest region, where spring comes earlier – hence the plastic tunnels on the south coast for hothousing winter fruit and vegetables. Cosmopolitan Ag. Nikólaos is the capital, set among spectacular cliffs around the Gulf of Mirabéllo and the swish villas and art hotels on the road to the fancypants resort of Eloúnda. To the east the little city of Sitía, at the end of a spectacular corniche road, offers a quieter, more 'Cretan' alternative. Away from the towns there is plenty more to see, in the lofty Lassíthi plateau with its windmills and the Diktean cave, the frescoed church of Panagía Kéra at Kritsá, the Dorian ruins of Lato, the fortified monastery of Toploú and the palm-lined beach at Vaï. Don't neglect Lassíthi's tiny and secluded off-shore islands, such as Koufounísi, 'the Delos of Crete', Spinalónga, sandy Chrisí or the wild Dionisádes, all reachable by small boat. The Minoans were here too, leaving behind the great unpillaged palace of Zákros and the ruined city of Gourniá, and a host of minor sites scattered around the coast and into the valleys.

Mythic Crete

...[the Cretans] declare that most of the gods proceeded from Crete to many parts of the inhabited world, conferring benefits upon the race of men and sharing among each of them the benefits of their own discoveries.

Diodorus Siculus

Roman mythographers and modern scholars alike have puzzled over the complex web of tales that involve Crete. These interlaced legends lie at the very core of Greek mythology's history and meaning, and they provide any number of fascinating hints about life and religion in the time of the Minoans. In their strange, indirect way they can tell us many things the scholars of archaeology alone would never find out.

Ever since the fuzzy sciences were invented, psychologists, anthropologists, sociologists and worse have had a high time smelting down Greek mythology in their various forges, generating a modicum of good glittering gold along with impressive heaps of slag. There is more in the old myths than can be explained by any of their more modern mythologies; storytelling is one of the basic ways the human mind works, conveying a wealth of meaning on many different levels and transcending the limitations of simplistic rational thinking. Between the lines of the myths, we can read a tremendous amount of information about the hidden corners of Greek history and religion, and their ultimate sources.

Myths have no author – not even Homer. Wherever the seed of a story comes from, it is polished and refined by each generation. Long before any of these stories were ever written down, innumerable poets in the oral tradition added bits on, and meaningfully deleted or repressed others, until the story as a whole became truly an evolving product of the whole Greek people.

The most important stories often serve to chronicle, in their fashion, important changes in culture and religious conceptions, especially those stories that explain how something 'came to be': how a city was founded, or where the gods came from, or why a particular religious ritual or dance was performed. Because so much of Classical Greek religion had its beginnings with the Minoans, a thousand years and more before the Parthenon was built, it is no surprise that the important Greek tales so often find their way back to Crete.

If there is an underlying conflict, a recurring theme in Greek myth, it is the oldest battle in the world – the one between men and women, on earth and reflected in the heavens. In the 'Greek Dark Age', northern invaders brought down their patriarchal warrior society and male, all-powerful sky god and imposed it on the older societies of southern Greece, such as that of the Cretans, which were ultimately matriarchal and conserved strong traces of the original, many-faceted 'great goddess', worshipped under a hundred names across the western world.

The Rise and Fall of Zeus

It is only natural that caves feature so prominently in the myths that involve Crete; cave sanctuaries were among the most important sites for Minoan religion before the building of the temples, and a Cretan cave was the birthplace of the ruler of the gods himself. But, to begin at the beginning of time, we have Uranus (Sky), son of

Mother Earth and Chaos. Uranus was father of the Cyclopes and the Titans. The latter rebelled against his tyrannical ways, goaded on by Mother Earth and led by the youngest Titan, Cronos (Time). They crept up on their father while he was sleeping, and castrated him with a stone sickle.

The dying Uranus cursed Cronos, declaring that one of his own sons would do him the same treat, so as a preventative measure Cronos swallowed every baby his wife Rhea, daughter of the Earth, presented to him. After this had happened five times (to Hestia, Demeter, Hera, Hades and Poseidon) Rhea determined on a different fate for her sixth child, Zeus. Once he was born she smuggled him to Crete and gave Cronos a stone instead, which the old fellow duly swallowed. Mother Earth hid the baby in the Diktean cave and set young Cretan warriors called the Kouretes (*kouroi*) to guard him, with orders to shout and dance and beat their shields to drown out the baby's cries.

In the cave, Zeus was nursed by the goat-nymph Amaltheia, whose single horn was the horn of plenty, or cornucopia; her son Pan was his foster brother. According to one account, though, Zeus had a golden cradle that was hung in a tree, so that Cronos could not find him on earth or in heaven. When Zeus came of age, his mother Rhea slipped Cronos a Mickey Finn that not only laid him out, but made him vomit up the swallowed siblings; Zeus then led them in a 10-year war against Cronos and the Titans, in which the new Olympians were finally victorious. The battle of the Gods and Titans was a favourite subject of Classical temple sculpture. It signified the founding of a new cosmic order, that of the more humanized gods of Olympos.

In Classical times, Cretans took visitors to see the birthplace of Zeus in the Diktean cave; centuries later they would do the same with northern European tourists of the Romantic era, rediscovering the ancient world and its myths. Even stranger, though, Cretans of the old days liked to show their guests the *grave* of Zeus, on Mount Júktas near Knossos. Such heresy helped considerably in giving the Cretans their ancient reputation as liars, but behind the curious fancy of the greatest of the gods actually dying lies an important insight into the roots of Greek religion.

A similar theme is explored in the first great work of anthropology, Sir James Frazer's *The Golden Bough*: the 'sacred king', the symbolic consort of the great goddess for a fixed period of time, who in the earliest stages of religion was fated to be supplanted and killed by a son or a rival. Remember that Zeus himself overthrew and killed his own father. In a less direct way, mythology records Zeus' worries about suffering the same fate through his dalliance with women or goddesses whom the oracles declared were destined to bear a son greater than his father. One such was Metis. Zeus couldn't resist, and after he had his way with her he avoided danger by simply swallowing her (unnecessary, in fact, since the only offspring was the girl later born from Zeus' head – Athene). For the same reason Zeus had to give up the nereid or sea-nymph Thetis; marrying a mortal, she became the mother of Achilles.

Behind all those apparently more human gods of Olympos stand ancient, shadowy figures, transcendent goddesses and the males who were their children, their lovers and finally their victims. Before Zeus fought his way to the top he was, like almost all the other gods, a *daimon* of the year. The *kouroi* were young warriors and, as a hymn records, Zeus was 'the greatest *kouros*'. In ancient Crete, they would have danced and clashed their shields at a ritual, perhaps where one of their number 'became' the god himself, or the god's representative as sacred king. Now – there's no way to put it gracefully – a sacred king's business is to give his life for the luck of the year and the crops: as *daimon* of the year, like Jesus or John Barleycorn, he must die.

Some anthropologists trace the beginnings of change in the old religion to men's discovery of the facts of paternity – that they, too, had something to do with life and growth and keeping the world going. Whatever, somehow the boys figured out that this brand of religion was giving them a bum deal, and they became increasingly intolerant of the domination of goddesses and priestesses. At one stage, the sacred king's reign on Crete was extended to a longer astronomical cycle, the eight-year agreement of lunar and solar months, the 'marriage of sun and moon' (*see* p.33). And later, when the men were more in control of things, a substitute was found for the sacrifice of the king. These may have been more lowly human sacrifices; evidence from Cretan digs hints at this. By the more civilized time of the palaces, it was the animal associated with the sacred kings that was sacrificed – the bull. In the ocean of Greek myth, the closer you look at the history of any important god – Zeus, Dionysos, Poseidon or whoever – the more you come to realize they are essentially all the same being, and that the shadows they cast all have horns.

So the Cretans were right about Zeus' demise, although it was heresy to Classical Greeks, who had begun to imagine deity as something perfect and eternal. They ensured Cretans kept a reputation as liars all through Antiquity. The clever Cretans, however, turned this reputation into a means for torturing the brains of Classical philosophers, and all of us since, with the simplest, neatest logical paradox of all time:

> *Epimenides the Cretan says: 'All Cretans are liars.'*

Europa and her Children

So Zeus started out as a fertility god, and throughout his career as an Olympian he certainly did his best to fertilize anything in a skirt he could get his hands on. His attentions once fell on a girl named Europa, a cowherd near Tyre (in Phoenicia, now Lebanon). One day, while she was grazing her herd near the seashore, Zeus turned himself into a a beautiful white bull and insinuated himself among them. Europa, struck by his gentleness, began to play with him, but when she climbed on his back for a ride the bull immediately thundered off into the sea and did not stop until he reached Gortyn, in Crete. There, Zeus changed himself from a bull to an eagle (God knows why) and ravished poor Europa; the result was three fine boys named Minos, Rhadamanthys and Sarpedon.

What may have begun as an image of a priestess leading a bull off to the sacrifice was turned into this pretty story by later mythographers. Or not a priestess, but the Middle Eastern moon goddess Astarte, who in art was often pictured riding the bull-god El. This myth is telling us something important in Cretan religion came from the East. Basically, this girl Europa, who gave her name to an entire continent, *is* Astarte; like the sacred kings, the great goddess is visible behind a hundred different names around the Mediterranean. In Classical times Zeus was worshipped at Gortyn as 'Zeus

Asterion' – a telling example of how the male Olympian gods took over the names of their female predecessors, just as they gradually took over their rites and functions.

Although it is generally recognized that Aegean culture, including the Minoans, Mycenaeans and Cycladic peoples, was an original and independent growth, elements of Aegean religion may well have been adopted from the East. Relations and cross-influences between the Minoans and the Egyptians and Anatolian peoples make up a subject that has still not been fully explored.

King Minos and the Birth of the Minotaur

The three brothers were adopted by King Asterius (there's that name again) of Crete. By some accounts, they began to quarrel over the love of a beautiful boy named Miletus, who escaped them all and founded the famous city that bore his name on the coast of Asia Minor. Their quarrel continued when they succeeded to the Cretan throne after Asterius' death. Minos claimed primacy for himself, and justified his arrogance by stating that he was the favourite of the gods and that they would grant him anything he asked. To prove it, he made preparations for a sacrifice to Poseidon and prayed for a bull to emerge from the sea as a sign. Poseidon delivered – a beautiful white bull, no less – and Minos liked it so much that he decided to keep it for himself instead of sending it to be sacrificed.

Now, for the Greeks, a sacrifice was always part religious rite and part barbecue. Gods were content with the fat and bones, and the aroma, while the celebrants took care of the rest of the animal (much tastier, if you think about it, than communion wafers). No doubt Minos' brothers were even more cross with him after missing out on the expected feast. But he was acclaimed king, and chased the unhappy Sarpedon off to Cilicia in Asia Minor (where he became king of the Milyans). More significantly, though, Minos had also incurred the wrath of Poseidon, and this ill-tempered deity found a truly novel way of getting his revenge. He caused Minos' new bride Pasiphaë to acquire an unnatural but extremely fervent passion for this white bull.

At first the poor girl didn't know what to do, but fortunately she was able to take her problem to the master problem-solver of the age, Daedalus, who had been exiled from his native Athens for the murder of his apprentice and rival Talos, and washed up on Crete. Daedalus agreed to help her, and constructed a wooden cow big enough for Pasiphaë to fit inside, with wheels under the hooves and a trap door in just the right place. They rolled it out to where the white bull was grazing, and Pasiphaë climbed in. The wooden cow must have been quite skilfully made and more than a little attractive, as before long Pasiphaë found herself in the family way. The result, if you haven't already guessed, was the Minotaur: the body of a man with a bull's head.

What Pasiphaë thought of her new baby is not recorded, but Minos was beside himself. In the dream time of mythology, as in any other age, appearances counted for everything, and the king's first thought was making sure the neighbours didn't find out. Daedalus came in handy once again. He built the famous Labyrinth under the king's palace at Knossos, to hold the monster and conceal him.

The kingdom of Minos prospered, ruling the seas and exacting tributes from across the Mediterranean. A son of Minos, Androgeus, once visited Athens to compete in the

Athenian games, and won the prize in every sport. Either out of jealousy or because he suspected Androgeus of aiding some Athenians who were in revolt, King Aegeus of Athens had him ambushed on his way to some funeral games in Thebes, and Androgeus died in the battle. In revenge, Minos ordered the Athenians to send seven youths and seven maidens to Crete every ninth year, and when they arrived he marched them into the Labyrinth to be devoured by the Minotaur.

Theseus and Ariadne

The Athenians had twice sent consignments (chosen by lot) to Minos, and on the third occasion Theseus, hero of Athens, decided to take his place among the 14 victims to see if he could end the humiliating tribute. Like the Minotaur he was to meet, this Theseus had an interesting conception; his mother Aethra had slept in the same night with King Aegeus and Poseidon. This happened in Troezen, across the Saronic Gulf from Athens. Aegeus abandoned mother and child, as Greek heroes were wont to do, and went back to Athens, leaving his sword and sandals under a stone altar of Zeus. If when the boy grew up he proved strong enough to lift the altar and recover them, he would be welcome at Aegeus' court. When the time came, Theseus did this easily and set off for Athens, dispatching monsters and miscreants along the way, sometimes with a club and sometimes with his bare hands – among his other accomplishments Theseus was the inventor of wrestling, and knew all the good holds.

Arriving in Athens, Theseus immediately had some trouble with a wicked stepmother – none other than the famous sorceress Medea, who had taken refuge with Aegeus. Medea, being a sorceress, knew who Theseus really was; Aegeus didn't. She had convinced the king to let her poison the stranger as a spy, but Aegeus noticed the serpents (Erechtheid royal symbols) carved on Theseus' sword – the one Aegeus had left him – and knocked the cup from his hands just in time.

When Theseus set out for Crete with the tribute ship, Aegeus gave him a black sail and a white one, and bade the sailors hoist the white one if Theseus was victorious, or the black one if he had been killed by the Minotaur. There are several different versions of what Theseus actually did in Crete. The original travel writer, Pausanias, wrote in the 2nd century AD that in the Theseion, a temple still standing in Athens today, there was a famous painting of Theseus emerging from the sea, holding a ring and a crown. The story goes that Minos doubted that Theseus was really a son of Poseidon and, to make him prove it, the king threw his ring into the sea and demanded that the hero bring it back to him. Theseus swam down to the bottom and found it, with the aid of dolphins and the nereids, who took him to their palace and gave him a golden crown with rubies shaped like roses that had belonged to Thetis.

Minos' daughter Ariadne had a look at Theseus and fell in love straight away. She promised to help him deal with the Minotaur if he would carry her off with him, and asked Daedalus for a little something to help Theseus find his way through the Labyrinth. The old magician came up with something no more complicated than a ball of string (although by one account it was a magic ball of string that threaded the maze by itself). Ariadne gave it to Theseus; unwinding the thread as he went, he made his way into the Labyrinth, slew the Minotaur with his bare hands, and used the thread to retrace his steps. With the princess' help, he next freed his 13 companions. They made their way to the Greek ship and sailed off. Minos' fleet soon appeared in pursuit, but when night fell the Athenians were able to slip safely away.

They landed first on the island of Náxos, and here the story takes a strange turn. Theseus left Ariadne on Náxos, and none of the poets and mythographers could ever explain why. Her laments when she awoke to find herself alone make a touching scene in the poetry of Ovid and others, and the abandonment was a common subject for Classical painting. As a consolation prize, she got the god Dionysos, who arrived on Náxos shortly afterwards with his ivy-crowned satyrs and maenads, cymbals and drums playing, and carried Ariadne away on his ship. Divine retribution, perhaps, caught up with Theseus while his ship was approaching Athens. He hoisted the wrong sail, the black one; his father took it to mean Theseus had been killed, and threw himself from the cliffs into the sea.

What Was That All About?

Could the story of Theseus in Crete be a distant echo of a Mycenaean raid on Knossos, or the capture and sacking of the city that historians have speculated about? Athens, too, was a Mycenaean city, the only one to survive intact through the post-Mycenaean dark age; it may have taken part in a revolt against Minoan overlordship. Plutarch records an altogether different version: no Minotaur and fairy-tale motifs, but a simple naval invasion in which Theseus lands while Minos is away, kills his son Deucalion and marries Ariadne to create an alliance between Crete and Athens.

In mythology, it is often the seemingly inconsequential details that give the biggest clues. The story of Theseus and the Minotaur is set at the time of the key event in Minoan religious life – the festival held every eight years, when Athens had to send its tribute of youths and maidens to Crete. Another myth records that, every eight years, Minos conferred with his father Zeus. There is an astronomical period, known in Classical times and undoubtedly to the Minoans too, of this length. More precisely, it is 99 lunar months, the period when lunar and solar months coincide, the 'marriage of sun and moon'. This would once have been the extent of Minos' – the sacred king's – reign; by the height of Minoan civilization the great festival would have been commemorated by some important sacrifice, instead of the death of the king himself. The famous 'bull vaulting' pictured on a Knossos fresco (in Heráklion's Archaeological Museum; *see* p.188), and so many other works, has a male figure, ceremonially dyed red, representing the sun while he passes through the crescent horns of the bull.

Most writers on Crete assume automatically that the courtyard at the centre of the palace at Knossos was the site of the bull vaulting. No one has ever stopped to wonder how they got the bulls inside. The bull vaulting may indeed have been performed at this festival, but the real purpose of the courtyard is clear enough:

> ...*a dancing floor like that which once in the wide spaces of Knossos Daedalus built for Ariadne of the lovely tresses...*
>
> *Iliad*, Book XVIII

The ancient 'Labyrinth', meaning 'house of the double axe', was probably named after the complex, spiralling dance that was performed in the courtyard, heart of the ritual that accompanied the sacred marriage every eight years. The famous Phaistos Disc (in the Heráklion Archaeological Museum) seems to be a very sacred object; if it is ever deciphered, its spiralling hieroglyphic inscription may have more to say on this.

The crown that Theseus brought up from the sea and gave to Ariadne was later placed by Zeus in the heavens, and you can see it there today – *Corona Borealis*, the Northern Crown. The handle of the Plough (or Big Dipper) points towards it, and it is close enough to the Pole to be visible most of the year. Interestingly, the Celts associated this circlet of stars with Arianhrod, a version of the great goddess who, in her worship as in her name, seems to have much in common with Ariadne. Only here the constellation was not a crown but a castle, the seven-towered silver castle of Arianhrod where Celtic warriors went after their deaths.

Although it isn't mentioned in most versions of the tale, the Minotaur had a name, Asterius, which besides its associations with Astarte can be translated as the 'starry way' – interestingly, the same as the original king of Crete who adopted Minos. All this brings up the intriguing question of astronomical connections with Minoan religion and myth. Besides Ariadne's crown, on a summer night you can go out and see Amaltheia, Zeus' goat-nymph nursemaid, with her cornucopia marked in stars – none other than Capricorn. As for the white bull, it turns up later in mythology breathing fire and devastating the countryside. Capturing it was the seventh of Heracles' Twelve Labours. He brought it into Greece, where it was later killed by Theseus. The Greeks said it was the Taurus of the zodiac.

Why did Theseus jilt Ariadne? Some accounts say he had another girl, but the most coherent version of the myth is that Dionysos cast a spell over Theseus while he slept on Náxos that made him forget; this would fit in with a common fairy-tale motif. In terms of religion, the abandonment makes perfect sense. Ariadne, like her mother Pasiphaë, is only another mask for the ancient Cretan great goddess – someone the Classical Athenians, worshippers of Olympian Zeus, would rather not have had around. Not just the helpful maiden of a fairy-tale, the real Ariadne was the mistress of the Labyrinth, the goddess of the double axe – even in Classical times she survived as an orgiastic goddess who had demanded human sacrifice, worshipped in many places around Greece and as far afield as the Crimea. If Theseus and the Athenians had no use for her, she was more than welcome in the cult of Dionysos – a throwback to the old religion, with its maenads, mountain revels and tearing of raw flesh.

The End of Minos

Minos was furious when he discovered the part Daedalus had played in this business, and threw the inventor and his young son Icarus into the Labyrinth. They managed to find their way out, but escape from Crete was impossible, as Minos controlled the seas. Daedalus, though, never at a loss, decided that what they could not accomplish by sea they would do by air. He fashioned wings of feathers and wax for himself and Icarus, and on the first fine day they flew towards Asia Minor. All went well until an exhilarated Icarus disobeyed his father's command not to fly too close to the sun. The wax in his wings melted, and he plunged into the sea and drowned off the island that took his name, Ikaría.

Minos heard of Daedalus' escape and pursued him all over the Mediterranean, hoping to trap the wily inventor by offering a great reward to whoever could pass a thread through a spiralling nautilus shell. Finally, at Heracleía Minoa in Sicily, Minos gave the shell to King Cocalus, and he brought it back threaded – Daedalus was indeed there, and had performed the task by tying the thread to an ant. At once Minos demanded that the king turn Daedalus over to him. The king hedged, and invited Minos to stay at his palace. Cocalus' daughters were dismayed at the thought of losing the man who had made so many enchanting mechanical toys for them, and while Minos was in his bath they put a pipe through the ceiling and poured boiling water through it, scalding him to death. Zeus then sent him down to Hades to judge the dead, a task he shared with his brother Rhadamanthys and his enemy Aeacus.

Talos and Daedalus

His name was Talus, made of yron mould,
Immovable, resistless, without end;
Who in his hand an yron flale did hould,
With which he thresht out falshood, and did truth unfould.

> The Faerie Queene, Book V, canto I

It took considerable poetic licence to convert Talos, the Bronze Man of Crete, into the iron companion of Spenser's Sir Artegall, who in the fifth book of *The Faerie Queene* wanders the world bashing miscreants with his 'yron flale', all in the name of Justice. In Spenser's hallucinatory verse it is hard to imagine Talos as anything more than a kind of sinister motorized dustbin, or maybe a Dalek. The original Talos, though, is even stranger. Some accounts say he had a single vein, running from his head to his heel, and that he 'ran around the coasts of Crete three times a day', guarding the land; whenever enemies appeared, Talos would sink their ships by casting great boulders at them. If any enemy made it onto land, Talos would hop into a fire until he was red-hot, then seize the invader and burn him alive in his fiery metal embrace, laughing like thunder. When Jason and the Argonauts sailed by, Medea cast a hypnotic spell over him, and pulled the pin from his heel, draining away his immortal *ichor*, or blood. After death he was transformed into a partridge.

It is generally agreed that Talos was Daedalus' nephew, and both (like Theseus) were members of the Erechtheid royal house of Athens (descended from Erechtheus, the first Athenian king, who was half man and half serpent). One mythological account has Talos as the nephew of Daedalus and the father of Hephaestus, the smith-god. According to Apollodorus, Talos was Daedalus' apprentice, a clever boy who invented the compass for drawing circles, the potter's wheel and the saw, this last from observing the bones of a fish. His talent made Daedalus tremendously jealous. The master finally murdered his pupil, and escaped or was exiled to Crete.

Somehow it is all tied together – everything in mythology that has to do with making things, with the male mysteries of crafts and metallurgy that aided men in gaining their eventual religious and cultural supremacy. In the Bronze Age Aegean, the smith's art was something veiled by magic and secrecy, conducted in the *andreion*, or 'men's house', the centre of these new mysteries. One of the things a master-of-all-trades such as Daedalus would be involved with, naturally, was casting in bronze. The Minoans were skilled at this and, like other peoples around the Mediterranean, they used what is called the *cire-perdue*, or 'lost wax', method. A wax model of the desired result is made, and then the mould is formed around it. Then the mould is heated, the wax melts and pours out through a hole left in the bottom – through the heel, for a figurine or idol – and the wax is replaced by molten bronze. Now think of our bronze man Talos, with his 'single vein', and his relation Hephaestus with his lame foot (any number of smith gods from different cultures have the same curious feature, not to mention Achilles' heel, or Oedipus' lameness). Curiously, in myth all this is connected to partridges, perhaps for the hobbling way they walk. This bird may have been a kind of totem animal of the smiths.

Like Zeus, Poseidon and many other gods of Classical times, Talos began as a year *daimon*, and Daedalus probably did too. But the enduring importance of these two is their works, a reminder of how ancient Crete with its advanced culture must have truly seemed a land of sorcerers to its simpler Greek neighbours. Talos had other duties, more to do with affairs of state. It is said he carried the laws of Minos around Crete on bronze tablets to instruct the people. His three daily circuits around the island may recall a system of signal beacons that really did guard the coast. In this curious figure, the functions of artisan, magician, soldier and lawgiver are combined. The great goddess may still have ruled Crete's heart and soul, but men with their imposing works were ever more insistent on a share of recognition and power.

Demeter

And I am come from Crete across the wide sea-water wave
Homeric hymn to Demeter

The familiar tale of Demeter and her daughter, of how Persephone was abducted and taken to the underworld by Hades, has more to do with Sicily than Crete (Lake Pergusa, where it happened, is not far from Heracleia Minoa), but Demeter, like her brother Zeus, was a Cretan, and another aspect of the great goddess. The sacred myths the Minoans knew are lost to us, but it has been established that their goddesses Diktynna and Britomartis correspond neatly to Demeter and Persephone.

One story tells how at a wedding feast Demeter was seized with a sudden passion for a Titan named Iasion. He couldn't wait either, and the two of them sneaked out together and made love in the open air, in the furrow of a 'thrice-ploughed field'. As Jane Harrison wrote, this is 'one of the lovely earth-born myths that crop up now and again in Homer, telling of an older, simpler world, of gods who had only half-emerged from the natural things they are, real earth-born flesh and blood creatures, not the splendid phantoms of an imagined Olympic pageant.'

The gods of Olympos, those later creations of a sophisticated, literary age, whose temples were by Classical times little more than glorified museums, never really had much to do with genuine religion. But though the Greeks were rarely as pious a people as, say, the Romans, the religious impulse definitely existed among them, evidenced in the Orphic and Dionysian cults and especially the worship of Demeter. Here we have something ancient and conservative, relics of an old matriarchal religion that survived and prospered in men's (and especially women's) hearts despite the coming of the Olympians and the patriarchal, warrior-based society they represented. Wherever you visit sites of the Greek world, from Sicily to Syria, you will find vast numbers of little plaques and figurines on display in the museums – *ex votos*, or thank offerings, left in Demeter's temples by the common people. No other gods or goddesses commanded such popular devotion.

The most important rites involving Demeter were the Mysteries, as practised at Eleusis, near Athens, at Samothrace and elsewhere. These initiation rituals, popular until their extinction at the hands of Christianity, were kept so secret that scholars today still puzzle over what went on in the mystery caves. One thing that seems sure is that they originated in Crete, and indeed may have been a direct survival of the religion of the Minoans. Diodorus Siculus, the excellent 1st-century BC historian who tells us much of what we know about the curiosities of the Classical world, mentions that the rites other people kept secret were in Crete completely open and available to all. This in a way is what the story of Demeter and Iasion illustrates. It is likely that the climax of the Mysteries (and of the old Cretan religion) included a sexual union between the sacred king (or the initiate) and a priestess representing the goddess.

Minoan Religion

Beyond what can be inferred from myth, extremely little is known for sure about Minoan beliefs and practices. Lacking definitive texts, writers on the subject are forced into ingenious interpretations based on the evidence of paintings, seals, bronzes and such. But what if the figure apparently engaged in a religious rite really represented a character in a popular legend, a scene from everyday secular life, or a flight of the artist's fancy? Nearly everyone emphasizes that the the Minoans were a god-ridden people whose every move was determined by rituals and priestesses. But this is only because the scholars themselves have chosen to interpret the evidence this way; imagining religious associations is always the easiest way out.

Most Minoan texts so far deciphered have been simple temple records, but at least they tell us the names of some of the gods. Often even these are only aspects (additional or alternative titles) of single deities: *Potnia*, for example, the most common name of the great goddess, means 'Lady', and is often used in conjunction with other names, such as *Atana* – the origin of the Greeks' Athena. Zeus' mother Rhea and his wife Hera seem to have originated as similar titles of the Lady. One extremely ancient and important aspect of the goddess is her role as the mountaintop 'mistress of the wild things', the way she is most frequently pictured in art, between two griffins, lions or other animals. She resembles the later divine huntress Artemis, and her common name, Britomartis, gives away the connnection. But these divinities hate being pinned down to a single identity and one form always seems to shade into the next, as in the aforementioned equation of Britomartis and Diktynna with Persephone and

Demeter. Sometimes seals and gems show a male 'master of the wild things', a consort of the goddess or a later male substitution for the original. Zeus doesn't appear at all under his common Greek name, but the male *daimon* of the year is called the greatest *kouros* or Velchanos. Other male gods, or perhaps aspects of a single god, are mentioned: *Poteidan* (Poseidon), who seems to have been the most important, and also *Palaiwon* and *Enualios*, forerunners of the Greek Apollo and Ares.

'Temple', incidentally, is a word that comes easily to us, but one probably very foreign to the religious practices of the Minoans. Even the Classical Greeks did not build proper temples until quite a late date, the 8th century BC. Before then they had only sanctuaries, sites for the most important rite: the sacrifice. This was probably true for the Minoans too. Their sanctuaries would have included an altar and perhaps a sacred tree or grove of trees: oaks and olive trees seem to have been especially revered. Similar enclosed shrines are very common on Minoan seals; occasionally, in place of a tree there is a sacred pillar, perhaps like those decorated with double-axes on the Ag. Triáda sarcophagus. The goddess as 'mistress of the wild things' was worshipped in shrines on sacred mountains. These, along with the caves, such as the Diktean cave, were the most important religious sites in early Minoan times, and gradually gave way to urban 'temples' as Minoan society grew more opulent and complex.

Four striking symbols, repeated over and over in Minoan art, may be keys to understanding Minoan culture. First and most importantly, the double axe. Plenty of them, small ritual gold or bronze models with no practical use, have been unearthed and they appear frequently in art, often placed between a bull's horns or atop a pillar. They are commonly associated with the Cretan goddess or goddesses; the double axe is the *labrys* in Greek, after which the Labyrinth was named. Bulls and bulls' horns are equally common, from those that appear on seal rings to architectural versions decorating the cornices of Knossos. A third symbol is the sacral knot, a looped strip of cloth with fringed ends extending downwards. These commonly occur on female figures, but the Minoans left us with no real hints as to their significance. The fourth is the shield, a figure-eight shape reminiscent of the double axe in its symmetry. These are the shields that the *kouroi* clashed in their dance at the birth (and death) of Zeus. Real ones would have been made, not surprisingly, from the hides of bulls.

Looking at Minoan art or trying to figure out the puzzle of their culture, it's only natural to ask sometimes 'What were these people on?' The answers are wine, obviously, as in the later cult of Dionysos, but also opium. Statuettes of goddesses with crowns of opium poppy heads have been discovered, and a common decorative motif usually called a 'rosette' probably represents the top of a poppy head as well. This, perhaps, explains a lot, but nevertheless there is still so very much about the Minoans that we may never understand. If the Minoans did in plain sight what were Mysteries for others, why should their ways remain so mysterious to us?

Contemplating other ancient cultures, we find it hard to resist the tendency to put their rulers, gods and celebrants into our shoes, and make them think and act as we would. With the Minoans this never seems to work; they are simply too *different*, and therein lies their special fascination. They remind us that this world of ours is a wide and a strange one, capable of more surprises and more delights than we know.

History

04

Crete has been called the 'Cradle of Europe', and the mysterious legends and above all the matchless art of Minoan Crete exert a special fascination. Poetically, we know the island first from Homer:

> One of the great islands of the world in midsea, in the winedark sea, is Krete: spacious and rich and populous, with ninety cities and a mingling of tongues. Akhaians there are found, along with Kretan hillmen of the old stock, and Kydonians, Dorians in three blood-lines, Pelasgians – and one among their ninety towns is Knossos. Here lived King Minos, whom great Zeus received every ninth year in private council.
>
> *Odyssey*, book XIX, translated by Robert Fitzgerald

Myths hinted obscurely at an age when Crete had been much more important than it was in Homer's time, but it was not until 1900 and the discoveries of Arthur Evans that Europe's first great civilization rose up again from historical oblivion. We learned in school to think of everything before the Dark Ages as 'Classical Antiquity', and everything before that as 'Prehistory', but the astounding archaeological discoveries of the 20th century have cast our horizons much further back in time. There was another dark age, the one from which Classical Greece grew, and before that another era of culture, another world full of marvels. Between 2000 and 1100 BC, this world saw many great civilizations thrive: the Mesopotamian, the Hittite, the Egyptian and, perhaps most marvellous of all, the Aegean civilization of Crete and Mycenae.

6200–1900 BC
In which a dinner of bread, wine and olives helps the Cretans to a culturally precocious start

The first radiocarbon dates for settlement in Crete are placed at 6200–5800 BC. It may seem surprising that people at that early date were able to make the sea voyage (most likely from modern Turkey) to get there, but Neolithic peoples seem to have liked messing about in boats. On Crete they developed their own Neolithic society, practising agriculture and living in mud-brick houses or in caves. They built villages at Knossos and other future Minoan sites, with rooms clustered around a central open area, presaging the layout of the famous palaces. They worshipped goddesses in the depths of caves and on top of mountains – the later peak sanctuaries of the Minoans.

Until recently it was believed Minoan civilization, like every other early European culture, appeared as a result of learning new techniques and ideas from the Middle East. But as the archaeological record fills out it becomes increasingly clear that growth and development were original and independent: the Aegean area is one of the true cradles of culture. Evidence is also accumulating that Minoan Crete was not a radical break with the past or a sudden dramatic blossoming of culture. Continuity was one of its prime features, change gradual and evolutionary. Most main centres of Neolithic Crete, though, were in the same locations as those used during the palace culture – so that when the palace builders changed the landscape around them for their new creations, they effectively destroyed any record of what had gone before.

Long before the palaces, though, before 2000 BC, Cretans practised metallurgy, built imposing buildings (like the one recently discovered at Vassilíki) and made excellent ceramics and jewellery, exporting them around the eastern Mediterranean. The population grew steadily through the third millennium BC, implying a relatively peaceful life and continual improvements in technology. Bronze casting was imported from the Balkans or the Middle East, resulting in better tools and weapons, but the great advances of the late Neolithic Aegean area were agricultural: the development of the essential Greek way of life, depending on the triad of the olive, the grape and an early form of wheat. All three can be easily stored, and olives and grapes require little labour. These three blessings of nature made greater surpluses and more leisure possible – a perfect diet for any Neolithic people looking for cultural advancement.

'Neolithic' is supposed to mean 'late Stone Age', but in many places Neolithic people already worked bronze – shouldn't they be in the Bronze Age? This is an indication of the re-evaluation archaeology is beset by these days, thanks to new discoveries and the refinement of carbon dating. Terms such as 'Bronze Age' and 'Copper Age', or classifications by tool use, have become very hard to define – although you still see them in books and museums. The past is getting more complicated all the time.

An alternative way to come to terms with it on Crete is to call the latter half of this era the **Pre-Palatial period** (2600–1900 BC), following Professor Níkos Pláton's useful revision of Evans' original chronology. This was when Minoan culture really took off, as evidenced by the first monumental *tholos* tombs (as at Archánes), the building of sanctuaries at the highest points of settlements, and the apparent beginning of a ruling or priestly (or priestess) class, dwelling in palaces or temples with red-plastered walls. Trade contacts were established with Egypt, the Cyclades and the Middle East. The Minoan taste for refinement shines through at the end of the period, in exquisite work in gold, semi-precious stones and miniature sealstones, some bearing the first signs of writing in ideograms. It is interesting to note that Crete in this era was already exporting, not importing, high-quality finished goods. More Cretan items are found in Egypt and the Middle East than items from those places in Crete. The island may not have produced great monuments like the pyramids and ziggurats, but in many other ways it may already have been the most advanced culture around.

1900–1700 BC
The Caphtorites found an empire, and build great palaces without telling anyone whom they were for

When Arthur Evans began excavating Knossos, he found a completely unknown culture and was forced to give it a name: he labelled it 'Minoan' after the legendary King Minos. And everyone will probably go on calling them Minoans, even though ancient records have finally provided the people of old Crete with a name of their own: the Egyptians called Cretans *Keftiu*, and they appear in Syrian inscriptions as the *Caphtorites*, who also feature in the Old Testament. 'Minos', incidentally, denotes a title rather than any individual, from the Egyptian *menes*, a royal title taken from the name of the founder of a contemporary reigning dynasty. Cretan kings, though, were probably religious figureheads with little political power (*see* **Mythic Crete**).

It is about 1900 BC that these Caphtorites begin to make a name for themselves. Pláton's **Old Palace period** (Evans' Middle Minoan: 1900–1700 BC) saw a hitherto unheard-of concentration of wealth and power in Crete. Built over the sites of simpler predecessors, the 'palaces' of Knossos, Mália, Phaistos and Zákros appear. Some argue these buildings are really temples, or even the shrines of a cult of the dead. We may never know their purpose, and it is likely the reality would not make a perfect fit with our conceptions of either a 'palace' or a 'temple'. They may have been a little of both. The rulers at Knossos may have been kings or queens or chiefs, colleges of priestesses or priests, or there may even have been citizen democracies like the later Greek city-states – the evidence gives so few clues that no idea can be totally discounted.

Whatever the truth may have been, 'palaces' seems as good a word as any for the great building complexes; they were kitted out with the first known plumbing, and lavishly decorated with frescoes and stylized sacred 'horns of consecration'. The vast storehouses on the lower levels at Knossos and (on a lesser scale) other palaces hint at a role as 'centres of redistribution': in other words, treasuries. Goods collected as taxes could be stored there and later redistributed among the needy, traded for profit or used to finance foreign adventures or public works. Some imaginative writers have seen the Minoan system as primitive communism, others as royal tyranny; again, we know little of the truth of the arrangement. Certainly the palaces were the economic centres of Cretan life, and in this era the new cities of Crete grew up around them.

Both towns and palaces were unfortified, suggesting political unity on the island, or at least close cooperation among various city-states, and supporting the references in myth to a thalassocracy, or sea empire; no walls were needed, thanks to the Minoans' powerful fleet. Their ships traded with Cyprus, Egypt and the Greek islands; Egypt in particular seems to have had a strong influence on Cretan religion and culture. Minoan colonies have also been found at Kéa, Mílos and Kýthera. There was a system of writing in ideograms, most famously on the undeciphered Phaistos disc in the Heráklion museum. Roads paved with flagstones crossed the island, and the first large irrigation projects were dug. Art reached new heights in stonecarving, fresco painting and pottery. In 1700 BC a huge earthquake ripped across the eastern Mediterranean and devastated the buildings, but this did not mean the end of Minoan culture, or even a serious setback. The best was yet to come.

1700–1100 BC
A great civilization reaches its height – and we still don't really know what was going on in it

Forced to start afresh, the Minoans rebuilt better than ever in the **New Palace period** (1700–1450 BC). Palace complexes were rebuilt in the same style: a warren of rooms, illuminated by light wells, around a central court where religious ceremonies took place. To build the new palaces with more 'give' in case of earthquakes, wooden beams and columns (the distinctive reversed cedar trunks, thin at the bottom and wide at the top) were combined with stone. Workshops and vast storerooms clustered around the palaces, the contents of the latter recorded on clay tablets in a writing system known as Linear A. Fancy villas were built outside the palaces, most famously at Ag. Triáda, and scattered throughout the countryside were farms, with pottery kilns, wine presses and looms. Densely populated towns have been excavated at Gourniá, Móchlos, Palaíkastro, Zákros and Psíra island. Some of the houses show traces of frescoes like those in the palaces – one of many clues that prosperity was widespread, not limited to the palace élite. Burials became more elaborate, their paraphernalia more monumental, more various; many people were interred in painted clay sarcophagi, or *larnaxes*, possibly an Egyptian influence. Impressive port facilities were built, especially along the north and east coasts, and shields, daggers, swords and helmets have been discovered, although land defences have never been found.

If Cretans themselves had little need for weapons or town walls, their nation was throwing a big shadow across the Aegean and perhaps beyond. New trade counters were established on Santoríni, Rhodes, Skópelos, and the mainland of Greece and Asia Minor; script similar to Linear A has been found as far west as Panarea, an island off the north coast of Sicily. Miletus, the very ancient city that was long the metropolis of western Asia Minor, seems to have been of Cretan foundation. Nearby peoples, the Lycians and Carians, had strong ties to Crete, as did the more distant Pulesati – the Philistines of the Old Testament. Greek myths are filled with echoes of Minoan colonization, or settlement, or conquest, or whatever it was – remember, for example, the story of Minos' brother Sarpedon going off to become king of Cilicia. Place names also give clues. Gaza, for one, a major religious centre in Classical times, was originally called Minoa, and there is a Heracleia Minoa on the southern coast of Sicily, near the place where Minos, searching for Daedalus, is said to have met his end.

One thing that's certain is that this Cretan 'empire' did not include Mycenaean Greece. Until about 1550 BC mainland Greeks had little culture to speak of, but from then on we see an impressive flowering of the arts, heavily influenced by Crete. The Mycenaean city-states grew rapidly in wealth and power, and one intriguing interpretation of the admittedly scanty evidence on Crete has the 17th century BC as a time of invasions, in which Greeks from the mainland conquered the island to head a mixed, Greek-run society that managed to maintain its prosperity and cultural brilliance. As we will see, this is just what most historians assume happened later, in 1450. Some day perhaps more sources will appear, and be deciphered, to clear all this up.

One of the longest-running arguments about ancient Crete centres on just what happened to bring the great Middle Minoan period to an end. Until recently the consensus was that the great eruption of Santoríni, c. 1450 BC, and its tidal waves and earthquakes left Crete in ruins – in some places on the north coast an eight-inch layer of *tefra* (volcanic ash) has been found. This was the time when Knossos and the other palaces were destroyed. Unfortunately, refinement in carbon dating now suggests the eruption took place about a half-century earlier. In another theory invaders from Mycenaean Greece torched the palaces and took over the country. But, as ever in Minoan affairs, theories are cheap and conclusive evidence completely lacking.

The end of the palaces marks the beginning of the **Late Minoan** or **Post-Palace period** (1450–1100 BC). Many scholars now believe that Mycenaean infiltration was much more gradual, and that for a long time the Mycenaeans co-existed peacefully with the Minoans. Since we know nothing of the politics of the time, this, too, is only speculation; the destruction of the palaces could as easily have been the result of civil strife or revolution. What is certain is that cultural and political supremacy passed to the Greek mainland, to Mycenae and other city-states of the Peloponnese. Of the Cretan palaces, only Knossos was rebuilt; interestingly, the only important new section from this time was the so-called 'throne room', perhaps implying a royal ruler and a more centralized state. The Knossos palace burned once and for all *c.* 1380 BC. In other places, such as Ag. Triáda, Mycenaean palaces or *megarons* have been found. Linear B became the primary script (in Mycenaean Greek, replacing the undeciphered native language in Linear A), and the free, natural decoration of Cretan art became more conventional and stylized, as it always was in Mycenae. The island maintained its great fleet, and according to Homer contributed 90 ships to the Trojan War.

The really big troubles began around 1200, a time of upheavals all around the Mediterranean world (the usual date given for the fall of Troy is 1180 BC; some now say 1250). The Egyptians were plagued by a host of invaders that included the 'Ahhiwasha' – Homer's Achaeans – who were Greeks, of course. Confusingly enough, archaeologists record that about the same time the Achaeans' Mycenaean civilization itself was destroyed. The champion hoodlums among the Greeks seem to have been the Dorians, a people with few manners but advanced iron weapons who came down from Epirus in northwestern Greece to conquer the Peloponnese about 1200 BC. Crete was spared for another century, but the Dorians conquered it too about 1100 BC.

1100–67 BC
A long period of conservative rule, under which Crete declines to participate in Greece's Classical Age

The coming of the Dorians brought a cultural Dark Age to the whole Greek world. On Crete the Minoans lived on as a subject people, although some, known as the *Eteocretans* or true Cretans, took to the hills, especially south of Sitía. Their art grew weird and misshapen in decline; in Praisós they left mysterious inscriptions in the Greek alphabet, still waiting to be translated. Other Cretans were treated according to the amount of resistance they offered the Dorians; those who fought the most were divided among the conquerors as slaves. Burials of this period begin to show a sharp difference between a small class of wealthy aristocrats and the impoverished masses – rather like the divisions of feudal society in western Europe in the later Dark Age.

For nearly a thousand years the Cretan cities were ruled as aristocratic republics, where a small class of Dorian landholders elected committees called *kosmoi*. As in Sparta, another Dorian land, the population was split into three castes: free citizens (mostly descendants of Dorian warriors); the *perioeci*, free people with no political rights, such as artisans, merchants and seamen; and slaves, of individuals or the state.

By 900 BC Crete was divided, like the Greek mainland, into autonomous city-states: a hundred, according to ancient writers. The Minoan goddesses were dragooned into the patriarchal Greek pantheon – Atana became Athena, Britomartis Artemis, her son and consort Welchanos Zeus, father of the gods. The 8th century brought rapid cultural and economic advance throughout the Greek world and, at least in the beginning, Crete seems to have shared fully in it. New towns were founded far from traditional Minoan centres (Lato, Dreros, Aptera, Polyrenia), nearly all perched high over the sea and bristling with walls, looking down to their harbours. Overcrowded Greek towns sent out colonies across the Mediterranean, and the Cretans with their maritime tradition seem at first to have been in the forefront. Doric Crete was also one of the art centres of Greece in the Archaic period (650–550 BC).

Something – there isn't enough evidence to know exactly what – happened about 600 BC; after that date the number and quality of finds drop off drastically. Herodotus and other writers hint at civil wars on the island, but the crucial factor in Crete's new decline was probably the expansion of Ionian influence in the Aegean. Athens, Miletus and the other Ionian cities were elbowing out Cretan manufactures and trade. Crete would have been hindered by its reactionary Doric constitution, which discouraged expansion and trade; as a kind of political Sparta, trying to play the cultural and economic role of an Athens, Crete could never have gone very far.

The rest of the Greek world was entering its Classical Age. During this period Crete sat out on the margins of history, its cities wasting their energies in countless petty wars against each other. Many Cretans fled their increasingly impoverished island for a soldier's life; Cretan mercenaries are frequently mentioned, from the Peloponnesian Wars to the campaigns of Alexander the Great and Julius Caesar. Spartan influence remained strong on Crete until about 250 BC, when much of the island became a protectorate of the Ptolemies, the Greek rulers of Egypt. Other towns fell under the sway of other Hellenistic states, such as Macedonia or the Seleucid Empire (both, like Ptolemaic Egypt, fragments of Alexander's short-lived empire). Still, warfare between the towns continued unabated, often reaching frightful excesses such as the total destruction of Lyttos by Knossos in 220 BC.

Not long after that event, an unusual attempt at unification was made under a pan-Cretan council called the *koinon*, in which all cities were to have equal rights. This *koinon* is not well documented, and it does not seem to have had much effect on the prevailing fratricidal anarchy. Some of the towns with fleets turned to piracy in this period, which brought in the Aegean's biggest maritime power, Rhodes, which built up a sphere of influence in the east of the island.

A menace much greater than Rhodes was already looming in the west. Fresh from its final victory over Carthage in the Punic Wars, the incredibly strange (from a Greek point of view) and bellicose Roman Republic was proceeding to its easy conquest of the Greek East. Gortyn, then the strongest Cretan city, was an early centre of pro-Roman sentiment (though it was briefly embarrassed when Hannibal took refuge there on his escape from the Romans). Knossos, Gortyn's arch enemy, logically became the leader of anti-Roman opposition. Pirates were still active in Cretan ports, leading Rome to plan the conquest of the island in 74 BC. The job was entrusted to a senator named Marcus Antonius – father of the more famous Mark Antony, no less. Unfortunately for him, the Cretans gave his fleet a sound whipping before it ever landed any troops, earning Marcus Antonius the derisive title of 'the Cretan'. Unfortunately for Crete, this only served to make the Romans thoroughly angry. They succeeded in landing a huge force in 69 BC and, despite the wholehearted resistance of a finally united island, the legions wiped out all resistance within two years.

67 BC–AD 1204

Thirteen rather nondescript centuries, decorated by dour Romans, piratical Arabs and perfumed Byzantines

Under Roman rule the centre of power on the island moved south to Gortyn on the fertile Mesará plain, which was made capital of the province of 'Crete and Cyrene' (Libya). Knossos, wrecked in the conquest, was refounded as a Roman colony, called *Colonia Julia Nobilis* and settled largely by Italians from Capua.

With peace established, Crete's population grew to some 300,000. The Romans, always more respectful towards Greeks than other subject peoples, largely left Crete and its institutions alone. The *koinon* continued to function, and towns minted their own coins and ran their own affairs. Wealth and trade increased, and public works appeared. Christianity came early; St Paul, who rarely had a good word to say about the Cretans, appointed one of his Greek disciples, Titus, to found the first church at Gortyn in 58 AD; this suggests Crete had a sizeable Jewish community. Christian Crete prospered especially after the founding of Constantinople in 330, when basilicas were built across the island, at Knossos, Chersónisos, Gortyn, Líssos, Sýia, Ítanos and Kainoúrios – although in these first years the church in Crete was subject to Rome.

After the collapse of Rome itself, Crete continued as a provincial backwater under the eastern, Byzantine empire. Chroniclers of this period mention only a few minor disasters: two terrible earthquakes that levelled most of Gortyn in the 6th century, a plague or two, and a raid by Slavic pirates in 623. This last event presaged Byzantine weakness and greater troubles to come. Muslim Arabs, expanding in every direction in the first generations after Mohammed, first raided the Cretan coast in 656. Their attacks on the island continued, until the Arabs took control of the entire island in 824, taking advantage of the distractions caused by the fury over the iconoclastic controversy on Crete. The new conquerors, however, had not come from nearby Egypt or Sicily: they came from, of all places, Spain. After some civil strife in the Caliphate of Andalusia, a losing faction under Abu Hafs 'Umar fled to the East in 40 ships. After briefly occupying Alexandria, they turned their attentions to Crete, as a safe refuge.

One lasting feature of their stay was the building of the first castle at Heráklion, called *al-Khandaq* ('the ditch'), or Candia, a name that grew to mean all of Crete in the Middle Ages (and eventually became synonymous with the sweet honey and nuts it exported, hence 'candy'). The century of the Arab Emirate of Crete is also remembered in some village names, such as Sarkenos and Aposalemis (Abu Salim), but the occupation was too short to effect substantial changes (or many religious conversions), nor did the Arab rulers achieve much in either culture or commerce. What they were good at, following the old Cretan tradition, was piracy. Cretan fleets ravaged the Greek islands, and even sacked Thessalonika and Mount Athos.

In 961 Byzantine general and later emperor Nikephóros Phokás reconquered Crete, with massacres and looting that put the pirates' best efforts to shame, and sent the pirates' treasure off to Constantinople. Victorious Greek soldiers were among the first new colonists given tracts of land, in an attempt at repopulation; Emperor Alexius I Comnenus later sent his own son and other young Byzantine aristocrats to Crete as a ruling class of landowning *archons*, which would dominate Cretan life for centuries.

1204–1669
In which the Lion of St Mark plants his heavy paw on the island, and keeps it there for 400 years

To a land power in any age, Crete is of little importance; this is why the Arab caliphs, never great seafarers, made little effort to keep it. To a state whose future lay in controlling the trade routes of the eastern Mediterranean, however, Crete meant everything. And just such a state was growing up at this time: a true thalassocracy King Minos would have appreciated – the Republic of Venice.

Venice engineered the conquest of Constantinople in the Fourth Crusade in 1204. In the division of the spoils Crete was given to a Frankish baron, Boniface of Montferrat. Having no use for it, he sold the island cheap to the Venetians who, after a brief tussle with arch-rival Genoa, occupied Crete in 1210. Venice did everything she could to hold on to it, as the key to her interests in the East, and kept the island until 1669.

The first two centuries of rule by the Most Serene Republic proved neither serene nor republican. The Venetians high-handedly imposed their model of government; the island was even divided into six *sestieri* like Venice itself and ruled by its own doge, or *duca*, based in Heráklion. Laws attempted to diminish the influence of the Orthodox Church and replaced the Orthodox hierarchy with a Catholic one. This, along with high taxes for defence and forced labour on Venetian galleys, caused over a dozen serious revolts, often led by the *archons*, the old Byzantine nobles. Nearly every time they won important concessions from the Venetians until, by the 15th century, the Greek Orthodox population and Venetian Catholics (some 10,000) lived in reasonable harmony – except of course for the majority, the *villani* or serfs, who in addition to working long hours for their lords were compelled to build the immense walls around the cities, even though they were not allowed to live inside them.

Cretan–Venetian relations were cemented with the fall of Constantinople in 1453, when the Venetians were keen to keep the Greeks on their side. In accordance with Greece's age-old tradition of absorbing the invader, many Venetians were hellenized, spoke Greek more than Italian and converted to Orthodoxy. A refuge for scholars and painters from Constantinople and mainland Greece, Crete became the centre of Greek culture and key point of contact between the East and the Italian Renaissance. In the 15th and 16th centuries Cretans were prominent among the large community of learned Greeks in Venice, giving the Renaissance a big push by reprinting and translating countless classical works previously unknown or inaccessible in the West. Crete produced, among other artists, Doménikos Theotokópoulos, who moved to Venice and later Spain, where he became known as El Greco. Creto-Venetian schools and academies, architecture, theatre, literature, song and romantic epic poetry blossomed, culminating in the dialect epic poem *Erotókritos* by Vicénzo Kornáros.

The fall of Constantinople, and the end of the Byzantine Empire, replaced Venice's old, decrepit Christian enemy with a young, ambitious and formidably strong Muslim foe: the Ottoman Turks. By 1500 they had a fleet to match that of Venice, designed to gain control of the eastern Mediterranean and perhaps areas beyond. Crete once again found itself living in interesting times.

Although pirate raids by such famous nasties as Barbarossa and his successor Dragut (both Greek by birth) were a constant menace in the 1500s, the tremendous coastal fortifications the Venetians had forced the Cretans to pay for finally proved their worth. The island held out until 1571, when the battle of Lepanto put an end to the first great wave of Ottoman expansion and ushered in a long period of relative tranquility. Even so, Crete was left in isolation as the only important bastion of Christian Europe in the East. By the 17th century Venice was entering on its own long economic and military decline, and it was clear that the Turks would be back as soon as they felt strong enough to try.

In 1645, Sultan Ibrahim declared war on the Knights of Malta after the privateering knights supposedly captured his wife and son as they sailed to Mecca. There is no evidence such a thing actually happened – it may have been just a pretext – but the sultan accused the Venetians on Crete of aiding the pirates and sent a fleet of 450 ships after them. They stopped in Kýthera to buy coffee and sugar, and the Venetian commander there sent word to his counterpart in Chaniá to allow the fleet safe passage. On 12 June, the sultan's ships turned their guns on the city, which fell after a siege of two months. Réthymnon shared its fate a year later. The Turks turned their attentions to the capital soon after, but Heráklion, with the strongest fortifications in the eastern Mediterranean, proved a tougher nut to crack. The siege dragged on for years, a major embarrassment for the Turks. In 1666 the sultan had his commander beheaded, replacing him with the extremely capable Grand Vezir Ahmet Köprülü.

Now the battle recommenced in earnest. The European powers, finally realizing the seriousness of the struggle, sent help. The Spaniards sent food, ships and money, and troops came from Italy, France and even some of the German states. It proved too little and too late, and the western commanders often made things worse by quarrelling among themselves. After 21 years of siege, one of the longest in history, Heráklion fell in September 1669. The Venetians negotiated a liberal surrender: they were allowed to leave in peace, and the entire population of the city with them. Venice continued to keep a few coastal strongholds, tiny islet pinpricks in the Ottomans' side, and refuges for rebellious Cretans, always hoping to recapture the island. In 1692 a Venetian force unsuccessfully attempted to retake Chaniá. This proved to be the last gasp. The remaining three Venetian toeholds, Spinalónga, Néa Soúda and Gramvoúsa, were handed over by treaty in 1715.

1669–1898

In which the Cretans come under Turkish rule – a marriage made in heaven

As the Greeks tell it, the period of Ottoman rule was one long night of indescribable cruelty and oppression. But, as always in this part of the world, their version is best taken with a large pinch of salt. Certainly, after the ravages of the long war, Crete was depopulated and its towns in ruins. The Ottomans piled on more misery with taxes perhaps even worse than Venice's, and quartered large numbers of their mercenary soldiers or janissaries on Crete – probably to get them far away from Constantinople. The janissaries, once the finest fighting force in the world, had degenerated into a lawless band only interested in enriching themselves. Their outrages against the population became legendary, and civilian governors could do little against them.

The Turks did expel Italian Catholics and restore the Orthodox Church to primacy, but their occupation was also marked by huge numbers of Cretans converting to Islam, often whole villages at a time – and often significantly motivated by the higher taxes levied against infidels. Turkish settlers were also encouraged to come to Crete, and by the late 18th century nearly half the population was Muslim.

The Turks attempted to restore Crete's towns and trade, but in a time of economic decline throughout the region the odds were hardly in their favour. Heráklion in particular recovered slowly, and travellers of the time report Crete looking sad and impoverished. Still, in the 1700s things began to pick up. Crete exported grain around the eastern Mediterranean and as far as France, while manufacture in the towns began to grow again, especially soap-making, a new use for Crete's excellent olive oil.

One small corner of Crete was not included in the regular Turkish system – Sfakiá, the wild mountainous region on the southern coast. After the Turkish conquest the sultan donated it to the holy cities of Mecca and Medina, and imposed a religious tithe on the Sfakians in place of the usual taxes. This wasn't the most generous of gifts; Sfakiá was near-inaccessible by land, with a long tradition of independence, and no ruler ever found it easy to squeeze cash out of it. In the 18th century the Sfakians began to build boats and go into the shipping trade – a phenomenon familiar on islands such as Chíos, and the beginning of modern Greece's shipping interests.

Sfakiá's tradition of freedom, its isolation and the progressive outlook fostered by trade made it the natural focus for a century of revolts – over 400 of them – until Crete won its independence. From the first years of Turkish rule, mountain bandits called *hayins* (similar to the *klephts* on the mainland) made trouble for the Ottoman government, but the first organized revolt did not come until 1770. The Daskaloyánnis Rebellion, which began in Sfakiá, was brutally repressed in 1771 when aid promised by the Russians – fellow Orthodox and the Turks' worst enemies – never materialized.

The next big outbreak came in 1821. While the rest of Greece was fighting for its independence, a revolt began once again in Sfakiá and spread across the island. The Cretans formed a general assembly and held most of the island, but the tide turned against them with the arrival of Egyptian troops led by Mehmet Ali. The Egyptians subdued the last rebels in 1824, but then the next year the revolt started up again.

A pattern was becoming familiar: the Cretans would liberate the countryside, while the Turks (or Egyptians) would wait inside the still-formidable Venetian walls of the towns for help to arrive. When it did, a few villages would be burned, the rebels would surrender, and next year the whole cycle could start again. By 1830 the Cretans were actually close to victory, but their fight was betrayed, as Cretans like to put it, by the new thalassocracy in the neighbourhood, Britain, which opposed Greece gaining control of Crete and forced a diplomatic solution under which Mehmet Ali would rule the island. British warships forced the surrender of rebel strongholds on the coast.

Egyptian rule lasted only a decade, but proved a surprisingly liberal and beneficial regime, under which some long-needed roads and public works were begun. This was not enough for the Cretans, who were set on union with newly independent Greece. The disruption and tensions caused by endless revolts had led many Muslim Cretans to emigrate by this time, and their numbers fell to under a quarter of the population.

The revolts continued, especially after military embarrassments in Syria forced the Egyptians to give Crete back to their Turkish bosses in 1840. The Cretans gained a charter and an elected assembly from the increasingly weak Ottoman state, but this only fuelled their campaign for freedom. An 1866 revolt witnessed a dramatic event. When Turkish troops were on the point of taking a rebel stronghold, the monastery at Arkádi, the revolutionaries ignited a munitions store inside, killing themselves, many Turks – and most of the 600 women and children who had taken refuge there. This bizarre act of mad bravery caught Europe's attention, and even gained sympathy for the rebels' cause. It was clear the 'Cretan Question' would finally have to be faced.

Another major revolt, in 1878, secured Cretans the right to a Christian governor. In 1898, Greece declared war on Turkey, and asked the Great Powers for aid. Britain did little, in spite of searing accounts of atrocities sent home by Arthur Evans, until the Turks made the fatal mistake of killing the British consul and 14 British soldiers in Heráklion. As British, French, Russian and Italian troops landed on the island, Prince George of Greece was appointed High Commissioner of an 'autonomous' Crete; the Powers, for their own reasons, were still not ready to permit union with Greece.

1898–the Present
The Nazis come for a Mediterranean holiday and find both the accommodation and service deplorable

Independent Crete is a curiosity perhaps known only to philatelists. The most long lasting effect of the brief but well-timed period of independence was a law to forbid the export of antiquities found on the island, allowing it to keep all the Minoan finds from the excavations of Evans and the others, instead of seeing them shanghaied off to the National Museum in Athens. At the start, the islanders worked in earnest to create all the institutions of an independent state. Prince George proved a repressive autocrat, and his high-handed actions resulted in the Revolution of Thérisso in 1905, led by his Justice Minister, Elefthérios Venizélos of Chaniá. Now Crete was fully independent, but a large majority still favoured *enosis*, union with Greece, and everyone knew this would be only a matter of time. Crete had become the hot political issue in Greece itself. In 1909 Venizélos was appointed Greek Prime Minister, a position that enabled him to secure Crete's union with Greece after the Balkan War of 1913.

Venizélos continued to be the dominant figure in Greece's political life well into the 1930s. Crete's history from this point follows that of the nation as a whole. The island was affected by the ghoulish 'exchange of populations' agreed by the Turkish and Greek governments in 1923, after Greece's failed invasion of Turkey. The remaining 30,000 Cretan Muslims were robbed of their property and forced from their homes, their places taken by a nearly equal number of Greek refugees from Asia Minor – part of the nearly two million Greeks who had suffered the same fate.

When the Nazis overran Greece its government took refuge on Crete (23 April 1941), the last bit of free Greek territory, defended by 30,000 British, New Zealand and Australian troops brought from Egypt. Crete's own battalions were trapped near Albania; the only Greek soldiers on the island were cadets and raw recruits. But then, no one suspected what Goering and General Student, his paratroop commander, had in store – although some writers now say the British command were well aware of their plans, but didn't think Crete worth the risk of betraying the fact that they had cracked the Germans' secret code. After a week of bombing, Nazi paratroopers launched the world's first invasion by air on 20 May. The Allied and Greek forces, along with hundreds of ill-armed men, women and children, put up such resistance that the Germans were forced to expend the cream of their forces to subdue the island – at the cost of 170 aircraft, 4,000 men and the decimation of their airborne division.

The Battle of Crete proved, if nothing else, the folly of attack by parachutists alone, and as Churchill wrote in *The Grand Alliance*:

The German losses of their highest class fighting men removed a formidable air and parachute weapon from all further part in immediate events in the Middle East. Goering gained only a Pyrrhic victory in Crete, for the forces he expended there might easily have given him Cyprus, Iraq, Syria and even perhaps Persia. These troops were the very kind needed to overrun large wavering regions, where no serious resistance would have been encountered. He was foolish to cast away such almost measureless opportunities and irreplaceable forces in a mortal struggle, often hand-to-hand, with the warriors of the British Empire.

In spite of brutal German reprisals, the Cretan resistance to occupation, aided by British and ANZAC agents, was legendary. It culminated in the sheer audacity of Major Patrick Leigh Fermor and Captain Billy Moss's abduction of General Kreipe, the German commander of Crete, from Heráklion in 1943. As a massive manhunt combed the island, Kreipe was relayed across the mountains and put on a submarine to Egypt from Rodákino on the south coast, earning a grudging compliment from the General: 'I am beginning to wonder who is occupying the island – us or the English.'

Because of its Venizélan, republican traditions, Crete was spared the worst of the civil wars between left- and right-wing factions that divided most of Greece in the years after the war; communist-dominated militias were simply not as popular as in the north of the country, although a few found refuge in the White Mountains (and a couple of old guerrilla groups stayed there in the wilds until 1974 and the end of the Junta). Just the same, Crete usually leans to the left in elections, and has always been one of the strongholds of PASOK (Pan-Hellenic Socialist Movement).

Crete Today, or Forty Whacks with the Double Axe

You, pilgrims of modern times, guard yourselves from the songs of Cretan sirens and their false allures.

Pausanius, 2nd century AD

Homer spoke of several 'Cretes', and the same is true at the start of the 21st century. Two predominate: the Crete of the villages and the Crete of the coasts. The first one is doing relatively well. EU agricultural subsidies that make the family olive groves and vineyards a viable alternative to waiting tables in Mália have something to do with it. Paved roads have replaced mule tracks, and Japanese pick-ups replaced the mules. In the mountains you can still find older men who cut a dash in their baggy breeches or *vráche*, black shirts and waistcoats, high jackboots and the black-fringed neckerchiefs, or *tsalvária*, which the Turks forced Cretans to wear as a sign of servitude but which, even after the law was rescinded, they continued to wear to show their defiance.

To be fair, the other Crete wasn't asked, back in the 1960s, whether or not it wanted to be a guinea pig for Greece's new vocation in mass tourism, but there's no turning back the clock. The lovely beaches of the north coast, especially around Heráklion, have been raped with toadstool strips of hotels, shops, restaurants and discos, in Euro-compounds most often run by Athenians or foreigners. The money was good, at least in the beginning, and much easier to make than olive oil. This of course has happened in numberless other sunny places, but it seems especially tragic on Crete, perhaps because it resisted so many other enemies for so long. More has been lost in the past 30 years than in 243 under the Turks. But the double axe of paradox is striking Crete's developers on the rebound, and they seem genuinely puzzled as to why many travellers have begun to ask for more than a plot of sunny sand for their holidays.

The past decade has seen moves in the right direction. High-rise hotels have been banned; old houses and villas in the villages are being restored, often as holiday homes or alternative tourism projects (the efforts made in Vámos, east of Chaniá, are a prime example). Funds from the Orthodox patriarchy and EU are seeping in to restore the best of the island's 850 frescoed churches and monasteries before they fall over. Cretan cuisine and wines enjoy new prestige in the restaurants, and Cretan music and dancing is alive and well. Environmentalists have pushed to the fore such issues as garbage disposal, clean seas, water conservation, alternative energy and wildlife and forest preservation. Even the rights of domestic animals get a mention – if mostly from British ex-pats. Old crafts (weaving, lacemaking, pottery, basket-weaving, jewellery) have yet to die out, and in some places are being revived. The revival of natural remedies has led to a new interest in the island's magical herbs.

Nor have the Cretans lost their pluck. A few years ago, an old man was asked: 'Grandfather, if you could relive your life, what would you do?' and he replied, unhesitatingly, in the old Cretan spirit: 'The same thing, and worse!'

Art and Music

05

Minoan art is the one thing that sets Crete's ancient civilization apart from every other – a vibrant, flowing art, 'infused with a lyrical carelessness and freedom, not only in subject, but also in execution', far closer to modern tastes than the stiff, hieratic figures of Middle Eastern cultures or even the self-consciously idealized art of Classical Greece. The Minoan frescoes and vases were a revelation when Sir Arthur Evans' men reconstructed them from the fragments of Knossos, and, even though we know more about their meanings and contexts today, they remain a revelation still.

Other cultures show us imposing monarchs, mysterious figures of gods and demons, vast funeral pomps and such; compared to these the Minoans often seem to have come from another planet. Even though their Linear A and B tablets suggest they had a bureaucratic, accounting streak in their souls as dry as dust, their art is free from political propaganda or state-worship; even works that are clearly religious seem more human, less threatening and shadowy. Many Minoan works even look almost like art for art's sake, born of a sense of delight so strong it catches our fancy too, despite the centuries that separate us from the enigmatic people who created it.

Its ancient visual arts may be more celebrated, but Cretans have also had music and dance in their souls since the warrior *daimons* the Kouretes sang and danced around the newborn Zeus, and Ariadne tripped across her dancing floor at Knossos. In modern times, Cretan music continues to occupy its own very special place within the great body of Greek music, an essential part of the island's rich flavour.

The Arts of Crete

Pre-Palatial (2600–1900 BC)

Handmade pottery was well established in Neolithic times on Crete. The first works attributed to the early Minoans were simple, graceful vessels decorated with discreet linear patterns painted in red or incised in the clay, but early in the Pre-Palatial period new ideas were picked up from Egypt and Asia Minor, one of which was that ceramics alone were rather second-rate. One of several styles, **Vasiliki ware**, uses a mottled red and black effect intended to imitate stone vases, while the sometimes extravagant shapes – 'teapots', for instance, with enormous horizontal spouts – were inspired by metal pots. Very few gold or silver vases have survived (most would have been melted down and re-used in later ages), but the early Minoans probably also had a good deal of gold and silver, judging by the quantity of imitative ceramics that have been found, some with fake rivets. Ceramic ship models were also common, suggesting Cretans may have believed in an after-death passage similar to that of the Egyptians.

Stone vases were a Minoan luxury speciality, from as early as 2500 BC. The early Minoans were stone connoisseurs, carefully selecting marble, serpentine and alabaster (mostly local, although they also used Liparite, imported from the Lipari islands, north of Sicily) to make into shapes such as a bird's nest vase or blossom bowl that emphasize the beauty of the stone. The technique used was learned from Egyptian masters: block out the stone by whacking it with even harder stone, grind it into shape with an abrasive, and then hollow out the interior with a copper drill.

Minoans from the earliest times liked gold jewellery, much of it made from thin sheets of gold and beads. In *c.* 2300 BC the first engraved seals appeared, in bone, ivory and steatite, for 'signing' documents inscribed on clay tablets and to mark wax-sealed stores to prevent tampering, although they also served as magic talismans. Their tiny, intricately carved designs formed one of the great arts of Crete, and have yielded a wealth of information on Minoan culture and religion. As for architecture, only fragments of Pre-Palatial buildings remain, but there is evidence that in them a simple kind of wall painting was practised, a forerunner of artistic triumphs to come.

Old and New Palace/Middle Minoan (1900–1450 BC)

As the Minoans made a name for themselves in the Mediterranean around 1900 BC, their art took off as well. Cretan pottery reached its apogee in what Evans called the Middle Minoan period, 1900–1450. The potter's wheel, introduced from Asia Minor or Egypt, allowed artists to make ever more attractive shapes, and as time went on they decorated them in vivid style with natural forms that flow freely around the contours of vases, in patterns derived from the backgrounds of contemporary frescoes. Black and white are the dominant colours, with rich red and yellow accents. Figurative motifs appear, mostly floral (palms, lillies, grasses) as well as scenes of marine life; human figures never, probably because they were judged unsuitable. The finer black and white **Kamáres ware** was popular throughout the Palace periods (and the bulk of it was found in the palaces). Textured **Barbotine ware** first appeared in the Middle Minoan as well; Arthur Evans thought it was influenced by marine surfaces such as barnacles, prickles, spines, scales and wave motions. While working on such refine-ments, Minoans also made the giant *pithoi* jars found in palace store rooms, to hold bulk quantities of oil and grain; standing some five feet tall, they were too large to be crafted on a potter's wheel, and had to be formed by hand. Their embossed decora-tion of ropes imitate the way in which they were transported, in rope hammocks.

The technique for making faïence had arrived in Crete, also from Asia Minor, in the Pre-Palatial period, when it was used to make beads. In the Middle Minoan period new uses for it were found, as in the three-dimensional figures of the Snake Goddess and appliqué relief plaques, including one of the masterpieces of the genre, a delicate plaque of a cow tending her calf, and the 'Town Mosaic', faïence plaques in the shape of houses. All were discovered in the so-called Temple Repository at Knossos.

The 'Mosaic' reveals the basics of Minoan architecture: mud-brick walls, perhaps plastered or stuccoed, interlaced with long, squared beams to create a pleasing effect. Good stone was largely limited to the important parts of the palaces, the greatest monuments Crete has to show. Their obvious and most unusual architectural feature is a disregard for any kind of monumental planning and symmetry, and this is another Minoan puzzle. Other cultures of the time built imposing shrines, large-scale sculptures and monuments to exalt their gods and rulers. The well-travelled Minoans surely saw examples, especially in Egypt, but seem not to have felt the same urge.

But there are the palaces. The lost upper storeys might have helped to make more architectural sense of these rambling piles, but nonetheless there is a pattern common to them all. Each was built around a rectangular central court, orientated slightly east of north (again, quite different from their contemporaries), and had a monumental entrance on the west side. Upper storeys and entrances were supported by wooden columns, tapering at the bottom and brightly painted. The northern part of the palaces commonly held banqueting rooms and kitchens, while the western parts contained the major shrines and rooms used for record-keeping and storage.

Some had **frescoes**; the famous ones in the Heráklion museum (from 1700–1450 BC) are mainly from Knossos. They have been called 'the world's first naturalistic art', although a close look at paintings from contemporary Egypt, or even older frescoes from Mari in Syria, shows that the Cretans weren't completely alone; in fact much of the style and subject matter derived from Egyptian sources. In Crete, however, the figures – whether human, bull, bird, fish, octopus, tree or flower – are sensuous and full of life; even mountains and seas seem charged with energy and *joie de vivre*. In their self-portraits, the Minoans portrayed themselves with wasp waists and long black curls, the men in codpieces and loincloths, women with eyes blackened with kohl and lips painted red, wearing their famous bodices that exposed the breast, flounced skirts decorated in complex patterns and wonderfully exotic hats. Boys are painted red, girls are white, a convention adopted from the Egyptians, perhaps because men were supposed to look robust and tanned and women more delicate from staying indoors; another possibility is that in religious ceremonies men dyed themselves (and women may have done themselves up with powdered alabaster).

Although the frescoes often seem to portray elite court or religious ceremonies, they were by no means limited to the palaces; fragments have also been found in villas and houses around Crete, and in Minoan colonies on Mílos and Santoríni. None of this is true fresco, which would have lasted better (paint was applied on dried plaster, rather than on fresh), but, considering next to nothing of Classical Greek painting has survived, the Minoans didn't do too badly. Some figures were moulded in the plaster before painting to create a relief effect. Mycenaean Greece learned its art from Crete, but by the end of the Old Palace era reverse influences are recognizable in a slightly stiffer approach on Crete, as in the heraldic griffons in the Throne Room at Knossos.

Jewellery, too, reached new heights in the Palace periods, with intricate work as ever based on a loving observation of nature. Two new techniques helped makers achieve their aims: filigree and granulation, in which thin golden wire and grains of gold were

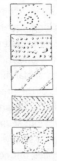

1 Vasilikí ware 'teapot'; 2 Barbotine-style designs; 3 Kamáres ware amphora from Knossos

used to create fine detail – as in the famous bee pendant from Mália. Seal engravers perfected their craft, turning to carnelian, jasper, rock crystal, amethyst, agate and other semi-precious stones to create a wide range of forms: round, prismatic (three-sided), oval, almond-shaped or discs with pierced centres that were worn on a chain. Beautiful gold signet rings became increasingly popular and were also worn on a chain, decorated with talismanic themes of the goddess and animals. The Minoans used crystals for magnifying glasses (one has been found) and created astonishing compositions in a quarter-inch field, with free, fluid, Matisse-like lines.

Stone vases were still made, including remarkable works originally plated with gold – the *Cup of the Chieftain* and *Harvester Vase*, the Mountain Shrine *rhyton* (drinking-horn) and beautiful tapered chalices from Zákros, and the serpentine bull's-head *rhyton* from the Little Palace of Knossos. As far as we know **sculpture**, as statues or reliefs, was never popular in Crete, outside of the mysterious 'horns of consecration' at some palaces. This is a bit surprising, seeing the care Minoan stonemasons took in cutting blocks and the virtuosity of their stone vases. Of small figurines, most that have survived are ceramic, although carving in ivory – easily obtained from the east, where people were busy driving the Syrian elephant to extinction (they succeeded in the 9th century BC) – was another great Cretan talent. However, ivory deteriorates, leaving the Snake Goddess now in Boston and the superb Bull Leaper in Heráklion as rare examples of the art. Around 1600 BC **lost wax casting** was invented (see p.36); Cretans liked to leave the surfaces of their bronze figurines rough (like Rodin) and saved their wonted precision for fine daggers and swords – the male status symbol of choice. Most Minoan daggers and swords, inlaid with fine gold, silver and niello work, were strictly ornamental, and made up a big part of Crete's luxury export trade.

Post-Palace/Late Minoan (1450–1100 BC)

It's always fascinating watching art deteriorate – as if weary of perfection, sated with imagery, a culture turns on the one hand to the strange and exotic, and on the other to shopworn, standardized versions of old favourites just to keep up tradition. After 1450 BC the Minoans seem to have maintained their prosperity in spite of difficult times (and perhaps foreign rule), but the vision that had animated the earlier stages of their culture seems to have vanished.

4   5   6

4 Kamares ware jug from Phaistos; 5 New Palace seal, of a deer; 6 Geometric-style jar from Zákros

In pottery, this era was marked by increasing stylization and stiffness, as the superb spontaneous flow of earlier times somehow drained away. The Late Minoan II period has been called 'baroque', an art straining for the ornate and grandiose. Also, many designs became standardized and lifeless when turned out in number, even if the Minoans resisted conforming to the full stylistic uniformity that characterized the Greek world in the Mycenaean era. The last stages of Minoan art saw a growing tendency towards abstract designs. One novelty is the quantity of *larnaxes*, small terracotta chests for burials; although they go back to Pre-Palatial times, they only became common in the Late Minoan, after 1400 BC (earlier ones may have been of wood, which had become scarce). The most fascinating *larnaxes* were painted with religious scenes, such as the famous Ag. Triáda sarcophagus (see p.187).

Perhaps the most characteristic works of this period are the strange, bell-shaped terracotta goddesses, usually with arms uplifted. Quite primitive, they represent a more 'popular' art (and are sometimes called 'household goddesses'). Nevertheless, there were also still craftsmen on Crete capable of making fine jewellery, bronzes, ivories and weapons. Often they went for export, and many Cretan artists seem to have emigrated to the mainland and the Mycenaean heartland of the Peloponnese.

After the Minoans

By the 12th century BC Minoan art was already in serious decline, and with the coming of the war-like Dorians, who had no interest in such decadent fancies, it nearly disappeared altogether. The few items that have been discovered were often imported, or showed a simple, almost barbaric style, much like the 'household goddesses'. The depths of Greece's Dark Age is represented by the **Proto-Geometric period** (1100–900 BC), with a simple, non-figurative decoration of pottery.

Art from the recovering **Geometric period** (900–700 BC) shows Eastern influences; work in bronze is especially fine, and Crete for a time was again an artistic centre. Towards the end of this period the first bronze 'Daedalic' statuettes appeared, characterized by wide eyes, thick hair and parted legs. Legend credits this Daedalos (not to be confused with Daedalus, the inventor of myth) with inventing the craft of making statues out of marble and hammered bronze. By the 6th century BC, however, Crete was once more in serious decline, spending its energy on building strong walls (as at Aptera, near Chaniá, see p.120) rather than gold jewellery and pretty pots, and in the centuries that followed the island had little to contribute to Greece's golden age.

Roman, Byzantine and Venetian

Time, earthquakes and pirates have wiped clean much of what followed in the **Roman** and **First Byzantine periods** (67 BC–AD 824). Only titbits remain to show that if Crete didn't hold high the torch of culture at least it muddled through with a 40-watt bulb: a few statues, mosaic floors, aqueducts, cisterns and remains of simple three-naved basilicas. The 7th-century cathedral of Ag. Títos at Gortyn provides eloquent witness that Cretans had completely forgotten how to build on a monumental scale.

The art purge of the **Iconoclastic period** in Byzantium (726–843) and **Saracen interlude** (824–961) ensured that Crete was well behind the rest of the Eastern empire at

Understanding Byzantine Art

Painted decoration in Greek churches often follows a set 'hierarchical' formula, to reproduce the universe symbolically. Christ *Pantokrator* ('all-governing') or the Christ of the Ascension reigns in the dome of heaven, surrounded by angels, while below the Virgin and John the Baptist intercede for humanity. The Virgin and Child occupy the central apse. Surrounding vaults and upper registers show the *Dodekaorton*, the 'Twelve Feasts' of the church, while in the lower, terrestrial zone are saints, prophets and martyrs (whose gory deaths are also a favourite subject in the narthex).

Yet even in the bloodiest Byzantine martyrdoms there is a certain trance-like detachment. Its saints reside on a purely spiritual plane; on church walls or icons their most striking feature is often their intense staring eyes. They never play on the heartstrings or ask the viewer to relive the pain of the Passion or coo over a baby Jesus; the Virgin (the *Panagía*, or 'all-holy'), cocooned in black or blue like an Orthodox nun, has none of the charms of a Madonna. 'The artistic perfection of an icon,' as Timothy Ware wrote, 'was not only a reflection of the celestial glory – it was a concrete example of matter restored to its original harmony and beauty serving as a vehicle of the spirit.' An intention wholly different from that of the ancient Greeks, who were infatuated with human beauty and intellect and made divinity in their own image. The calm Classical gaze of their gods was a reflection of earthly mathematical perfection; the Byzantine stare belongs to the visionary, abstract and ascetic. Curiously, this stare annoyed the Turks no end – in many churches you'll find frescoes more or less intact except for the eyes, gouged out by their knives.

the turn of the millennium, although it soon caught up. The old Roman basilica plan for churches was jettisoned once and for all in favour of the classic Byzantine style: a central Greek-cross plan crowned by a dome, elongated in front by a vestibule (*narthex*) and outer porch (*exonarthex*) and at the back by a choir and three apses. Frescoes and icons of the 9th–12th century Macedonian period (named after the Macedonian emperors in Constantinople) are on the austere side. In Crete, only a few Macedonian frescoes survive (at Myriokéfala, and Kéra Panagía in Kritsá).

The Venetian arrival on Crete coincided with the **second golden age of Byzantine art**, under the Comnene emperors. As in Italy, this period saw a renewed interest in antique models: the stiff, elongated figures with staring eyes were given more naturalistic proportions in graceful, rhythmic compositions. Itinerant artists on Crete – only a few left names behind, such as Ioánnis Pagoménos, from western Crete – were influenced by Italian artists brought by the Venetians to decorate Catholic churches; the 14th was the century of plague, when *Second Comings* were especially prominent.

This cultural cross-fertilization, and the arrival of artists from Constantinople fleeing from the Turks, encouraged a vibrant school of painting in 16th- and 17th-century Venetian Crete, as local artists began to wander from the abstract spiritual plane of Byzantine art. In the works of Michális Damaskinós, whose finest paintings (you can hardly call them icons) are in Ag. Ekaterína in Heráklion, you have the Byzantine equivalent of Renaissance painting in Italy, a not entirely comfortable synthesis. Other painters of the time, such as Ioánnis Kornaros and Giórgios Klontzas, stuck closer to Byzantine tradition. The one genuinely original artist Crete produced, Doménikos Theotokópoulos (El Greco; see p.202) didn't synthesize at all but picked up the most extreme, late 16th-century thread of Italian Mannerist painting, moved to Toledo and took it to a spiritual edge no other Byzantine painter ever imagined.

By 1669, when Crete fell to the Turks, the Venetians had given it fine architectural souvenirs: impressive fortifications, lighthouses, fountains, arsenals, public buildings, town houses and country manors. It had an incredible 1,000 active monasteries, of which no two are alike. Many have façades and gates inspired by the Venetians (Moní Arkádi is the finest example), and although over half are ruined they contain a large proportion of Crete's reputed 800 more-or-less-intact frescoed churches. Nor did figurative art completely perish under Crete's Muslim rulers: see for example Ioánnis Kornáros' magnificent icon *Great is the Lord* (1770), with its cast of thousands, at Moní T@@oploú. Crete's meagre **Turkish** heritage is concentrated in a few small mosques, fountains and houses in Réthymnon and Chaniá, and in the Heráklion Historical Museum, where you can also see much of the finest **movable art** produced in Crete in the last 2,000 years. Much of it was made by women: weavings, rugs, silks and lace are beautiful. Nor have they died out completely, for along with icon painting and jewellery-making these crafts are undergoing a revival. The provincial capitals have a growing number of galleries and exhibition centres (notably the Centre of Contemporary Art in Réthymnon) where you can see the work of contemporary Cretan artists.

Cretan Music and Dance

The strength of Crete's musical culture is shown in part by the fact that the island has provided many of Greece's best-known modern composers, such as Hatzidákis (famous for *Ta Pedia tou Pirea*, alias *Never on Sunday*), Ioánnis Markopoúlos, whose haunting music is based on traditional instruments and songs, Ioánnis Xenákis, who is just the opposite, a friend of Le Corbusier who composes on computers in Paris, and Míkis Theodorákis, most famous internationally as the composer of *Zorba the Greek*, but most celebrated in Greece for his long collaboration with deep-voiced Maria Farandoúri and his lavish orchestral settings of modern Greek and other poetry.

You can hear all kinds of Greek music on Crete, from big bouzoúki tunes in clubs outside Heráklion or Chaniá that showcase popular Greek singers (don't arrive before midnight, and bring lots of money). Small bars, especially in Chaniá, host everything from *rembétika* (born in the hashish dens of the old Greek towns in Anatolia) to Greek jazz. But what many Cretans like most of all is Cretan music, a passion not always shared by visitors, who, missing the poetry of the lyrics, may find it droning and monotonous, an acquired taste – a bit like *stáka*, Crete's fresh goat's milk butter.

Cretan music, like most Greek music, began as the product of ancient, Byzantine and eastern inspirations. The arrival of the Venetians from the 13th century on introduced a new wave of western trends, and in particular the three-stringed *viola da braccio*. After the fall of Constantinople in 1453 scores of Greek musicians took refuge on Crete and established schools of Byzantine music, while Venetian musicians visited on tours. Local musicians adapted all these sounds to form a unique style; 16th-century travellers often mentioned 'boisterous' dancing in the streets. The oldest surviving Greek folk song compositions, from the 17th century (housed in the libraries of Mount Athos) are Cretan, and are still sung today in modified form in western Crete.

It was under the Turkish occupation in the 17th century that the lyre or *lýra*, adapted from the violin, became the main stringed instrument of Crete. The original version came in two sizes: a small, pear-shaped *lyráki* to play the high notes, accompanied by the bass *vrodólyra* or 'thunder-lyre'. Falcon-bells (*gerakokoundoúna*), the same used by Byzantine falconers, were attached to the bows to keep time. Both lyres had three strings and were set on the knee. Other instruments popular up until the 1940s were the *violólyra* (the violin-lyre) and the *boúlgari*, a stringed instrument that came to Greece with refugees from Anatolia, and kept time better than the falcon bells.

In the old days musicians carved their own *lyráki* or *vrodólyra* out of ivy wood or mulberry. The modern Cretan *lýra* was only born in 1940, when Manólis Stagakís, an old player, carved himself a cross between the *lyráki* and the *vrodólyra*. Able to express a wide range of moods, from slow brooding to lightning improvisation, it fast took hold as the Cretan national instrument. At the same time, the **boúlgari** was gradually replaced by the more versatile, deeper-pitched lute (*laoúto*), which had come to Crete with Renaissance Venetians, but was now modified for a new role. The *laoúto* usually introduces a song, setting the rhythm and tone, then provides rhythmic accompaniment to the *lýra*'s fireworks; occasionally solo *laoúto* is used to accompany ballads and love songs. Sometimes other instruments – guitar, fiddle, *bouzoúki*, small drums – may join in. Selíno is the only place on Crete where the clarinet is popular.

Other factors also contributed to a renaissance of Cretan music. In 1913, union with Greece coincided with a new technology, electric recording. At the same time, in the general enthusiasm over union, people also wanted live music, and lots of it. Amateur and professional performers were in great demand across the island, and their influence only increased with the advent of radio. Cretan music reached a peak of popularity in the 1960s and 70s, with the film of *Zorba the Greek*, and the rise of Níkos Xyloúris, the 'Nightingale of Crete' (1936-80), whose fine voice, highly personal style and protest lyrics against the junta found an audience all over Greece. Many *lýra* players initially saw them as traitors to tradition, but in retrospect musicians recognize that Xyloúris and his brother Psarantónis did much to rejuvenate Cretan music.

Things changed abruptly in the 1980s when the island was transformed almost overnight by tourism. Easy prosperity lured Cretans away from their traditions and customs, or perhaps more soul-destroying, into bartering these traditions and music just like any other commodity. Suddenly any and everything could be commercialized, and what had been an essential part of Crete's identity found itself transformed into a cheap folkloric item for the entertainment of coach-loads at 'Greek Nights'.

Since then a reaction has set in, and today traditional music seems to be holding its own; everywhere in Crete posters advertise performances at Cretan music halls (*Kentro Kritiko*). Among the new crop of traditional performers look for Nektários Samólis, Stélios Bikákis, Dimítrios Vakákis, Níkos Eliákis, Giórgios Tsantákis and Geórgios Lekákis. Established recording stars include Manólis Alexákis, composer

Michális Alefantínos, Níkos Gonianákis, Giórgios Manolioúdis, Vangélis Pitharoúlis, whose passionate, erotic songs are popular throughout Greece, *laoúto* player Michális Tzouganákis and youthful sensation Giórgios Zervákis. If you're looking for CDs, check out classic performances by the greats: Kostás Moudákis, Vasilís Skoúlas, Baskevanís, Spíros Sifogiorgákis and Giórgios Koustourélis (*laoúto*). The ultimate in Cretan music are two ten-CD sets, the *Great Masters 1922–55* and the *Great Masters 1955–95*.

If Cretan music can seem a bit monotonous to the uninitiated, Cretan **dances**, among the most vigorous and ancient in Greece, and fuelled by shots of rakí, are anything but. Favourites include the *pentozáli*, a furious machine-gun five-step that in the old days Cretans used to dance fully armed to show off their war-like prowess, and the *pedektó*, which requires energetic jumping and stamping and every last drop of adrenalin; dancers hold hands up high, elbows bent, while a leader, 'always dark, handsome and 20 years old', performs astonishing leaps that prove at least some white men – heirs to bull-leaping Minoans – can jump. Among others you might see at a village *panegýri* (saint's day festival) or wedding are *malevyzýtikos, ortses, chaniotíkos, siteiakos* or a *siganos*, characterized by its slow movements. Ioánnis Kondylákis' 19th-century *Patouchas*, a comic novel set in a Cretan village, describes a typical party:

> The sound of feet echoed together so loudly one thought the ground was shaking. There were moments when the lyre positively barked... Then the dancers seemed to grow into giants whose heads almost touched the ceiling. The daggers shook in the belts of the young men, and breasts of the female dancers trembled and throbbed under the silk bodices. In the meantime couplets crossed back and forth like arrows with the fast pace of the dance...

These arrow-like Cretan couplets are famous for being double-edged, and masters of the genre can let them fly impromptu. The tradition of improvised poetry goes back at least to Homer's day, but medieval Cretans assimilated Western-style rhyming couplets from the Venetians, then set them to age-old Greek iambic 15-syllable metre in a new form, the *mantináda*. The masterpiece of the genre, the *Erotókritos*, the Cretan national epic, was composed entirely in *mantinádes* by Vicénzo Kornáros in the 17th century (*see* p.256); to this day some old shepherds can recite it off the tops of their heads. Even many young Cretans know at least parts of it, thanks to a popular recording by Níkos Xyloúris, Chistodoúlos Chalaris and Tánia Tsanakioú.

Mantinádes, usually accompanied by the *lýra*, can be funny (often at the expense of fellow villagers), erotic, melancholy or patriotic – ethnologists have come up with over 200 thematic classifications, including some inspired by the Battle of Crete. Song contests test a singer's invention, and the ability to come up with a *mot juste* from the vast *mantináda* repertoire. Another, older genre, *rizitika* or 'songs from the roots', are usually unaccompanied (they were often sung to pass the time on long journeys on foot) and are mostly heard in western Crete, especially in Sfakiá and Selíno; usually one person begins a song and the others sing the chorus. Even if you don't understand a word, attending an improvisation session in a village, if you're lucky enough, is a moving experience, a last relic of a 3,000-year-old European tradition, still surviving, at least for the time being, in Europe's southeasternmost corner.

The Fauna and Flora of Crete

Balanced on the shelf between the African and Eurasian tectonic plates, Crete, as small as it is, has nearly a continent's-worth of environments, habitats and micro-climates, from lofty mountains to sub-tropical lagoons. Distinctive biotopes in the island's 35 sizeable gorges provide homes fpr rare indigenous plants and birds. Some very scarce native Cretan animals survive, if barely: Cretan horses (*kritikos ihnilatis*), the Cretan spiny mouse, Cretan bees (*kritiki melissa*), the only recently rediscovered 'ghost' cat and the long-horned wild goat or ibex, known locally as the *kri-kri* or *agrimi*, a direct descendant of the first flocks that were brought to the island by Neolithic herdsmen. A favourite motif in Minoan art, the *kri-kri* now survives mainly on offshore island refuges and in the White Mountains. Even there, however, numbers have sadly fallen to an estimated 2,000 or so, thanks in part to loss of habitat but mainly due to their habit of mating with domestic goats.

Heráklion's Museum of Natural History concentrates on Crete's own wildlife and natural environments (*see* p.191). There are also are a number of specialist holiday firms (*see* pp.84–5) that offer nature tours, especially between March and early June, when the island's wildflowers are at their peak.

Birds

Spring is also the best time to see birds, when residents are supplemented by many other species that visit Crete on their return to Europe. Look for migrant and resident herons, marsh harriers, egrets and the occasional pelican by **Lake Kournás** (Crete's only natural lake), down by the Kourtaliótis river below **Moní Préveli**, or near the coastal islands and lagoons of western Crete, especially at **Balos**. Crete's mountains are one of the last bastions of the lammergeyer or bearded vulture, with the widest wing-spans in Europe (nearly 10ft/3m) and the striking habit of dropping bones on rocks, to break them open for their marrow. Smaller vultures, eagles, buzzards and falcons are often seen, floating high over the gorges; Eleanora's falcons, almost as rare, thrive on the islands off Crete's north shore, especially **Día** and the **Dionysádes**. There aren't many songbirds on Crete, but you may hear the 'hoop hoop hoop' of the hoopoe, and several warblers live in the olive and fruit groves, most prominently the black-capped Sardinian warbler. By the sea cliffs, look out for swift crag martins and red-rumped swallows, and the red-beaked Aegean gulls, which are found exclusively in the Mediterranean.

Snakes and Lizards

The only snakes you're likely to see on Crete are ceramic ones, clutched by the Minoan snake goddess. Of the island's four species, only the grey, blotchy, chequer-board cat-snake is poisonous, but as its venomous fangs are at the back of its mouth it's very unlikely to do you any harm. The most spectacular reptile is the Balkan green lizard, one and a half feet long and emerald-green; smaller lizards and geckos, as well as more elusive chameleons, are present in the woodlands and brush. Loggerhead sea turtles (*caretta caretta*) like to nest on sandy beaches west of **Chaniá**, around **Réthymnon** and **Mátala**, where they are officially protected. However, the fact that the turtles nest in peak tourist season in July and August makes co-existence tricky.

Trees

Crete has millions of trees, but these days most are olives. Deforestation is nothing new here: the Minoans only made their *larnaxes* (*see* p.58) out of clay once timber was running low, and 15th-century Venetian writers tell of a fire in the White Mountains that burned for three years. Most trees these days are typical Mediterranean species, but some are worth a special mention. In the past, Crete's mountains were covered with wild cypress (*cypressus horizontalis*), growing to heights of up to 100ft (30m), its name derived from the branches that grow horizontally from the trunk to form a pyramid-shaped tree. Cypress oil, extracted from its aromatic resin, was prized by Egyptian embalmers, and the long-lasting wood was equally prized by Minoan palace builders; depletion continued apace until 1414, when the Venetians enacted Crete's first conservation measure by banning its export. Impressive stands remain in the White Mountains. Several spots on the coast are home to Europe's only native palm trees (*phoenix theophrastii*), named after Aristotle's philosopher colleague Theophrastus of Lésbos, who was the first to make a note of them; **Vaï** on the east coast has a 30-acre grove, and there are others, especially around **Prevéli**. Not as popular on the travel posters but equally rare are forests of sea juniper, found above all on the islands of **Gávdos** and **Chrisí**.

Although tall Calabrian pines are the main species of conifer, efforts are under way in the gorges and coastal mountains near Ierápetra to protect Crete's last native pines. The little evergreen maple, which grows as high as 5,250ft (1,600m) above sea level, provides the first colour in autumn, the red that made it sacred to Ares, the god of war; look for them and oaks in the forest of **Rouvas**, above **Gérgeri**. Rarer by far (because of overgrazing) is the short, deciduous *zelkova abelicea* (ampelitsa) that blooms on rocky slopes in May and June. Shepherds once used its hard wood to carve their twisted crooks; there are only four species of zelkova in the world, and Crete has the only one that grows in Europe. The only deciduous forests are the chestnuts of western Crete, growing around **Élos**, and in several places, such as **Áno Viánnos** and **Krási**, there are magnificent plane trees well over a thousand years old.

Wildflowers and Herbs

Most tourists who come in summer only see Crete as sunburnt as they feel at the end of an afternoon on the beach, never suspecting that wild flowers are one of the island's glories. Some 1,500 different species, including 210 that are endemic only to Crete, brighten the landscape in the spring with the intensity of 1950s Technicolor. March through June is the peak period, when yellow anemones, white arum lilies, wild violets, blue campanulas, pink periwinkles and white cyclamens cover the hills and mountains. If you come earlier, you'll find the first flowers along the coast, especially in the arid east; if you come later, you can still find a fair amount of blooms by heading into the mountains, especially the **Omalós, Nida** and **Lassíthi** plateaux and the **Amári** valley. Fascinating *chasmophytes* grow safe from predators and competition, in impossible niches or clinging to the bare walls of Crete's gorges; nearby, *xerophytes* have adapted to the dry, hot climate by developing fleshy, water-storing leaves. Wild orchids trick insects into their boudoirs to pollenate them.

Early bloomers include yellow spiked Cretan mullein, the first flower of winter (but only in the west), Cretan ricotia, on pebbly wastelands, and the delicate Cretan tulip, green outside with white-rosy petals inside, which grows at low altitudes and blooms from January to June. Mountain crocuses burst open just as the snows melt, including the superb, large, white- and violet-striped Sieber's crocus in subalpine regions, the source of saffron that has been prized by the Minoans (as in the fresco, the *Saffron Gatherers*, now in the Heráklion museum) and everyone since. Another valuable flower is the pink and white Cretan cistus, or rock rose, which blooms on hillsides from March to May. One appears in the *Blue Bird* fresco from Knossos; the balsam that was used for ointments, perfumes and incense in ancient times (and is called *ponikijo*, or Phoenician incense, on Linear B tablets) was harvested by plucking the sticky stuff from goats' legs and beards. You may occasionally still see women gathering it in with special rubber-edged rakes.

In April–June, look for masses of little white flowers known as mouse ears. *Anchusa caespitosa*, with its long narrow leaves and dark purple flowers, blooms in the **White Mountains** at 3,800–6,500ft (1,150–2,000m), and Cretan calaminth, which also likes alpine altitudes, has tiny white-pinkish flowers in June and July. Fragrant alpine violets, of a type that is endemic to Crete, nearly always have yellow flowers. Other unusual flowers of April and May include Scorpion vetch or coronilla, with round white flowers hanging from the sides of the gorges; Burnet saxifrage (*pimpinella tragium*), a shrub known as Cretan ebony, with fragrant stalk cluster flowers once used to stuff pillows; and large white peonies, named after the Minoan god Paeon and reputed to cure madness and nightmares. Wild aromatic herbs, which come into their own in June, include the famous Cretan dittany (*see* p.228), oregano, savory, mint, sage, marjoram, thyme, lavender and Greek mountain tea made from the flower stems of *sideritis syriaca*, another Cretan endemic that grows at over 3,000ft (900m) and is a remedy for everything from the common cold to indigestion.

Later in the year, the mountains are graced with Cretan squill in white or blue varieties, pink *prunus prostrata* (a creeping dwarf wild cherry) or shade-loving Cretan symphandra, which has lovely pinkish-violet bell-shaped flowers and blooms in the western gorges in July and August – a cousin to the almost extinct purple and white bellflower on the walls of the **Gorge of Samariá**. Far more common are the little white star-shaped flowers of the asphodel that grows on the hills, once famed as the food of the dead, and fragrant sea daffodils (Mediterranean lilies) and sea squill, with tall spirling white spikes that bloom beside even the busiest beaches during August and September. Come autumn, crocuses and cyclamen pop their heads up in the meadows with the first rains.

Food and Drink

'...well, you just fill yourself up with more heaps of luscious food, which doesn't all turn into dung. There's something which stays, something that's saved and turns into good humour, dancing, singing, wrangling even – that's what I call Resurrection'.
Níkos Kazantzákis, *Zorba the Greek*

As Zorba himself says, true eating in Crete is more than an intake of calories, but rarely is it like the gourmet epiphanies you expect from the culinary temples of Italy or France. Rather, on Crete, dining is not an end but a means, the always-good excuse to get together with as many family members and friends as can squeeze around a table; a meal out is not the prelude to an evening out, it often *is* the evening out. In spite of the great revival of Cretan recipes in the island's restaurants and the arrival of 'New Cretan Cuisine' (the old recipes given a *nouvelle cuisine*-Mediterranean accent) this remains true: dining is still primarily a social affair, only now the food in the restaurants and tavernas is often much better than it was even a decade ago.

Because of the intense heat in summer, Cretans tend to eat a late lunch (2 or 3pm), followed by a siesta or *mesiméri*. Housewives spend all morning cooking, but in the evening, especially at weekends, everyone will head out of doors, working up an appetite and meeting friends, and dine late, rarely before 10pm. Meals can go on into the small hours, often increasingly boisterous, punctuated with fiery discussions and maybe bursts of song or dance, if there's sufficient *kéfi* or 'soul' in the air. Across Crete you'll find large, outdoor country tavernas called '*Kentro Kritiko*' which offer live Cretan music, dancing and singing, and sometimes exuberant pistol shots in the air (and there have been accidents, hence the signs you see: Do Not Shoot Aimlessly!).

The Food of Greece

Crete, of course, is part of Greece, and a large percentage of the dishes you'll find in its restaurants are the national mainstays. Many of these need no introduction – *tarama*, moussaká, *gýros*, retsina, vine leaves, Greek salads with feta, Greek yoghurt and baklava have all achieved the universality of lasagne and chicken tikka. However, though some of the food may be familiar, if you've not been to Greece before you may find eating different from what you're used to, with a big emphasis on informality.

Meals begin with bread and starters (*mezédes*), to be communally shared: olives, *tzatzíki* (cucumbers and yoghurt), prawns, *tirosalata* (feta cheese dip), *koponistá* (a pungent cheese dip), salted fish, roasted sweet peppers, cheese or spinach pies, meat-balls or *saganáki* (fried cheese sprinkled with lemon). These are followed (often before you've finished the starters, unless you specify otherwise) by a shared salad and pota-toes, and your main course. This could be a **'ready dish'** (already prepared) such as moussaká, *pastítsio* (baked macaroni, layered with mince, cheese and cream and topped with béchamel), roast lamb or chicken, *makaroniá* (basically spaghetti bolog-nese, which has been sitting there but isn't bad), *yemistá* (stuffed tomatoes or peppers), *stifádo* (spiced beef stew with baby onions), *lagostifádo* (rabbit stew, similar to the beef version but flavoured with orange), *kokinistó* (beef cooked with tomatoes), lamb or veal *youvétsi* (baked with tomatoes and with tear-drop pasta), *chirinó me* *sélino* (pork with wild celery, in egg lemon sauce), or *kréas stin stamna* (lamb or beef baked in a clay dish). **Grilled meats** come under the heading *tis óras* ('the On Times') – pork chops (*brizóles*), lamb cutlets (*paidákia*), kebabs (*souvláki*), minced steak (*biftéki*), meatballs (*keftédes* or *sousoukákia*), sausage (*lukániko*) or chicken (*koutópoulo*).

Seafood is fresh and delicious, but relatively expensive, although you can usually find cheapies like fresh whitebait (*marídes*), fresh sardines (*sardínas*), cuttlefish stew (*soupiá*) and squid rings (*kalamári*). Baked or fried *bakaliáros* (fresh Mediterranean cod) is a treat that shouldn't break the bank. Some places offer soups – *psarósoupa* (with potatoes and carrots) or spicy, tomato-based *kakávia*. Prawns (*garídes*) are lightly fried or baked with garlic, tomatoes and feta as *garídes saganáki*; spaghetti with lobster (*astakomakaronáda*) is another delicious recent addition to Greek menus. Note that fish portions are priced by weight; often you'll be asked to pick out the one you want cooked and the owner will put it on the scale in front of you.

Cretan Specialities

Cretan agriculture is dizzying in its variety and richness. Nearly every kind of fruit, from apples to oranges to bananas, grows on the big island – the plastic-tunnel farms along the west and south coasts may not be very aesthetic, but they provide many of Greece's winter vegetables. The large markets at Heráklion and Chaniá have heaving counters of produce and herbs grown on the island (many prettily packaged to make inexpensive gifts). Cretan mountain honey has enjoyed a deservedly high reputation

Vegetarian and Vegan Dishes

In the old days, Orthodox fasts (still followed in the monasteries) decreed that the faithful refrain from meat, and sometimes fish, wine and even olive oil, for a third of the days of the year. Consequently, over the centuries Greeks have devised plenty of dishes suitable for vegetarians and vegans ('vegetarian' is *chortofágos*); if you're a vegan, Lent is an ideal time to come, because restaurants go out of their way to prepare purely vegetarian dishes (especially artichokes, *anginárẹs*). Any time of the year you should find pulses, in starters such as *gigántes* (giant butter beans in tomato sauce) or *revíthia* (chick peas, baked or in soups or fritters), bean soups (*fasoláda*) and occasionally lentils (*fakés*). Other stand-bys are ratatouille-like *ládera* (fresh vegetables cooked in olive oil), a host of salads, sometimes enlivened with a handful of *kápari* (pickled caper plant), *yemistá* (peppers or tomatoes stuffed with rice), *bríams* (potato and aubergine or courgette, baked with olive oil), *imams* (aubergine stuffed with tomato and onion), various *keftédes* (vegetable fritters from carrot to courgette), *dolmádes* (rice and dill-filled vine leaves), *oftés patátes* (potatoes roasted in their jackets) and everywhere, endless supplies of chips. *Skordaliá*, the classic garlic dip served with fried vegetables or beetroot, is traditionally made simply with puréed potatoes and olive oil, but some places now do it with soft cheese. On Crete, you'll typically find a wide array of salads and some unique dishes, such as *sofegátha*, similar to ratatouille, or fried pies filled with spinach and greens.

since antiquity: the ultimate snack, served in many *kafeneía*, is thick homemade sheep's milk yoghurt sweetened with wild thyme honey.

As the island's honeymoon with tourism matures, there has been a remarkable renaissance of traditional Cretan cuisine; rather than clobber visitors with yet more wiener schnitzel and chips, new restaurants offer a selection of Cretan dishes on their menus. Essential ingredients are herbs and spices (the usual Greek dill, mint, oregano, thyme and cinnamon, but also basil, coriander and caraway seeds, long abandoned in the cuisine of the mainland) and locally grown (often organic) vegetables and fruits, including some unusual greens for the salad or pot such as *stamnágathi* (spine chicory), *avroníes* (black byrony), *glistrída* (purslane, a common garden weed that's remarkably good for you), *askolymbr* (Spanish oyster plant, with spiky leaves), *rodíkio* (similar to wild dandelion) and *papoúlos* (vetchling or bird's pea). Most of the time when you see people poking around in fields, they're hunting for one or the other.

Cretans, in spite of their ancient fixation with bulls, rarely touch beef, but they do delicious things with **lamb**, usually combining it with other ingredients as in a *toúrta* or *kriotópita*, where titbits are baked with four kinds of cheese in pastry topped with sesame seeds. Other classics are lamb baked in a tangy yoghurt and egg and lemon sauce, lamb sausages (*spilogáradiyna*), served with a creamy sauce called *áfogalo*, and *arní kleftíko*, 'bandits' lamb', with meat, vegetables and often a bit of cheese baked in paper (to conceal the aroma, and the bandits' whereabouts).

The local love of **yoghurt** and its widespread use in cooking is perhaps the most obvious Turkish influence in the Cretan kitchen. Rabbit baked with yoghurt, or suckling pig baked in yogurt, lemon, thyme and oregano, are delicious. Kid and game dishes, traditional Cretan staples, are stewed in orange and quince juice or served with a rice pilaf. Cretans eat far more snails than most Greeks, served as a *mezéde* or a ragout, or cooked with rice, tomatoes, garlic and cinnamon. *Souchília* are veal pies, often served as a starter. An old Cretan dish is *kefalgraviéra*: made with *graviéra* cheese, tomatoes, aubergines and artichokes stuffed with mince, and flavoured with bay and nutmeg. Chicken, once a big luxury, is especially tasty; try *kokkinistó koukli*, a variation on *coq au vin*. Cretan women also make pasta (*mangíri* or *makarónia skiofichta* or *chylófta*), rolled into shape by hand and topped with grated cheese.

Traditionally inward-looking as islands go, Crete has fewer **seafood** specialities, although the island does good *kakávia* (fish soup), *achinosaláta* (sea urchin salad, your revenge for stepping on them, although their presence signals that the water is unpolluted), parrot fish (*skáros* – the same scarus so prized by the Roman emperors), which is sometimes so fresh when it comes out of the Libyan sea that you may be offered it with all its innards intact except for the gall bladder, and various fish dishes with vegetables, such as *rofo me bamiés* (grouper with okra). If you see it on the menu, try *saláta tis yialias*, 'seashore salad', made from pickled seaweed.

Local **cheeses**, many aged in caves in baskets, may not be eaten in large quantities but do lend an unmistakable authenticity to many Cretan dishes. The best known Cretan cheese, *myzíthra* (or *anthótyro* in Western Crete), a fresh white whey cheese sold in bags, is similar to fresh ricotta and is used as a favourite ingredient in sweet pastries or served on round barley rusks (*dákos*); with a glass of *rakí*; a *koukouvágia*

The Cretan Diet, Old and New

In 1947, researchers for the Rockefeller Foundation noted with astonishment how healthy elderly Cretans were compared to their American counterparts. In spite of the privations of the war and their 'primitive' way of life, people in their 90s were still running up mountains and working in the fields. In 1956, the Foundation launched a 15-year study under an American doctor, Anzel Keys, in Japan, Finland, Yugoslavia, the USA, Holland, Italy and Corfu comparing their diet, lifestyle and the incidence of cardiovascular disease and cancer with a group of some 700 rural Cretan men. If health were a race, Crete lapped the competition several times over; the differences in death rates, even compared with Corfu, another Greek island, were striking. And this despite the fact that the Cretans consumed as much fat as the Finns, who did the worst in coronary disease; in fact, the only Cretan who died of coronary disease during all the years of the study was a butcher. Perhaps even more striking, when the researchers went around in 1991 as a final follow-up, 50 per cent of the Cretans were still alive and well. All the Finns had died.

Extra-virgin olive oil (the main source of all the fat), lots of cereals (whole wheats, barley and rye breads and rusks), pulses, greens and fresh vegetables and fruit, and notably smaller quantities of cheese, eggs, fish and meat, with a couple of glasses of wine at every meal, proved the secret of the diet that nutritionists and now the Cretans have actively begun to promote – even among themselves, as the younger generation has begun to eat like the rest of Europe, and suffer the consequences in heart attacks and cancer. Plus, the average Cretan now walks 2km a day, compared to the 13km logged by Cretans of old, so lighter, less fatty versions of the classics are being devised, with some imagination – the so-called New Cretan Cuisine.

('owl'), the favourite 'New Cretan' snack, is a rusk topped with *myzíthra*, olive oil, chopped tomato, olive oil, salt and oregano, and with a black olive in the centre. Hard or dried *myzíthra* (*anthótyro xeró*) tastes much stronger and is grated on pasta; sour or *xino myzíthra* has an acidic taste, and is a favourite in savoury pies such as the famous cheese pies of Sfakiá; or there's very soft and fresh *galomyzíthra* from Chaniá, made from goat's milk and sometimes served as a *mezéde*. Other Cretan cheeses include hard, yellow, holey and slightly rubbery *graviéra*, made from ewe's milk, and *malaká*, a softer ewe's milk cheese. Powerful *stáka* is a real test of one's ethnic credentials: fresh goat's-butter cream, with a bit of salt, often baked with vegetables or meats. **Omelettes** here contain a variety of cheeses, but if you're really hungry order a *sfougáto*, a Cretan omelette stuffed with potatoes fried in olive oil.

Crete has a **sweet** tooth, and again everything tends to be baked into an olive oil-based pastry. Two favourites are *amygadalópitta* or almond pie and *myzithropitákia*, baked with sweet *myzíthra* cheese and served with honey. *Kalitsoúnia* are little tarts, made with cheese, honey and cinammon; *mamoúlia* are even more decadent, made of walnuts, honey and *rakí*. *Xerotígana* are fritters like long coils in a honey and nut syrup and *tiganites* are little golden cakes fried in a pan, topped with honey or grape-must syrup, sesame seeds and walnuts. At Christmas, look for *melomakárona*, cakes made with walnuts, cinammon, oranges and cloves and dipped in honey syrup.

Eating Out and Café Life in Crete

Because dining is an integral part of social life, Greeks eat out more than most Europeans – twice a week is the national average. And on Crete you can find a huge range of places to choose from, large or small, in which to eat a hefty lunch, knock down a tangily enjoyable snack, spend a sociably laid-back evening dining and drinking or just sit in the shade with a coffee or a cool drink watching all the locals watch the world go by. The old differences between *estiatória* (restaurants) and *tavernas* are fading quickly, although traditionally tavernas are generally more informal, or at least less likely to have white tablecloths. *Mezedopoieíons* specialize in a host of little dishes, which you can build up into an entire meal.

In seaside towns and villages you'll find the fish tavernas, *psarotavérnes*, specializing in all kinds of seafood; most also carry one or two meat dishes for fish haters who may be dragged along. If on the other hand you're a red-blooded meat eater then head for a *psistariá*, specializing in charcoal-grilled chicken, lamb, pork, beef or *kokorétsi* (lamb's offal, braided around a skewer). Even the smallest resort will have at least one *gýros* or *souvláki* stand for cheap greasy fills, many now offering chicken as well as the usual pork. Bakeries sell an array of sweet and savoury hot pies. For something sweet, just look at the lovely displays in any *zacharoplasteío* or pastry shop.

Every village larger than a dozen houses will have a *kafeneíon*, which is a café or coffee house, but more importantly a social institution where men (and increasingly women as well) gather to discuss the latest news, read the papers, nap or play cards, and incidentally drink coffee. Some men seem to live in them. They are so essential to Greek identity that some villages, where property prices seem to make private cafés unprofitable, have opened a municipal *kafeneíon*. The bill of fare is fairly standard, and features Greek coffee (*café ellinikó*), which is the same thick stuff as Turkish coffee, prepared in 40 different ways, although *glykó* (sweet), *métrio* (medium) and *skéto* (no sugar) are the basic orders. It is always served with a cold glass of water. Other coffees, unless you find a proper Italian espresso machine, won't make the earth move for you: 'nes' (Nescafé) has become a Greek word, and instant coffee comes either hot or whipped and iced as a *frappé*, which was invented in Greece but so far hasn't conquered many other taste buds, except in Malaysia and Thailand. Tea, soft drinks, brandy, beer and *ouzo* round out the old-style *kafeneíon* fare. Newer **cafés** usually open earlier and close much later than *kafeneíons*. In resort areas they offer breakfast, from simple to complete English, with rashers, baked beans and eggs. They also serve mineral water (Crete bottles its own: ETANAP from the White Mountains and Zaros, both still and carbonated, from Psilorítis) ice-cream concoctions, milkshakes, wonderful fresh fruit juices, cocktails and thick creamy yoghurt and honey.

Also, even the most flyspeck town these days tends to have at least one music **bar**, usually playing the latest hits (foreign or Greek). They come to life at cocktail hour and again at midnight; closing times vary but dawn isn't unusual in the summer. In general, bars are not cheap, and sometimes outrageously expensive; it can be pretty disconcerting to realize that you paid the same price for your gin fizz as you paid for your entire meal earlier in the taverna next door. However, remember that the usual measures will be at least triples by British standards. If in doubt, stick to beer (Amstel or Heineken are available most of the time, or the Greek brands: the slightly sweet *Mýthos*, and a recently revived old favourite, *Fix*).

Wine and Rakí

Crete is not only one of Greece's biggest wine producers, but was first off the mark; in **Vathýpetro** near Archánes you can see the oldest known wine press in Europe, where some 4,000 years ago the Minoans made their favourite plonk. The Venetians exported large quantites of their beloved *malvasia*, and today's Cretans all seem to have a family vineyard somewhere. The eastern half of the island has several appellations ('AO' is the equivalent of the French AOC). Chief of these is **Pezá**, south of Knossos, the only place in the world where *vilana* grapes grow, producing a thirst-quenching white wine. The slightly spicy reds from **Archánes** (part of the Pezá appellation) are a blend of low acid, low tannin *kotsífali* (usually about 80 per cent) and tannin-rich black *mandelará* grapes, one of Greece's most ancient varieties. Top Pezá producers include Minoikos, both red and white (and both costly) and Ktima Lyraki; less expensive labels include Minos Palace, Logado and Xerolithia. Other estates in Heráklion province, such as Fantaxo-Metocho in **Skaláni**, have planted nearly forgotten varieties such as the once-prized *malvasia dia di Candia*. Crete's second appellation area is **Sitía**, which chiefly produces dry white wines from *liátiko* grapes; Myrto, one of Sitía's better labels, comes in red, white and rosé, all of them around 11.5 per cent proof. The area of western Crete around **Chaniá** and **Kastélli-Kíssamou** may lack an appellation but produces good wines (the white has a distinct sherry tinge) and **Ostria**, a fortified (20 per cent) red wine drunk chilled as an apéritif.

The **house wines** of Crete are good – look for *krasí varelísio* or *krasi chéma* (barreled or loose wine). Although Crete in the past never had much use for **retsina**, Greece's best known wine, the Chaniá co-operative and EKABH in Pezá have started to produce it by popular demand for tourists. Traditionally loose wine or retsina is served by the kilo or half kilo, and chilled (even the red) in copper-anodized jugs. Expect small tumblers instead of stem glasses; etiquette requires that they are never filled to the brim or drained empty, and so you keep topping up your colleagues' glasses, as best you can. *Avíva* or *áspro pato!* ('bottoms up!') are favourite Cretan toasts.

Rakí (or *tsikoúdia*), an eau-de-vie distilled from grape skins and seeds in a hundred mountain stills, is Crete's firewater, its moonshine, quintessence and pure hot-blooded soul. Unlike sweetish, anise-flavoured ouzo, a shot of *rakí*, a *sfyráki*, is always as clear as water and should never be diluted, and never refused; it is synonymous with hospitality, whether offered in a village *kafeneíon* or a monastery. In October, the *kazaniasma* takes place: old-fashioned stills in communal huts, usually hidden in the mountains, come to life with a huge stoking fire, a blast of steam and a continuous party of barbecued meats and song, fuelled by fresh still-warm *rakí*: if you get an invitation to see how it's done, it's not to be missed. But whatever you do, don't light up a cigarette immediately after a shot of the home brew!

The Greek Menu (Καταλογοσ/*Katálogos*)

Ορεκτικά (Μεζέδες)	Orektiká (Mezéthes)	Appetisers
τζατζίκι	tzatziki	yoghurt and cucumbers
ελήές	eliés	olives
κοπανιστί (τυροσαλάτα)	kopanistí (tirosaláta)	cheese purée, often spicy
ντολμάδες	dolmáthes	stuffed vine leaves
μελιτζανοσαλατα	melitzanosaláta	aubergine (eggplant) dip
σαγανάκη	saganáki	fried cheese with lemon
ποικιλία	pikilía	mixed hors d'œuvres
μπουρεκι	bouréki	cheese and vegetable pie
τυροπιττα	tirópitta	cheese pie
αχινοί	achíni	sea urchin roe (quite salty)

Σούπες	Soópes	Soups
αυγολέμονο	avgolémono	egg and lemon soup
χορτόσουπα	chortósoupa	vegetable soup
ψαρόσουπα	psarósoupa	fish soup
φασολάδα	fasolada	bean soup
μαγειρίτσα	magirítsa	giblets in egg and lemon
πατσάς	patsás	tripe and pig's foot soup (for late nights and hangovers

Λαδερά	Latherá	Cooked in Oil
μπάμιες	bámies	okra, ladies' fingers
γίγαντες	yígantes	butter beans in tomato sauce
μπριαμ	briám	aubergines and mixed veg
φακηές	fakés	lentils

Ζυμαρικά	Zimariká	Pasta and Rice
πιλάφι / ρύζι	piláfi/rizi	pilaf/rice
σπαγκέτι	spagéti	spaghetti
μακαρόνια	macarónia	macaroni
πλιγγούρι	plingoúri	bulgar wheat

Ψάρια	Psária	Fish
αστακός	astakós	lobster
αθερίνα	atherína	smelt
γάυρος	gávros	mock anchovy
καλαμάρια	kalamaria	squid
κέφαλος	kefalos	grey mullet
χταπόδι	chtapóthi	octopus
χριστόψαρο	christópsaro	John Dory
μπαρμπούνι	barboúni	red mullet
γαρίδες	garíthes	prawns (shrimps)
γοπα	gópa	bogue (boops boops)
ξιφίας	ksifias	swordfish
μαρίδες	maríthes	whitebait
συναγρίδα	sinagrítha	sea bream
σουπιές	soupiés	cuttlefish

φαγγρι	*fangri*	bream
κιδόνια	*kidónia*	cherrystone clams
σαρδέλλα	*sardélla*	sardines
μπακαλιάρος (σκορδαλιά)	*bakaliáros (skorthaliá)*	fried hake (with garlic sauce)
σαργός	*sargós*	white bream
σκαθάρι	*skathári*	black bream
στρείδια	*stríthia*	oysters
λιθρίνια	*lithrínia*	bass
μίδια	*mídia*	mussels

Εντραδες	*Entrádes*	**Main Courses**
κουνέλι	*kounéli*	rabbit
στιφάδο	*stifádo*	casserole with onions
γιουβέτσι	*yiouvétsi*	veal in a clay bowl
συκώτι	*seekóti*	liver
μοσχάρι	*moschári*	veal
αρνί	*arní*	lamb
κατσικι	*katsíki*	kid
κοτόπουλο	*kotópoulo*	(roast) chicken
χοιρινό	*chirinó*	pork

Κυμάδες	*Kymadhes*	**Minced Meat**
παστίτσιο	*pastítsio*	mince and macaroni pie
μουσακά	*moussaká*	meat, aubergine with white sauce
μακαρόνια με κυμά	*makarónia me kymá*	spaghetti Bolognese
μπιφτέκι	*biftéki*	hamburger, usually bunless
σουτζουκάκια	*soutzoukákia*	meat balls in sauce
μελιτζάνες γεμιστές	*melitzánes yemistés*	stuffed aubergines/eggplants
πιπεριές γεμιστές	*piperíes yemistés*	stuffed peppers

Της Ωρας	*Tis Oras*	**Grills to Order**
μριζολα	*brizóla*	beef steak with bone
μπριζόλες χοιρινές	*brizólas chirinés*	pork chops
σουβλάκι	*souvláki*	meat or fish kebabs on a skewer
κοκορέτσι	*kokorétsi*	offal kebabs
κοτολέτες	*kotolétes*	veal chops
πάιδακια	*paidakia*	lamb chops
κεφτέδες	*keftéthes (th as in 'th')*	meat balls

Σαλάτες	*Salátes*	**Salads and Vegetables**
ντομάτες	*domátes*	tomatoes
αγγούρι	*angoúri*	cucumber
ρώσσικη σαλάτα	*róssiki saláta*	Russian salad
σπανάκι	*spanáki*	spinach
χωριάτικη	*choriátiki*	salad with feta cheese and olives
κολοκυθάκια	*kolokithákia*	courgettes/zucchini
πιπεριεσ	*piperiés*	peppers
κρεμιδι	*kremídi*	onions

πατάτες	patátes	potatoes
παντσάρια	pantsária	beetroot
μαρούλι	maroúli	lettuce
χόρτα	chórta	wild greens
αγκινάρες	anginάres	artichokes
κουκιά	koukiá	fava beans

Τυρια	**Tiriάv**	**Cheeses**
φέτα	féta	goat's cheese
κασέρι	kasséri	hard buttery cheese
γραβιέρα	graviéra	Greek 'Gruyère'
μυζήθρα	mizíthra	soft white cheese
πρόβιο	próvio	sheep's cheese

Γλυκά	**Glyká**	**Sweets**
παγωτό	pagotó	ice cream
κουραμπιέδες	kourabiéthes	sugared biscuits
λουκουμάδες	loukoumáthes	hot honey fritters
χαλβά	halvá	sesame seed sweet
μπακλαβά	baklavá	nuts and honey in filo pastry
γιαούρτι (με μελι)	yiaoúrti (me méli)	yoghurt (with honey)
καριδοπιτα	karidópita	walnut cake
μήλο	mílo	apple
μπουγάτσα	bougátsa	custard tart

Miscellaneous

ψωμί	psomí	bread
βούτυρο	voútiro	butter
μέλι	méli	honey
μαρμελάδα	marmelátha	jam
λάδι	láthi	oil
πιάτο	piáto	plate
λογαριασμό	logariazmó	the bill/check

Drinks

άσπρο κρασί	áspro krasí	wine, white
άσπρο/κόκκινο/κοκκινέλι	áspro/kókkino/kokkinéli	white/red/rosé
ρετσίνα	retsína	resinated wine
νερό (βραστο/μεταλικο)	neró (vrastó/metalikó)	water (boiled/mineral)
μπύρα	bíra	beer
χυμός πορτοκάλι	chimós portokáli	orange juice
γάλα	gála	milk
τσάί	tsái	tea
σοκολάτα	sokoláta	chocolate
καφέ	kafé	coffee
φραππέ	frappé	iced coffee
πάγος	págos	ice
ποτίρι	potíri	glass
μπουκάλι	boukáli	bottle
καράφα	karáfa	carafe
στήν γειά σας!	stín yásas (formal, pl)	to your health! Cheers!
στήν γειά σου!	stín yásou (sing)	

Travel

08

Getting There

By Air

Crete has two main airports, and each summer a steady stream of direct charter flights run from at least seven UK airports to **Heráklion** and to a lesser extent to **Chaniá**. Coming from outside Europe, your best hope for a bargain route to Crete is to get a discount flight to London, and from there a cheap charter to the island; another alternative is to fly to Athens, from where connections to Crete are easy and frequent. **Olympic** has five to six flights daily from Athens to Heráklion and two or more to Chaniá, as well as several flights weekly to Heráklion and Chaniá from Thessaloníki and Rhodes. **Aegean Airlines** also has frequent flights between Athens and Chaniá and Heráklion, which usually underprice Olympic (for more on flights via Athens, *see* p.80).

From the UK and Ireland

Charters provide virtually all the direct flights to Crete, but, as competition across Europe increases, don't automatically assume charter flights are your best buy, as prices on scheduled, no-frills flights with a change in Athens onto a Greek domestic flight can also work out as very competitive. The one rule seems to be that the sooner you buy your ticket, the more you will save. Always check out the deals currently offered through local travel agents, the websites of easyJet and other low-cost airlines, and the discount flight websites listed below.

Airline Carriers

UK and Ireland

Aer Lingus, t 0845 0844 444; Ireland **t** 0818 365 000, *www.aerlingus.com*.

British Airways, t 0845 77 333 77, *www.britishairways.com*.

easyJet, t 0870 6000 000, *www.easyjet.com*.

Excel Airways, t 0870 998 98 98, *www.excelairways.com*.

KLM, t 0870 5074 074, *www.klm.com*.

Lufthansa, t 0845 7737 747, *www.lufthansa.com*.

Monarch, t 0870 0405 040, *www.flymonarch.com*.

Olympic Airways, t 0870 6060 460; Dublin **t** (01) 608 0090, *www.olympic-airways.gr*.

USA and Canada

Air Canada, t 1 888 247 2262, *www.aircanada.ca*.

British Airways, USA and Canada **t** 1 800-AIRWAYS, *www.britishairways.com*.

CSA–Czech Airlines, t 1 800 223 2365, *www.czecharlines.com*.

Delta, t 1 800 241 4141, *www.delta.com*

KLM, USA **t** 1 800 225 2525, Canada **t** 1 800 447 4747, *www.klm.com*.

Olympic Airways, USA **t** 1 800 223 1226; in Canada: Montreal, **t** (514) 878 9691; Toronto, **t** (416) 920 2452, *www.olympic-airways.gr*.

Charters and Students

UK and Ireland

Avro, t 0870 558 2841, *www.avro.co.uk*. Charter flights to Crete from London Gatwick, Manchester and some other airports.

Balkan Tours, t (028) 9024 6795, *www.balkan.co.uk*. Charter flights to Crete and other parts of Greece from Belfast.

Delta Travel, t 0870 22 00 727, *www.deltatravel.co.uk*. Based in Manchester, Birmingham and Liverpool, this agency specializes in Greece and has good deals on scheduled routes to Athens and Greek domestic flights, plus charters to Crete.

Eclipse Direct, reservations **t** 0870 501 0203; **t** (01293) 554 400; **t** (0161) 742 2277. Charter flights from London Gatwick, Birmingham and Manchester.

Holiday to Crete, t 0870 745 0677, *www.holiday-to-crete.co.uk*. Part of the Holiday Warehouse group, this agency is a good place to look for late package deals, self-catering holidays, flight-only bookings and other bargains on Crete.

JMC, flights **t** 0870 0100 434, holidays **t** 0870 7580 203, www.jmc.com. Giant agency with flights from several UK airports.

STA Travel, central phoneline **t** 0870 1600 599; also Bristol, **t** 0870 167 6777; Leeds, **t** (01132) 459 400; Belfast, **t** (02896) 241 469, *www.statravel.co.uk*. The largest student

Scheduled and No-Frills Flights

Olympic and **British Airways** (both from Heathrow) and budget carriers **easyJet** (from Luton and Gatwick) fly to Athens, from where it's easy to pick up a connecting flight to Crete. In the peak season Olympic flies three times daily from Heathrow and twice weekly from Manchester, and also has direct flights several times a week from London Gatwick to Thessaloníki. Scheduled flights with one stop can also be booked with **Lufthansa** (via Munich) and **KLM** (via Amsterdam), and Lufthansa especially sometimes has very good late price deals. Return prices range from around £80 off season to £250 high season.

Scheduled flights from Ireland to Athens on **Aer Lingus** and **Olympic** involve a change in London and are a lot pricier than charters.

Charter Flights

The great advantage of charters is that they fly from many regional UK or other European airports straight to Crete. And, with all the recent changes in the airline business, the differences between charters and scheduled flights are much less than they once were. With some charter airlines, notably **Monarch** (which flies to Heráklion from Gatwick, Manchester and Dublin, and to Chaniá from Gatwick) and **Excel** (Heráklion from Gatwick and Glasgow, and Chaniá from Gatwick) you can book online, just as you would with a scheduled carrier. Many flight-only charters can also be booked through discount flight websites, as well as through travel agents. Check out, too, newspaper travel sections and *Time Out* for last-minute standby deals.

travel specialist in the UK, with over 60 branch offices throughout the country.
Trailfinders, London, **t** (020) 7937 1234; Birmingham, **t** (0121) 236 1234; Manchester **t** (0161) 839 6969; Glasgow, **t** (0141) 353 2224; Belfast **t** (028) 9027 1888; Dublin **t** (01) 677 7888, *www.trailfinders.com*. Bookings of any level of complexity worldwide.

Websites

All these sites are good places to look for good-value flight deals.
www.cheapflights.com
www.cheap-crete-flights.co.uk
www.cheap-flight-offers.co.uk
www.dialaflight.com
www.flights4less.co.uk/crete.htm
www.lastminute.com
www.onlinetravellers.co.uk
www.skydeals.co.uk
www.thomascook.co.uk
www.travelocity.co.uk
www.travelselect.com

USA and Canada

Air Brokers International, USA **t** 1 800 883 3273, *www.airbrokers.com*. Discount flight agency.
Homeric Tours, **t** 1 800 223 5570, *www.homerictours.com*. Greek specialists offering flight-only charter flights and custom tours throughout mainland and island Greece from the USA.

Last Minute Travel Club, USA **t** 1 800 527 8646, Canada **t** 1 877 970 3500, *www.lastminute club.com*. Canada-based travel service offering bargain flights and also extra-low-cost stand-by deals for those who pay an annual membership.
New Frontiers, **t** 1 800 677 0720, *www.newfrontiers.com*. Good prices on flights to every part of Europe and especially good low-season deals.
STA Travel, **t** 1 800 781 4040, in New York, **t** (212) 627 3111, *www.statravel.com*. The North American arm of the worldwide student travel specialists, which now has offices throughout the US and Canada.
Travel Avenue, **t** 1 800 333 3335, *www.travel avenue.com*. Bargain flight agency.
Travel Cuts, Canada **t** 1 866 246 9762, USA **t** 1 800 592 2887, *www.travelcuts.com*. Canada's largest student travel specialist, which now also offers bargain flights and tours from most parts of the US.

Websites

www.air-fare.com
www.expedia.com
apps.flights.com
www.orbitz.com
www.priceline.com
www.smarterliving.com
www.travellersweb.ws
www.travelocity.com

Note that most charters still fly only from May to October, but some firms offer early specials, often from Gatwick and Manchester, in March and April, depending on when Greek Easter falls. Otherwise the chief remaining difference between charter and scheduled services is that charter tickets are nearly always issued for a fixed, minimum period, usually of seven days, 14 days or any other multiple of a week, with little flexibility. There's also little choice on departure and arrival times, which may be in the wee hours.

Returning from Crete, be sure to confirm your return flight three days prior to departure. Visitors to Greece using a charter flight may visit Turkey or any neighbouring country for the day but must not stay overnight, at the very real risk of forfeiting your return ticket home. Travellers with stamps from previous holidays in Turkey will not be barred entry, but if you have Turkish Cypriot stamps, check with the Passport Office before you go.

Student and Youth Discounts

If you're under 26 or a full-time student under 32 with an **International Student Identity Card**, you're eligible for student/youth charters; these are exempt from the usual charter voucher system and can be sold as one-way tickets, enabling you to stay in Greece longer than would be possible with a regular charter. Students under 26 are sometimes eligible for discounts on scheduled flights as well, especially with **Olympic**, who currently offer 25% discounts to ISIC holders on all flights from Athens to the islands.

International Student Travel Service, 11 Níkis St, Athens, t 210 323 3767.

From the USA and Canada

Olympic and **Delta** both offer non-stop flights from New York to Athens year-round, with more frequent services in summer; Olympic also flies direct to Athens from Toronto and Montreal. US economy fares (Apex and SuperApex/Eurosavers, booked at least three weeks in advance) range from $800 return New York–Athens in low season to $1,200 high season; Canadian economy fares from Toronto or Montreal range from CAN$1,000 low season to CAN$1,400–1,900. When calling around, take into consideration the hefty discount offered by travel agents on

domestic flights within Greece for travellers arriving in the country on Olympic.

From many US or Canadian cities European airlines such as **KLM** or **Czech Airlines** offer good deals to Greece, with changes (and possibly stopovers) in New York or Boston and one other European city. Internet travel companies often come up with the best deals.

Flights between Athens and Crete

Flights from Athens to Crete are run by **Olympic Airways** and **Aegean Airlines**. North Americans who do not have a local Olympic office should call t 1 800 223 1226 for information. In the last few years Olympic have also been offering **island-to-island flights** in the summer season, a pleasant innovation that can preclude the need to go to Athens; routes between Crete and Rhodes, Santoríni and Mýkonos are fairly well-established. It's also possible to get a scheduled 'open jaws' ticket to Athens and on to any permutation of islands, but you will still have to return home from Athens. At time of writing the **prices** of one-way economy-class flights from Athens to Crete run from around €45–70.

Changing Flights in Athens

Athens' new **Elefthérios Venizélos Airport** – opened only in 2001 – is 25km northeast of

---

Airlines in Athens

Aegean Airlines, 572 Vouliagménis, Glyfáda, low-cost reservations line t 801 11 20 000; airport t 210 353 4289, www.aegeanair.com.

Air Canada, 8 Zirioi, Maroússi, t 210 617 5321, f 210 610 8919.

British Airways, 1 Themistokléos, Glyfada, t 210 890 6666, f 010 890 6510.

CSA–Czech Airlines, 65B Vouliagménis, Glyfada, t 210 969 4331, f 210 961 2712.

Delta, 4 Óthonos, special reservations line t 800 4412 9506, office t 210 331 1668, f 210 325 0451

easyJet, t 210 967 0000.

KLM, 41 Vouliagménis, Glyfáda, t 210 960 5010, f 010 964 8868.

Lufthansa, 10 Zirioi, Maroússi, t 210 617 5200, f 210 610 8919.

Olympic Airways, 96 L. Syngroú, among many branches; low-cost reservations line t 801 11 44 444, www.olympic-airways.gr.

the city centre and has shops, restaurants, banks, car rental and a tourist information kiosk, on Level o. There is a charge for luggage trolleys, so try to bring euro coins with you

The new airport is huge, with some long distances between international and domestic gates, and Athens' airports (old and new) have long had a reputation for delays, so be sure to allow for at least **90mins–2hrs** between your arrival time and an ongoing connection to Crete. If possible have your luggage booked through to Crete so that you don't have to re-check it in Athens, which will also cut down on potential delays.

If you are stopping over in Athens, a light rail link between the aiport and the Athens metro system is slated for completion in 2003; until then there are **express buses** to the city that leave 24hrs a day from the main terminal; tickets cost €3 and are valid for 24 hours on all other forms of Athens' public transport.
Airport information, t 210 353 0000. Operates 24 hours a day in English and Greek.

By Train

The best route by train from the UK to Greece is via Italy. Starting with a Eurostar train from London Waterloo to Paris (3hrs), the journey to Brindisi in the south of Italy should take about 24 hours. From Brindisi you can take a ferry to Pátras in the northern Peloponnese, or you can also go by train to Venice and then take a ship to Pátras from there; once in Pátras you can get a train to Piraeus and from there a ferry for Crete.
Eurostar, UK **t** 08705 186 186, USA **t** 1 800-EUROSTAR, *www.eurostar. com.*
Rail Europe (UK), 179 Piccadilly, London W1V 0BA, **t** 08705 848 848, *www.raileurope.co.uk.* For information on trains between the UK and Greece, and the rail passes available.
Rail Europe (USA), 226 Westchester Ave, White Plains, NY 10064, **t** 1 800 438 7245, *www.raileurope.com.* Take your passport.

By Bus

Taking a coach from London through Europe to Greece is another possible alternative for those who decide that a train trip is too expensive and maybe are seriously averse to

flying. It should be said that nowadays a coach to Greece can work out only marginally cheaper than a standby flight, and can easily take four days instead of four hours, but it gives you a chance to see Munich, Belgrade and other fine bus terminals en route. As with the trains, the easiest route to take is via Italy, where ferries can be picked up in Venice, Ancona, Brindisi and Bari.
Busabout, London Traveller's Centre, 258 Vauxhall Bridge Rd, London, SW1V 1BS, **t** (020) 7950 1661, **f** (020) 7950 1662, *www. busabout.com.* Popular hop-on, hop-off service for backpackers who want to take in various European cities, using bus passes that cover travel from 2 weeks to 2 months.
Eurolines, 52 Grosvenor Gardens, London SW1W 0AU, **t** 08705 143 219, *www.gobycoach.com.* The largest international bus network operating from the UK no longer has a service direct to Athens, but still offers a wide array of other interconnecting routes that will transport you through various European cities to Athens or Italy, where you can catch a connecting ferry.

By Sea

The most popular sea routes to Greece are from Italy: there are ferries daily from Ancona and Brindisi and slightly less frequent services from Bari and Venice. Brindisi ferries connect with a night train from Rome, and arrive in Igoumenítsa in northwestern Greece or Pátras in the Peloponnese the next morning. Lately ferries have been picking up speed: **Ventouris** has a fast catamaran from Brindisi that goes to Corfu and Igoumenítsa in under 4hrs. Passengers are usually allowed a free stopover in Corfu, if that is not their final destination, before continuing to Igoumenítsa or Pátras, but make sure this is stated on your ticket.

The different companies (*see* p.82) offer a range of **discounts**. On all of them, fares for children aged 4–12 are half the adult fare and under-4s travel for free or for only a minimal fare so long as they do not occupy their own berth. There are also special family fares, and discounts of 10% for over-60s and of 30% on return tickets for people travelling with a car who book in advance, and also occasional special discounts for students and under-26s.

Ferries to Crete

Piraeus, the port of Athens, is the natural hub of the giant ferry network connecting the Greek mainland and islands. Local companies run the large, clean and comfortable ships – among the best in Greece – that provide the most frequent services to Crete, nightly at 9 or 10pm from Piraeus to Heráklion. The 9-hour journey through the night, in a cabin or, on a warm night, out on deck, can be very pleasant, besides reminding you that Crete, after all, is an island. There are also high-speed ferries that take about 6hrs, but which still allow you a couple of extra hours to snooze in your cabin on arrival – which is usually at 5.30am.

While **Piraeus–Heráklion** is the busiest route, there are also slightly less frequent sailings from Piraeus to other ports on Crete (**Chaniá, Réthymnon, Ag. Nikólaos, Sitía**) and from other parts of the mainland and islands (**Thessaloníki–Heráklion** via Santoríni and Náxos, **Ag. Nikólaos to Rhodes** via Kárpathos and other islands). ANEK has twice-weekly boats between **Gýthio** in the Peloponnese and **Kastélli-Kíssamou** in western Crete.

If you arrive at **Athens airport** and want to get a boat straight to Crete, one of the airport buses (**E96**) runs every 15–30mins straight through to Piraeus harbour; from central Athens, take metro line 1 to the end of the line, Piraeus station. From late 2003–4, it should be possible to take the metro all the way from the airport to the harbour. A **taxi** from the airport to Piraeus should cost around €14.50.

The Greek National Tourist Office publishes a **free weekly list** of all the many ferries around the country, both international and to the islands; serious island-hoppers can also ask for their free booklet, *Greek Travel Routes: Domestic Sea Schedules*. Otherwise, you can find pretty comprehensive lists of current Greek island ferry routes, times and fares on the **websites** *www.ferries.gr* and the *Greek Travel Pages* (*www.gtp.gr*). Bear in mind, though, that schedules change quite frequently, and that any number of factors (weather, health emergencies and unforeseen repairs) can throw timetables out of the window; if, for example, you have to catch a flight home from Athens, allow for the eccentricities of the system and give yourself plenty of time (a day early, if possible) to be safe.

Ferries to Greece and Crete

Italy to Greece

Tickets can be booked in advance via travel agents in Greece and abroad or through *www.greekferries.gr*, which conveniently lists all the ferry companies and allows you to compare prices and schedules.

ANEK Lines, 54 Amalías, ✉ 10538 Athens, **t** 210 323 3481, **f** 210 323 4137, *www.anek.gr*. From Ancona and Trieste.

Blue Star Ferries, 26 Aktí Possidónos, ✉ 18531 Piraeus, **t** 210 891 9800, **f** 210 891 9938, *www.bluestarferries.com*. From Ancona, Venice and Brindisi.

Minoan Lines, 2 Vass. Konstantinoú, ✉ 15125 Athens, reservations **t** 801 11 75000, **f** 210 752 0540, *www.minoan.gr*. From Ancona and Venice.

Superfast Ferries, 30 Amalías, ✉ 10538 Athens, **t** 210 331 3252, *www.superfast.com*. From Ancona and Bari.

Ventouris Ferries, 91 Pireós/2 Kýthiron, ✉ 18541 Piraeus, **t** 210 482 8001, **f** 210 481 3701, *www.ventouris.gr*. From Ancona and Brindisi.

Mainland Greece to Crete

Handy sources of information on current routes are *www.ferries.gr* and *www.gtp.gr*.

ANEK Lines, Piraeus, **t** 210 419 7420, Chaniá **t** 282 127 5004, *www.anek.gr*. Piraeus–Heráklion, Piraeus–Chaniá, both daily, and Piraeus–Réthymnon 3–4 times weekly; the subsidiary **ANEN Line** (**t** 282 102 4148) operates between Kastélli–Kíssamou and Gýthio and other small ports in the Peloponnese.

Blue Star Ferries, Piraeus, **t** 210 891 9800, Crete **t** 281 022 1166, *www.bluestarferries.com*. Piraeus–Chaniá, daily Mar–Oct, check schedule at other times.

Lane Line, Piraeus, **t** 210 427 4011, Crete (Ag. Nikólaos) **t** 284 102 5249. Piraeus to Ag. Nikólaos and Sitía, both five times weekly (less frequent in summer), and Rhodes–Ag. Nikólaos, stopping in Sitía and other islands.

Minoan Lines, 26 Aktí Possidónos, Piraeus, reservations **t** 801 11 75000, Heráklion **t** 281 039 9800/**t** 281 022 9602, *www.minoan.gr*. Piraeus–Heráklion daily, Thessaloníki–Heráklion 4 times weekly.

It is obligatory to have a ticket before boarding all ferries, as they are no longer sold on board. They can be bought from many small agencies, and before buying a ticket it's worth comparing the different companies. For up-to-date and 'non-partisan' information on sailing schedules, the best places to enquire are the **Port Authorities** (*Limenarchion*) of each harbour (they don't often speak English, however, so if you phone you may have to get a Greek to help). The number of the Piraeus authority is given below, and Port Authority phone numbers on Crete are included in the **Getting Around** sections in each chapter.

Prices have been rising but are still reasonable; deck-class from Piraeus to Heráklion costs around €24, a berth in a 4-bed cabin from around €45; other routes are often a bit cheaper. Children under four travel free or for very little, and aged 4–10 for half fare. Taking a car to Crete will cost from around €65 one-way, but there are discounts for return tickets.

Comfort on Greek ferries has improved by leaps and bounds, and some now boast shops, video rooms, disco bars and even small swimming pools. On the big Piraeus–Crete ferries cabins are air-conditioned and divided into two or three classes: the first, 'distinguished' class, with a plush lounge and private cabins (which can cost as much as flying); second class, often with its own lounge, too, but much smaller cabins, segregated by sex; and third or tourist class, with big rooms of airline-type seats and access to shops and snack bars. On summer nights old-fashioned 'deck class' can be a cheap and fun alternative, especially if you have a sleeping bag (it can get chillier than you might expect); if you aim to sleep out it's worth getting on board an hour early, to claim some quiet deck space. Also, bottled water, snacks and so on tend to be expensive on the ferries, so take some with you.

In August, buy tickets well in advance if you have a car or want a cabin. If you miss your ship, you forfeit your ticket; if you cancel in advance, you will receive a 50% refund, or 100% in the case of major delays or cancellations. If you are 'greatly inconvenienced' by a delay, you're entitled to compensation: contact the Ministry of the Merchant Marine (*www.yen.gr*), or the Piraeus port police. **Piraeus Port Authority, t** 210 422 6000/ **t** 210 459 3000 (for ferry schedules).

By Car

Driving from the UK to Athens at a fairly normal pace, with a ferry from Italy to Greece, takes around 3½ days. An **International Driving Licence** is not required for EU citizens, but is useful for nationals of other countries; obtain one at home from a motoring organization (such as the AAA, in the US) before you leave. The minimum age is 18 years.

Under EU law all motor **insurance** policies give basic third-party cover in any EU country, but before taking a car to Greece it's advisable to obtain extended comprehensive and breakdown cover. Alternatively, the **Motor Insurance Bureau**, 10 Xenofóntos Street, Athens, **t** 210 323 6733, can provide additional cover for Greece.

Customs formalities for bringing in a car are very easy; you must have with you the registration and insurance documents and the car should have a hazard warning triangle and a fire extinguisher. You are allowed six months' use of a car in Greece before it must leave the country; if you intend to stay more than a few weeks, to avoid difficulties when you leave, make sure the car details are stamped in your passport on arrival.

The **Greek Automobile Club (ELPA)**, 395 Messógion, Ag. Paraskeví, Athens ☑ 153 43, **t** 210 606 8800, operates a breakdown service within 60km of Athens and Heráklion (**t** 104). The AA and RAC in Britain both have affiliate arrangements with ELPA. It has a medical assistance helpline, **t** 166, and a 24hr information line, **t** 174. An alternative private breakdown service is Express Service, **t** 154.

Entry Formalities

Passports and Visas

European Union citizens can stay in Greece indefinitely. The only reason you would need special permission to stay would be if you wanted to work or carry out any banking procedures that require proof of residence; if so, apply at a local police station.

Formalities for **non-EU** tourists entering Greece are very simple. US, Australian and Canadian citizens with a valid passport can stay for up to three months. If you decide you want to stay any longer, take your passport, 20 days before your time in Greece expires, to your local police station, and be prepared to prove you can support yourself, with bank statements and the like. If you overstay the three months, be prepared for a fine that's currently around €150 for overstaying three months, €300 if over six months.

Customs

Duty-free allowances have been abolished within the EU. For travellers arriving in Greece from outside the EU, the duty-free limits are 1 litre of spirits or 2 litres of liquors (port, sherry or champagne), plus 2 litres of wine and 200 cigarettes. Much larger quantities – up to 10 litres of spirits, 90 litres of wine, 110 litres of beer and 3,200 cigarettes – bought locally, can be taken through customs provided that you are travelling between EU countries and can prove that these goods are for your private consumption only.

For more information, US citizens can phone the **US Customs Service**, t (202) 354 1000, or see the pamphlet *Know Before You Go*, available from *www.customs.gov*.

Getting Around

The bibles for travel around Crete are the *Greek Travel Pages* (updated monthly, *www.gtp.gr*) and *www.gogreece.com*, and the Crete-only site *www.cretetravel.com*.

By Bus

The Greek national bus service (**KTEL, ΚΤΕΛ**) in Crete is efficient, regular, punctual, recently computerized and relatively cheap. Buses run between main towns and from provincial capitals out to the villages, with a first bus on most routes early in the morning, around 6–7am, and a last bus back around 9–10pm; between then, there are frequent services on major routes, but maybe only one or two a day in each direction on quiet country roads.

If there's a bus station or ticket booth, you purchase your ticket before boarding; if not, the driver will sell you one on board. In August, it's worth booking on long-distance

Specialist Tour Operators

For agencies specializing in self-catering villa rentals, *see* pp.96–7.

From the UK

Amathus Holidays, 2 Leather Lane, London EC1N 7RA, **t** (020) 7611 0901, *www.amathus holidays.co.uk*. Villas, packages and special interest holidays.

Argo Holidays, 100 Wigmore St, London W1H 9DR, **t** (020) 7331 7070, *www.argo-holidays.com*. Villa rentals and special interest trips, from painting to watersports.

Artemis Travel, 157 El. Venízelou, Mália, ✉ 72200, Crete, **t** (+30) 289 703 3767, *www.crete-holidays.net*. Local company with a range of facilities, tours and car rental.

Explore Worldwide, 1 Frederick St, Aldershot, Hants GU11 1LQ, **t** (01252) 760000, *www.exploreworldwide.com*. Walking and caique tours on Crete.

Filoxenia/Grecofile, Sourdock Hill, Barkisland, Halifax HX4 0AG, **t** (01422) 375999/371796, *www.filoxenia.co.uk*. Comprehensive Greece-only agency with tours, flights and 'couture' holidays, including archaeological, walking

and nature tours. Its **Grecofile** section tailors trips to all kinds of individual requirements.

Greek Islands Club, Upper Square, Old Isleworth, Middx TW7 7BJ, **t** (020) 8568 4499, *www.sunvil.co.uk*. Helpful and friendly company with a choice of villas and activity holidays, including sailing and watersports.

Headwater Holidays, The Old School House, Chester Rd, Northwich, Cheshire CW8 1LE, **t** (01606) 720 033, *www.headwater-holidays. co.uk*. Special-interest tours on Crete: walking, cycling, cookery, adventure tours.

Hidden Greece, 47 Whitcomb St, London WC2H 7DH, **t** (020) 7839 2553, *www.hidden-greece. co.uk*. Off the beaten track, small group trips.

Island Holidays, Drummond St, Comrie, PH6 2DS, **t** (01764) 670107, *www.24islandholidays. com*. Birdwatching and nature tours.

Martin Randall, Barley Mow Passage, London W4 4PH, **t** (020) 8742 3355, *www.martin randall.com*. Prestigious cultural tours specialist with small-group trips guided by experts, including one on Minoan Crete.

Naturetrek, Cheriton Mill, Cheriton, Alresford, Hampshire SO24 0NG, **t** (01962) 733051, *www.naturetrek.co.uk*. Birdwatching and nature trips, especially in spring.

buses, but this is often not possible on local routes. There are never enough seats in summer, nor is it customary to queue, although if you have a ticket with a seat number you can claim your rights (note that the numbers are on the back of each seat, not on the seat in front). Buses are rarely crowded early in the morning.

Different timetables apply at weekends and on holidays; bus schedules for the whole of Greece can be found on *www.ktel.org*.

By Car or Motorbike

Buses are fine for travel to Crete's larger towns and best-known sites, but many others can only be reached with your own transport, be it shoe-leather, motorbike or car. Cretan roads have a terrifying accident rate, so be careful. Most mishaps happen along the E75 highway east of Heráklion, especially when old and new roads merge in the middle of resorts like Gouvés (where 50 people, mostly pedestrians, were killed in one five-year stint). Crossroads, tipsy tourists, Greeks speeding or gesticulating while driving, low visibility in mountains and flocks of goats or sheep are the greatest hazards. Don't be shy about sounding a horn on blind mountain corners.

Traffic regulations comply with standard practice on the European continent, and most signs are in Greek and Roman script (if you can read them through the bullet holes – Cretan hunters like to use them for target practice). Where there are no right-of-way signs at a crossroads, give priority to traffic coming from the right. There is a speed limit of 50kph (30mph) in towns and villages; other speed limits are indicated by signs in kilometres.

The good news is that **petrol/gasoline** is cheaper in Greece than in almost any other EU country, around €1 a litre; unleaded (*amólivdi*) is even less. If you're exploring, it's a good idea to have a spare can of petrol with you, as petrol stations can be scarce, and only open during shop hours. A good map, such as the ROAD map of Crete, is essential for exploring.

Ramblers Holidays, Box 43, Welwyn Garden City, Herts AL8 6PQ, **t** (01707) 331133, *www.ramblersholidays.co.uk*. Walking tours emphasizing archaeology and wildflowers.

Solo's Holidays, 54–58 High St, Edgware, Middx HA8 7EJ, **t** 0870 0720 700, *www.solosholidays.co.uk*. Group holidays for singles', in 4-star hotels, for different age brackets.

Waymark Holidays, 44 Windsor Road, Slough SL1 2EJ, **t** (01753) 516477, *www.waymarkholidays.com*. Guided hiking groups and treks.

Yoga Plus, 177 Ditchling Road, Brighton BN1 6JB, **t** (01273) 276175, *www.yogaplus.co.uk*. Yoga and other holistic therapies in beautiful locations in southern Crete.

From the USA and Canada

Archaeological Tours, 271 Madison Ave, New York, NY10016, **t** 1 866 740 5130, **t** (212) 986 3054, *www.archaeologicaltrs.com*. Tours of the Minoan and other historic sites with special guest lecturers.

Classic Adventures, P.O. Box 143, Hamlin, NY 14464, **t** 1 800 777 8090, **t** (716) 964 8488, *www.classicadventures.com*. Cycling-based tours of Crete, with guides who are also well informed on archaeology.

Cloud Tours, Newtown Plaza, 31-09 Newtown Ave, 3rd Floor, LIC, N.Y. 11102, **t** 1 800 223 7880, **t** (718) 721 3808, *www.cloudtours.com*. Greek specialists with several tours and cruises.

EcoGreece, P.O. Box 2614, Rancho Palos Verdes, CA 90275, **t** 1 877 838 7748, *www.ecogreece.com*. Hiking tours of Crete, yacht sailing tours around the islands and more.

Goddess Pilgrimage to Crete, Ariadne Institute, P.O. Box 791596, New Orleans, LA 70179-1596, **t/f** (504) 486-9119, *www.goddessariadne.org*. Tours of ancient holy places in Crete, for small groups of women 'in search of the goddess'.

Greece 101, *www.greece101.com*. Net-based operator offering hiking tours and other activities in Crete and other parts of Greece.

Meander Adventures, P.O. Box 4168, Park City, UT 84060, **t** 1 888 616 7272, **t** (435) 649 6015, *www.greece-travel-turkey-travel.com*. Organized tours, sailing holidays, honeymoons and also personalized itineraries.

Metro Tours, 484 Lowell Street, Peabody, MA 01960, **t** 1 800 221 2810, **t** (978) 535 4000, *www.metrotours.com*. Honeymoons, cruises, yachting and adventure trips in Greece; customized itineraries are a speciality.

Hiring a Car

There are so many rent-a-car companies on Crete it's hard not to fall over them. Many are family-run, and many are rip-offs: read all small print with care and, if it's off season, don't be shy about negotiating (arriving at an agency with brochures from the competition can help). Most firms require that you be at least 21, but for some the minimum age is 23 or 25; anyone with a driving licence from any EU country will have no trouble hiring a car, but non-EU citizens may be asked to show an **International Driving Licence** (*see* p.83). Most agencies do not include **tax** or personal and collision damage waiver (CDW) **insurance** in their advertised prices, so check this carefully; it is always advisable to take out CDW, as the obligatory minimum insurance cover is very limited. Check, too, that your deal gives you **unlimited mileage**, as anything else will waste you money. As usual, a credit card is effectively essential to hire a car, but many agencies will give discounts if you eventually pay in cash.

Hiring a small car averages €45–55 a day in summer, with Jeeps 30% more. You can save money by booking in advance with your flight or via the Net (try *www.interdynamic.net*, *www.dilos.com* or *www.crete-holidays.net*).

Motorbikes, Scooters and Mopeds

Motorbikes and ever-more popular scooters and mopeds are ideal for getting around Crete in summer. It almost never rains, parking is easy and what could be more pleasant than a thyme-scented breeze freshening your trip over the mountains? Scooters and mopeds (Greeks call them *papákia*, 'little ducks', for the noise they make) are more economical and practical than cars; they fit into almost any boat and travel paths where cars fear to tread. Rental rates vary (count on at least €15 a day), and should include third-party insurance, but as with car hire (*see* above) it's a good idea to take out extra cover. You will need a valid driving licence (non-EU nationals may need an international one, *see* p.83) to hire a basic bike and for bikes over 75cc may be asked to show a motorcycle driver's licence.

The downsides: many hospital beds in Crete are occupied every year by careless tourists (the accident rate is even worse for bikes than for cars), and the noise drives everyone buggy.

By law, **helmets** are required at all times and should be provided by the rental agency, but in practice the only ones you'll see are worn about the elbow. When renting, **check out the state of your bike**; maintenance standards are very patchy. And above all, be careful.

Hitchhiking

Greek taxi-drivers have convinced the government to pass a law forbidding other Greeks from picking up hitchhikers, so you may find it slow going. Perhaps because of this, motorized holidaymakers now seem to stop and offer rides more than locals.

By Bicycle

Cycling has not caught on in Crete, as a sport or a means of transport, but you can hire bikes in most larger resorts and at **Trekking Bike** in Chaniá (*see* p.102), and **Hellas Bike** in Réthymnon (*see* p.153) runs excursions into the mountains. If you have your own, planes carry bikes for a small fee, and ferries generally take them along for nothing.

On Foot

Crete's many gorges offer the island's most celebrated walks, but keen walkers might like to take on part of the **E4 long-distance footpath**, which runs the length of Crete from Kastélli-Kíssamou in the west to Káto Zákros in the east. It is marked on the maps in this guide, and for more on the E4 and other aspects of walking in Crete, *see* p.94.

Caiques and Local Ferries

Traditional sailing boats (**caiques**) and more modern **water-taxis** provide transport to outlying islands around Crete and to isolated beaches inaccessible by road, especially from south-coast towns like Paleochóra and Chóra Sfakion. Some caique-routes have schedules, others are less predictable; to get the current picture, ask at the quayside in each harbour. New safety regulations mean that caiques are increasingly being replaced by more modern craft, but travelling to a beach by caique is still one of the great Greek experiences.

Practical A–Z

Climate

Crete manages to squeeze in three different climates: a typical Mediterranean one in the north, hot and dry in the south and cool and temperate up in the mountains in the middle. In general, the ideal time to visit is towards the end of April, when you'll avoid the worst crowds; the Libyan Sea is usually warm enough for swimming, the wild flowers are glorious and the higher mountains are still capped with snow. Note that the Gorge of Samariá doesn't open until 1 May, when its torrent recedes sufficiently for safe passage. Mid-summer is, predictably, the most popular time for visitors, but on the south coast it can be fiercely hot, so be prepared; if you aim to do much walking, it's generally better to come earlier or later in the year. In northern Crete in summer, though, especially in August, *meltémi* winds from the Aegean tend to whip the coast head-on for days at a stretch, making for slightly cooler temperatures and frothing seas. Earlier in the year southern Crete gets the benefit of a southerly wind from Africa, the *nótos*, which is said to make the sap rise in the spring, in trees and men.

Crete's first rains usually begin at the end of September, fall hardest in November and December and practically come to a halt by May. October is another good month, with many perfect, comfortably sunny days and a lingering warm sea.

For all the attractions of the warm spring, balmy autumn and hot summers, an increasing number of people (mostly Greek) who are more interested in Crete's nature, archaeology and people than in hot sun and beaches now come to the island in winter. Expect driving winds, rain and snow in the mountains, but also many bright, clear spells. Most of the island's roads will be almost empty, but many hotels and restaurants, especially in the main towns, stay open.

Disabled Travellers

Hotels in Greece increasingly have facilities for wheelchair users, as do major museums, but getting around Crete can still be hard. Access to buses and ferries can be a challenge, and the steepness of the terrain means that many villages have plenty of steps for streets, and/or cobblestoned pavements. *See* box opposite for organizations that can be helpful.

Eating Out

A Greek menu (*katálogos*) often has two prices for each item – with and without tax. In most restaurants there's also a small cover charge. Note that if you eat with Greeks, there's no nit-picking over who's had what. You share the food, drink, company and the bill, *to logariasmó*, although hosts will seldom let foreign guests part with a cent.

In 'ordinary' Greek restaurants there's not much variation in prices: an average taverna meal – if you don't order a major fish dish – runs to **around €10–15 a head**, with carafes of house wine. In sophisticated restaurants, or blatantly touristy places with views, costs may be much higher. In the 'Eating Out' sections of this book, prices are only given for places that do not fall into the usual taverna price category, and are per person with house wine. Some places now offer set-price meals with a glass of wine included, often for under €10.

In many resorts, waiters are paid a cut of the profits (so some obnoxiously tout for custom); **tipping** is discretionary but very appreciated. By law, there's a book by the door for registering complaints. A law against tax evaders insists that on leaving a restaurant you must retain a receipt (*apóthixi*) within 150m of the door; the police make occasional checks.

For more on food in Crete and local specialities, and a menu decoder, *see* pp.67–76.

Average Monthly Temperatures in °C

Jan	Mar	May	June	July	Aug	Sept	Oct	Dec
12.3	13.8	20.4	24.4	26.4	26.4	23.6	20.3	14

Average Monthly Sea Temperatures in °C

Jan	Mar	May	June	July	Aug	Sept	Oct	Dec
15.2	16	20.6	24.0	25.9	25.6	23.0	22.4	16

Organizations for Disabled Travellers

Greece
Panhellenic Association for the Blind,
31 Veranzérou St, ✉ 10432 Athens,
t 010 522 8333, *www.pst.gr.*

UK
Thomsons and other major package holiday companies usually offer a few suitable tours. Otherwise, consult:

Access Travel, 6 The Hillock, Astley, Lancashire, M29 7GW, t (01942) 888 844, *www.access-travel.co.uk.* Specialist travel agent for disabled people; in Greece, it currently only has Rhodes as a main destination, but can advise on other trips.

Chalfont Line Holidays, 4 Providence Road, West Drayton, Middx UB7 8HJ, t (01895) 459540, *www.chalfont-line.co.uk.* Escorted or individual holidays for disabled people.

Filoxenia-Opus 23, Sourdock Hill, Barkisland, Halifax HX4 0AG, t (01422) 375999/371796, *www.filoxenia.co.uk.* Greece specialist Filoxenia has an 'Opus 23' section for travellers with special needs, and can advise on access possibilities around Greece.

Holiday Care Service, 7th Floor, Sunley House, 4 Bedford Park, Croydon, Surrey, CR0 2AP, t 0845 124 9971, *www.holidaycare.org.uk.* A good general information and facilities service, with plenty of links on its website.

RADAR (Royal Association for Disability and Rehabilitation), 12 City Forum, 250 City Rd,

London, EC1V 8AS, t (020) 7250 3222, , *www.radar.org.uk.* As well as providing other facilities, publishes *Holidays and Travel Abroad: A Guide for Disabled People.*

Tripscope, t 0845 758 5641, *www.tripscope. org.uk.* Helpline and information website on travel for disabled people.

USA
Alternative Leisure Co, 165 Middlesex Turnpike, Suite 206, Bedford, MA 01730, t (718) 275 0023, *www.alctrips.com.* Organizes a range of vacations for disabled people.

Mobility International USA, PO Box 10767, Eugene, OR 97440, USA, t (541) 343 1284, *www.miusa.org.* Information on international exchange programmes and volunteer service overseas for the disabled.

SATH (Society for Accessible Travel and Hospitality), 347 Fifth Avenue, Suite 610, New York NY 10016, t (212) 447 7284, *www.sath.org.* Non-profit organization providing a wide range of information.

Other Useful Contacts

Access Ability, *www.access-ability.org.* Web-based information service for disabled people, with travel links.

Emerging Horizons, *www.emerginghorizons. com.* Online travel newsletter for people with disabilities.

Global Access, *www.geocities.com/Paris/1502.* Excellent online resource for disabled travellers: links, contacts, tips and information.

Electricity

The **electric current** in Greece is 220 volts, 50Hz; plugs are the usual European two-pin type. If you have any appliances with British three-pin plugs take plug **adaptors** with you, as they are pretty hard to find in Greece. North Americans with any 110 volt equipment will need adaptors and current transformers.

Embassies and Consulates

Australia: 37 D. Soútsou, Athens,
t 210 645 0404.

Canada: 4 Ioannoú Gennadíou, Athens,
t 210 727 3400.

Ireland: Consulate on Crete, 10 G. Papandreoú, Heráklion, t 281 022 0537;
Athens Embassy, 7 L. Vassíleos, Athens,
t 210 723 2771.

New Zealand: 268 Kifissías, Athens,
t 210 687 4700.

UK: Consulate on Crete, 16 Papa Alexándrou, Heráklion, t 281 022 4012;
Athens Embassy, 1 Ploutárchou, Athens,
t 210 727 2600.

USA: 91 Vassilísis Sofías, Athens,
t 210 721 2951.

Festivals and Events

Every church has its *panegýri*, or saints' day festival, celebrated with various degrees of enthusiasm – the most enjoyable are spectacular events running over several days, with plenty of food, wine, singing and dancing. Most of the best *panegýria* are up in the interior villages; along the coast, events tend to be organized with tourists in mind, although Cretans attend them as well. There are listings of local festivals in the text throughout this guide; in addition, the main annual events on Crete, including some of the bigger *panegýria*, are listed below. Note that festival dates for saints' days vary over a period of several given days, or even weeks, due to the Greek liturgical calendar's movable calculations for Easter; check these locally.

It is also important to remember that the main partying happens the night *before* the saint's day, which is more of a day for religious processions and observances.

Health and Emergencies

For local **police** in an emergency, call **t 100**.

For **first aid**, go to the nearest Local Health Centre (**ESY** or '*kentro e-yiée-as*'), which will be well-equipped to deal with snake bites, jellyfish stings, stomach bugs and so on, and treats foreigners for free. Where there's no ESY, rural **doctors** (*iatrós*) do the same, also for free. ESY and doctors' offices tend to be open Mon–Sat 9–1, 5–7, but some may open longer. For more serious incidents, you'll need a **hospital** (*nosokomío*); each of Crete's four provincial capitals has one. They are open all day every day, and usually have an outpatient clinic open in the mornings.

EU citizens are entitled to free **emergency medical care**; travellers are often urged to carry an **E111 form**, available in the UK from health centres and post offices, but note that in Greece this will entitle you only to the most basic level of treatment in IKA (Greek health service) hospitals, and will not cover the cost

Calendar of Events

April
Good Friday Big fair at Voukouliés (Chaniá).
Easter Ag. Nikólaos: Resurrection service, burning in effigy of Judas and other celebrations; also a major festival at Moní Toploú monastery and Chersónisos.
23 St George's Day, Así Goniá: Shepherds bring cattle to be blessed in the church and fresh milk is distributed to all, followed by a huge feast. Also celebrated in Plakiás.

May
21 Ag. Konstantínos and Ag. Elena (Constantine and Helen's Day), at Nóchia, near Kastélli-Kíssamou: religious service and feast of seafood, cheese and wine, with traditional songs (*tavlas*) and dances.
Last Sunday Virgin of Thymiánis, Chóra Sfakíon.

June
20–30 Klidónas, Chaniá: traditional feasts celebrating the old Cretan custom of water-divining for a husband, with comic songs and dances.

All-Summer Festivals
June–Sept Lato Festival: celebration of traditional culture, music and handicrafts, in Ag. Nikólaos and the ancient city of Lato.
June–Sept Crete International Festival, Chaniá: a large-scale arts programme with Greek and foreign dance troupes, exhibitions and traditional local celebrations.
June–Sept Irákleio Festival, Heráklion: Crete's largest arts festival, with traditional and international performances and events.
July–Aug Kýrvia Festival, Ierápetra: music, arts exhibits, dances and other events celebrating one of the town's ancient names.
Kritsá Festival, Kritsá, near Ag. Nikólaos: a smaller-scale traditional folklore festival.
July–15 Aug Kornária Festival, Sitía: varied cultural events in honour of Crete's 15th-century poet Kornáros, in his birthplace.
July–Sept Renaissance Fair, Réthymnon: a range of cultural events all around the city.

July
First week *Yakinthéia* Festival, Anógia (Réthymnon): spectacular mix of traditional music, exhibitions and Greek drama 'in celebration of Zeus', near the god's birthplace.

of medicines or nursing care – and on top of that, many Greek clinics look on the E111 with total disregard in any case. In general, expect to pay up front, and get receipts in the hope that you can be reimbursed back home. For this reason, in Greece it's more than usually advisable not to rely on the state system, but to have a private **travel insurance policy** with medical and repatriation cover. For non-Europeans the best advice is, similarly, to have full travel insurance against all eventualities.

The good news is that Greek doctors' **fees** are usually reasonable, and most pride themselves on their English. **Pharmacists** (found in the *farmakeío*) also give good advice on minor ailments. **Condoms** (*kapótes*) are widely available from *farmakeío*, kiosks and supermarkets, with lusty brand names such as 'Squirrel' or 'Rabbit'. You can also get the pill (*chápi anti-siliptikó*), morning-after pill and HRT over the pharmacy counter without a prescription. Take your old packet to show the brand you use. For some reason Greeks buy more **medicines** than

anyone else in Europe (hypochondria? an old hoarding instinct?) but you shouldn't have to. The strong sun is the most likely cause of grief, so be careful, and stay hatted and sunscreened. *See* pp.63–6 for possibly unkind wildlife. If anything else goes wrong, do what Greeks have done for centuries: pee on it. In case of a health emergency, call **t 166**.

Internet

The Internet is big in Greece, and even in small towns some kind of access is available, through Net cafés, travel agencies or hotels.

Money and Banks

Greece now uses the **euro** (pronounced *evró* in Greek), with notes of €5, 10, 20, 50, 100, 200 and 500, and coins of €1 and €2, then 1¢, 2¢, 5¢, 10¢, 20¢, 50¢ (cents in Greek are *leptá*). The word for **bank** is *trápeza*, derived from the

---

17 Ag. Marína, specially celebrated at Ag. Pelagía and Ag. Marína.
Late July–early Aug Gavalochóri Folk Festival, Gavalochóri, near Vrises, Chaniá: events are organized by the village's Folk Art Museum.
Last 10 days Réthymnon Wine Festival.
26 Ag. Paraskévi, especially in Kalýves and Falassarná (Chaniá).
27 Ag. Pantéleimon, in Kaló Chório (Lassíthi), Fournés (Chaniá), Árvi (Heráklion)

August
First week The *Anogéia*, Cretan song, dance and *lýra* competitions, Anógia (Réthymnon). Also, Grape Festival, at Epano (Heráklion).
First 10 days Musical August, Paleochóra.
6 *Metamórfosis* (The Transfiguration): big celebrations in Eloúnda and Georgioúpolis.
10–25 Cultural events, dances and fish-feasts in the evenings at Tymbáki (Heráklion).
15 *Apokímisis* (Assumption of the Virgin Mary), the biggest *panegýri* of all: most spectacular at Palaíkastro, Neápolis, Koxáre, Ierápetra, Chrysoskalítissa Monastery, Kolimbári, Therísso, Archánes, Veneráto, Mochós, Kali Liménes and Koudoúma Monastery.
15–18 Sultanina Grape Festival, Sitía.
26 Ag. Ioánnis (St John), in Balí (Réthymon).

September
14 Tímios Stávros, Alikianós (Chaniá).
15 Ag. Nikítas, Frangokástello.
First Sunday after the 20th Chestnut Festival, Élos (Chaniá). Merry-making and old songs, and chestnut sweets are offered to visitors.
24 Panagía Myrtidiotíssa, Spiliá (Chaniá). One of Crete's largest, most enjoyable *panegýria*.
End of month Raisin Festival, Peramá (Réthymnon).

October
7 St John the Hermit, Gouvernétou (Chaniá): Day-long feast including improvised singing.

November
First weekend Tsikoudiá Festival, Voukoliés (Chaniá): a chance to taste the local *tsikoudiá*, slightly less powerful than rocket fuel.
30 Ag. Andreas, Malaxa (Chaniá): a pot-luck lunch is offered to all after a church service.

December
6 Ag. Nikólaos: especially celebrated in Ag Nikólaos and Pánormos (Réthymnon).
14 Ag. Várvara, in the village of the same name (Heráklion).

word *trapézi*, or table, used back in the days of money-changers. Most towns have several; normal **banking hours** are Mon–Thurs 8.20–2, Fri 8–1.30. If there's no bank, travel agents, tourist offices or post offices will change cash and traveller's cheques. Beware that some resorts have only one bank, where changing money can take forever: beat the crowds by going as they first open, at 8.20am.

The number of 24hr automatic cash machines (**ATMs**) grows every year, and are what most people now use for their holiday cash. Major hotels, luxury shops and resort restaurants take **credit cards**, but small hotels and tavernas rarely do.

Traveller's cheques are still useful here, in case the machine eats your card, even though commission rates are less for cash. The major brands (Thomas Cook and American Express) are accepted in all banks; take your passport as ID, and shop around for commission rates.

Museums, Ancient Sites and Churches

All significant archaeological sites and museums have regular admission hours. **Nearly all are closed on Mondays** and open on other weekdays from 8 or 9 to around 2, while outdoor sites tend to stay open later, until 4 or 5pm or even sunset. Hours are shorter in winter. As a rule, plan to visit cultural sites in the mornings. All close on 1 Jan, 25 Mar, Good Friday, Easter Sunday, 1 May, 25 Dec and 26 Dec.

Entrance fees are still reasonable: count on €2–3 in most cases, exceptions being Knossos (€6), Phaistos (€4) and the Heráklion Museum (€6). **Students** with an ID card and anyone over 65 often get a discount, and admission is generally **free** for all on **Sundays**.

Because of a surge in thefts, **churches** are only open when there is someone around, often in the late afternoon (6–7pm); at other times you may have to hunt down the key (*kleethEE*). **Monasteries** tend to close for a couple of hours at midday. If you're visiting a church or monastery, it's good manners to dress decently. In the old days this used to mean no shorts or sleeveless tops, but these days all the monks and sacristans tend to require is any kind of shirt at all and something bigger than your bathing suit down below.

National Holidays

1 January New Year's Day, *Protochroniá*; also *Ag. Vassílis* (Greek Father Christmas)
6 January Epiphany, *Ta Fóta/Theofánia*
February–March 'Clean Monday', *Katharí Deftéra* (precedes Shrove Tuesday and follows a three-week carnival)
25 March Annunciation/Greek Independence Day, *Evangelismós*
late March–April Good Friday, *Megáli Paraskeví*, Easter Sunday, *Páscha* and Easter Monday, *Theftéra tou Páscha*
1 May Labour Day, *Protomayá*
40 days after Easter Pentecost (Whit Monday), *Pentikostí*
15 August Assumption of the Virgin, *Koímisis tis Theotókou*
28 October *Ochí* or 'No' Day (in celebration of Metaxás' 'no' to Mussolini in 1940)
25 December Christmas, *Christoúyena*
26 December Gathering of the Virgin, *Sináxi Theotókou*

National Holidays

Most businesses and shops close down for the afternoon before and the morning after a religious holiday. If a national holiday falls on a Sunday, the following Monday is observed.

In Greece **Easter** is the biggest national holiday, the equivalent of Christmas and New Year in northern climes, when far-flung relatives return to see their families back home. Orthodox Easter is generally a week or so after the Roman Easter. It's a good time to visit for atmosphere, with fireworks, feasting and shooting rifles at the moon. After the priest has intoned *'O Christós Anésti!'* – Christ has risen! – families walk home with lighted candles, often amid fireworks, to tuck into *magirítsa* (lamb innards) soup. On Easter Sunday the Paschal lamb is spit-roasted, and music and dancing goes on day and night. On 1 May, Spring (*ánixi* – the opening) officially arrives, and everyone goes into the country to picnic and weave garlands of flowers.

Packing

Even in the height of summer, evenings can be chilly in Crete, especially when the *meltémi* wind is blowing. Always bring at least one warm sweater and some long trousers. Those who venture off the beaten track into thorns and rocks should bring sturdy and comfortable footwear – trainers (sneakers) are fine much of the time, but for walking down the gorges serious trekking footgear is in order. Cover the ankles, too, as scorpions and harmful snakes can be a problem. Plastic swimming shoes are recommended for rocky beaches, where there are often sea urchins; you can buy them near any beach if you don't want to carry them around with you.

Serious sleeping-baggers should bring a Karrimat or similar insulating layer to cushion them from gravelly Greek ground. A torch (flashlight) is very handy for moonless nights, caves, frescoed churches and rural villages.

On the **health** side, seasickness pills, insect bite remedies, antiseptic wipes, band-aids, tablets for stomach upsets and aspirin will deal with most difficulties. Women's sanitary towels and sometimes Tampax are sold from general stores, but in remote areas you'll need to seek out the *farmakeio*; if there isn't one, you've had it, so plan ahead. Soap, washing powder, a clothes line and especially a towel are necessary if you're staying in class C hotels or lower; most importantly, buy a universal-fitting **sink plug** for rinsing your clothes; Greek sinks rarely have them. A Swiss army-style knife is a good idea for picnics and *panegýria*, where you are often given a slab of goat meat and just a spoon or fork to eat it with.

Unless you completely isolate yourself you can buy whatever you forgot to bring in cities or resort towns; toilet paper and anti-bug defences are the most popular buys on arrival. Follow this theory: however much money and clothing you thought you needed, try to halve the clothing and double the money.

Photography

Crete lends itself to beautiful photography, but fees are charged for taking pictures at archaeological sites and museums. At sites, with a camcorder or movie camera, you will be encouraged to buy a ticket for the camera; with a still camera and tripod you pay per photograph. Cameras (especially tripod-mounted ones) are officially not allowed at all in museums, for no particular reason other

than maintaining a monopoly for the museum's own (usually dull) postcard stock.

Print and slide film can be found in many shops, but it tends to be expensive and the range of film speeds limited. Disposable and underwater cameras and digital cards are on sale in larger resorts. One-hour developing services now exist everywhere, although again prices will be higher than at home.

The light in summer is often stronger than it seems, and is the most common cause of ruined photographs; opting for slow film (100 ASA or less) helps. Cretans usually love to have their pictures taken, and although it's more polite to ask first, it's best to go ahead and take the photo if you don't want them to beautify themselves and strike a pose. Avoid taking pictures of all **military installations**, including communications systems on mountain tops; the 'Photography Forbidden' sign shows a camera with a cross through it. As British plane-spotters famously discovered a while ago, Greek officialdom is very suspicious of anyone photographing military hardware.

Post and Post Offices

Signs for post offices (*tachidromio*) and postboxes (*grammatokivótio*) are bright yellow and easy to find. Post offices (which are also useful for changing money) are **open** Mon–Fri 7.30–2, but in large towns may be open till 7.30–8pm and on Saturday morning, too. **Stamps** (*grammatósima*) can also be bought at kiosks and in some tourist shops; **postcards** cost the same as letters and are given the same priority (they take about three days to the UK). If you're in a hurry you can send letters **express**, for a small extra charge.

If you do not have an address, mail can be sent to you *poste restante* to any post office in Crete, and picked up with proof of identity. After one month all unretrieved letters are returned to sender. If someone has sent you a **parcel**, you will receive a notice of its arrival, and must go to the post office to collect it; you will have to pay a handling fee of €2, and customs charges if necessary. 'Fragile' stickers attract scant attention. To **send** a package, try to use larger, city post offices. In **villages**, mail is usually not delivered to houses but to the village post centre, either a café or a bakery.

Shopping

Official **shopping hours** in Greece are Mon and Wed 9–3; Tues, Thurs and Fri 9–7, Sat 8.30–3.30 and Sun closed; in practice, tourist-orientated shops stay open as late as 1am in season. Leather goods, gold and jewellery, traditional crafts, embroidery and weaving, onyx, ceramics, alabaster, herbs and spices and tacky knick-knacks are all favourite purchases; check each chapter also for local specialities.

Non-EU residents tempted by Greek jewellery, carpets and other big ticket items can have the sales tax (VAT, currently 18%) reimbursed. Make sure the shop has a 'TAX FREE FOR TOURISTS' sticker in the window and pick up a **tax-free shopping cheque** for your purchases. When you leave Greece, you must show the purchases and get a customs official to stamp the cheques (allow an hour for this), and then cash them in at the refund point as you leave. If you are flying out of another EU country, hold onto the cheques, and get them stamped again by the other country's customs and reclaim your money there. You can also post the tax-free cheques back to Greece for refund (10 Níkis, 10563 Athens, t 210 325 4995), but they skim off 20% on commission.

Sports

Watersports

These take first place among the activities available on Crete. All popular beaches these days hire out **pedal boats** and **windsurf boards**, and some have **paragliding**, **banana boats** and **jet skis**. Large resort hotels can usually get you on a pair of **waterskis**.

Scuba diving, once strictly banned to keep divers from snatching antiquities and to protect Greece's much-harassed marine life, is permitted between dawn and sunset in specially defined areas; local diving operators will take you there. For information contact the **Hellenic Federation of Underwater Activities**, t 210 981 9961, or the **Owners of Diving Centres**, 67 Zeas, Piraeus, t 210 411 8909.

Nudism is forbidden by law in Crete, except in designated areas; in practice, however, many people shed all in isolated coves, at the far ends of beaches, or ideally on beaches accessible only by private boat. **Topless**

sunbathing on the other hand is now legal on the majority of popular beaches away from settlements, but do exercise discretion. It isn't worth wounding local sensibilities: you could be arrested on the spot and end up with three days in jail or a stiff fine. Canoodling on public beaches in broad daylight can also offend.

Walking and Climbing

Away from the water these are far the most popular activities on Crete. If you plan on any serious trekking bring sturdy boots and a hat, and pick up a **Harms-Verlag** Crete map, based on Greek Army ordnance surveys, with paths well marked. The biggest challenge, for its arid, rugged conditions, is the **trans-European Long Distance Footpath E4** (marked by white signs with a yellow diamond) which has its southernmost segment in Crete, extending 320km from Kastélli-Kíssamou in the west to Káto Zákros in the east, with side-paths near the Samariá Gorge and Anógia. **It is marked on the maps in this guide.** The E4 affords superb views, but has tough stretches: the northern section requires alpine experience, while further south the track is very rough. On any part of the path, expect to carry your own supplies (especially water). A detailed map is a must, and it shouldn't be attempted alone; ideally you should have someone keeping track of your progress, to notify authorities if you fail to show up at any point.

A growing number of local walking guides are on sale on Crete, or pick up Sunflower Books' guides by Jonnie Godfrey and Elizabeth Karslake (*see* p.270). Several companies offer guided walks on Crete (*see* pp.84–5). If you're venturing into the White Mountains or Psilorítis, local climbing organizations (**EOS**) are good sources of information: in Heráklion (53 Dikeosínis, t 281 022 7609), Chaniá (90 Tzanakáki, t 282 102 4647) and Réthymnon (12 Dimokratías, t 283 102 2655).

Other Land Sports

Resort areas have **tennis** courts, nearly every village has **basketball** nets, and the Greek National Tourist Organization is helping to fund four **golf** courses in Crete, the first of which is due to open outside Chersónisos in June 2003. You can also watch Heráklion's first division team *Ofi* in the Greek **football** league, or even **ski** down Psilorítis, above Anógia.

Telephones

The new improved *Organismós Tilefikinonía Elládos*, or **OTE**, has replaced most of its phone offices with card phones. Cards (*télekartas*), sold in kiosks, come in denominations from €2.90 to €24.60; another, the *Chronocarta* (€5, €13 or €25), is good value for long-distance calls. Some street kiosks (*períptera*) also have a phone *me métriki* (with a meter), which tend to be more costly. Several companies hire out mobile phones; *www.greecetravel.com/phones* will deliver them when you arrive.

Since 2002 all Greek **phone numbers** have **10 digits**, with no separate area codes, so you dial the whole number wherever you are in the country. Numbers beginning 2 are for standard lines, any with 6 are for mobiles. To call abroad direct, dial 00, then the country code; to **phone Greece from abroad**, the country code is **30**, after which you dial all ten digits.

Time

'God gave watches to the Europeans and time to the Greeks,' they say, but if you need more precision, **Greek time** is two hours ahead of Greenwich Mean Time, seven hours ahead of Eastern Standard Time in North America.

Toilets and Plumbing

Greek plumbing has improved greatly in the past few years. Tavernas, *kafeneíons*, bus stations and sweet shops almost always have facilities (it's good manners to buy something), and there are often public pay toilets in strategic areas of towns. Do not tempt fate by disobeying any notices 'the papers they please to throw in the basket', or it'll lead to trouble.

If you stay in a private house or pension you may need to have the electric water heater turned on for about 20 minutes before you take a shower. In many smaller pensions, water is heated by a solar panel on the roof, so the best time to take a shower is late afternoon or early evening (before other residents use up the hot water). In larger hotels there is often hot water in the mornings and evenings, but not in the afternoons. But 'cold' showers in summer aren't that bad, because the water is generally lukewarm, especially after noon.

Tourist Information

You can contact the Greek National Tourist Organization (**EOT**) at the offices listed here. EOT **websites** are *www.greektourism.com* (for North America) and *www.gnto.gr*; other good sites are the *Greek Travel Pages* (*www.gtp.gr*), *www.gogreece.com*, *www.cretetravel.com* and *www.west-crete.com*.

Australia and New Zealand: 51 Pitt St, Sydney, NSW 2000, **t** 9241 1663/4.

Canada: 1300 Bay St, Toronto, M5R 3K8, **t** (416) 968 2220; 1233 De La Montagne, Suite 101, Montreal, H3G 1Z2, **t** (514) 871 1535.

UK and Ireland: 4 Conduit Street, London W1R 0DJ, **t** (020) 7734 5997.

USA: Olympic Tower, 645 Fifth Avenue, 5th Floor, New York, NY 10022, **t** (212) 421 5777; 168 N. Michigan Avenue, Chicago, Il 60601, **t** (312) 782 1084; 611 West Sixth Street, Suite 2198, Los Angeles, CA 90017, **t** (213) 626 6696.

On Crete there are EOT offices in the provincial capitals and Sitía, and many resorts have local tourist offices and/or **tourist police** units, which also give general information. There is a national **tourist police phoneline** based in Athens (**t** 171, or **t** 210 171 from other parts of Greece) that's a handy source of information.

Where to Stay

Hotels and Hotel Grades

All hotels in Greece are divided into six categories: luxury, A, B, C, D and E. This grading system bears little relation to the quality of service; it's more to do with how the building is constructed, size of bedrooms and so on (a marble-clad bathroom gets a higher rating). For this reason, some D and C class hotels can be better than Bs. Pensions, some without restaurants, are a confusing subdivision in the

Hotel Price Ranges

Accommodation is listed in this guide in the price bands below, according to the price for a **double room in high season**. Expect to pay a good deal less in May–June or late Sept–Oct.

luxury €90 to astronomical
expensive €50–€90
moderate €35–€50
inexpensive up to €35

Villa and Self-Catering Holiday Operators

In the UK

Catherine Secker (Crete), 102A Burnt Ash Lane, Bromley, Kent BR1 4DD, t (020) 8460 8022, f (020) 8313 1431. Home-run agency with a personal touch featuring luxury villas with pools on the Akrotíri Peninsula: Secker offers all mod cons in quiet beachside villages, with everything from hairdryers to toyboxes.

CV Travel, 43 Cadogan Street, London, SW3 2PR, t (020) 7581 0851, f (020) 7584 5229, www.cvtravel.net. Upmarket villas at fair prices, with maid service, and cooks available.

Direct Greece, Granite House, 31–33 Stockwell St, Glasgow G1 4RY, t 0870 516 8683, www.directgreece.co.uk. A choice of villas and flats, with good low-season specials. The reps are very helpful and knowledgeable.

Filoxenia/Grecofile, Sourdock Hill, Barkisland, Halifax HX4 0AG, t (01422) 375999/371796, www.filoxenia.co.uk. Not so much tailor-made as *couture* holidays: Suzi Stembridge and family have scoured Crete for unusual locations and can arrange stays in villas or tavernas, fly-drive and personal itineraries, and cater to special needs and interests.

Freelance Holidays, Hill House, Pathlow, Stratford-upon-Avon, Warks. CV37 0ES, t (01789) 297705, www.freelance-holidays.co.uk. Villas, apartments and hotels around Crete, plus whale- and dolphin-watching trips in the Libyan Sea.

Greek Islands Club, Upper Square, Old Isleworth, Middx TW7 7BJ, t (020) 8568 4499, www.sunvil.co.uk/sites/gic. Well-run, helpful company; their 'Private Collection' features exclusive villas and hideaway hotels.

Igluvillas, 165 The Broadway, Wimbledon, London SW19 1NE, t (020) 8544 6401, www.igluvillas.com. Net-based company offering a big choice of cottages, villas and flats on Crete, mainly on the south coast.

Island Wandering, 51A London Road, Hurst Green, Sussex TN19 7QP, t (01580) 860733, www.islandwandering.com. Fly-drives with villa rental, flying on charters from most UK airports or scheduled flights via Athens.

classifications, especially as many call themselves hotels. They are family-run and more modest (an A class pension is equivalent to a C or D class hotel and priced accordingly).

On the **Internet**, www.greekhotel.com lists 8,000 hotels and villas throughout Greece Most large hotels have their own websites.

Prices and Hotel Reservations

Hotel prices are set and strictly controlled by the tourist police. **Off-season** you can generally get a discount, sometimes of as much as 40%. Bear this in mind when looking at the **price categories** used in this book (*see* p.95), and remember that, in the off season, if you just walk in off the street and ask you may well get a lower rate than the official one that will be quoted on the phone. In the summer season prices will be up to 20% higher. Other charges include an 8% government tax, a 4.5% bed tax, a 12% stamp tax, an optional 10% surcharge for stays of only one or two days, an air-conditioning surcharge and sometimes a 20% charge for an extra bed. All these charges are listed on the door of each room. If your hotelier fails to abide by the posted prices, take your complaint to the tourist police.

Generally speaking, a hotel's official 'grade' determines its price, so that a Luxury or A class hotel will charge the highest rates, whereas a B class will fall into the *expensive/moderate* band. However, this isn't always the case: sometimes a B class will be pricier than an A and so on, as the lines between each grade become more and more blurred with the improvement of services and facilities.

Hotels down to class B all have **bathrooms** in each room; in C and D most do; E will have a shower down the hall, and neither towels nor soap will be supplied. In summer, hotels with restaurants may require guests to take meals in the hotel, on **full pension** or **half pension**, with no refund for an uneaten dinner. Twelve noon is the usual check-out time. Most Luxury and class A, if not B, hotels far from a town or port supply buses or cars to pick up guests.

In July and August and at some other busy times (such as Easter) it is essential to **reserve a room** in advance. Off-season, as mentioned, the situation is often much more flexible.

Rooms (*domátia*) in Private Homes

These are for the most part cheaper than hotels, and are often more pleasant. Cretan

Pure Crete, 79 George Street, Croydon, Surrey CR0 1LP, **t** (020) 8760 0879, *www.pure-crete.com*. Small Anglo-Cretan company offering restored farmhouses and other individual places for rent, mainly in western Crete. Also special turtle-watching tours.

Travel Club of Upminster, Station Road, Upminster, Essex RM14 2TT, **t** (01708) 225000, *www.travelclub.org.uk*. Personal service and a distinctive selection of high-standard villas, flats and hotel bookings.

Villa Villas, **t** (01202) 503950, *www.villavillas.com*. Net-based service offering all kinds of rentals on Crete, from rustic farmhouses to luxury villas with pool.

In the USA and Canada

Apollo Tours, 1701 Lake St, Suite 260, Glenview, IL 60025, **t** 1 800 228 4367, *www.apollotours.com*. Greece specialists with villas and apartments around Crete.

European Escapes 111 Av. Del Mar, Suite 220D, San Clemente, CA 92672, **t** 1 888 387 6589, *www.europeanescapes.com*. Luxury villas with every comfort, across Europe.

Omega Tours 3220 Broadway West, Vancouver, British Columbia V6K 2H4, **t** (604) 738 3433, *www.oti.bc.ca*. Villa and apartment rentals and tours around Crete.

Rentvillas, 700 E Main St, Ventura, CA 93001, **t** 1 800 726 6702, *www.rentvillas.com*. Net-based company with good-value rates.

Tourlite-Zeus Tours 120 Sylvan Avenue, Englewood Cliffs, NJ 07632, **t** 1 800 272 7600, *www.zeustours.com*. Tours and independent accommodation in various parts of Crete.

In Crete

Crete Direct, Sabbáticos, Drapaniás, Chaniá ✉ 73400, **t** (+30) 282 203 2030, *www.crete-direct.com*. Villas and farmhouses of all sizes, from basic farmhouses for two to multi-family villas with space for 10, for rent all around Crete.

Crete Travel, PO Box 1433, Heráklion ✉ 73400, **t** (+30) 281 081 1966, in UK **t** 0870 133 0536, *www.cretetravel.com*. Internet company based in Crete, offering luxury seaside villas and also remote hideaways in the White Mountains.

houses often don't look like much in comparison with other European homes, mainly because people spend so little time inside them; they are clean, though, and an owner will often go out of his or her way to ensure maximum comfort for their guest. Staying in someone's house can also offer rare insights into Greek domestic taste, from near-Japanese simplicity to a clutter of bulging plastic cat pictures. Increasingly, rooms to rent to tourists are built in a separate annexe, which can mean a rather characterless concrete barracks, although some nice surprises can be found among the newer ones as well.

Rooms for rent are generally well advertised in each village. Depending on facilities, a double room in high season will cost between €25 and €35 with bath, a studio €35 to €75. Until June and after August prices are always negotiable. Owners will nearly always drop the price per day the longer you stay, especially for a stay of three days or more. Prices also depend on local 'fashion'. Speaking some Greek is the biggest asset in bargaining, but not strictly necessary. Always remember that you are staying in someone's home, and don't waste water or electricity. The owner will

generally give you a bowl for washing your clothes, and there is always a clothes line.

Renting a House, Villa or Apartment

On Crete you can rent village houses, beach villas or apartments for one week, two weeks or a month or more at a time. Generally, the longer you stay the more economical it becomes. You may be able to find something on the spot in a mountain village, but don't count on finding anything near the coast in summer without using a rental agent or holiday company; alternatively, another place to look for less formal rentals is in the weekly *Kriti News*, available at newsstands. If you are arranging your rental yourself, things to look out for are leaking roofs, damp, water supply (the house may rely on a well) and a supply of lamps if there is no electricity.

In any case, an ample choice of house rentals on Crete is available through specialist self-catering holiday companies. Most are small agencies belonging to the **Association of Independent Tour Operators**, which tend to advertise in Sunday papers or depend on word-of-mouth recommendations; the Greek National Tourist Organization (*see* p.95) also

Campsite Prices

These are not fixed by law, but below are some approximate guidelines, per day:

adult €5
small/large tent €3–€4
child (4–12) €3
car €3
caravan €5
sleeping bag €2

has a list of operators. A selection of villa and self-catering specialists is listed on pp.96–7; most offer 'loosely packaged' holidays that combine the freedom of your own villa with the convenience of pre-arranged flights, coach or ferry transfers and often hire cars.

Youth Hostels

None of the hostels in Crete (in Chaniá, Réthymnon and Heráklion towns, and Plakiás, Chersónisos, Mália and Sitía) is 'official' and affiliated to the International Youth Hostelling Federation (although some pretend they are). The up-side of this is that no membership cards are required, they have no irksome regulations and admit anyone, and most are still quite pleasant. Most charge extra for showers, some for sheets. Expect to pay €6–12 a night, depending on hostel facilities and services.

Camping Out

Crete's summer climate is perfect for sleeping out of doors, and in July and August you only need a sleeping bag to spend a pleasant night on a remote beach, cooled by the sea breezes that also keep the mosquito menace at bay. Note though that unauthorized camping is illegal in Greece, although each village enforces this ban as it sees fit. Some couldn't care less if you put up a tent at the edge of their beach; in others the police may pull up your tent pegs and fine you. All you can do is ask around to see what other campers or friendly locals advise. Naturally, the more remote the beach, the less likely you are to be disturbed. If a policeman does come by and asks you to move, it's best to comply. A great many beaches have privately operated camping grounds. They are reasonably priced, though some have only minimal facilities.

One of the reasons behind the camping law was that beaches have no sanitation facilities for crowds of campers; another was the threat of forest fires. If the police can be lackadaisical about enforcing the camping regulations, they come down hard on anyone lighting any kind of fire in a forest, as fires damage huge swathes of land in Crete every year.

Women Travellers

Crete holds no great barriers for women travellers, but foreign women travelling alone may still be viewed as an oddity. Be prepared for a fusillade of questions: Greeks tend to do everything in groups or pairs, and can't understand people, especially women, who want to go solo. All Greek men from 16 to 60 like to chat up foreign women, but extreme coercion and violence is rare. A rape case near Chaniá a while ago was resolved as they always have been: the woman's family had two of the rapists killed, and the third is sure to be shot down the minute he shows his face in public.

Kamáki means harpoon in Greek, and it's what Greeks call Romeos who roar about on motorbikes, hang out in bars and hunt in pairs or packs. Their aim is to collect as many women as possible, notching up points for different nationalities. There are professional *kamákia* in the big resorts, gigolos who live off women tourists. Other Greeks look down on them and consider them dishonourable.

Nowadays many young Greek women have jobs and are beginning to travel alone, too, but this is no indication that traditional values are disappearing. Old marriage customs still exert a strong influence. 'Poverty and nakedness are nothing, provided you have a good wife,' is an old Cretan saying. Not a few old Cretan customs relate to young women guessing who they might marry: the *klidónas*, looking into the water to see the face of a future husband, or the custom of the beans. On New Year's Eve at midnight, they take three beans: one raw, one shelled, one peeled. With eyes closed a girl chooses a bean: the raw one means a young husband, a shelled one means a widower, and a peeled one, a poor man.

Chaniá

10

Unless you have only a few days on Crete and want to concentrate on the big resorts or the high shrines of Minoan culture around Heráklion, consider easing yourself gently into this complex island by starting with Chaniá (XANIA), urbane, seductive, lively and easily the most elegant of the four provincial capitals. With the ghostly snow-capped forms of the White Mountains hovering over its palm trees and rooftops, Chaniá is exceedingly old, its urban fabric like a wall encrusted with circus posters, peeling here and there to reveal its depths: Venetian, Turkish and neoclassical monuments line its streets and quays. Many, unfortunately, were lost to bombs during the Battle of Crete, but perhaps more fortunately many war-scarred ruins have stood neglected for so many decades that they have become part of the landscape and been made into unique garden settings for bars and restaurants, while beautiful hotels now fill some of the old palazzi. Splendid beaches are a short bus ride away to the east of Chaniá on the Akrotíri peninsula or all along the coast to the west; in town, the lovely inner and outer Venetian Harbours are magnets for evening strollers, where unwinding over a drink in the quayside bars is wonderfully addictive.

History

The ancient historian Diodoros Siculus wrote that Chaniá was founded by Minos and that it was one of the three great cities of Crete. Buildings in the Kastélli quarter go back to 2200 BC, and archaeologists are pretty sure that the Minoan palace and town, *KY-DO-NI-JA*, referred to on a Linear B tablet found at Knossos, lie hidden under the modern town. Kydonia was so important that for a time its name referred to all of Crete. In modern Greek *kydónia* means quince, a fruit loved by the Minoans: the word (like 'hyacinth', 'labyrinth' and 'sandal') may have come from the Minoan language.

Quince Town survived to get a mention in Homer, know glory days in the Hellenistic and Roman periods, and then to decline so far that by the 13th century it was better known as 'Rubbish City'. The Venetians, who Italianized its name as *La Canea*, rebuilt it and fortified the centre (now Kastélli), and by the 1500s it was so splendid that it was known as the 'Venice of the East'. It underwent major expansion in the mid-16th century, when Venice's master engineer Sammichele designed the walls and moat. The shipyards, warehouses and new streets were laid out at the same time, and an outer ring of forts was built on the islets of Ag. Theodóri, Néa Soúda and Gramvoúsa.

Captured none the less by the Ottomans in 1645, Chaniá became the seat of one of the three ruling Pashas of Crete, and a mostly Turkish town – in the last Ottoman census in 1881, it counted 9,469 Turks, 3,477 Orthodox Greeks, 485 Jews, 159 Catholics and a handful of Protestants and Armenians. Made the island's capital in 1849, Chaniá became Crete's cosmopolitan window on the outside world, with consulates and embassies, and later prospered as the personal fief of Greek national statesman Elefthérios Venizélos. Chaniá and its old airport at Máleme bore the brunt of the Battle of Crete in 1941, and then lost capital status to arch-rival Heráklion in 1971, but it remains Crete's second city (pop. 73,000); one recent contribution to national life was Néa Demokrátiki Prime Minister Konstantínos Mitzotákis, elected in 1990 when Greece got fed up with the scandals around the late Andréas Papandréou and PASOK, only to be voted out in 1993 for trying to make Greece bite the economic bullet.

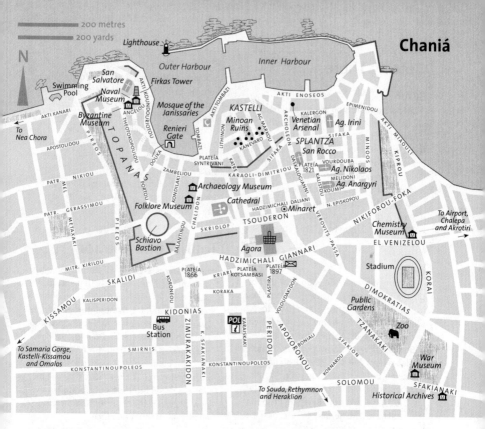

Into Old Chaniá: The Market and Chalídon

The vortex of daily life in Chaniá, its 1911 cruciform covered market or **Agora** neatly separates the new city from the old. Here locals shop every morning for food – a couple of stalls even offer fresh fish soup, made on the spot – and wonder about the sanity of all those Germans videoing slabs of meat and cheese. Old Chaniá lies just to the north of the Agora; from the back stairs of the market hall a left turn will lead to **Skrídlof** street, a narrow lane jam-packed for as long as anyone can remember with shops selling leather goods. This has long been an important traditional craft in Chaniá, although nowadays many of the bootmakers have changed over to sandals, bags and belts for the tourists. Skrídlof opens up onto bustling **Chalídon** street, Chaniá's main tourist-and-jewellery-shop-lined funnel to the sea.

The Archaeological Museum

t 282 109 0334; open Tues–Sun 8.30–3; adm.

The 14th-century Gothic church of San Francesco at 21 Chalídon doesn't look like much from the outside, but it's had a hard life. Used as a mosque (the stump of a minaret and a pretty fountain survive), its cells and refectory converted beyond all recognition into shops, and bombed during the war, it has been beautifully restored for its new role of housing a sumptuous collection of treasures found in western

Getting There

By Air

Chaniá's **airport** is on the Akrotíri peninsula, about 12km east of the city (for airport information t 282 106 3264). A taxi from there to the city centre will usually cost about €15, depending on the state of the traffic. The **Olympic Airways** office is in the new city at 88 S. Tzanakáki, t 282 105 7700; buses run to and from there to coincide with Olympic flights. **Aegean Airlines** has offices at the airport, t 280 120 000, and in town at 12 El. Venizélou, t 282 105 1100.

By Sea

The **ferry terminal** is in **Soúda**, the port of Chaniá, 5km east of the city (*see* p.120). Local buses meet arriving ferries and run into Chaniá; ANEK ferries from Piraeus arrive early in the morning, Blue Star in the evening. Buses to Soúda follow the same route. Tickets are available from **ANEK** offices at Plateía S. Venizélou, by the market square in Chaniá, t 282 102 7500, and at the Soúda terminal, t 282 108 9856, and from **Blue Star** in Soúda, t 282 108 9229. The number for the local **Port authority** is t 282 104 3052.

By Bus

The **bus station** is on Kidonías street, in the new city just west of Chaniá's main central square of Plateía 1866. Inside it, whiffs of faded grandeur mingle with those from plugged-up toilets; black-bordered death notices posted outside merge imperceptibly with ads for campsites. Buses travel at least once a day to all the larger villages of the *nomós*, and there are also hourly departures for Heráklion and Réthymnon, services at least every hour and often more frequently along the Stalos/Ag. Marina/Platanías/Gerani route and buses almost as often to Kolimbári. For bus information call t 282 109 3052.

Getting Around

There are **taxi** stands in central Chaniá in Plateía 1866 and Plateía Eleftherías in Chalepa, or you can ring for a cab on t 282 109 8700, 282 109 8701 or 282 108 7700.

Car and Bike Hire

Nearly all the local travel and tour agencies hire out cars: try **Diktynna Travel**, 36 Sfakión St, t 282 104 1458, *www.diktynna-travel.gr*; **Europrent**, 87 Chalídon, t 282 102 7810 (as well as standard cars, they also have jeeps and mini buses), or **Kyriákis Travel**, 78 Hadzimicháli Giannári, t 282 105 0500 and at the airport, t 282 106 3803.

Mountain bikes can be rented from the **Trekking Plan** shop, on Karaóli-Dimitrioú street and open daily.

Tourist Information

Internet access: E-Café, 59 Theotokopoúlou, is an impressive new venue with plenty of quiet cubicles where you can log on until 2am; **Sante** and the **Manos Internet Café** are two useful Net cafés on Aktí Koundouriotoú, on the harbour. **Ideon Andron**, 26 Chalídon, is a more-attractive-than-most Net café in a pleasant garden setting, with a restaurant. **Tourist police**: 23 Irákleio, t 282 105 3333. The office is rather inconvenienty located in the new city, but is the nearest thing there is to an official information office.

Festivals

Mid–end of May: Anniversary commemorations of the Battle of Crete. For information, call t 282 108 7098.

June–Sept Crete International Festival: the island's largest arts festival, with performances and exhibitions of traditional and modern arts in many venues around Chaniá.

24 June: St John's Day.

15 August: Pan-Cretan Festival.

Shopping

Chaniá has no shortage of shops: where they used to specialize in the making of shoes and hand-carved chairs (the latter in particular are still available here and there, but they tend to be daunting to cart home), jewellery now rules the roost. Leather, though, still predominates on Skridlóf street, and there are several traditional knifemakers along Sífaka.

Nearly all the shops and workshops listed here are located in the Old Town.

Anatolia, 5 Chalídon, **t** 282 104 1218. A big, beautiful shop with modern and ethnic designs in jewellery.

Antonioú, 22 Kondiláki. An engaging display of handmade necklaces, bracelets and earrings based on traditional Greek designs.

Apogio, 80 Hadzimicháli Giannári. For books, new or old, tapes and CDs.

Apostolos Pachtikos, 14 Sífaka, **t** 282 105 4534. Mr Pachtikos began working in 1946 at the age of 13 and still makes traditional Cretan knives, tempered on a tiny forge and anvil at the rear of the shop. In addition to knives, he also offers mountain goat horns and a collection of battered Nazi helmets.

Diamantopoulou, 51 Potié. An idiosyncratic shop full of chess and backgammon sets.

Eólos, 7 Chalídon. Beautiful creations in lapis lazuli.

Gaia, 2 Dimitrakáki, **t** 282 102 8783. Organic foods, including Cretan specialities.

International Shop, Plateía Syntrivani. Chaniá's best choice of books and papers in English.

Lefteris Klidaras' Herb Centre, Agora (indoor market). This market shop offers not only a wide range of spices but also an excellent selection of Cretan wines.

Metamorphosis, 50 Theokotópolou, **t** 282 107 0545. Showcases the work of some eminent contemporary Greek jewellery designers.

Mythos, 30 Betolo, **t** 282 105 7776. Jewellery and objets d'art, mostly by modern Cretan designers. Betolo street is an alley just beside the Cathedral.

Neféli, 20 Kondiláki, **t** 282 108 1967. A very similar neo-traditional jewellery range to its neighbour, Antonioú.

Roka Carpets, 61 Zambéliou, **t** 282 107 4736. Carpets are handmade by the owner on a 17th-century loom.

Top Chanas, 3 Angélou (Old Town), **t** 282 109 8571. A lair of traditional Cretan weavings and blankets.

Sports and Activities

Watersports and Water Parks

Around the quays of the Venetian Harbour you will find several companies that offer **boat trips** to the nearby islands of Theodorir and Lazaretta, most of which include stops for swimming and snorkelling. **Evagélos Cruise Lines**, **t** 294 5087 4283, has both regular cruise boats and a glass-bottomed boat that offers a glimpse of the fascinating wealth of marine life in the area; they also sail right over a plane that went down in the Battle of Crete.

There are also several **scuba diving** centres in Chaniá that give you the chance to explore Crete's vibrant underwater world from closer up. Most offer trips for complete beginners as well as experienced divers, and provide short training courses leading to an internationally-recognised PADI certificate. **Blue Adventures Diving** is at 69 Daskologiánni, **t** 282 104 0608; **Fun Dive** is at 6 Akti Papanikoli, **t** 282 107 2512.

Water parks are increasingly popular in Crete and there are two near Chaniá, which as well as the usual spaghetti of water slides offer sports such as tennis and mini-golf.

Limnopoulis Water Park, Varypétro, 6km south of Chaniá, **t** 282 103 3246. Ten hectares of pools, waterslides, whirlpools and more. Open April–Oct daily 10–7.

Atlantis, Akrotíriou, just east of Chaniá, **t** 282 103 9777. A slightly smaller park.

Climbing and Outdoor Sports

Mountaineering Club of Chaniá, 90 S. Tzanakáki, **t** 282 107 4560/282 104 4647. The club organizes excursions in and around the Chaniá area (open to non-members), but if your adventurous streak doesn't run to mountain climbing, they also run skiing, canoeing and caving trips.

Where to Stay

Chaniá ✉ 73100

Chaniá's hotels have more character than any others in Crete, but be aware that some of the most picturesque places around the Venetian Harbour can be noisy at night.

Association of Rented Rooms & Apartments, 12 Isódion, **t** 282 104 3601, **f** 282 104 6277. Provides a list of inexpensive quality lodgings, with a map to help you find them.

Luxury

Casa Delfino, 9 Theofánous, **t** 282 108 7400, *www.casadelfino.com* (*B*). A very classy conversion of a 17th-century town house, full of marble and palatial touches; its suites are all individually designed and some feature hi-tech business extras such as data ports for modem link-up as well as luxuries like jacuzzis. The public areas include a lovely rooftop terrace and a courtyard café.

Villa Andromeda, 150 El. Venizélou, **t** 282 102 8300, *www.villandromeda.gr* (*B*). One of the fanciest hotels in Chaniá, out on the east side of the city in the Chalepa quarter. The villa was formerly the German consulate, and has now been divided into eight air-conditioned suites; in addition, a lush garden, Turkish bath and swimming pool are just some of the other amenities.

Expensive

Bozzali Studios, Gavaládon (a quiet lane off Sífaka), **t** 282 105 0824 (*A*). 15 elegant rooms in a lovingly restored old house in old Chaniá. *Open Mar–Nov.*

Contessa, 15 Theofánous, **t** 282 109 8566, **f** 282 109 8565 (*A*). This small hotel has the intimate air of an old-fashioned guesthouse, furnished in traditional style. The owners speak little English, but make up for it by being extremely helpful. *Book well in advance.*

Doma, 124 El. Venizélou, **t** 282 105 1772, **f** 282 104 1578 (*B*). One of several hotels on Eleuthériou Venizélou, on the east side of town towards the beach, with comfortable rooms in a neoclassical mansion, decked out in antiques and Cretan rusticana. The owner has an unusual collection of hats from all over the world. *Open Mar-Oct.*

El Greco, 49 Theotokopoúlou, **t** 282 109 0432, **f** 282 109 1829, *hotel@elgreco.gr* (*B*). A pretty and popular place draped in creepers on Chaniá's prettiest street, named after the same artist. *Book well in advance.*

Halepa, 164 El. Venizélou, **t** 282 102 8440, **f** 282 102 8439, *www.halepa.com* (*B*). This villa once housed the British counterpart of the Andromeda (*see* above), as the Consulate. Renovated in 1990, it now offers 49 very comfortable, fully air-conditioned rooms and a quiet, palm-lined garden.

Nóstos, 46 Zambelíou, **t** 282 109 4743, **f** 282 109 4740 (*B*). A small refurbished Venetian house on a busy lane in the heart of the old city; many rooms have nice views.

Pandora, 29 Lithínon, **t** 282 1043 589, *www.pandorahotel.gr* (*A*). A neoclassical building with comfortable rooms and studio apartments furnished with period pieces, very well located in Kastélli not far from the harbour; there are great views from the terrace.

Rodon, 92 Akrotíriou, **t** 282 105 8317, *www.interkriti.net/hotels/acrotiri/rodon* (*B*). A modern family-run hotel with a pool and pretty garden on the east edge of the city, not far from beaches and with views of Chaniá and the White Mountains.

Moderate

Palazzo, 54 Theotokopoúlou, **t** 282 109 3227, **f** 282 109 3229 (*A*). For anyone seeking divine inspiration this is the place, with each room named after a god. Most have balconies, giving them a lot of charm.

Pension Kastélli, 39 Kanenáro street, Kastélli, **t** 282 105 7057. Pleasant rooms and small apartments with kitchen facilities, priced near the bottom of this category.

Pension Theresa, 8 Angélou, **t/f** 282 109 2798 (*B*). Charming rooms and studios oozing with character, and a tempting roof terrace with great views in another restored Venetian house.

Vranas Studios, 23–25 Ag. Déka, **t** 282 105 8618 or 282 104 3788. On a quiet side street near the old port, these bright studio apartments have recently been done up, in an attractive, traditional style .

Inexpensive

Chaniá has a vast selection of pensions and inexpensive rooms, and most are located within a few streets of the Venetian or inner harbour. Those listed here are some of the nicer ones among the many.

Esta, 6 Kondiláki, (no phone). Simple rooms in a charming pink house .

Konaki, 43 Kondiláki, **t** 282 108 6379. Eight rooms in a quirky, tastefully renovated house – the two on the ground floor have bathrooms and open onto a garden of banana palms.

Kydonia, 20 Chalídon, **t** 282 107 4650. Well-designed doubles, triples and quads in a quiet courtyard, next to the Archaeological Museum.

Maria, 4 Angélou, t 282 105 1052. One of several small pensions in a location full of life near the harbour, the Firkas Tower and the Naval Museum, this one has lovely views from some of its rooms across the port to the White Mountains.

Meltémi, 2 Angélou, t/f 282 109 2802. In the same area as the Maria and with similar views, this pension sits above the mellow Meltémi café and offers space enough to swing several cats in its bigger rooms.

Monastíri, 18 Ag. Markoú, t 282 105 4776 (*E*). Occupying part of the ruined cloister of a Venetian church, this little place is unusually serene; some rooms have nice views towards the Venetian Harbour.

Stella, 10 Angélou, t 282 1073 756. Airy, mostly traditional-style rooms with air-conditioning and fridges, in an old building and perched above an eponymous shop selling psychedelic hand-blown glass.

Venus, 42 Sarpáki (no phone). On a quiet street in Splántza, the old Turkish quarter, this basic pension has simple but clean rooms in a lovingly restored house.

Rent Rooms 47, Kandanoléou, t 282 105 3243. In a cul-de-sac in Kastélli, this is another place set back from the main night scooter routes. Rooms are plain but decent.

Youth Hostel, 33 Drakonianoú, t 282 105 3565. Decent and exceptionally quiet, because it's almost out of the city limits: to get there, take an Ag. Ioánnis bus, which leaves every 15 mins from the square beside the market. Youth Hostel cards are not needed.

Camping

There are two campsites near Chaniá, but you'll need a bus to reach them, as they're both on the road towards Ag. Marína and Plataniás west of the city. Both are within easy walking distance of fine beaches:

Camping Ag. Marína, t 282 106 8596. On the way to Ag. Marína, 8km west of the town; buses leave from the main bus station. *Open Mar–Oct.*

Camping Chaniá, Ag. Apóstoli, 5km west of town, t 282 103 1138, f 282 103 3371 (city bus from Platéia 1866). This modern site is loaded with amenities including a pool and a bar, both of which, though, can be noisy in the evenings. *Open Mar–Oct.*

Eating Out

It's actually hard *not* to find a restaurant in Chaniá – all around the harbour is one great crescent of tavernas.

Dinos, 3 Aktí Enóseos and Sarpidónos, t 282 104 1865 (€20–25). A long-time favourite overlooking the inner harbour, specializing in fish, but which also has a good selection of meat dishes to choose from.

To Pigadi tou Tourkou ('The Well of the Turk'), 1 Kalliníkou Sarpáki, t 282 105 4547 (€18–22). In the heart of the old Turkish quarter of Splántza, this excellent establishment has been delighting taste buds for years. The bias is, of course, Middle Eastern, with specialities from Egypt, Lebanon and Tunisia. Dishes include various Arabian pies (try the spinach pie with lemon, walnuts and raisins), humous and lamb with lemon.

Mirovólos, 19 Zambéliou, t 282 109 1960 (€18–22). In the lovely courtyard of a Venetian building dating from 1290, this restaurant provides ample well-prepared dishes accompanied by Cretan dancing and live music.

Monastíri, t 282 105 5527 (€20). Behind the Mosque of the Janissaries by the port, Monastíri serves fresh fish, fine Cretan food and wine from the barrel. It's frequented by ex-prime ministers and the like.

Tholos, 36 Ag. Déka, t 282 104 6725 (€18–20). Excellent Greek specialities are served in the picturesque ruins of an old Venetian town house, with mellow music. *Open April-Oct.*

Ela, 47 Kondiláki, t 282 107 4128 (€12–15). Good for Cretan specialities, occasionally accompanied by live traditional music.

Apovrado, Isódon, t 282 105 8151. Chaniot specialities are a strong point of the menu, including local wine and country sausages.

Aeriko, Aktí Miaoúli, t 282 105 9307. A good choice by the seafront and excellent value, with fresh seafood on the menu as well as spit-roasted chicken.

Akrogiáli, 19 Aktí Papaníkoli, t 282 107 3110. On the east side of the city: grab a taxi for excellent seafood at excellent prices.

Hippopotamos, 6 Sarpidónos, t 282 104 4128. For a change: Chania's only Mexican restaurant, off the Venetian Harbour, has all the favourites from burritos to fajitas, and pizza.

Ideon Andron/Chin Chin, 26 Chalídon, **t** 282 109 8591. Two restaurants in one, giving you the choice of a Greek or Chinese menu, or even a mix of the two. It's also a popular, mellow café-bar, with jazz or classical music playing around a pretty courtyard.

Suki Yaki, 28 Chalídon, **t** 282 107 4264. Chinese and Thai dishes, served in a garden.

Tsikoudadiko, 31 Zambéliou, **t** 282 107 2873. A place to go to for a distinctly Cretan experience, in a 16th-century Venetian loggia: homemade *tsikoúdia*, excellent *mezédes* and Cretan dishes, great wines and live music.

Tamam, 49 Zambéliou, **t** 282 109 6080. Set in an old Turkish hammam, Tamam offers vegetarian dishes including zucchini rissoles and *dakós* with olives and spices.

Iordánis, 96 Kydonias, **t** 282 109 0026. Ever since 1924, this has been *the* place to go in Chaniá for a perfect (bargain) cheese pie.

Kariátis, 12 Plateía Katechaki, **t** 282 105 5600. Good-value, enjoyable pizza or pasta, served on a terrace near the Venetian Harbour.

Entertainment and Nightlife

Cinema

Kípos Municipal Cinema, A. Papandréou , **t** 282 105 6450. Occupying the Public Gardens each year, this popular open-air summer movie season features a wide mix of Greek and foreign films. *Open June–early Oct.*

Bars and Cafés

Dio Lux, Sarpidónos, **t** 282 105 2515. An arty café by the Venetian Harbour, with a wide choice of teas and coffees.

Monastíri tou Károlou,22 Hadzimicháli Daliáni (behind the market), **t** 282 104 0950. The fomer 16th-century monastery of Santa Maria Misericordia has recently been restored, making use of old etchings, and houses an exhibition gallery, theatre, café and library, plus a smart hairdressing salon.

Neorion, Sarpidónos. A trendy place just off the Venetian Harbour, one of several nearby that are favoured by young Chaniots.

Santé, Aktí Koundouriotoú. Fairly traditional *kafeneíon* on the Inner Harbour (named 'health' after the famous, bizarrely labelled

Greek cigarette brand) where young Cretans hang out and play *távli*, with music at night.

Synagogi, Kondiláki, **t** 282 109 5242. An atmospheric lounge bar housed in the old Jewish baths, near the Schiavo Bastion.

To Mikro Kafeneio, 6 Aktí Miaóuli, Koum Kapi, **t** 282 105 9321. Charming café with great drinks: beautiful Chaniots decorate this and neighbouring seafront venues on the east side of town, the place to be to watch the world pass by into the early hours.

Music Bars and Clubs

For a night on the tiles, many head west out to the clubs in **Plataniás** (*see* p.123).Be warned though, that the police are out in force on the coast road in the early hours, so be sure to have a designated driver (or take a taxi).

Anagénnisis, Chalídon and Skalídi, **t** 282 107 2768. Lively disco housed in some restored Venetian storerooms

Café Kriti (Lyrákia), 22 Kallergón, **t** 282 105 8661. A hole-in-the-wall local institution, one street back from the harbour, where from 8.30pm on you can hear Cretan music for the price of a rakí, accompanied by *mezé* and, usually, impromptu dancing.

Ekentro Club, 16 Sourméli. Everything from hip-hop to trance turns up here.

The Face, 12 Kallergón. The newest and (reputedly) the best real dance club in town.

Fedra, 7 Isóderon, **t** 282 104 0789. Music bar that hosts a mix of live rock and jazz.

Fírkas Tower. Traditional Greek dance shows are put on in the tower on summer nights.

Fortezza, t 282 104 6546. Isolated out by the lighthouse is this live Greek music bar, with its own shuttle boat to ferry guests from the quay, and a restaurant. *Open April–Oct.*

NRG, Schiavo Bastion, www.otenet.gr/nrgclub. The only real mega-club in town: basspounding techno beats and celebrity DJs.

Plateía, Venetian Harbour. Long-running venue that frequently hosts blues (westernstyle) and other kinds of live music.

Street, 51 Aktí Koundouriotoú, **t** 282 107 4960. Very popular music bar, one of the oldest in Chaniá, with DJs after midnight.

Volcano, 6 Sourméli. Air-conditioned club in an old Venetian building by the outer harbour, with a magnificent lofty ceiling; music is split between Greek pop and techno.

Crete. At the entrance, there's a recent acquistion – a carefully reconstructed altar of Poseidon from Lissos, together with its clay bull votive offerings. Finds discovered in Chaniá itself, relics of Minoan Kydonia, are intriguing, and as usual raise more questions than they answer: especially the celebrated clay seal in high relief (*c.* 1450 BC) showing the commanding figure of a young Minoan proudly holding a staff, standing high above a sea breaking against the gates of a city – Kydonia itself, perhaps – with roofs crowned with horns of consecration. One guess is that it portrays the chief Minoan male deity, *Poteidan* (Poseidon), master of the sea, earth, bulls and earthquakes; another is that the curious sea or rock underneath him is really a tidal wave or *tsunami*, perhaps the very one that is believed to have clobbered Crete when Santoríni flipped its lid around 1450 BC.

Other cases contain Minoan jewels and vases, and ceramics that were imported from Cyprus by ancient Kydonians; most of the polychrome clay sarcophagi, or *larnaxes*, in the museum come from the cemetery of Arméni, near Réthymnon (*see* p.164). From the Classical period there are statues and ex-votos from the shrine of Diktean Artemis, and a finely moulded 4th-century BC terracotta Tanagra statuette, still bearing traces of her gilt and paint (in ancient times these figurines were as popular, and as often forged, as Cartier watches are now). A 3rd-century AD house in Chaniá yielded the series of beautiful mosaic floors on the legend of Dionysos. Lastly, in the middle of the nave, there are cases with Linear A and Linear B tablets. Kydonia is the only town in western Crete where both scripts have been discovered.

The Folklore Museum and the Cathedral

In the courtyard adjacent to the Archaeological Museum, a set of steps leads to a sweet little **Folklore Museum** (*t* 282 109 0814, open daily 9–3 and 6–9), full of traditional weavings and needlework and run by a charming lady. Across the street is an old Turkish **hammam** covered with baby bubble domes, standing next to a large square holding the **Trimartyr**, Chaniá's cathedral. In the 1850s a soap factory belonging to Mustafa Nily Pasha stood here; when he became Prime Minister of the Ottoman Empire he donated it to local Christians as a gesture of reconciliation, along with a large sum of money (100,000 Ottoman *curus*) to erect a church. His son, who became the next governor of Crete, donated another 30,000 *curus*, and the Tzar of Russia donated the bell. A little further seawards, the stone building at the corner of Chalídon and Zambéliou is believed to have been the **Venetian Loggia**; it later served as a Turkish military hospital, and even later as Chaniá's town hall.

The Topanás District

Chalídon street flows into the crescent of the **Outer Harbour**, lined with handsome Venetian buildings. The neighbourhood on the west side of the port, Topanás (from the Turkish word for 'cannons', which were kept here), has landmark status, although this has not stopped nearly all its interiors being converted into bars, pensions and restaurants. The **Fírkas Tower** at the far western end of the port saw the official

Translating the Minoans

The great fires that ravaged the Minoan palaces around 1450 BC had the side-effect of baking the clay tablets on which the Minoans scratched their mysterious script. Three types of writing have been found: the earliest, unfathomable 'pictographic' script of the Phaistos disc (*see* p.184); Linear A, used from the 18th to the 15th centuries BC; and Linear B, current after the rise of the Mycenaeans (*c.* 1450 BC). Few examples of Linear A script have been found, and nearly all were at the major temple sites in Eastern Crete. On the other hand, thousands of Linear B tablets have been uncovered, both in Crete (some 3,000 at Knossos alone) and on the Greek mainland.

Ancient scripts fired Arthur Evans's imagination: accidental finds of Linear B writing were what propelled him to Crete in the first place (*see* p.193). By the time he died in 1941, he could claim to have been the discoverer of Europe's first civilization, but he never accomplished what he had set out to do: translate the Minoans.

Yet, before the Second World War Evans had unknowingly planted the seed that would lead to a breakthrough when he gave a lecture on the Minoans in Athens. He fired the imagination of one listener in particular, an English teenager named Michael Ventris. Ventris grew up to be an architect, but his hobby was the Minoan script; the British cracking of Hitler's secret code was one inspiration. But how could anyone hope to decipher the writing of a long-lost language? A few notations (man, horse, spear) could be easily picked out, but there were many more signs that didn't

raising of the Greek flag over Crete in November 1913 in the presence of King Constantine and Prime Minister Venizélos, godfather of the union, and the erection of a marble plaque that reads 'Turkish Rule in Crete 1669–1913. 264 years, 7 months and 7 days of Tribulation.' Long used as a prison, the tower now contains a summer theatre (*see* p.106) and the **Naval Museum** (*t 282 109 1875; open April–Oct Tues–Sun 9–4, Nov–Mar Tues–Sun 10–2; adm*), founded in 1973 by a local admiral. Crete, naturally, is the main focus; among the photos, don't miss those showing another ruler, Prince George, who landed at this very spot on 9 December 1898 to become High Commissioner of autonomous Crete. Kazantzákis describes this electrifying moment in his *Report to Greco*: 'The Cretans sang and danced in the taverns, they drank, they played the *rebec*, but still they did not find relief. Unable to fit any longer inside their bodies, they grasped knives and stabbed themselves in the arms and thighs so that blood would flow and they would be unburdened.' The museum also has models of Venetian galleys and fortifications, and mock-ups of key Greek naval victories in history, all described in slightly hysterical nationalistic translations. The first floor contains an evocative collection of photos and items from the Battle of Crete, including a Wehrmacht-issue chess set.

Behind the tower, simple little **San Salvatore** belonged to a Franciscan monastery under the Venetians and then, like most of Chaniá's churches, was used by the Turks as a mosque. Near here begins Topanás' main street, **Theotokopoúlou**, the most picturesque in the city, lined with Venetian houses that were remodelled by the Turks, who added their favourite lattice work and wooden balconies. Behind the San look like anything at all. In 1952 an idea occurred to Ventris that had escaped all the scholars. Perhaps, after all, it wasn't a long-lost language; perhaps the widespread Linear B, at least, was Greek, and the symbols were phonetic, each representing a syllable. Together with John Chadwick, an expert in ancient forms of Greek, Ventris set to and found enough instances where the system worked for scoffers to start paying attention. Although problems still remain, nearly everyone now admits that Ventris (who died in a car accident not long after his discovery) was on the right track. And, after all the fuss, what did the Minoans and their Mycenaean peers have to say? 'Five jars of honey, 300 pigs, 120 cows for As-as-wa' – inventories of goods. Imagine if modern civilization were obliterated and only our shopping lists survived.

Nevertheless, the deciphering of Linear B has opened up a whole range of tantalizing new questions: on cultural exchanges between the Minoans and Mycenaeans, on the origins of the earliest known names of gods and places, on the functions of the palaces and the governments that operated from them. Symbols borrowed from the older Linear A (believed by Chadwick and others to be in the native, non-Greek language of the Minoans) have led to tentative translations; scholars think it could be related to ancient Anatolian languages, perhaps Hittite. Examples are so rare and brief that linguists will just have to sit tight and wait for archaeologists to come up with some longer and more connected texts. It is known that the Minoans used ink. A volume of poetry by their Shakespeare would be especially nice.

Salvatore bastion at 72 Theotokopoúlou is the **Byzantine Museum** (*t 282 109 6046; open Tues–Sat 8.30–3; adm, combined ticket with Archaeological Museum*), which has a good collection of Cretan icons, frescoes, pottery, inscriptions, sculptures, coins and mosaics that fleshes out a long period of the island's history, from the early centuries AD into the post-Byzantine era (as the Greeks prefer to call the Turkish occupation).

On Theofánou street (off Zambéliou, itself lined with handsome Venetian façades) the **Renieri Gate** bears a Venetian coat-of-arms of 1608 and the curious inscription *Multa tulip Fecitus et studarit dulces pater, sudavit et alsit semper requies serena* ('the sweet father had worked hard and studied, sweated and froze; may he always rest in joy'). This gate stood by the Palazzo Renieri, which has all but vanished, except for the remarkably well-preserved little private **chapel** near the gate. Another house nearby has another inscription, reading *Nuli parvus est cui magnus est animus* ('No one is poor when his soul is big').

Further south stood the old ghetto of Chaniá, the **Ovraiki**, although the dilapidated former synagogue on Kondiláki street burned down a few years ago (the Taverna Ela marks the spot). In fact, it has been said that the only surviving physical sign of Crete's Jewish population, already reduced through emigration from around 1,600 under the Venetians to 400 on the eve of the Second World War, is the two lists of Jews in the city compiled not long before the war by Chaniá's rabbi that are now in the Historical Archives (*see* p.112). The Germans used these lists to round the Jews up, along with other undesirable Greeks and Italians, and put them all on a ship, the *Danaë*, which set sail on 7 June 1944 and was never seen again.

At the top of Kondiláki, along Portoú Lane, is the big, round **Schiavo Bastion**, the last surviving tower of the stretch of **Venetian walls** that still defend the district. It was in 1538, just after the pirate admiral Barbarossa had left his calling card of death and desolation in Réthymnon, that the Venetians decided to surround Chaniá with a complete set of walls and a moat that was more than 147ft (45m) wide and 30ft (9m) deep. As it turned out, though, these precautions did little to keep out the Turks in 1645, when they captured Chaniá after a siege of just two months. Nowadays, one of the functions of the old fortress is as a setting for the **NRG** dance club, one of Chaniá's biggest, noisiest and hippest nightspots (*see* p.106).

Kastélli

The east end of the old Venetian port, the **Inner Harbour**, has Chaniá's two most photographed landmarks: a graceful Venetian **lighthouse** in golden stone that was restored under the Egyptians in the 19th century, located at the tip of the breakwater and enclosing the inner harbour, and the **Mosque of the Janissaries** (1645), crowned with its distinctive ostrich- and chicken-egg domes. Here the Christian-born slave troops of the Ottoman Empire worshipped, although little did it improve their character; not only did they terrorize the Greeks, but in 1690 they murdered the Pasha of Chaniá and fed his body to the dogs. In 1812, even the Sublime Porte of Constantinople had had enough and sent Hadji Osman Pasha, 'the Throttler', into Crete to hang the lot of them – an act that so impressed the locals that rumours flew around the town that 'the Throttler' must be a crypto-Christian.

Behind the mosque lies the Kastélli quarter, spread across a low hill above the Inner Harbour. This slight rise was the acropolis of ancient Kydonia, and **excavations** by a Greek-Swedish team along Kaneváro street have revealed a complex of Middle Minoan buildings, most of them with second storeys, flagstoned floors and grand entrances that opened on to narrow streets. The presence of nearly 100 Linear B tablets among the ruins suggest the proximity of a palace; a large deposit of Linear A tablets was found in a dig on **Katre** street nearby. The name 'Kastélli' itself derives from the first, inner fortress that was built by the Venetians here in the 13th century, and which sheltered their palazzi; according to the 'Concession of Chaniá' of 1252 these first colonists (there were 90 of them, and all of them well off) were obliged to rebuild the city in return for their privileges. Although Kastélli and its once lovely palazzi took the brunt of the Luftwaffe bombs, you can still pick out the odd Venetian architectural detail, especially along **Kaneváro** (once the Venetian main street, or *Corso*) and **Lithínon** streets; at the end of the latter are the Renaissance gateway and courtyard of what was once the palace of the Venetian Rector and, later, the Turkish Pasha. At the top end of Ag. Markoú street you can see the ruined walls and windows of the old Catholic cathedral of Venetian Chaniá, Santa Maria degli Miracoli, from 1615. Below, overlooking the inner harbour, rise the vaults (1600) of the Venetian **Arsenali**, hub of Venice's military establishment here when Chaniá was the Republic's great stronghold in western Crete, though only seven of its originally 17 shipyards survive.

Splántza and Koum Kápi

Splántza, just east of Kastélli, was Chaniá's main Turkish quarter. Some interesting churches are concentrated here, such as the recently discovered, underground **Ag. Iríni**, dating from the 15th century, in Plateía Roúgia (Kallinikou Sarpani street). South in Vourdoúba street, near an enormous plane tree, is Ag. Nikólaos, which began life as a Dominican monastery church built in the early 14th century and was subsequently converted by the Turks into an Imperial mosque to shelter the 'Sword of the Conqueror', which the Imam would hold up while leading Friday prayers (surprisingly, it's still there). Note the *tugra* or emblem of the Sultan, on the entrance and the minaret (formerly the Venetian campanile) and, if the church is open, on the coffered ceiling inside. Close by on Daskalogiánni street is **San Rocco** (1630), a little church covered with weeds, although in its day it was charged with protecting Chaniá from the plague. The little **mosque of Ahmet Aga** with its mihrab and and minaret still stands in Hadzimichali Daliani street, back towards the modern Orthodox cathedral.

The area just to the east of the mosque was another little Christian quarter, named after the modest 16th-century **Ag. Anargýri** in Koumi street, which served as the town's 'cathedral' from 1646 to 1859, when it was the only church in Chaniá allowed to hold Orthodox services; its prize is a superb icon of the *Second Coming*, with a dramatic crowd of tormented sinners, by Amvrósios, a pupil of Damaskínos.

Another large section of Sammichele's wall survives along **Mínos** street, along with the **Koum Kapissi** (or **Sabbionari**) bastion, less imposing than the Schiavo Bastion but emblazoned with the date 1590 and a Lion of St Mark. Just outside of the wall here is the district of **Koum Kápi** (Turkish for 'Beach Gate'), a quarter that was first settled by Bedouins who migrated here during Crete's Egyptian interlude (1831–40) and again later on in the 1870s, when extra hands were required to construct the island's new capital. Today it houses several hotels, and the cafés along Koum Kapi's seafront, **Aktí Miaoúli**, are choc-a-bloc every evening with young Greeks, meeting up to take the breeze before heading out to the clubs in Plataniás.

Chaniá's Newer Quarters and Beaches

The blocks of 'new' Chaniá extend south and inland from the Agora and the broad, relatively businesslike main square of **Plateía 1866**, hub for many of the local bus services. From the covered market, **Tzanakáki** street leads southeast to the private gardens of Reouf Pasha, now the cool and shady **Public Gardens**, with a small **zoo** (your chance to see a *kri-kri*) and outdoor cinema, often showing films in English (*see* p.106). Another curiosity in the area is the small **Chemistry Museum**, north of the gardens and the stadium at 34 El. Venizélou street (*t 282 104 2504; open Mon–Fri 7–2.30*), in the house where 200 years ago the first chemist in Greece set up shop. The curator Michaíl Amoutzákis, himself a chemist, will talk you through the variety of apparatus on show, including a long tubed contraption that can detect the difference between real and synthetic honey.

South of the Public Gardens, on the corner of Tzanakáki and Sfakianáki, is the **War Museum** (*t 282 104 4156; open Mon–Fri 9–1*), which chronicles Crete's remarkable battle history, while a villa just to the south houses the **Historical Archives of Crete** (*open Mon–Fri 9–1*), at 20 Sfakianáki. It contains Greece's second largest collection of archival material, dating from the Venetian occupation to the liberation of Crete in 1944. Nearly all the material, though, is in Greek, with few concessions made to non-Greek-reading visitors.

Further east from Koum Kapi along the sea shore is the fancy **Chalepa** quarter, a much more plush side of Chaniá, dotted with 19th-century neoclassical mansions and gardens, many of which were built as consulates during Crete's years of autonomy. On the district's main square of **Plateía Venizélos** stands the house (and statue) of Venizélos, built in 1880 by Eleftheriós' father, together with the **government palace** built for Prince George as ruler of autonomous Crete (now the main courthouse) and the rather exotic church of **Ag. Magdalení** (1901) with its little onion dome. It was donated by the Russian Grand Duke George, on the site of the former home of his wife. The waterfront area nearby is called the **Tampakariá**, named after its tanneries, which kept Chaniá's traditional leather trades supplied with their essential raw material. Some of the district's tanneries have been in business continuously for well over a century.

Chaniá's town beach of **Néa Chorá** is over on the opposite, western, flank of the old city and the harbour along the waterfront of **Akti Papanikóli**, beyond the Firkas Tower and San Salvatore. It's a 15-minute walk from the Inner Harbour, or you can get there by city bus from Plateía 1866. The sands improve the further west you go. The whole coast is well developed, with good swimming and windsurfing, cafés and tavernas, and fills up with Chaniots at weekends. The golden sands of **Chrýsi Aktí**, 5km from Chaniá, are popular with families and older tourists; **Ag. Apostolí** (7km) has three sandy coves and a lively beach bar. For beaches at Ag. Marína, Plataniás and further west, *see* pp.121–3.

Nomós Chaniá

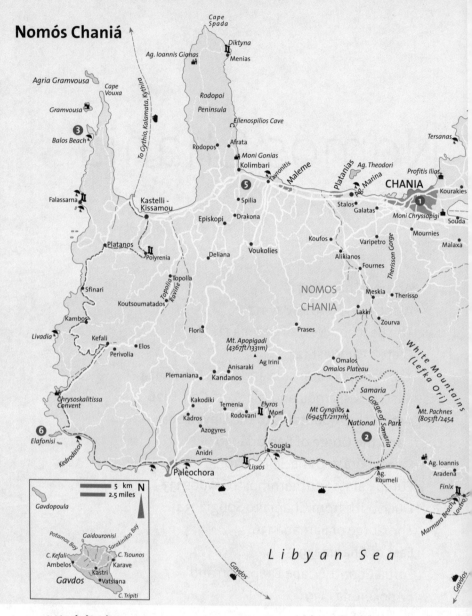

Nomós Chaniá

Cape Spada

Diktyna

Menias

Ag. Ioannis Gionas

Agria Gramvousa

Cape Vouxa

Rodopoi Peninsula

Gramvousa

Ellenospilios Cave

3 Balos Beach

Rodopos

Afrata

Moni Gonias

Kolimbari

Tavronitis

Maleme

Platanias

Ag. Theodori

Tersanas

Profitis Ilias

CHANIA

Kourakies

5 Spilia

Ag. Marina

Stalos

Galatas

Moni Chryssopigi

Souda

Falassarna

Kastelli - Kissamou

Episkopi

Drakona

Koufos

Varipetro

Mournies

Malaxa

Platanos

Polyrenia

Deliana

Voukolies

Alikianos

Fournes

Therisson Gorge

Meskla

Therisso

Sfinari

Topolia Kavité

Koutsoumatados

Floria

Prases

Lakki

Zourva

Kambos

Livadia

Kefali

Elos

Perivolia

Mt. Apopigadi
(4367ft/1331m)

Ag Irini

Omalos

Omalos Plateau

White Mountains
(Lefka Ori)

Anisaraki

Plemaniana

Kandanos

Samaria

Mt Pachnes
(8051ft/2454

Chrysoskalitissa Convent

Kakodiki

Temenia

Elyros

Moni

Rodovani

Mt Gyngilos
(6945ft/2117m)

Gorge of Samaria

National Park

Kadros

Azogyres

6 Elafonisi

Kedrodasos

Anidri

Sougia

Lissos

Ag. Roumeli

Ag. Ioannis

Aradena

Paleochora

Finix

Marmara Beach

Loutró

Gavdos

Libyan Sea

5 km
2.5 miles
N

Gavdopoula

Potamos Bay

Gaidouronisi

Sarakinikos Bay

C. Kefali

Ambelos

C. Tsounos

Karave

Kastri

Vatsiana

Gavdos

C. Tripiti

Gavdos

Highlights

1 Venetian Chaniá, Crete's most evocative city

2 The spectacular Gorge of Samariá, the longest in Europe

3 The white sands and turquoise waters of Balos Beach, on the Gramvousa peninsula

4 The homeland of Zorba, in the old town of Vamos and the nearby hamlets

5 Frescoed Byzantine churches among the orange groves south of Kolimbári

6 The stunning lagoon of Elafonísi and the chestnut groves just inland

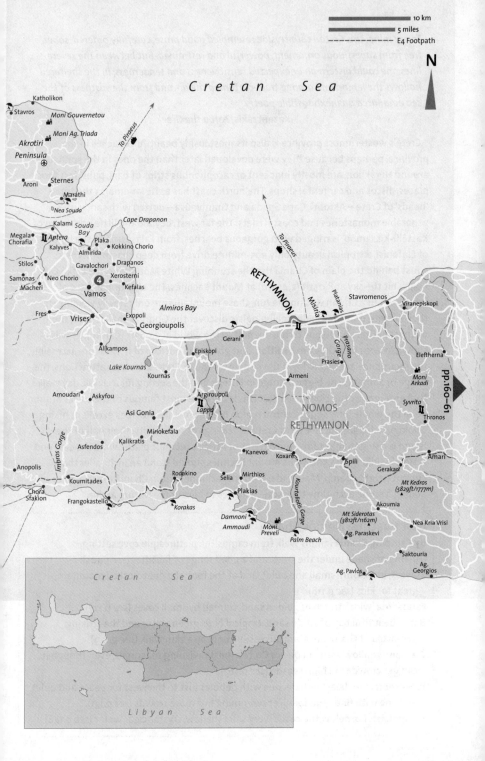

To my mind, this Cretan countryside resembled good prose, carefully ordered, sober, free from superfluous ornament, powerful and restrained. But between the severe lines one could discern an unexpected sensitiveness and tenderness; in the sheltered hollows the lemon and orange trees perfumed the air, and from the vastness of the sea emanated an inexhaustible poetry.

Kazantzákis, *Zorba the Greek*

Crete's westernmost province is also its most lushly beautiful. Beaches in the province, perhaps because they were developed later than the ones in the sprawl around Heráklion, are mostly innocent of cacophonous strips of bars, pubs, fast food places, discos and car rental shops. The north coast has as its landmarks the three 'heads' of Crete – Akrotíri, Cape Spada and Gramvoúsa – dotted with sandy coves, venerable monasteries and coastal islets. The far west, beyond the little port town of Kastélli-Kíssamou, is fringed with gorgeous beaches, from Falassarná to the lagoon of Elafonísi, a tropical beauty only a 15-minute drive from deep chestnut forests.

Just behind the plain of Chaniá rise the stunning White Mountains, the Lefká Óri, which hit the sky at 8,051ft (2,454m) at Mount Pachnés. The traditional place of refuge when a Cretan was on the run, these mountains are only slowly yielding up their secrets; only in 1991 did speleologists discover the Gourgouthákas cave, the deepest in Greece and one of the deepest in the world at 3,963ft (1,210m), as was shown in 2001 by a Greek expedition that got to the bottom of it. Far more accessibly, the mountains are sliced down the middle by one of Crete's five-star attractions, the Gorge of Samariá, the biggest gorge in Europe and the setting for a classic day walk that emerges by the Libyan Sea. But this is only the most famous of the tracks around here: the whole lofty south-central region of the province provides excellent hiking. Geology helps support western Cretans' feelings of superiority; their half of the island is rising thanks to the movement of Africa's tectonic plate, while the east end is slowly sinking. In 1,500 years Mount Pachnés should stand an inch taller than current height champ, Mount Ida; mountain-climbers from Chaniá make a point of adding a stone each time they scale Pachnés to encourage Nature along.

Best Beaches: Nomós Chaniá

By Camping Chaniá (2mins walk from campsite): picturesque cove setting, plenty of shade under the trees, and a good range of facilities (*see* p.105).

Stávros, in Akrotíri: small and quiet, and at the foot of a goat-flecked mountain; great for kids (*see* p.118).

Falassarná: wide stretch of golden sand, framed by small coves (*see* p.127).

Balos: beautiful bay of white sand, tropical blue-green water and the striking peninsula of Gramvousa, and accessible only by a 2km walk (*see* p.129).

Elafonísi: shallow water in one of Crete's most ravishing seascapes, even though it can get crowded in high season (*see* p.129).

Paleóchora: two beaches here, one with pebbles just to the west for peace and quiet, and one with fine sand for nicer swimming but more crowds (*see* p.131).

Frangokástello: below the castle: very safe, shallow, crystal-clear water (*see* p.148).

A few small towns on the Libyan coast have grown into modest resorts; Paleochóra is the largest but still pretty low-key, while Loutró, on a smaller scale, owes a great deal of its charm to the fact that it's only accessible by sea. Once fierce Chóra Sfakíon, the blazing centre of Cretan resistance, has mellowed to the point that it looks like any other Greek island port, while just east of it, under a haunted Venetian castle, stretches the delicious beach of Frangokástello. Some people never get any further.

Around Chaniá

Akrotíri (ΑΚΡΩΤΗΡΙ) and Soúda Bay

Akrotíri, the most bulbous and busiest of the three headlands that thrust out of Crete's northwest coast, wraps around to shelter the island's biggest and safest port at Soúda from northerly winds. Its strategic position has assured it plenty of history, and now that Crete is safe from imminent invasion the steep access road (Eleftheríou Venizélou) from Chaniá's Chalepa quarter is often choc-a-bloc with locals heading out to Akrotíri's beaches, restaurants, nightclubs and seaside villas. Outside these suburban tentacles, Akrotíri is a moody place, dusty and junky in the military zones towards the airport, lonely and wild by its famous monasteries.

First stop on Akrotíri should be little **Profítis Ilías,** a former monastery church 4.5km from Chaniá that's better known today as the **Venizélos Graves.** Elefthérios Venízelos died in exile in Paris in 1936, and as the then Greek government refused to let his body lie in state in Athens, it was brought here for a low-key funeral. Venizélos (1864–1936) and his son Sophoklís (1896–1964) both asked to be buried on this spot to enjoy superb posthumous views over Chaniá, but they had patriotic reasons as well: in the rebellion of 1897, the monastery was briefly a Revolutionary Military Camp, located just within the 6km exclusion zone around Chaniá set by the Powers, there to police the volatile Greeks and Turks rather like nowadays in Bosnia. To rout out the Greeks, the English, French, Italian and Russian navies bombarded the camp; in response they raised the Greek flag. The admirals were so impressed by the sheer audacity of the Cretans, who held up the flag with their bare hands after it was shot off its pole, that they stopped firing and applauded. Later a Russian shell destroyed the monastery, but the Prophet Elijah, not one to turn the other cheek, took revenge by blowing up the Russian ship the next day. The news that the Powers were bombing Christian Greeks caused a great stir in Europe and led the Allies to offer Crete its autonomy. There are two cafés nearby with splendid views, especially at sunset.

If it's Easter Day afternoon, head east for the spotless convent of the **Prodrómos** (St John the Baptist) at **Kourakiés,** where the bishop of Chaniá reads the 'Vespers of Love' in a score of languages to the crowd in the flower-bedecked courtyard. It was abandoned after several rampages by Chaniá's Janissaries, but the nuns returned in the late 19th century; the wife of the then British ambassador taught them embroidery and lacework as a means of supporting themselves, work that continues to this day.

To the north is Akrotíri's first sandy seaside playground, **Kalathás** (Καλαθάς) and its nearby, quieter beach of **Tersanás**, rimmed with villas. **Stavrós** (Στάυρος), further north, is the end of the trail for buses from Chaniá and owes its growing popularity for longer stays to a lovely sheltered circular bay, resembling a shallow lake, that makes it an ideal spot for young kids. The beach scenes in *Zorba the Greek* were filmed here, including the finale when Anthony Quinn taught Alan Bates how to dance the *syrtáki*; the steep slope to the sea was the site of Zorba's half-assed cableway that collapsed like a row of dominoes under the first plummeting tree trunks. A nice way to explore the area is on horseback, and there is a riding centre in Tersanás (*see* below). Another good beach on Akrotíri, **Maráthi**, is just east of the airport – a pretty crescent of fine silver sand with small fish tavernas, near the ruins of the ancient city of Minoa; one end of it is occupied by a naval base, but no one seems to mind.

Akrotíri's Monasteries: Ag. Triáda and Gouvernétou

East of Stavrós, Akrotíri has two venerable, faded but still barely active monasteries that well repay a visit. several of the roads across the headland eventually converge on the immaculate monastic olive groves and cypress-lined avenue that announce the peach-coloured walls of **Moní Ag. Triáda** (or Tzagaróliou) (*open officially 6–2 and 5–7, but beware, as many afternoons the gate doesn't re-open at all; adm*). The cruciform church has an austere, colonnaded Venetian façade, with a frieze of Greek letters evoking depth, knowledge and the supremacy of God; in the narthex an inscription in Greek and Latin tells how Ag. Triáda was refounded in 1634 by Jeremiah and Lavréndios Zangarola, Venetians who had become Orthodox monks. The monastery's museum contains two fine works from the 17th century, *The Second Coming* and *The Last Judgement*, later icons and hoary manuscripts, including illuminated parchments. Ag. Triáda was responsible for the ecclesiastical school of Crete until 1974, and there is talk of renewing the tradition. For now, the five monks and their cats seem content just to contemplate eternity from the shade of the tangerine trees in the courtyard.

The second and even older monastery, fortified **Moní Gouvernétou** (or *Gdernetto*, as the Venetians called it) stands on a remote plateau, 5km above Ag. Triáda along a narrow road that just squeezes through the wild terrain with no room for oncoming traffic. Gouvernétou (*open 7–2 and 4–8; adm*) played a major role in reconciling the Cretans and Venetians at the end of the 16th century; the grotesque sandstone heads of the portal, blasted by the sun and wind, are curious Venetian fancies far from home. The church, impregnated with old incense, has a few icons and frescoes.

Have a torch and water on hand to visit the two intriguing holy places that Gouvernétou supplanted. A shadeless but easy path from the car park leads in 10 minutes to the ruined walls and arches of the hermitage outside a cave known as **Arkoudiótissa** ('Bear'), due to its striking, bruin-shaped stalagmite, worshipped since pre-Minoan times as part of the cult of Artemis, Mistress of Wild Animals. The stone bear leans over a cistern of water, filled by dripping stalactites; the ceiling is blackened with centuries, or millennia, of candle-smoke. A walled-off corner in the cave contains a 16th-century chapel dedicated to **Panagía Arkoudiótissa**, 'Our Lady of the Bear', who shares the same feast day as Artemis once did: 2 February, or Candlemas.

Getting Around

There are **buses** more or less every hour from Chaniá bus station to villages around the Akrotíri peninsula, and several buses each hour between Plateia 1866 and Soúda ferry harbour, from early morning till late.

Sports and Activities

Zefirós, Tersanás, **t** 282 103 9366, *besthander@hotmail.com*. A friendly riding centre that offers both free-style and group-trek trips around the Akrotíri coast.

Where to Stay and Eat

Korakiés ✉ 73100

Nikterida, ('Bat'), 3km east of Chaniá, **t** 282 106 4215 (*around €16*). In the evening Chaniots head up here to one of the best tavernas in Crete, open since 1938; the first owner gave Anthony Quinn his Greek dancing lessons. There's music and dancing every Saturday night; book well ahead. *Closed Sun.*

Kalathás ✉ 73100

Sunrise, Tersanás, **t** 282 106 4214 (*moderate*). On the hillside above Tersanás beach, with pleasant rooms in a pretty location.

Taverna Kalathás, on the beach, **t** 282 106 4729, Good Cretan and Greek food, and live music on Friday nights. *Open April–Oct.*

Stavrós ✉ 73100

Perle Resort, **t** 282 103 9400 (*L, luxury*). A very recently opened (2002) upscale hotel and bungalow complex, complete with state-of-the-art thalassotherapy centre, fitness club and every kind of sport, including riding.

Rea, **t** 282 103 9001, **f** 282 103 9541 (*B; expensive*). A little way back from the sea, this air-conditioned resort complex head-

lines on sports and facilities for families, with basketball, tennis and a very nice pool. *Open April–Oct.*

Zorba's Studio Flats, **t** 282 103 9011 (winter **t** 282 105 2525), **f** 282 104 2616 (*moderate*). Well located by the beach, these apartments are well suited to families, with a pool, tennis courts, garden and a playground.

Blue Beach, **t** 282 103 9404, **f** 282 103 9406 (*moderate*). This villa-flat complex also offers a pool, restaurant and bar, plus BBQs, Cretan nights and sea sports. *Open April–Oct.*

Kavos Beach, **t** 282 103 9155 (*inexpensive*). Has some of the nicest rooms to rent in the village, and an enjoyable pool and bar.

Taverna Thanasis, **t** 282 103 9110. Between Zorba's and the Blue Beach, this taverna provides a varied food and wine selection and free sunbeds for customers.

Taverna Christiana, on the beach. A favourite for lunch that has live music on Thursday evenings; don't miss the Oscar won in 1964 by Walter Lassally (now a local resident) for his photography in *Zorba the Greek*.

Soúda ✉ 73200

Adelfi Vlacháki, **t** 282 108 9219; (*€25*). Mainly a seafood taverna, but one that also offers lots of vegetable dishes and Cretan cheeses; try their prawn omelette. *Open evenings only.*

Kiassos, 4 Ellis, Káto Soúda, **t** 282 108 9786. By the fishing harbour, with great seafood *mezédes* and local meats. *Open all year.*

Megála Choráfia and Stílos ✉ 73003

Taverna Aptera. Fresh blue and white décor and good food, just outside the Aptera ruins.

Kastro, **t** 282 503 2164. Also near Aptera, this family-run taverna has fine views and dishes fresh from the oven; try lamb *giovétsi* and cheese *kalitsouniá*. *Open Apr–Oct, eves only.*

Kritiko Kentro tou Moustakia, Stílos, **t** 282 504 1190. Live Cretan music, dance and barbecues most summer weekends.

From here the path continues down, down, down, another rough and steep 20 minutes or so, past hermits' huts and a crag above the sea shaped like a boat (a petrified pirate ship, they say, although coincidentally Candlemas also marked the beginning of the navigation season in the Mediterranean). The path ends with 150 steps carved in the rock, which leaves you by the dark, complex **cave of St John the Hermit** (or '*Xénos*', the Stranger) who sailed to Crete from Egypt on his mantle, founded a score of monasteries and retired here, becoming so stooped from his poor diet of roots and vegetables that a hunter shot him, mistaking him for an animal. The saint managed to crawl back to his cave, where the hunter tracked him down and found him bleeding to death, on 7 October 1042. The anniversary still draws crowds of pilgrims here. Also tucked in this inhospitable ravine is the **Katholikón of St John the Hermit**, a striking church and buildings with cells so low you have to crawl inside it, gouged into the living rock of the precipice, straddled by a stone bridge. Thought to date from the 6th or 7th century, this may be the oldest surviving church in Crete; St John was only one of the anchorites who lived here, until 17th century pirates made it too hot. Across the bridge, the path continues down to a rocky but delightful swimming nook, especially enjoyable when you contemplate the walk back up.

The Port of Chaniá: Soúda (ΣΟΥΔΑ)

Greater Chaniá trickles scrubbily all along the road to **Soúda**, the main port for western Crete, tucked into a magnificent sheltered bay (you can also drive there from Akrotíri, through a fenced-off military zone). Thanks to the military, Soúda will never win a beauty prize, in spite of its setting; its largest features include an active Greek naval base behind yellow walls and a now-inactive former NATO one, for years the source of local gripes. But NATO was hardly the first to appreciate Soúda Bay: the Venetians fortified the islet of **Néa Soúda** in the mid 16th-century, and when they and the Greeks who took refuge there finally surrendered in 1715 (50 years after the Turkish conquest of Crete) it was only by way of a treaty, in spite of many attacks and a gruesome pyramid of 5,000 Christian heads the Turks piled around the walls.

Signs in Soúda point the way to the immaculate lawns and flowers of the seaside **Commonwealth War Cemetery**, where 1,497 British, New Zealand and Australian troops who died in the Battle of Crete are buried, many of them too young to vote or lying anonymous under tombstones inscribed 'A Soldier of the 1939–1945 War, Known unto God'. The silence is in marked contrast to the Greek families frolicking a few yards away on the beach. Two km west of Soúda towards Chaniá, a road forks south for the 16th-century walled **Moní Chryssopigí** (*open 3.30–6*), founded by Ioánnis Chartophylákas, a doctor ennobled by the Venetians for his tireless work in a devastating epidemic that struck Crete in 1595. The church and its museum contain an exceptional collection of icons and a superb, intricate cross decorated with golden filigree and precious stones. Confiscated by the Germans in 1941, the monastery was repopulated in 1977 by nuns, who restore icons and books and operate a prestigious icon-painting workshop (*open by appointment only*). On the same artistic note, you can call in at the **Verekythnos Artists' Village** in Soúda's Industrial Park, **t** 282 108 1261, where local craftsmen (potters, weavers, goldsmiths and more) have their workshops.

Ancient Aptera

Heading east from Soúda, Crete's main highway, the E75, skirts Soúda Bay. The Turks had an excellent if rather frustrating view of the defiant islet of Néa Soúda and the entire bay from their fortress of **Idzeddín**, on the precipitous promontory of **Cape Kalámi**. Now Chaniá's prison, Idzeddin was built by a Turkish governor in the 19th century, when the Cretans seemed to be revolting every other week, and he named it after the son of the current Ottoman Sultan, Abdul-Aziz I.

The stone for Idzeddín was cannibalized from ancient **Aptera** (*open Tues–Sun 8.30–3*), high on a plateau 8.5km east of Soúda above **Megála Choráfia**. The site is reached by heading up the steep road from the Taverna Aptera. Mentioned in Linear B tablets found at Knossós (A-pa-ta-wa) and dedicated to Artemis, Aptera remained one of the chief cities in western Crete until shattered by an earthquake in AD 700. Cyclopean walls, often compared to those of Mycenaean Tiryns, squirm 4km over the slopes, standing over 10ft (3m) high in places. Pick your way through the weeds and fences to find a theatre, the base of a Temple of Demeter (1st century BC) and the skeleton of a Roman Senate House, with its decrees carved on the ruined wall; the **Monastery of Ag. Ioánnis Theológos** sits atop two magnificent if crumbling Roman cisterns the size of cathedrals. The city's name (*aptera* or 'wingless') came from a singing contest held between the Muses and the Sirens: the Sirens were sore losers and tore out their wings and plunged into the sea, where they turned into the *Léfkes* ('white') islets far below in Soúda Bay. From the stylish Turkish fortress of 1866, built on the edge of Aptera, there are tremendous views down over them and of the heads of the cons in Idzeddín prison.

Aptera's modern heir, Megála Choráfia, has its share of British holiday homes. To the south, the village of **Stílos** saw the ANZAC forces' last stand in the Battle of Crete, which permitted most Allied troops to escape to the south coast and boats for Egypt. To this day a special relationship survives with New Zealand, where many Chaniots emigrated after the war. Stílos is a quiet place, with lazy coffeehouses under massive plane trees, although they heat up with Cretan song and dance on summer weekends. North of the village, real explorers can walk to the gorge of **Diktimo** (signposted from the road) or the massive, half-ruined Byzantine church of **Panagía Zerviotíssa**.

From Stílos it's a 5km hairpin drive up to the village of **Samonás**, where archaeologists are unearthing a Late Minoan settlement, but the main reason for the difficult drive is the 11th-century church of **Ag. Nikólaos**, with ravishing 13th-century frescoes by an unknown hand, located just above Samonás in **Kyriakosélia**. Come in the morning or late afternoon and ask the café owner in Samonás to ring the key holder. Lastly, you can backtrack north of Stílos to pick up the road west to **Maláxa**, an ancient mining centre. Ruins of two Byzantine churches, **Ag. Saránta** and **Ag. Eleoúsa**, remain, but the most spectacular sight is the ravine to the south, riddled with caves.

Beaches West of Chaniá

Along the coast west of Chaniá town is one of Crete's most popular summer-fun beach zones, which took off rather later than the resorts east of Heráklion but is fast catching up. Not a single one of the hotels along this sandy stretch of coast and fertile plain existed when a rain of white parachutes fell on 20 May 1941. 'Out of the sky the winged devils of Hitler were falling everywhere,' wrote George Psychoundákis in *The Cretan Runner*. Few signs of the battle remain, although 2km west of Chaniá stands the monument of the diving eagle, known locally as the **Kakó Poulí** or 'Bad Bird', the German memorial to the 2nd Parachute Regiment. The biggest battle took place a kilometre south in **Galatás**, where Greek soldiers and civilians (armed with rusty old hunting guns and stones) and New Zealanders battled the parachutists.

Just beyond the reach of Chaniá's city bus lines, the rooms and restaurants of **Káto Stálos** (with a quiet beach) merge with bigger **Ag. Marína**, an old town with a smattering of Venetian and Turkish houses and a long, partially-shaded beach with bars and watersports. It looks out over the islet of **Ag. Theódori**, a refuge for the wild Cretan ibex, the *kri kri*; excursion boats make the trip from Chaniá. The vast gaping mouth of its cave originally belonged to a sea monster, bearing down on Ag. Marína

Getting Around

There are **buses** at least every half-hour from Chaniá bus station (**t** 282 109 3052) to all the resorts as far as the Louis Creta Princess Hotel; roughly every hour they continue to Kastélli-Kíssamou.

Tourist Information

There is any number of companies that run sightseeing tours through the beach villages and up into the hills, mostly in open-sided 'road trains'. Try the **Plataniás Express**, Plataniás, **t** 282 402 2920.

Festivals

17 July Ag. Marína.
14 September Tavronítis.

Sports and Activities

Watersports are not hard to find along the coast, with most larger hotels offering facilities; otherwise, your best bet is the waterfront at **Ag. Marína**. If you want something a bit wilder, you can make a mess of each other at **Kolimbári Paintball Club**, **t** 282 408 3051.

Where to Stay and Eat

Galatás ✉ 73100

Panorama, **t** 282 103 1700, **f** 282 103 1708, *www.panorama-hotel.gr* (A; *luxury*). A very attractive hotel built in modern Mediterranean style; all rooms have air-conditioning and balconies with sea views.

There are two pools, if the 50m walk to the sea is too strenuous, and a fine restaurant, which hosts gastronomic evenings.

Áno Stalós and Káto Stalós ✉ 73012

Alector's Rooms, Káto Stalós, **t** 282 106 8755 (*moderate–inexpensive*). Up the hill away from the noisy main coast road, this garden villa is immaculately run by the delightful Cretan-Californian Helen Zachariou.

O Levendis, Áno Stalós, **t** 282 106 8155 (*around €12*). One of the very best places to dine in western Crete: an old stone taverna, with hard to find seasonal, truly authentic Cretan dishes including homemade sausages flavoured with vinegar (*xidata*), wild onions and *stamnagathó* (spikey chicory), with wine from the barrel. *Open all year.*

Stavrodromi, **t** 282 106 8104. By the coast road, this straightforward taverna serves delicious fried squid.

Ag. Marína ✉ 73100

Ilianthos Village, **t** 282 106 0667, **f** 282 106 0721, *www.ellada.net/ilianthos* (A, *luxury*). Small, luxurious complex on the beach and within walking distance of all the coastal action. Accommodation varies from maisonettes to studios, all with kitchens. There is a pool and other amenities.

Santa Marina, **t** 282 106 8460, **f** 282 106 8571, *www.grecian.net/santamarina* (B, *expensive*). Also on the beach, and set in a lovely garden with a pool and gym. They can often come up with a room even when the season is in full swing.

Alexia Beach, **t** 282 106 8110 (C, *inexpensive*). A small and attractive beach hotel with a pool, and fridges in every room.

with an appetite as big as all Crete before Zeus spotted the threat to his home island and petrified the monster with a thunderbolt.

West of Ag. Marína, **Plataniás** has two faces as well: an old village above and a resort town by the sandy-pebbly beach, the most popular in the province, crammed with recliners and parasols and pounding music, drowning out the rustling of the cane forest planted to protect orange groves from the wind. The Battle of Crete began at **Máleme**, where Chaniá airport was at the time. There's a German war cemetery as a grim reminder, and, down a nearby lane, a monumental **Post-Palatial Minoan tomb** with a well-preserved *dromos* entrance, discovered by accident in 1966. Beyond, the resort and farming village of **Tavronítis** is the crossroads for Paleochóra (*see* p.131).

Angelika, t 282 106 8642 (*inexpensive*). A simple place with rooms with kitchenettes.

Villa Margarita, t 282 106 8581 (*inexpensive*). A good-value but basic option.

Villa Thodorou, t 282 106 0665, **f** 282 106 8342 (*inexpensive*). Straightforward rooms, facing the sea and with fridges and balconies.

Plataniás ✉ 73014

Aegean Palace, Pýrgos Psilónerou, **t** 282 106 2668, **f** 282 106 2647, *www.aegean-palace.gr* (*A, luxury*). Minimalist designer suites (some with their own private pools) and rooms on a quiet estate 200m from the sea; an added feature are little electric golf carts for pootling about. *Open April–Oct.*

Geraniotis, t 282 106 8681, **f** 282 106 8683 (*B, expensive*). One of the more attractive of Plataniás' many beach hotels, standing amid lush green lawns. *Open April–Oct.*

Kronos Apartments, t 282 106 8630, **f** 282 106 8574 (*C, expensive*). Well-kept complex of 53 self-catering units, with a pool and near the sea. *Open April–Oct.*

O Mylos tou Keratas, t 282 106 8578 (€20–25). In a converted 15th-century water mill, this is a lovely traditional restaurant with superb Cretan and Greek spit-roasted meats, where desserts are always on the house.

Haroupia, Áno Plataniás, **t** 282 106 8603 (€15). In the old village above the beach resort, this not only enjoys lovely sunset views from its creeper covered terrace, but also has delicious Cretan food.

Máleme ✉ 73100

Louis Creta Princess Club Hotel, t 282 106 2702, **f** 282 106 2406, *www.louishotels.com* (*A, luxury*). Shaped like a giant trident to give each of its 414 rooms a sea view, this giant beach hotel is very well set up for families, with windsurfing facilities and an excellent restaurant, **Presvia**; open evenings only, it offers delicious New Cretan dishes for around €30. *Open April–Oct.*

Louis Creta Paradise Beach Resort, t 282 106 1315, **f** 282 106 1134, *www.cretaparadise.gr* (*A, luxury*). In Geráni, between Máleme and Plataniás, this hotel is even slicker and glossier than the same owners' Princess, if half the size. *Open April–Oct.*

Máleme Mare, t 282 106 2121, **f** 282 109 4644 (*C, expensive*). Modest, perhaps unexciting but decent-value apartments by the beach, with a pool. Nearby are the tables of the **Maleme Taverna**, set on the grass by the beach.

Nightlife

Plataniás, especially, is one of the Cretan coast's summer-fun hubs, with plenty of big discos that gear up after midnight.

Virgin, Káto Stálos. A large club playing the latest Greek hits.

Eclipse, Plataniás. Plays tunes that are a little more Greek than at most venues nearby.

Mylos Club, Plataniás, **t** 282 106 0449. Next to Utopia, in a water mill from 1800, is this ultra-popular club with guest DJs in summer, playing mainstream dance music. *Open June–Sept.*

Privilege, Plataniás, **t** 282 106 1196. Near the town bridge, a club that boasts Crete's biggest laser show.

Utopia, Plataniás, **t** 282 106 0033. Bamboo-and-palm jungle décor, blasting out disco and house, and Greek music much later on.

Crete's Far West

The line of resort-villages and fairly broad beaches west of Chaniá comes to an end at the foot of the rugged Rodópoi peninsula, the 'middle head' of Crete. Beyond it lies the ancient province of **Kíssamos**, dominated by a beautiful coastal plain densely planted with olives and vineyards, with knobbly hills rising just behind and planted with the same: the difference between its lush greenery and the arid hills of the far east couldn't be more striking. As relatively few visitors make it out this far, the unruly west coast offers not only some of Crete's loveliest beaches, but a chance to find a lonesome strand of your very own. The chief town and port here is **Kastélli** or, officially, **Kastélli-Kíssamou (ΚΑΣΤΕΛΛΙ ΚΙΣΣΑΜΟΥ)** a dusty, workaday wine town charmingly devoid of any tourist attractions whatsoever.

The Rodópoi Peninsula and Cape Spada

The next big village along the coast after Tavronítis is **Kolimbári (Κολυμπάρι)**, at the neck of the Rodópoi. It has a quiet beach of large smooth pebbles, and a bust in the centre of the village of Timoléon Vássos, the commander of the 1,500 Greek volunteers who in 1897 landed in Kolimbári and declared Crete's union with Greece. This attempt proved distinctly premature, but the revolt he ignited led directly to the granting of the island's autonomy the following year.

A short walk just to the north of the village is the most important monastery in western Crete. **Moní Gonías**, or Odigítrias (*open Sun–Fri 8–12.30 and 4–8, Sat 4–8*), was founded in 1618 by several groups of monks and hermits, who decided to club together and found a central religious house, which they built in the form of a fortress high above a little sandy cove (*gonías*, in Greek). The patriotic monks were often besieged by the Turks; a cannon ball fired in 1866 is still embedded in the seaward wall. The church contains a fine gilt iconostasis carved with dragons, a venerable *Last Judgement* and a beautifully drawn St Nicholas, although the juju seems to be concentrated in an icon of the Virgin, covered with votive *tamata*, jewellery and a digital watch. The small museum holds excellent post-Byzantine icons from the 16th and 17th centuries: note especially the *Genesis* triptych (1662) by Demítrios Sgoúros and a *Crucifixion* (1637) by Konstantínos Paleokápas.

Next to the monastery is the Orthodox academy, with a memorial to the cadets killed in the Battle of Crete. Beyond, the road veers dizzingly up and up the coast of the peninsula to **Afráta**, the last village accessible by car, where you can visit the cave of **Ellenóspilios**, its 300ft-long corridors lined with stalactites and stalagmites. From Afráta you can either pick your way down to rocky coves for a swim in the idyllically clear water, or follow an unpaved, treeless track to the north on foot or with a four-wheel-drive (here and there still using an old Roman road) or, easiest of all, take a caique from Chaniá to **Diktyna**, in ancient times the holiest sanctuary in Western Crete. Its little port, **Meniás**, is rocky but the sea is transparent, and seaside caves offer shelter from the sun. Diktyna's celebrated shrine to Artemis probably dates back to

Getting Around

Kastélli's **port** (which is 2km west of the town centre – take a taxi) is linked by **ANEN Line** (t 282 102 4148, *www.anen.gr*) ferries to various ports in the Peloponnese: three times a week to Kalamáta, twice to Monemvassía and Neápolis and once to Gýthio; there are also two sailings a week to Piraeus and three to Kythira and Antikythira. Tickets can also be bought from **Xyroukákis Travel Agency**, Kastélli, t 282 202 2655, or **Omalós Tours**, Plateía 1866, Chaniá, t 282 109 7119.

Buses cover the area from Kastélli: there are three a week (*Mon, Wed, Fri*) to Polyrénia, three a day to Falassarná, five to Chóra Sfakíon, six to Paleochóra, three to Omalós and one morning bus to Chrysoskalítissa and Elafonísi.

The **Elafonísi Boat**, t 282 304 1755, connects Elafonísi to Paleochóra every afternoon in summer. There is also a daily **bus** to Elafonísi from Chaniá bus station, leaving at 7.30am.

Festivals

Early Aug Kastélli wine festival.
14–15 Aug The *Apokímisis* (Assumption) is a huge festival at Chrysoskalítissa monastery.
15 Aug, 29 Aug Kolimbári: pilgrimage to the chapel of St John the Hermit.
First Sunday after 20 Oct Chestnut festival in Élos.

Sports and Activities

From Kastélli-Kíssamou harbour (Port Authority t 282 202 4344) there are daily boat trips to Gramvoúsa Island with its Venetian fortress, and the lagoon of Balos Bay.
Kissamos Diving Centre, t 282 202 4248. On the main road through Kastélli, this centre offers diving and snorkelling trips to see mantas, moray eels and lobsters in the crystal-clear waters of the gulf. They do not, though, give PADI-certificated courses.

the Minoans, and continued to have a following up to the end of the Roman Empire; the Diktean mountains in eastern Crete were named after her. There are just enough remains of her unexcavated shrine to make it worth a scramble, if it's not too hot.

Inland from the shrine of Artemis are the Venetian-era ruins of the monastery of **Ag. Geórgios** and a frescoed church. Another monastery, **Ag. Ioánnis Giónas**, overlooks the bay of Kíssamos, and every 29 August attracts crowds of pilgrims (especially if their name is John), who make the three-hour walk from **Rodopós** village, have a bite and walk back.The nearest sandy beaches are at **Plakálona**, just west of the Spáda peninsula, where some of the densest olive groves in Crete provide a silvery backdrop.

Inland from Kolimbári

The farming villages south of Kolimbári can boast some fine churches. One of them is at **Marathokéfala**, only 2km south of Kolimbári; just beyond the church a short path leads back to a grove of plane trees and the cave that was frequented around the turn of the last millennium by one of Crete's favourite saints, John the Stranger (Ag. Ioánnis Xénos); his is the small chapel near the entrance, and he left some divine magic in the shape of one of the stalactites inside. Nearby **Spiliá** has a 12th-century church of the Panagía with 14th-century wall paintings; others from the same period, on the *Life of St Stephen*, are further south in **Drakóna**'s 9th-century Ag. Stéfanos. But most interesting and oldest of all is a golden stone church in **Episkopí**, known as the **Rotunda**, dedicated to St Michael. Seat of a bishop in early Christian times, the Rotunda has the only concentric stepped dome in Crete. Inside there are still sections of its original mosaic floor and a stone baptismal font; at least five layers of frescoes cover the walls. Lastly, the church in **Delianá** southwest of Episkopí has interesting if

Strata Tours, t 282 202 2433,
www.stratotours.com. Guided hikes around
the area, some lasting for up to four days.

Where to Stay and Eat

Kolimbári ✉ 73007

For eating in Kolimbári, there's a line of large
grill houses along the main road that do a
roaring trade with the locals.
Aphea Village, t 282 402 3344 (*B,
expensive–moderate*). 300m above the
village, this quiet, pastel-coloured complex
has 30 furnished apartments, a pool and bar.
Arion, t 282 402 2440, (*B, expensive–moderate*).
Smack beside the sea, and with a good pool.
Dimitra, t 282 402 2244 (*E, inexpensive*) A
straightforward pension with decent rooms.
Open all year.
Paleo Arkontiko, t 282 402 2124. Popular
seafront taverna with excellent fresh fish.

Kastélli -Kíssamou ✉ 73400

Stavroula Palace, Plateía Teloneiou, **t** 282 202
3620, **f** 282 202 2315 (*C, expensive*). A recently
opened apartment complex in the town,
with a pool. *Open April–Oct.*
Galini Beach, t 282 202 3288, *www.galinibeach.
com* (*inexpensive*). At the far end of Kastélli
beach, this hotel has quiet rooms and
organic breakfasts from their own farm.
Nopigia Camping, t 282 203 1111, **f** 282 203 1700.
A well-equipped campsite just east of
Kastélli, with an amply-sized swimming
pool. *Open April–Oct.*
Mythimna Camping, Drapánias, **t** 282 203
1444, **f** 282 203 1000. In farmland 3km east of
Kastélli, near the sand and pebble beach,
this is quieter than most campsites; it also
has pleasant rooms and bungalows, and
beautiful sunsets. *Open April–Oct.*
Coco Beach Camping, t 282 402 2940,
katntagk@otenet.gr. Just before Kastélli on
the main road in from Chaniá, this campsite

damaged medieval paintings of the *Last Judgement*, where Heaven's elect swan
around in Byzantine court dress. **Voukoliés**, a little to the southeast, holds a flea
market that's famous throughout Crete, every Saturday.

Kastélli-Kíssamou and the West Coast

Set at the bottom of a deep, rectangular gulf, **Kastélli-Kíssamou**'s long beach (pebbly
below town, and sandy just to the west) brings in the kind of tourists who shun the
fleshpots. Its double-barrelled name, which has never really caught on, recalls its
ancient predecessor Kissamos, inhabited since Mycenaean times; excavations of the
acropolis, a half-hour walk to the west of the modern town, have revealed a
Mycenaean sanctuary that, just perhaps, might have been the one that in legend was
built by Agamemnon. Later it became the port of Dorian Polyrénia (*see* below).
Excavations of the Roman-era city behind the health centre have unearthed a lovely
mosaic floor from the 2nd century AD; the town has an **Archaeological Museum**, with
other finds from ancient Kissamos, which is currently being re-ordered and renovated
inside the former Venetian commandery.

Ancient Kissamos' temple and theatre were dismantled by the Venetians in 1550,
and refashioned as a castle – hence Kastélli. This castle has a melodramatic history:
when the Cretan Kaptános Kantanoléo captured it from the Venetians, the latter
pretended to recognize Kantanoléo's authority and offered a highborn Venetian girl
as his son's bride. At the wedding, in Alikianós, the Cretans were given drugged wine,
and the Venetians slit their throats and retook Kastélli's fort.

is inexpensive and has plenty of facilities, including access for the disabled.

Kalabriani, t 282 202 3204. A taverna on a beautiful terrace overlooking the sea, 5km west of town, with excellent food. It also has rooms (*inexpensive*).

Stimadóris, t 282 202 2057. By the west end of town, a friendly place with fresh fish caught by the owners, and a tasty pickled seaweed salad. *Open eves, and lunch in summer.*

Taverna Plaka, t 282 202 3322. A local favourite for lunch, set in a garden by the beach, which has live Cretan music twice a week.

Castell Restaurant, Main Square. An institution that's very popular with locals.

Bakaliarakia, t 282 202 2734. A charming, quiet taverna, around a corner from the square.

Polyrénia ✉ 73400

Kastro, Grigorianá. In a hamlet on the road up to Polyrénia is this pleasant, isolated taverna with rooms to rent (*inexpensive*).

Perivoli, Grigorianá. In the same village there is also this classic old-fashioned taverna, set in a pretty garden.

Taverna Odysseas, Polyrénia. The food here is average, but the giant view over the olive terraces is wonderful.

Falassarná ✉ 73400

Plakures, t 282 204 1581, **f** 282 204 1781, *plakures@otenet.gr* (*expensive*). A small, stylish, quiet haven, with a pool; the restaurant has fine Greek and Cretan specialities. *Open April–Oct.*

SunSet Rooms and Studios, t 282 204 1204 (*moderate*). Apartments right on the beach, with a good taverna alongside.

Falassarná Beach Apartments, t 282 204 1257 (*moderate*). Plusses here are fine sea views.

Romantica, summer **t** 282 204 1089, winter **t** 282 109 4710 (*moderate*). Small apartments for 4–5 people, with verandas, sea views and kitchenettes.

A scenic drive 8km south of Kastélli leads to **Polyrénia** (Πολυρρήνια), 'many flocks', set on a natural balcony and as old-fashioned as a Cretan village can get; if your first contact with Greece predates the 1970s, the little footpaths and whitewashed rocks, the mingled smells of home cooking and coffee with potted flowers, jasmine, basil and donkeys will give you a serious dose of nostalgia.

But Polyrénia is even older than it looks at first, even older than the Roman tower (itself a collage of older bits and bobs) that stands at the village entrance. Founded in the 8th century BC by colonists from the Peloponnese, Polyrénia had the usual Dorian arrangement: a main centre high up and easily defensible, overlooking the sea and its port at Kissamos. It's a stiff climb up through the back gardens to the acropolis, with 360° views, an evocative tumble of overgrown, inscrutable walls and houses scattered over tawny terraces and natural rock formations. Although the city survived the Romans (Polyrénia's attitude to the legions was that if you can't lick them, join them), it fell prey to the Saracens in the 9th century AD. The most tangible memory of its centuries of prosperity is the massive base of a **4th-century temple** and **altar** of beautifully dressed stone, supporting the church of the 99 Holy Fathers. Down in the village, ask directions to **Hadrian's aqueduct**, a reservoir hewn out of the living rock, a present from the emperor.

Falassarná and Gramvoúsa

Crete's west coast is wild and dramatic, starkly outlined by mountains plunging sheer into the sea. They give way to a fertile coastal plain coated in plastic tomato tunnels, at **Falassarná** (Φαλασαρνά), 15km from Kastélli. Endowed with beautiful wide sandy beaches and coves that are among the finest in Crete, Falassarná has more

Adam Rooms, t 282 204 1729 (*moderate–inexpensive*). More apartments with good views, and the essential taverna below.

Aqua Marine, t 282 204 1414, *aquamarine@kissamos.net* (*moderate–inexpensive*). Newly renovated and spotless hotel, with en suite bathrooms in all rooms.

Stathis, t 282 204 1480 (*inexpensive*). A budget beach option with reasonable rooms.

Anastasia, t 282 204 1480 (*inexpensive*). Owned by the same people as the Stathis, with similarly decent rooms but set further back from the beach.

Panorama, t 282 204 1 336. True to its name, this taverna has gorgeous views; it serves simple Greek favourites and also has rooms to rent (*inexpensive*).

Sfinári ✉ **73012**

Taverna Delinia, t 282 204 1632. A friendly, delightfully simple fish and seafood taverna next to the village's free campsite.

Elafonísi ✉ **73012**

Innahorio, t 282 206 1111. Wonderful taverna (2km above the beach), serving lots of good home produced dishes, including their own bread and cheese. *Open April–Oct.*

Élos ✉ **73012**

Mília, Vlátos Kissámou, **t/f** 282 205 1569, *www.milia.gr* (*moderate*). Experience the rural Crete of centuries past: ecologically sound, traditional rooms in restored stone dwellings by the chestnut forest, furnished with antiques, heated by wood stoves and lit by candles. One house serves as a refectory, with delicious organic food, mostly produced on site. Vlátos is on a side road about 6km north of Élos. *Open all year.*

Kastanofolia, Élos village, **t** 282 206 1258 (*inexpensive*). Ten bright, spacious rooms to rent.

Filoxenia, Élos village, **t** 282 206 1322. A traditional restaurant favourite with the locals for *mezédes*.

tavernas and rooms to rent every year. North of the beach at Koutrí stood ancient **Phalassarna**, founded in the 6th century BC (although its name is pre-Hellenic). Long Polyrénia's most bitter rival, it was an important seafaring town, and minted coins with a trident and FA on one side and a lady with earrings on the other. You can measure how much this western end of Crete has risen – the ancient port of Phalassarná, with its mighty defence towers, is now 650ft (200m) from the sea. Bits of the ancient city lie scattered around the stranded port, while further up archaeologists have recently unearthed a bathhouse (now under a shelter). Most curious of all is a **stone throne**, resembling a giant arm chair, believed to date from Hellenistic times. Some scholars speculate that it was dedicated to the sea god Poseidon.

From Kastélli you can hire a caique to sail around the top of the wild, barren, uninhabited **Gramvoúsa** (or **Tigáni**) peninsula and its tip at **Cape Vouxa** to the sheltered harbour of the triangular islet of **Iméri**, better known by the name of its mighty Venetian fortress, **Gramvoúsa**. Like Néa Soúda and Spinalonga to the east, it held out against the Turks until the 18th century, when the Venetians finally gave up their last hopes of ever reconquering Crete. In 1821, during the Greek War of Independence, refugees from the devastated islands of Psará and Kássos managed to capture the fort, along with Cretan rebels. Forced to make a living in troubled times, the 3,000 put their fate in the hands of the *Panagía Kleftrína* (Our Lady Little Thief) and took to pirating so successfully on English and French shipping that the head of independent Greece's first government, Iannís Capodístria, had to intervene personally to prevent a diplomatic row, and the Powers oversaw the island's return to the Turks. Today the fort is more than half-ruined, but the Venetians' Renaissance church is more or less intact, and the huge reservoirs, unused for over a century, are full to the brim. Last but not least, the peninsula has one of Crete's most beautiful if shadeless strands, **Balos Beach**, a lovely oasis of white sand in a shallow turquoise sea, spread out on either side of the Tigáni ('Frying pan') peninsula. The boat tours from Kastélli stop there, or you can also drive most of the way, on a dirt track, by way of Kalyvianí. At the end there's a 2km walk; stock up on provisions at the cantina at the end of the road.

Down to Elafonísi

South of Falassarná the partially paved but easy coastal road takes in spectacular scenery rising up above the sea; try to do it in the morning to avoid the glare. In sprawling **Plátanos** a proto-Geometric tomb was unearthed during road construction, while down in the picturesque little fishing village of **Sfinári** there's a pretty pebble beach, a free campsite under huge eucalyptus trees and simple places to stay to drink in the gorgeous sunsets. Further south, the road rides a corniche high over the sea to **Kámbos**, a small village which won't detain you long, although you may be tempted by the 3km track leading down a ravine to the wild sandy beach of **Livádia**.

The road becomes increasingly rough as it winds south to the Libyan Sea and the sheer, 130ft rock pedestal of the windswept, bleached convent of **Chrysoskalítissa**, 'Our Lady of the Golden Stair' (*open 7am–8pm*), built over Minoan remains. The story goes that only persons without sin, or, according to some, non-liars can see which of the 90 steps is made of gold; a rather more prosaic version says that the Patriarch in Constantinople ordered the monks to sell off the golden step in the 15th century to pay off his debts. Its venerated icon of the Virgin is said to date from the 11th century. Tour buses from Chaniá have besieged the last nun who lives there.

The prime attraction in this remote corner of Crete, however, lies another 5km south, the enchanting islet of **Elafonísi** (Ελαφονίσι). It's a magnificent place to while away a day, set in a shallow, almost tropical lagoon that comes in a spectrum of turquoise, blue and violet, rimmed by pinkish white sand, sea shells and white lilies of the sea. The water is only 2ft deep, so you can wade to sandy Elafonísi, and beyond it to beaches with a few waves. Idyllic out of season, in August it overflows with baking bodies; besides the buses, caiques sail from Paleóchora and Kastélli. If they get on your nerves, take the dirt track 1.5km from the Innachorio taverna to the lovely bay and beach of **Kedródasos**, surrounded by green sea juniper (be sure to take water).

Inland in Kíssamos: the Chestnut Villages

Rather than backtrack along the coast, consider returning to Kastélli from Elafonísi and Chrysoskalítissa via Crete's chestnut country, its lush, dramatic, mountainous beauty reminiscent of Corsica. Fertile and well watered, its nine villages, the *Enneachoria*, live off the chestnut and agriculture; in July they host some of the best weddings in Crete. Some are worth a stop year-round: driving up from Elafonísi, you can pay your respects to the 14th-century frescoed church of Michaíl Archangelos and the older, twin-sailed Ag. Geórgios in **Váthi**. **Kefáli** has magnificent sea views from its porch and even better frescoes in its church, **Metamórfosis tou Sotírou** (1420), located just down a track at the end of the village; note the English graffiti on the walls from 1553. Nearby **Perivólia** is a charming green oasis, home of a private ethnographic museum, and delightful **Élos**, the largest and highest of the nine villages, is set in a forest of ancient plane and chestnut trees – a perfect antidote to the sunbaked sands of Elafonísi. It has a small hotel if you want to linger; one temptation is the chestnut cake baked in late October and served at Élos' chestnut festival. Six kilometres beyond there, a road forks off eastwards towards Strovlés and Paleóchora (*see* below).

The main road north descends leisurely to **Koutsoumatádos** and skirts the dramatic 1.5km **Topólia** (or Koutsoumátados) **ravine**, excellent walking territory. A sign by the road points up a rock stairway to the massive stalactite cave of **Ag. Sofía**, a holy place since Neolithic and Minoan times, still sheltering a little trogloditic church. **Topólia**, at the end of the ravine, is a handsome village with a frescoed church (Ag. Paraskeví).

Across the Mountains to the Libyan Sea and the Gorge of Samariá

The White Mountains only permit a few north–south roads to breach their rocky fastnesses. Those to the southwest run into the Eparchy of Sélino, where the growing but still very attractive resort town of Paleochóra is the central attraction, along with a score of decorated medieval churches that have escaped the ravages of time, especially around Kándanos. Most of the churches are locked, but asking in the nearest *kafeneíon* mornings or late afternoons usually produces an open sesame.

Further east, equally winding roads that begin among some of Crete's loveliest villages climb, dip and curve through the crags and valleys to end at one of its most seductive coastlines. All along it is a string of small villages and secluded, rocky coves – many only accessible by boat – with, nearby, the island's most celebrated and dramatic natural feature, the giant chasm of the Samariá Gorge.

Paleochóra and the Sélino

Of the three roads from the north that wriggle down to the Sélino, the main one from **Tavronítis** (*see* p.123) gets the most takers. It's not the most dramatic, but still more than likely to distress anyone subject to travel sickness. There are hosts of Byzantine churches en route, beginning in **Flória**, where the 15th-century frescoes in Ag. Patéras are well worth a look. Further south, **Kándanos** has a name that means 'the city of victory', and can claim the highest rainfall in Crete. Although it has been inhabited since Roman times, nothing here today is over 55 years old; in the Battle of Crete the townsmen, women and children, armed with whatever weapons they could find, resisted the Nazi advance with such stubborn ferocity that the rest were forced to retreat and return with reinforcements the next day, shooting everyone they could find and burning the village to the ground. Among the memorials is the original sign erected by Germans: 'Here stood Kándanos, destroyed in retribution for the murder of 25 German soldiers.' Excavations carried out here in the 1990s revealed a building believed to be a Roman praetorium.

Getting Around

Paleochóra is served by five **buses** a day from Chaniá, and a 6.15am bus runs from the town to Omalós for the Gorge of Samariá. Small **boats** leave Paleochóra for Gávdos (*see* p.133); on Friday and Sunday a larger boat sails to Soúgia, Ag. Roúmeli and Gávdos, and boats also run regularly to Chóra Sfakíon, Loutró, Soúgia and Elafónisi.
Port authority, t 282 304 1214.

Tourist Information

Paleochóra: town tourist office, El. Venizélos, **t** 282 304 1507; *open Wed–Mon 10–1 and 6–9*. Has a list of rooms with a big choice in the €18–25 range.
Internet access: **PC-Corner, t** 282 304 2422, *pc-corner@cha.forthnet.gr*.

Festivals

1–10 Aug Paleochóra's 'Musical August'.

Where to Stay

Paleochóra ✉ 73001
Anthea, t 282 304 1594 or 282 304 1596 (*expensive*). Classy studios and larger apartments.
Elman, t 282 304 1412, **f** 282 304 1412 (*B, expensive*). On the sandy beach, this attractive hotel has big, modern apartments, in a garden setting. *Open all year*.
Aris, t 282 304 1502, *arishotel@cha.forthnet.gr* (*B, moderate*). A modest hotel that's a good bet near the beach.
Polydoros, t 282 304 1150, **f** 282 304 1578 (*C, moderate*). On Paleochóra's main street between the beaches, this is an old favourite, with self-catering suites.
Pension Lissos, t 282 304 1266 (*C, moderate*). Near the bus station, the Lissos has the oldest lodgings in town, but it often has a place if everything else is full.
Ostria, t 282 304 1055 (*inexpensive*). Just by Pachía Ammos beach is this taverna with rooms, and Greek dancing, Thursday nights.

From Kándanos, take the left turn on the Soúgia road for **Anisaráki**. There are five Byzantine churches within the next three or four kilometres. Taxiárchos Michaíl, near **Koufalotó**, was frescoed in 1327 by one of the best artists working in western Crete, Ioánnis Pagoménos. Anisaráki itself has three 14th-century churches: the Venetian-Byzantine Panagía, with well-preserved paintings, Ag. Ioánnis and Ag. Paraskeví, with more frescoes. The paintings and iconostasis in a fourth church here, Ag. Anna, date from the 1460s; the dedication is intact, and among the pictures is a fine one of St Anne nursing the baby Virgin and St George on horseback. Just south in **Plemanianá**, Ag. Geórgios has frescoes of the *Last Judgement* from 1410. **Kakodíki** to the southwest has a hundred springs with soft mineral waters known for curing kidney stones, and two small frescoed churches, Taxiárchos Michaíl (1387) and Ag. Isódoros (1420). Further south, a sign (actually, thanks to local hunters, it looks more like a sieve) points out the road to **Kádros**, where a late 14th-century church of the Panagía has more frescoes.

Paleochóra (ΠΑΛΑΙΟΧΩΡΑ)

The Venetians called it *Castello Selino*, the Bride of the Libyan Sea. The Greeks call it simply the Old Town, Paleochóra. If no longer nuptially fresh, Paleochóra still attracts suitors, and although the hippies of yesteryear have upped sticks, it continues to draw mostly young, independent travellers. It has the rare advantage of straddling two beaches – **Pachía Ámmos**, wide, sandy and lined with tamarisks, the other pebbly **Chalíkia** – which are never wind-smacked at the same time, allowing you to pick up your towel and move according to the weather, unless you want to enjoy the superb windsurfing the sandy beach provides.

Kalypso, t 282 304 1429 (*inexpensive*). In the centre of town, with rooms with kitchens in an old stone house.

Oasis, t 282 304 1328. Simple rooms at very low prices.

Paleochóra Campsite, Chalíkia Beach, t 282 304 1120, f 282 304 1744. A simple campsite with shade; good breakfasts can be had at a taverna next door, but a club opposite can make nights noisy. The owners also have apartments and family bungalows. *Open April–Oct.*

Eating Out

Calypso, t 282 304 1429. On the east coast road: Paleochóra goes organic and fusion.

Oriental Bay, t 282 304 1322. Pretty setting, and with a good reputation for well-prepared, inexpensive Cretan dishes. *Open April–Oct.*

Taverna Dionysos, El. Venizelou St, t 282 304 1243. It may look touristy, but it's usually full of locals who know what's what.

The Third Eye, near Pachía Ammos beach, t 282 304 1234. Here vegetarians can forgo their usual Greek salad and cheese pie for spicy Asian and Mexican specialities; carnivores can also choose from barbecued meats.

Pizzeria Niki. In the centre, Niki offers good, fresh, cheap pizza, and some outside tables.

Knossos, El. Venizelou St. Cheap, tasty food.

Entertainment and Nightlife

Music Pub. Up by the castle, so with lovely views to go with its drinks and snacks.

Jetée Cocktail Bar. Near the Elman hotel, this is a trendy place to linger by the beach.

Nostos, Chalíkia beach, t 282 304 1523. A bar, and a popular dancing spot after 1am.

Paleochóra Club. By the campsite, an open-air disco with live Greek acts August.

Cine Attikon. An outdoor cinema that shows a different, subtitled film every day of the week in summer.

On the tip of the peninsula the Venetians built Paleochóra's **Castello Selino** in 1279, more to police the ornery Greeks than protect their new territory. When tested in 1539 by Khair Eddin Barbarossa, Castello Selino failed to measure up and was captured and demolished, leaving only empty walls to defend the poppies that fill it each April. To get away from it all, there are sand and pebble coves with crystal water all along the road west towards **Kountoúra** and **Ag. Kyriakí**, although the presence of greenhouses keep them off the postcards. Look for the **Karavópetra**, a pebble beach by what looks like a petrified rock, and one facing a monolith rising from the sea, the **Psilós Volakás**.

Inland from Paleochóra: Ánidri and Azogyrés

If you're spending any time at all in Paleochóra, delve into the interior and its pretty, unspoiled mountain villages. **Ánidri** to the northeast is one of the prettiest, home to the church of Ag. Geórgios, built in the 1300s and beautifully frescoed in 1323 by Ioánnis Pagoménos. From the village a marked path heads down the scenic **Anydron Gorge** to the beach at **Prótos Pótamos**, from where you can follow the coastal path (**E4**) back to Paleochóra. In the same direction as Ánydri, but on the winding road through cypress forests towards Teménia and Soúgia, **Azogyrés** has several claims to fame: the pleasures of its deep green setting and gurgling stream; a fascinating one-room **historical museum** (*ask in the village for Mr Prokopi, the keyholder*); and, down the shady path at the bottom of the village, one of Crete's rare **evergreen plane trees**, an enormous specimen growing next to the 19th-century chapel of the Ag. Páteres, built into the cliff (Mr Prokopi has the key). The highlight is the iconostasis, carved by a naïve local sculptor. Two km above Azogyrés is the **cave of Souré** (bring a torch), said to have been the temporary home of the 99 *Agii Páteres*, or Holy Fathers, who came out of Egypt after the Byzantine reconquest of Crete. The entrance, marked by a cross, is a short walk up from the road. An iron stair leads steeply down to the little chapel; instead of hermits (actually, it's hard to see how 99 of them could ever have fitted in), the cave shelters at least 99 pigeons.

Europe at its Southernmost: Gávdos (ΓΑΥΔΟΣ)

If you really suffer from *mal de civilisation*, catch one of the small ferries from Paleochóra or Chóra Sfakíon that sail 50km over the (often rough) Libyan Sea to the triangular, maquis-matted islet of Gávdos. Its current year-round population is less than 100 – down from 8,000 in its heyday in the 1200s. Gávdos was known as *Clauda* in ancient times, and it puts in a fairly limp claim to have been the home of the fair Calypso, but its very limited tourist amenities are most seductive for anyone seeking the Greek island of decades ago. Beware that it can get truly hot down there, and that the sea can easily leave you stranded for longer than you intended to stay. Outside the June–September season ferries can be so irregular you just have to stick around Paleochóra or Chóra Sfakíon and wait for one to appear.

Karavé, the port of Gávdos, is as dinky as can be, cupped in barren hills. Water is scarce, all electricity is supplied by generators and nearly all food, with the exception of honey, wine and fish, has to be imported from the big island. Minibuses usually meet the ferry, but renting a moped or bike on Crete to take with you isn't a bad idea; none are available on Gávdos. In the centre of the island is **Kastrí**, the 'capital', made of low stone houses, which has the post office, a few rooms, basic shops, an empty prison, the school (with one pupil) and the not terribly overwhelming ruins of Clauda. Most of the houses are empty in the other settlements: **Ámbelos**, near the island's highest point (1,250ft/381m), was reputedly named after the vineyards of King Minos, and has a path down to the little north coast beach of **Potámos**; in **Vatsianá** (with a charming little **Folk Museum**, the life's work of the island's priest) a rather longer

Getting There

In the main June–Sept season **small boats** run to Gávdos three times a week from Paleochóra and four times weekly from Chóra Sfakíon, mostly around weekends; on Fridays and Sundays there is also a larger ferry from Paleochóra. Sailings are less frequent in spring and autumn, and very scarce in winter.

Where to Stay and Eat

Gávdos ✉ 73001
Travel agents in Paleochóra seem determined to make sure that Gávdos becomes less lonely all the time and can arrange a room for you if you're not prepared for the possibility of camping out by one of the beaches. If you do camp, you'll still probably want to stay near to one of the tavernas, to buy water.

Quite a number of tavernas, many of them with a few basic rooms attached, open up on Gávdos just for the summer season, especially near Sarakiníkos beach.

Konsola Studios, t 282 504 2182 (*inexpensive*). Pleasant rooms, and the 'smartest' place to stay on the island.

Metochi, t 282 504 4457 (*inexpensive*). A taverna with rooms, and simple traditional food; a beachcomber's ideal.

path leads to the lovely sandy beach of **Tripití** or 'Three Holes' where a rock pierced by three arches marks the southernmost point of Europe, at 35°10'. There are other good beaches, especially sandy **Sarakiníkos**, a 40min walk north of Karavé, **Kórfos**, reached by one of Gávdos' few roads to the south, and lovely and peaceful **Lavrákas**.

Due South from Chaniá to Soúgia

The Citrus Villages and the Thérisson Gorge

If you're itching for a leisurely bike ride on relatively flat ground, the **Keríti Valley**, only just south of Chaniá, may be your ticket. The best oranges in Crete grow here and, as the locals will tell you, Cretan oranges are the best in the world; the entire valley has an estimated million trees. During the Battle of Crete it was nicknamed Prison Valley, for the big white prison near **Alikianós**, just off the main Chaniá–Omalós road. This evokes a bloodstained past: a memorial honours the Greeks who kept on fighting here, cut off and unaware that the Allies elsewhere were in retreat; their ignorance helped a majority of the British and ANZAC troops to be safely evacuated from the Libyan coast. During the Occupation, prisoners were also executed in a killing ground near the crossroads. The infamous wedding massacre of Kantanoléo's Cretans (*see* p.126) took place at Alikianós' ruined Venetian tower of Da Molino; although the historical truth of this story can't be confirmed, the medieval Venetians certainly played similar dirty tricks on other *signori* with attitude problems in Verona and Padua. Next to the tower, the little church of Ag. Geórgios (1243) has exceptional frescoes painted in 1430 by Pávlos Provatás. In nearby **Koufós**, the early Byzantine church of Ag. Kyr-Yánnis is decorated with more superb frescoes, added over centuries.

Fournés, back on the main road, alone claims over 120,000 shimmering orange trees, and makes wine so delicious, villagers say, that they can't bear to sell it. After Fournés the road to Omalós begins to rise rapidly to **Lákki**, another picturesque village immersed in greenery, set like a horseshoe into mountain terraces and with a pair of rooms and tavernas. Alternatively, take a 5km detour southeast of Fournés for **Mesklá**, a lovely village in lush green countryside, where one glossy orange grove succeeds another. The little church of the Panagía (next to a big modern church) has traces of mosaics from a Temple of Aphrodite left by the ancient city of Rizinia; another, Sótiros, has frescoes from 1303 by Theódoros and Michaíl Véneris. Above Mesklá a rough four-wheel-drive road leads up to **Zoúrva**, a whitewashed village with amazing views, to circle around into the dramatic, red-tinted 18km-long **Thérisson Gorge**. This is famous in Cretan history as a scene of battles and revolts, in particular the Revolution of Thérisso in 1905, led by Venizélos in response to the reactionary policies of his boss Prince George –an act that launched his career as a national figure. The village of Thérisso, burnt by Mustapha Pasha in the 1866 revolt, preserves his headquarters.

The gorge can also be reached easily from Chaniá (5km); near the entrance you can stop by the large, sleepy village of **Mourniés**, birthplace of Venizélos, Greek Prime Minister most of the time between 1910 and 1932. Before he was born, his mother had a dream that her son would liberate Crete, and so named him Elefthérios ('Freedom').

Getting Around

There are two **buses** daily each way between Chaniá and Soúgia. Small boats and sometimes caiques run fairly frequently to Soúgia from both Paleochóra and Chóra Sfakíon, and there are also boats every day to and from Ag. Roúmeli when the Samariá Gorge is open.

Tourist Information

Roxana Travel, t 282 305 1362. A helpful local travel agency, with boat tickets and tours.
Festivals: 8 Sept, Soúgia's main *panegýri*.

Where to Stay and Eat

Soúgia ✉ 73009

Many people camp at the eastern end of the beach. There's also a pretty good choice of good-value and inexpensive rooms.

Santa Irene, t 282 305 1181, f 282 305 1182 (*moderate*). A small and friendly complex of apartments and rooms, with good views and a popular bar that serves breakfast.
Pikilassos, t 282 305 1142 (*B, moderate*). Next to its taverna, this has just nine good bedrooms and a tame pelican.
Captain George, t 282 305 1133, f 282 305 1194 (*moderate, inexpensive in low season*). Well furnished studio flats sleeping up to four with air-conditioning, in a quiet garden setting. *Open April–early Nov.*
Lissos, t 282 305 1244 (*inexpensive*). Good-value pension: rooms have fridges and air-con.
Taverna Liviko. On the waterfront in Soúgia village, this popular place serves excellent Greek favourites; try the delicious stuffed courgette flowers. Live music every night.
Lotos, t 282 305 1191. A taverna with some unusual dishes, plus a bar and Internet café.
Fortuna Bar. The place to go hereabouts for after-dinner 60s rock, Latin, African and jazz.

The **Venizélos Museum** (*open Tues–Sun 8.30–3; adm*) at his birthplace, is dedicated to his life and times. Two kilometres from the village is the path up to the **Sarakína cave**, a place of worship in Minoan times; you'll need good walking shoes and a torch, and don't wear your best clothes – the cave entrance is on the small side.

Through Ag. Iríni to Soúgia and Lissós

You can get to Soúgia from Paleochóra in a caique-ride, but if you're coming from Chaniá a newish road branching off at Alikianós (*see* left) will get you there quicker. It ascends the western edge of the Omalós plateau to **Ag. Iríni**, a pleasant village immersed in trees at the top of a beautiful, walkable 8km gorge. From Ag. Iríni the road then descends into the Selíno, passing **Rodováni**, a village just west of ancient **Elyros**, one of the largest and most pugnacious Dorian settlements on Crete. In legend Elyros was founded by two sons of Apollo, Philakides and Philandros; it is known with certainty that it exported bows, arrows and bronze, and had risen to the level of a bishopric by the time the Saracens destroyed it in the 9th century. The English traveller Robert Pashley was the first to pinpoint its location, in 1834. Walls and the acropolis lie scattered on the hill, waiting to interest some archaeologist. The church of the Panagía was built on top of an ancient temple, re-using its mosaic floor.

Four km west is **Teménia**, a muscat-producing village with a photogenic old stone church of the Sotír, and, on its outskirts, the double cyclopean walls of ancient **Irtakina**. Its name is pre-Hellenic; it minted coins with bees, deer, dolphins and eight-pointed star motifs, and in 170 BC signed a treaty with Pergamon. But, that's about all anyone knows about it. East of Rodováni, **Moní** has another church, Ag. Nikólaos, finely frescoed by the indefatigable Ioánnis Pagómeno.

The paved road south of Rodováni ends up at **Soúgia** (Σούγια), a higgledy-piggledy, laidback little resort endowed with a long, long pebbly beach that never gets too crowded. This was the port of Doric Elyros. Its ancient name, *Syia*, means 'pig town', from the porkers it raised, back long ago when this region was covered with oak forests; to this day its nudist beach is known, rather unflatteringly, as the 'Bay of Pigs'. The ruins that still stand are a modest blast from Syia's Roman past: walls, vaulted tombs, an aqueduct and baths. The port itself vanished with the rising of Western Crete. Prettiest of all, however, is the 6th-century mosaic floor, which has been re-used in the foundations of the modern church. Ag. Antónios (1382) has frescoes and a cave near Soúgia, **Spyliára**, is one of a multitude in the Mediterranean that claims to have belonged to the Cyclops Polyphemos.

From Soúgia you can sail in 20 minutes or take a very pretty hour-and-a-half walk to **Lissós**, the tiny port of ancient Irtakina, set in a green landscape. In ancient times Lissós enjoyed a certain renown for its medicinal springs, and it attracted enough trade at its Doric *Asklepeion*, or healing sanctuary, to afford to mint gold coins. The Asklepeion was built in the 3rd century BC and has a fine pebble mosaic floor of geometric forms and animals. The pit here once held snakes, a sacred symbol of immortality and of the renewal of life through death; gliding in and out of holes in the earth, they seemed to have an uncanny contact with the underworld and were often seen around tombs (eating the mice that ate the grave offerings). You can see their descendants in any modern doctor's office, twisting around the caduceus. The population of Lissós these days is exactly one: the caretaker, who watches over the theatre, baths, houses and two old Christian basilicas with more mosaic floors, rebuilt in the 1200s as the chapels of Ag. Kyriakí and the Panagía.

The Gorge of Samariá (ΦΑΡΑΓΓΙ ΣΑΜΑΡΙΑΣ)

The single most spectacular stretch of Crete is squeezed into the 18km Gorge of Samariá, the longest in Europe and the last refuge of many species of the island's unique fauna and flora, especially rare chasm-loving plants known as *chasmophytes*. Once considered an adventurous trek, the walk is now offered by every tour operator, and the Gorge has been spruced up as a National Park; in short, forget any private communion with Nature before you even start out. The walk takes most people 5 to 8 hours, going down from Omalós south to Ag. Roúmeli on the Libyan Sea, and twice as long if you're Arnold Schwarzenegger, or just plain crazy, and walk up.

Omalós and Around

Just getting there is part of the fun. If you're on one of the early buses, dawn usually cracks in time for you to look over the most vertiginous section of the road as it climbs 3,937ft (1,200m) to the pass before descending to the **Omalós Plateau**, 25 sq km in extent and itself no shorty at around 3,540ft (1,080m). Snows from the fairy circle of White Mountains often flood this uncanny plateau, but its one village, **Omalós** (Ομαλος), manages to stay dry. However, like a bathroom sink, this plateau

Getting Around

Buses leave Chaniá for Omalós at 6.15, 7.30, 8.30am and 4.30pm; from Kastélli-Kíssamou at 5, 6 and 7am; Réthymnon at 6.15 and 7am; others leave early each morning from Plataniás, Ag. Marína, Tavronítis, Kolimbári and Georgioúpolis. Organized tour buses leave almost as early (you can, however, get a slight jump on the crowds or at least more sleep by staying overnight in Omalós).

Once through to Ag. Rouméli, **boats** run all afternoon in season to Paleochóra, Soúgia and Chóra Sfakíon, where you can pick up a late afternoon bus back to the north coast. Consider paying the bit extra for a tour bus, especially in mid-summer, to make sure you have a seat on the return journey; your tired dogs could turn rabid if you make them stand up for 2 hours on a bus after doing Samariá.

Practicalities

The gorge is open officially **1 May–31 Oct**, **6am–4pm**, when the water is low enough to ensure safe fording of the streams and when the staff of the National Forest Service patrols the area (it's for their services that you're asked to pay admission). **Last admission to the gorge is at 3pm**, but almost everyone starts much earlier, to avoid the midday heat, and to make the walk a single day's round-trip. It is **absolutely essential** to wear good walking shoes and socks; a hat, a bite to eat and water are only slightly less vital, and binoculars a great bonus for flower and bird observation. Dressing appropriately is difficult: it's usually chilly at Omalós and sizzling at Ag. Rouméli. It's a good idea to remove rings in case your hands swell. Early and late in the season fresh streams provide good **drinking water** at regular intervals; beware, however, that early in the year the stream that runs through the

centre of Samariá can be high and quite dangerous – drownings have happened in flash floods. Tickets are date-stamped and must be turned in at the lower gate, to make sure no one is lost in the park or tries to camp out; several mules and a helicopter landing pad are on hand for emergency exits.

If you haven't the energy for the whole trek, you can at least sample Samariá by going down only a mile or so into the gorge down the big wooden stair (the rub is you have to walk back up again). A less strenuous (and less rewarding) alternative, proposed by tourist agencies as 'the lazy way', is walking an hour or so up from Ag. Rouméli to the Sideróportes.

For Gorge information and walking conditions, call **t** 282 106 7179.

Where to Stay and Eat

Omalós ✉ 73005

Neos Omalós, t 282 106 7590, **f** 282 106 7190 (*C, inexpensive*). A recently built, small and pretty hotel, with centrally heated rooms, a bar and a restaurant. *Open all year.*

To Exari, t 282 106 7180, **f** 282 106 7124 (*C, inexpensive*). A bit larger than the Neos, and almost as nice.

Drakoulaki, t 282 106 7269 (*inexpensive*). Simple village-style rooms.

Ag. Rouméli ✉ 73011

Ag. Rouméli has plenty of rooms to choose from, but prices tend to be over the odds.

Ag. Rouméli, t 282 509 1241 (*C, inexpensive*). A combined taverna and pension. *Open Mar–Oct.*

Tara, t 282 509 1231 (*inexpensive*). A more basic taverna-rooms combination.

Lefka Ori, t 282 509 1219. Simple pension-style rooms.

Taverna Samaria. A popular standby for weary hikers, with good Cretan cuisine.

basin has a drain – a sink-hole cave system called **Tzanis**, which funnels the water through 3km of galleries before regurgitating it up in resurgent mountain streams. The mouth of Tzanis regularly floods up, exactly like Greek plumbing when too many tourists have ignored the little signs about flushing down paper; the rumbling of its subterranean bubbling makes the earth shake, and when the trapped air finally reaches the surface it sounds like dynamite.

The **Tourist Pavilion** for the Gorge of Samariá is a few kilometres south of Omalós. Some of the most spectacular views are from the pavilion, hanging over the edge of the chasm, overlooking the sheer limestone face of mighty 6,834ft (2,808m) **Mount Gýnglios**, a favourite resort of Zeus when the gods on Olympos got on his nerves. If you come prepared and have a bit of mountain experience under your belt, you can go up from here rather than down: a 90-minute trail from the pavilion leads up to the Greek Mountain Club's **Kallergi Shelter** (*contact t 282 107 4560, book in high season*); among the easier ascents nearby is the one up to Zeus' Gýnglios hideaway, through a natural rock arch and past the coldest, clearest spring on Crete.

Walking Down the Gorge

In early morning the pavilion fills to the brim as coaches pull in from across half Crete. Then the first of up to 2,000 people a day begin to trickle down the **Xylóskalo**, a zigzag stone path with a wooden railing, a fairly gentle descent into the Gorge, with scenic lookouts along the way. The name Samariá derives from **Ossa Maria**, a chapel (1379) and abandoned village halfway down the gorge, now used as the guardians' station and picnic ground. There are several other abandoned chapels along the way, as well as traditional stone *mitáto* huts (used by shepherds as shelter or for cheese-making) and, near the end, the famous **Sideróportes** ('iron gates'), the most oft-photographed section of the gorge where the sheer rock walls rise almost 900ft on either side of a passage only 10ft wide; you almost feel as if you can touch both walls.

Not a few people return from Samariá having only seen their own feet and the back of the person in front, the path down is that rough. Planning to stay in Ag. Roúmeli can be the answer, allowing you more leisure to enjoy the unique beauty of the gorge and rare cliff-hanging flowers and herbs that infuse Samariá with an intoxicating fragrance in the summer. Although the Gorge is in the **White Mountains National Park**, which is one of the last refuges of the *kri-kri*, the long-horned Cretan ibex, no one ever sees one here any more; the few that survived a 1993 epidemic of killer ticks, or *korpromantakes*, are shy of the hordes. Birds of prey (rare Griffon vultures, very rare Lammergeiers, buzzards and eagles) are bolder, and often circle high overhead.

Ag. Rouméli, Past and Present

At the southern end of the Gorge waits old **Ag. Rouméli** (Αγ. Ρουμέλι), as isolated as any village in Crete and more or less abandoned after a torrent in 1954 swept much of it away. Recently, some of its empty houses have been recycled as stalls selling very expensive cold drinks, which may be hard to pass up. When tourists began to walk through Samariá in the 1960s, a new (or lower) Ag. Rouméli obligingly rose out of the cement mixer like a phoenix (ugly duckling may be a more apt description), only in a new spot on the coast, another blistering 2km away. This last tortuous haul, however, makes Ag. Rouméli look as inviting as an oasis straight out of Hollywood, with its cool blue sea, fine pebble beach and snack bars with fridges stuffed with drinks.

New Ag. Rouméli stands on the site of ancient **Tarra**, inhabited since Minoan times, where legend has it Apollo hid from the wrath of Zeus after slaying Python at Delphi. While sojourning here he fell so passionately in love with a local nymph that he forgot to make the sun rise, and got into an even bigger jam with his dad. A sanctuary of Tarranean Apollo marked the spot, and on its foundations the Venetians built a church, **Panagías**. From Ag. Rouméli caiques will take you to Paleochóra (*see* p.131), Soúgia (*see* p.136) or Chóra Sfakíon (*see* p.145). If you linger, the beach to aim for is **Ag. Pávlos**, a 90-minute walk (or caique ride) away, with fresh springs and a little 10th-century church of red and pink stone; if it's open, have a look at its pretty frescoes.

East of Chaniá

East of Chaniá, Soúda Bay and the austerity of the Akrotíri peninsula there's one last bump, pointy **Cape Drápanon**. Extending between the cape and the White Mountains is the pretty, fertile region of **Apokorónas**, much favoured by the Venetians and increasingly by visitors to Crete in search of an alternative to sautéing on the beach; lively local initiatives in the charming villages are leading the way in reviving and treasuring many aspects of Cretan culture. The Almirós river flows along the south of Apokorónas to the sea, forming a wide beach at Georgioúpolis, while a bit further east is a surprise: the big island's only lake. Nearby, a road cuts off south to one of the most famous regions of Crete, **Sfakiá**, near-legendary haunt of rebels and bandits, and nowadays one of the island's best places for having an utterly relaxing time.

Zorba Country: Cape Drápanon and Apokorónas

Once east of Aptera and Megála Choráfia, the north coast highway dives inland, missing much of the area's finest scenery. A pair of resort towns just off the highway dot the somewhat exposed north coast: **Kalýves** ('huts', perhaps named after the first village built by the Saracens when they conquered Crete) has a long beach under the Apokorónas fortress, built by the Genoese when they tried to pinch Crete from the Venetians; it made enough of an impression to give its name to the area. Further east, **Almiría** is smaller and more attractive, with a curved sandy beach flying the Blue Flag, good for windsurfing and water sports, a few tiny boats in a tiny harbour and a very enjoyable set of fish tavernas. A fenced-off area by the entrance to Almiría shelters the exceptional mosaic floor of a 13th-century basilica, and on the hill behind the village, **Finikiás**, there are remains of a Hellenistic-Roman town. Nearby are two pretty beaches with caves, for seekers of more solitude, at **Neróspilia** and **Koutalás**.

East of Almiría the road swings in from the rocky coast and continues up to picturesque **Pláka** and more straggly **Kókkino Chório**, celebrated as the Cretan village used for most of the village scenes in *Zorba the Greek*. A road continues from there to Cape Drápanon, where bold swimmers can visit the big and colourful **Elephant Cave**.

Inside Apokorónas

Apokorónas, between the White Mountains and Soúda and Almirós Bays, is a lovely corner of Crete. Vineyards, olive groves and cypresses drape rolling hills, fragrant maquis fringes the rocky coast, and sleepy villages reek of past grandeur, with their old stone villas, towers and gateways. All are soon to be protected under a Natura 2000 scheme. From Almirída, it's 4km to the old village of **Gavalochóri**, named after the noble Byzantine family of the Gavalades, who won it back in 1182, when Crete was divided between twelve princes. Its excellent **Museum of Folklore** (*t 282 502 3222; open Mon–Sat 9–7, Sun 10–1.30 and 5–8; adm*), has exhibits of village life in days of yore, as well as local wood carvings and weavings; of particular interest is a wine press that converted into a bed. The local women's agrotourism co-operative (in the

Getting Around

Buses between Chaniá and Réthymnon (every hour) all stop in Vríses and Georgioúpolis, and many also do so in Vámos. Many smaller destinations can be reached with a change of buses at Vríses.

Sports and Activities

Almirída and **Georgioúpolis** have the widest choice of watersports facilities. From Georgioúpolis excursion boats sail daily to Maráthi beach on Akrotíri (*see* p.118), and there are also more 'specialized' trips on offer.

UCPA Watersports Club, on Almirída beach, t 282 503 1443. Windsurfing facilities and training, and catamarans, canoes and bodyboards for rent.

Yellow Boat Company, by the chapel jetty in Georgioúpolis, t 282 506 1472. Hires out paddle boats to explore Almirós Bay, home to turtles and plenty of birds.

Zoraida Farm, Georgioúpolis, t 282 506 1778. Horses for hire and rides with guides.

Where to Stay and Eat

Kalýves and Almirída ✉ 73003

For a choice of villas in the Almirída area, check out *www.villascrete.co.uk*.

Dimitra Hotel, Almirída, t 282 503 1956, f 282 503 1995 (*A, expensive*). A stylish hotel, with pool, beach bar and tennis courts.

Kalýves Beach, Kalýves, t 282 503 1285, f 282 503 1134 (*B, expensive*). By the sea, this is the pick of the village's hotels.

Almyrida Beach, Almirída, t 282 503 2128, f 282 503 2139, *almyrida_beach@internet.gr* (*B, expensive–moderate*). A modern hotel on the beach, with an indoor pool.

Villa Armonia, Almirída, t 282 503 1081 (*moderate*). Pleasant seafront apartments.

Psaros, Almirída, t 282 503 1401 (*around €18*). A beachside restaurant that has been deservedly popular for its beautifully prepared fresh fish since 1954. *Open all year*.

The Enchanted Owl, Almirída, t 282 503 2494. English owners serve dishes (Mexican, Indian, Italian) not offered by their Greek neighbours, and even roast dinners Sun.

Erotokritos, Almirída. On the seafront, this taverna has delicious lamb, direct from the owner's own farm.

Koumos Taverna, in the hills above Kalýves, t 282 503 2257. A fascinating folly built by an imaginative stone mason over 13 years. Originally a shepherd's hut, it now incorporates a small church as well as a taverna.

Vámos ✉ 73008

Vámos S.A. Pensions, t 282 502 2930, f 282 502 2266 (*expensive*). A cooperative run by locals, who have converted old stone olive presses and stables into traditional-style accommodation with kitchens and living rooms. In addition, they organize walks and offer courses in Greek dancing, cooking, language, ceramic making and icon painting.

Iliopetra, Douliraná, t 282 102 2555, f 282 102 2740 (*moderate–expensive*). In a garden setting, 10 traditional cottages, with handmade furniture and a pool. *Open all year*.

The Old Girl's School (Parthenagogio), t 282 502 2931, f 282 502 2266, (*B, moderate, breakfast included*). In a school built in the 1860s, a pleasant guesthouse with en suite rooms, run by the community.

Taverna I Sterna tou Bloumosofi (*around €20–25*). Another initiative of Vámos S.A., a restaurant in the centre of the town serving Cretan specialities made from mostly organic ingredients. *Open all year*.

main square, **t** 282 502 2038) sells their beautiful lace, an art that is still going strong. In late July or early August the museum also organizes old-fashioned Cretan evenings and other events; ask about the pretty 'Venetian wells' walk in the environs.

The big town of the area, **Vámos** (Βάμος), has been officially designated as a 'traditional community', but seems quite urban in comparison with the villages nearby, its main street dark with the shade of trees, a godsend on an August day. Made the capital of Sfakiá prefecture in the 1780s, it once had several stately buildings, but

Macherí ✉ 73009

Kamares, t 282 504 1111, **f** 282 504 1224 (*luxury–expensive*). Seven lovely flats in a Venetian monastery, with stunning views up towards Aptera. A pool sits in the centre of a courtyard garden of bananas and jasmine, and local organic produce often appears on the breakfast table. *Open all year.*

Vríses ✉ 73007

The town's rooms tend to be simple.
Orfeas, *t* 282 506 1218 (*C, inexpensive*). A small hotel with modest rooms.
Spiridakis. A pretty taverna by the river, with great light lunches and grilled meats.
Progoulis. On the main road through Vríses and in the shade of eucalyptus trees, this taverna has fine spit-roasted meats.
La Luna. A trendy bar with a cosy little garden.

Georgioúpolis ✉ 73007

Come prepared: it's not unusual to see hotels here advertising their mosquito nets. For meals, Georgioúpolis has no lack of places cooking up 'chicken kari', but it also has more *ouzeries* with *mezédes* than the typical resort.
Mare Monte, t 282 506 1390, **f** 282 506 1274 (*A, luxury*). One of this coast's most luxurious hotels. *Open Mar–Oct.*
Vanataris Palace, t 282 506 1783, *www.ellada. net* (*A, luxury–expensive*). Large modern hotel set amid lawns, with views of the enormous beach. *Open April–Oct.*
Mythos Palace, t 282 506 1713, **f** 282 506 1757 *www.ellada.net* (*A, luxury–expensive*). Large, modern hotel, with bright rooms and lots of sports, children's activities and hydrotherapy on offer. *Open April–Oct.*
Pilot Beach, t 282 506 1002, **f** 282 506 1397, *resv@pilot-beach.gr* (*A, expensive*). Stylish complex made up of several buildings and a nice pool, and well-equipped for families.

Sofia Apartments, t 282 506 1325 (*moderate*). Near the river, and attractively built in a more local style than most holiday flats.
Almyros, t 282 506 1349 (*E, inexpensive*). An unfussy pension 100m from the sea.
Zorba's Rooms, t 282 506 1381, **f** 282 506 1018. Rooms above a taverna, close to the sea. *Open all year.*
Villa Maria, t 282 506 1342. One of the cheapest pension options in town.
Poseidon. Away from the hurly-burly of the main road, a taverna with great fish.
Georgios. A similarly straightforward place with the town's best charcoal-grilled meats.
Taverna Arolithos, Just up from the beach, with a wide choice of starters and pasta, followed by Greek or international mains.
Naos Café & Music Bar. In the middle of town, this bright, modern-style café bar has a suitably modern range of snacks and salads.

Kournás ✉ 73007

Korissia, t 282 506 1653, **f** 282 506 1753 (*inexpensive*). A small hotel with 11 rooms with lovely views over the lake, and a taverna serving full Cretan breakfasts and fine local fare. *Open all year.*
Omorphi Limni, t 282 509 6221 (*inexpensive*). Rooms on the lake and delicious plates of spit roasted meat with pitta bread.

Argiroúpoli ✉ 73007

There are two simple 'rooms' places in the village, both enjoying wide views over the mountains.
Lappa Apartments, t 283 108 1204. A family-run little establishment; ask for Dimitris.
Zografaki, t 283 108 1269. Near the town's folk museum.
Paleo Myli. The best place to eat on the Asi Gonía road, in an old mill down a steep lane, serving good Greek and Cretan specialities.

most burned in the revolt of 1896. Nevertheless many stone houses along the narrow lanes have been restored, and in August a local cooperative puts on exhibitions and concerts at the **Fabrika**, in an old olive press. One cottage industry they have revived is white olive oil soap, one of Crete's main products in the 18th and 19th centuries. You can find it in the Myróvolon general store, which also sells other local produce.

In **Karýdi**, 4km southeast, the **Metóchi Ag. Georgíou** (*open 7–3 and 4–7, Wed 3–7, Sun 4–7*) is a working monastic dependency in an impressive set of Venetian buildings including a huge, ruined, dome-topped olive press. Another pretty place is **Doulianá**, with fine old houses on narrow streets, many now restored as holiday homes.

West of Vámos, beyond **Néo Chorío** at the foot of the White Mountains, is **Macherí** (Μαχαιροί), with a gorge on either side of the village and an outdoor theatre that's used for summer concerts; eastwards, the road leads through lovely landscapes and another beautiful village, **Xerostérni**, which hosts a traditional festival on 4–5 August. **Kefalás**, near the sea, dates mainly from the 19th century, with many houses from the Turkish period and a charming 16th-century church of Timioú Stavroú. Further south towards Georgióupolis, **Exópoli** enjoys breathtaking views over the sea.

Vríses, Georgioúpolis and Lake Kournás

Just south of the highway, **Vríses** (Βρύσες) is a major crossroads and the bus interchange between Chaniá, Réthymnon and the route south to Chóra Sfakíon. It's a pleasant place that grew up around a pair of merchants' inns, with lofty plane trees and café terraces all along the torrential Almirós river, dotted with busts of heroic, moustachioed Cretans. Just east of the village on the Réthymnon road there's a Hellenic (or possibly Roman) bridge, known as the **Ellinikí Kamára**. One of the oldest cypress trees in Crete is by a ruined Venetian house in **Fres**, just west.

The road from Vríses more or less follows the Almirós river as it flows down to the genteel resort of **Georgioúpolis** (Γεωργιούπολη), shaded by old eucalyptus trees that were planted in the 1880s to dry up the swamps and eradicate the malaria that long kept the area uninhabited. Named in honour of King George, who was on the throne when Crete was united to Greece, it has Crete's longest sandy (if sometimes rough and windy) beach, part of the intermittent strand that extends all along Almirós Bay to Réthymnon. Although a minute's walk from the coastal highway and a favourite with hotel builders, Georgioúpolis hasn't been entirely swamped in cement; perhaps the best advertisement for it are the many people who return year after year. Beware that strong undercurrents can make swimming hazardous outside the area sheltered by the breakwater. Several companies offer boat trips from the resort, up to Akrotíri and around the Almirós, home of turtles and an impressive array of birds.

Inland from Georgioúpolis, the narrow (and surprisingly busy) old Chaniá–Réthymnon road heads into the barren hills. These form a striking amphitheatre around Crete's only freshwater lake, **Kournás**, deep and eerie, but clean enough for a swim. A path encircles it, and a place on the lake shore hires out boats for a closer look; in ancient times it was known as *Korissia*, and there is a story of a lost city dedicated to Athena in its environs, but not a trace has been found so far. Winter is a lovely time to come here, when wild swans, storks and ducks flock to its shores.

Zorba: Forty Years On

In the summer Kókkino Chório (*see* p.139) seems too bright to fit the bill; come back in winter for the brooding atmosphere that kept the black-and-white movie from looking anything like a tourism poster. They say Cretans themselves only got to know Kazantzákis' novel from the film, and were rather shocked to see how conditions in the 1920s were portrayed. A visit to the *kafeneíon* in the village (where the rainy scene with the goat took place) revealed most of the local talent recruited for the film sitting in the dappled shadows, playing cards, or rather slapping them the way Greeks do. Of the six, only one had all arms, legs and eyes intact, usually the sign of misadventures with dynamite, although it seemed indiscreet to ask. There used to be stills and photos of the stars on the walls, but the owner (who played the role of the priest) took them down a few years ago, 'But I still have a video somewhere.' 'The best bit was slitting Irene Papas' throat, down there in the square. Like this he did it.' Another man acted it out, pretending to twist a woman's long hair around his arm to pull her head back for the knife. 'The movie was nothing though, compared to that tunnel those German bastards made us dig, big enough for 30 cannons. You can still see it, up that mountain. Now that's a wonder.' 'Yes,' said another. 'But young people don't want to know about those things any more.' They all shook their heads, and slapped their cards so hard the sound shot down the empty lanes.

The tunnels, by the way, were built by the Germans to watch over Soúda Bay in security and comfort. Located by the watchtower, 2km west of Kókkino Chório, they were equipped with amenities such as a cinema and restaurant, now all derelict.

A Detour to Argiroúpoli, Asi Gonía and Miriokéfala

From Kournás a road continues east to Réthymnon, but if you're not in a rush consider the lovely detour south (turn at **Episkopí**) to Asi Gonía and Miriokéfala. This road forks just beyond **Argiroúpoli**, a handsome hill town overlooking the sea. In ancient times this was the Dorian city of **Lappa**, destroyed in 67 BC by the Romans. In the later war between Octavian and Mark Antony, Lappa supported Octavian, who then gave it the money to rebuild once he became Emperor Augustus. To the south-east of the village you can still see ruins of the baths and aqueduct; a canopy protects a geometric mosaic in the upper village. Note the Venetian doorway inscribed *OMNIA MUNDI FUMUS ET UMBRA* ('All things in this world are smoke and shadow').

Just a little further down the Asi Gonía road is a spectacular set of springs, the **Pigés tis Argiroúpoli**, a cool, green oasis where Réthymnon's drinking water comes spilling through the little trogloditic chapel of Ag. Dýnami and down a stepped waterfall. A grove of immense plane trees and a clutch of outdoor tavernas make this a favourite stop for Greek visitors, who love cool, fresh, shady places like this.

From here the road rises through a narrow gorge under inhospitable mountains, where the boulders are softened by plane trees, oleanders and often tendrils of mist. Cut off from the Cretan mainstream, a nest of daredevil courage, the mountain village of **Asi Gonía** today seems a bit introspective as it goes about its business, especially now there isn't an enemy at hand for its black-clad *pallikari* to fight. Busts of old heroes overlook the square, but so far there hasn't been one erected to native son George Psychoundákis, whose tireless treks over the mountains delivering messages from one outpost to another (as described in his *The Cretan Runner*) was crucial to the Resistance. If you're in Crete on St George's Day (23 April), come here to see an age old custom: the shepherds bringing their flocks down to be blessed by the priests.

A deteriorating road from Asi Goniá loops around a tight mountain valley to remote **Kallikrátis**, before switching back as a track to **Miriokéfala**; by car you're better off backtracking to the crossroads near Argiroúpoli. What puts Miriokéfala on the map is its venerable monastic church, **Panagía Antifonitria** (Our Lady Who Replies): not long after the reconquest of Crete in AD 960, St John the Stranger came upon an ancient building at Miriokéfala and was immediately struck blind. He prayed for a week, and on the seventh day a voice bade him look east and found a church to the Virgin where he first saw light. The very early frescoes inside the church have a naïve, cartoonish charm, witness to local artists' attempts to get back in touch with Byzantine tradition.

South to Sfakiá

Sfakiá, long isolated under the White Mountains in the southeast corner of Chaniá province, was the cradle of Crete's most daring and most moustachioed desperados, who clobbered each other in blood feuds, but in times of need became the island's bravest freedom fighters. Now connected to civilization by a good (and dramatically beautiful) road, the Sfakiots have put their daggers away, and prey no more than any other Cretan on invading foreigners. Most tourists see the chief town, Chóra Sfakíon, only as a place to catch the bus after the boat ride from the Gorge of Samariá, but you may well want to linger on this sun-bleached coast, dotted with beaches, other gorges and places to explore, but perhaps most congenial for being incredibly lazy.

Through the Mountains from Vríses to Chóra Sfakíon

The twisting but good mountain road to Sfakiá begins at Vríses. After 5km, a left turn leads up (1.5km) to **Alíkampos**, where the church, the Panagía, has well-preserved frescoes (1315) by Ioánnis Pagoménos. The main road ascends the Krapí valley (prettier than it sounds) to the edge of the **Langos tou Katre**, the 2km ravine nicknamed the Thermopylae of Sfakiá. This was a favourite spot for a furious Cretan ambush, one that spelt doom to 400 Turkish soldiers after the capture of Frangokástello (*see* p.148), and again in 1866 to an army of Turks fleeing south after the explosion of Arkádi.

The road and ravine give on to the mountain plateau of **Askýfou**, where the grey ruins of the fortress of **Koulés** cast a long shadow over fields of wheat and potatoes, and where a monument on the edge of the main village, **Amoudári**, commemorates Sfakiá's uprising in 1770. Further south, a turn left leads to **Ásfendos**, a seldom-visited mountain village along a roaring brook; not far beyond the Ásfendos crossroads the blue Libyan Sea sparkles into view, seemingly miles below as the road noodles through the steep, wooded **Ímbros Gorge** before zigzagging sharply down to Chóra Sfakíon. There's a pretty walk down the stream bed: the path begins by the last *kafeneíon* in Ímbros, and takes about three hours; in June, it brims over with butter-flies. However, unless you arrange with a friend or taxi to pick you up in **Koumitádes**, you then face a long hour or so's trek down from the gorge's mouth to Chóra Sfakíon.

You could linger to visit two churches. In Koumitádes, hunt up the key to the village church of **Ag. Geórgios**, with frescoes by Ioánnis Pagoménos from 1314, with the patrons' inscription intact. Just east of Koumitádes, **Moní Thymiani** is a Cretan shrine: in May 1821, when revolution was in the air across Greece, the chieftains of Crete gathered here and vowed to take up arms. The monks blessed their rifles; typically, of the 1,200 guns the Cretans could muster, 800 belonged to Sfakiots. By September the Turks had come to pay a visit of their own, pillaging and putting the monastery to the sack; today only the whitewashed church stands, with some old carvings on its belfry.

Chóra Sfakíon (ΧΩΡΑ ΣΦΑΚΙΩΝ)

When spring takes hold of earth again, and when the summer comes,
Then I will take my rifle, my silver-mounted pistols,
I will go down to Omalos, the highway of Mousouri,
I will make the mothers childless, and motherless the sons.

An old song from Sfakiá

Legendary for its ferocity, a viper's nest of feuds, vendettas and hot-blooded revolutionaries, Chóra Sfakíon today is hardly distinguishable from other coastal villages given over to the needs of tourists. At one time, however, it was the capital of its own province, one that, with few resources of its own, turned to taking everyone else's: smuggling, sheep rustling and piracy brought home the bacon for centuries. To police the locals, the Venetians built the fortress at Frangokástello just to the east in 1317; then, after the revolt of 1570, they added the now-ruined castle on the pine-clad hill over Chóra. Chóra Sfakíon once had 100 churches, they say, not so much for piety's sake but to enable the Sfakiots to gather at seemingly harmless *panegýria* every few days to plot the next moves of a revolt. Only a couple survived the fires and bombardments in the 19th century. The tradition of resistance continued in the Battle of Crete, when locals helped the Allied rearguard to flee to North Africa; a monument by the sea commemorates the mass evacuation, while a memorial along the road just above town honours locals summarily executed by the Germans for their role in the same.

Getting Around

Chóra Sfakíon is linked by **bus** to Chaniá 3–4 times a day each way; there are also 4 buses daily to and from Omalós, Georgioúpolis and Réthymnon, and two to Plakiás. From Chaniá there are also 2 or 3 buses daily to Anópolis, Frangokástello and Skalotí.

From May to October **ANENDYK Lines** (t 282 109 5511 or 282 109 5530) run ferries 4 times daily between Chóra Sfakíon and Ag. Roúmeli, and 3–4 times a day to Soúgia and Paleochóra.

Services are intermittent at other times of year. Morning **trip boats** run to Sweetwater or Marmara Beaches, and in summer there are 4 ferries a week to Gávdos (*see* p.133). **Port authority, t** 282 509 1292.

Festivals

Last Sunday in May Chóra Sfakíon.
15 Aug Alíkampos.
15 Sept Ag. Nikítas, at Frangokástello.

Not long afterwards a German tourist is said to have gone to a village here and met a farmer: 'Don't you remember me?' asked the German. 'I was here in the war.' 'Oh, were you now?' the farmer said. 'Wait here, please.' He went inside, got his gun, and shot him. The locals buried the German, and no one was the wiser. Moreover, the 'big war' was only an intermission in a private local war between two Sfakiot clans known as the 'Omalós feud' or the 'Vendetta of the Century', which took 90 lives until 1960.

Anópolis and the Gorge of Arádena

If you like the idea of tripping down a ravine to the Libyan Sea and the Samariá Gorge is too crowded, the Gorge of Arádena is probably your most awe-inspiring alternative. It's shorter but almost as beautiful, and never crowded. On the other hand, if you aren't too fit, suffer from vertigo, don't have decent climbing shoes or a nimble buddy, don't even think about it: there are death-defying sections that require a firm hand on the rope ladder. If you're game, the easiest way to do it is to catch a bus from Chóra Sfakíon (at 11am or 6pm) up to **Anópolis** (Ανωπολη), a rustic village on a plateau offering a handful of rooms and a couple of places to eat, with delicious Sfakian cheese pies. In the centre a statue honours Daskaloyánnis ('Teacher John'), a native of Anópolis and first Cretan to organize a revolt against the Turks (*see* p.148).

From Anópolis, follow the road 4km west to the new bridge (1986) that spans the dizzying gorge and makes the once-arduous journey up and down the steep rock-face to **Arádena** a snap. Ironically, the bridge arrived too late for Arádena, now a near-ghost town after a particularly bloody Sfakiot feud caused everyone to leave; however, it does allow the road to continue west to another village, **Ag. Ioánnis**, with a taverna and frescoed church. Arádena also has a famous Byzantine church, the **Astratigos**, dedicated to Archangel Michael in his role as heaven's *generalissimo*, and sporting a dome like a tiled toupée. Of all the saints on the Orthodox calendar, Michael is the most remorseless; one of his duties is collecting and weighing souls. Not even a Sfakiot would dare shuck and jive in his presence, and whenever one was suspected of rustling flocks he would be brought here to be quizzed. The church is built of stones from the ancient autonomous city of *Aradin*, which gave the gorge its name.

If you're walking down the **Gorge of Arádena**, the partly-stepped track down is about a half-kilometre inland from the bridge and descends in a zigzag down the rockface to the stream bed, closed in by tremendous walls. It is well marked with red dots, and brings you down in under four hours to charming sandy **Mármara Beach**: the sea is inviting, but beware that there's nothing to drink. In summer you can catch an afternoon boat to Loutró; otherwise, it's about an hour's hike along the coast by way of **Líkkos**, a sleepy back-of-beyond town, with rooms, tavernas and a stony beach.

Loutró (Λουτρό) and Around

Linked to the rest of the world only by ferry (in summer several a day sail to Ag. Roúmeli to the west and Chóra Sfakíon to the east) or by a moderately difficult 2-hour path from Chóra Sfakíon, **Loutró** may well be the civilized, totally car-free get-away-from-it-all spot you've been looking for. Set under dramatic mountains, Loutró's horseshoe bay is sheltered and transparent, but it doesn't have much of a beach, a failing not too dismal as there are a number of coves a short walk or canoe ride away. Besides the regular boat trips to the aforementioned Mármara Beach, others will take you to the isolated strand of **Glykó Neró**, or **Sweetwater Beach**, cut off on one side by sheer cliffs and on the other by deep blue sea. True to its name, small springs provide fresh water, and there's a taverna when you need something more substantial; bathing suits are optional. Other boat services to Sweetwater run out of Chóra Sfakíon, so beware, it can get busy. A path from Loutró also leads straight up to Anópolis and its plateau (about 90 minutes) if you seriously need to stretch your legs.

The main port around here in Roman times was *Finikas* (modern **Fínix**, or Phoenix), a 15-minute walk west, where the ship carrying St Paul as its prisoner put in to wait out a storm. It has a rocky beach, a taverna and, on a headland, a lonely Venetian outpost, supplied by an elaborate cistern filled with water. The environs of Loutró and Fínix are pitted with caves. **Drakoláki cave** is noteworthy – an underground labyrinth with a bottomless lake that requires both a torch and Ariadne's ball of string to explore.

Where to Stay and Eat

Asýfou Sfakíon ☑ 73011
Lefkoritis Resort, Askýfou Plateau, t 282 509 5454, f 282 509 5455, *askyfou@otenet.gr* (*expensive*). High up in the White Mountains, this ultra-modern complex of stone-built apartments, all with open fires, specializes in hunting trips. There's a target range, a gym, indoor pool, sauna and billiards room.

Chóra Sfakíon ☑ 73011
Vritomartis, t 282 509 1222, f 282 509 1222, *vritnat@otenet.gr* (*B, expensive*). A self-contained holiday complex north of the village, on a ledge overlooking the sea, with a pool, tennis courts and frequent minibus service to Chóra Sfakíon. *Open April–Nov.*
Livikon, t 282 509 1211 (*C, moderate*). On the quayside in town next to one of the best harbour tavernas, this is a recently-opened, stylish and comfortable small hotel.
Xenia, t 282 509 1202 (*B pension, moderate*). One of the oldest hotels in the village.
Delphini Restaurant. On the beach, this little place has first-class service and a great view.
Limani. On the harbour, and one of the best bets for a fish fry or mixed grill and salad. The nearby bakery has Sfakiá's famous *myzithrópittes* (myzíthra cheese pies).
Cave, Koumitádes. Retreat from the heat in this atmospherically relaxing cave taverna, above Chóra Sfakíon.

Loutró ☑ 73011
One note: bring cash – not many places in Loutró take credit cards.
Porto Loutró 1 & 2, t 282 509 1433 or 282 509 1444, f 282 509 1091 (*C, expensive*), Two hotels with the same owners, English Alison and Greek Stavros; both have simple, airy rooms with gorgeous views, breakfast, bars and water sports. *Open April–Oct.*
Sifis, t 282 509 1346 or 282 509 1337 (*moderate–inexpensive*). A more basic alternative.
Blue House, t 282 509 1127, f 282 509 1035 (*moderate–inexpensive*). Pleasant rooms and a likeable restaurant.
Old Phoenix, Fínix, t 282 509 1257. 15mins from Loutró, this taverna serves good fish and salad. and its simple rooms are candidates for the most peaceful on Crete (*inexpensive*).

Frangokástello ☑ 73011
Fata Morgana/Paradissos Studios, t 282 509 2077, f 282 509 2362 (*A, moderate*) Studio flats by Órthi Ámmos beach. *Open April–Nov.*
Artemis, t 282 509 2096. Fresh fish served on a shady terrace, and rooms with air-con (*inexpensive*).
Oasis, t 282 509 2136. Great taverna on the road west of Frangokástello. *Open April–Oct.*
Galini, t 282 509 2295, Taverna on the beach at Skalotí, providing tasty dishes and pies made from homegrown ingredients and the owner's homemade cheese.

Daskaloyánnis' Sacrifice

Because of the rugged terrain and even more rugged inhabitants, the Ottomans were content to leave Sfakiá alone in exchange for the payment of a heavy poll tax, collected by a local representative and sent off to Mecca. In the 1760s this representative was one Daskaloyánnis, a wealthy, well-educated ship owner. In his travels he met emissaries of Catherine the Great who, keen to divert the attention of the Ottomans from their own schemes, convinced him that Russia would aid Crete if it rebelled against the Turks. In 1770, after two years of planning, Daskaloyánnis and 2,000 well-armed Sfakiots drove off the Ottoman tax collector and began to harrass the Turks north of the White Mountains. At first things went fairly smoothly, to the extent that Daskaloyánnis even minted coins of free Crete in a cave above Chóra Sfakíon. However, when the promised Russian fleet failed to materialize, the Turkish response was swift: 15,000 men were sent down to Sfakiá. Women and children had already been sent to Kýthera, leaving Daskaloyánnis and his troops holed up in mountain strongholds, to watch in despair as the Turks systematically destroyed their villages. In March 1771, Daskaloyánnis gave himself up, hoping to spare Sfakiá from the worst; he was taken to Chaniá, where the pasha ordered he be flayed alive.

The Ghosts of Frangokástello (Φραγγοκάστελλο)

The oldest fortress in Sfakiá is austere, crenellated Ag. Nikítas, better known as **Frangokástello**. Once splendidly isolated on its beach 14km east of Chóra Sfakíon, the castle is now joined by a straggle of accommodation places and tavernas. Built in 1317 by the Venetians, it established some law and order in the area, plagued by feuding Byzantine families. It knew its most dramatic moment in 1828, during the Greek War of Independence, when an Epirot insurgent, Hadzimichális Daliánis, took and held Frangokástello with 650 Cretans. Soon 8,000 Turkish troops under Mustafa Pasha arrived to force them out, and all the Greeks inside were slain, including Daliánis. But this victory had a price: other bands of Cretans had stayed outside the fort and taken the mountain passes, and wreaked havoc on the Turkish army as it marched north.

The Massacre of Frangokástello has given rise to one of the most authenticated of the million or so Greek ghost stories. On 17 May, anniversary of the massacre (or, some say, during the last ten days of May), the phantoms of the Cretan dead, known as the *Drosoulités*, the 'dew shades', rise up at dawn, fully armed, on horseback, from the cemetery of the nearby monastery of **Ag. Charolámbos** and proceed silently towards the empty shell of the fortress, before disappearing into the sea. Thousands have seen them, but many more haven't; the morning must be perfectly clear. Meteorologists pooh-pooh the ghosts – heat mirages from the Libyan desert, they say. Another time to visit is 15 September, when the church of Ag. Nikitas celebrates its saint with old-fashioned contests among the young men – foot races, shooting matches, and so on.

On other days of the year, Frangokástello is fairly quiet, popular for its long sandy beach and shallow sea, and there are other beaches nearby as well; east of the castle, the 500m track to Ag. Charolámbos continues down to the sand dunes of pretty **Orthi Ámmos** ('Standing Sands') **Beach**. There's a good road east of here, used by the daily bus to Plakiás (*see* p.164). passing another quiet beach, **Lakkoi Skalotí**.

Réthymnon

12

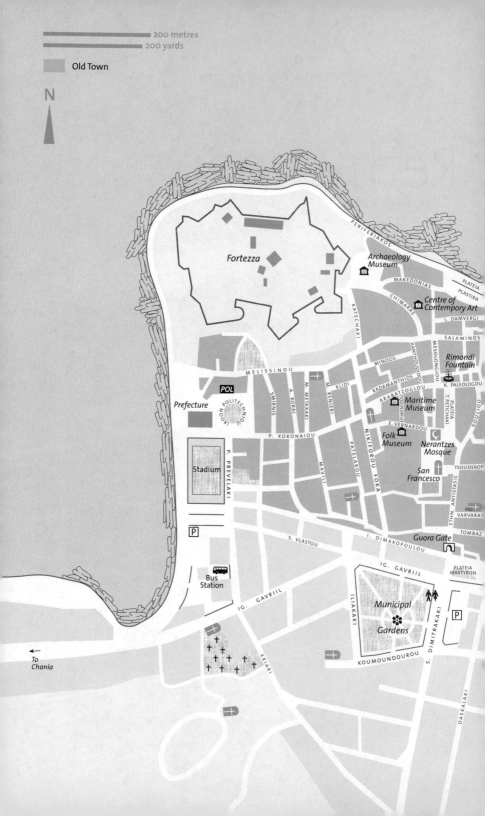

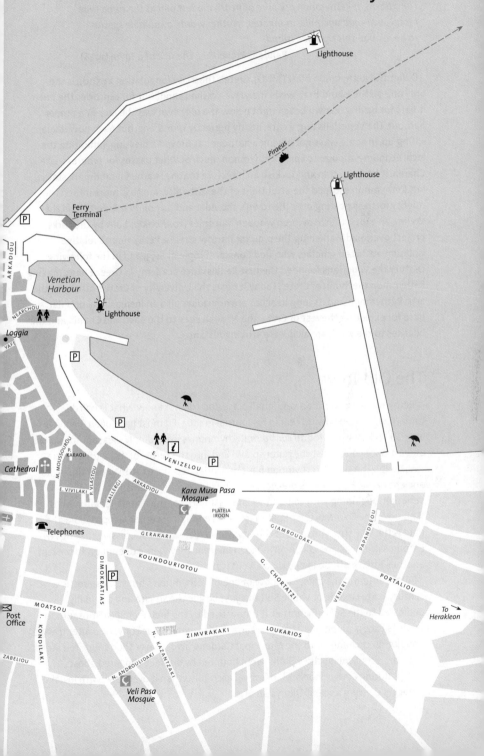

Réthymnon

Lighthouse

Piraeus

Lighthouse

Ferry
Terminal

P

ARKADIOU

Venetian
Harbour

NEARCHOU

Lighthouse

Loggia

YAFE

P

P

P

P

E. VENIZELOU

Cathedral

M. MOUSSOUROU

P. KARAOLI

E. VIVILAKI

P. VLASTOU

KALLERGI

ARKADIOU

Kara Musa Pasa
Mosque

PLATEIA
IROON

GIAMBOUDAKI

PAPANDREOU

Telephones

GERAKARI

P. KOUNDOURIOTOU

G. CHORTATZI

VENERI

PORTALIOU

DIMOKRATIAS

P

MOATSOU

I. KONDILAKI

Post
Office

ZIMVRAKAKI

LOUKARIOS

To
Herakleon

ZABELIOU

N. ANDROULIDAKI

N. KAZANTZAKI

Veli Pasa
Mosque

The citizens of Réthymnon are pure at heart, modest and at the same time proud, well-read and mild-mannered; in other words, a valuable species to have upon this troubled island.

Pandelís Prevelákis, *The Tale of a Town* (1938)

Delightful Réthymnon (ΡΕΘΥΜΝΟ), Crete's third city (population 23,500), is the only one on the island that 'weds the wave-washed sand', but for centuries the price it paid for having its own beach right below the old town was the lack of a proper harbour. The Venetians dug a cute, nearly perfectly round one, but even now it keeps silting up. In some ways not having a harbour has proved a blessing, inhibiting the local economy enough to spare Réthymnon much of what passes for progress. Like Chaniá, it has Venetian and Turkish architecture that has earned it landmark status, but Réthymnon escaped the attentions of the Luftwaffe and so is more intact. The mighty fortress peering over the town's shoulder and its pointy minarets lend the skyline an exotic touch; covered wooden balconies (*koultoukia*) built by the Turks project overhead, darkening the piquant narrow streets. Réthymnon's relative isolation attracted scholars who fled Constantinople in 1453, and in the following century the Venetians founded the first Renaissance academy in Greece here, making Réthymnon the 'brain of Crete'; today it hosts the University of Crete's faculty of the arts. Réthymnon and its long beaches are nowadays also an increasingly popular base for exploring the rest of Crete: the Minoan sites to the east, and Chaniá and the beaches to the west, are all in easy striking distance.

The Old Town

'Réthymnon is certainly a very small place and I do not know what I shall do tomorrow,' fretted Edward Lear in his journal in 1864. Ed must have been feeling less limerickal than usual, for, *au contraire*, Réthymnon is exceedingly pleasant to explore, at least once you're past the outer sprawl and into the kernel of its historic centre.

Although the site of Réthymnon has been inhabited since Late Minoan times (its ancient name, *Rithymna*, is pre-Hellenic), the oldest monuments in town are Venetian, beginning with the **Guóra Gate**, just north of the Plateía Téssaron Martyron (Square of the Four Martyrs). Built in 1566 by Venetian governor Jacopo Guóra, the gate is the sole surviving part of the city walls erected after successive sackings by Barbarossa in 1538 and Uluch Ali in 1562. However, they were not enough to prevent another Turkish attack, led by Uluch Ali in 1571.

Before entering the gate, take note of one of Réthymnon's finest mosques, the 17th-century Porta Grande or **Valide Sultana**, just beside the square and originally dedicated to the Sultan's mother. It is now used by the archaeological museum to store its excess amphorae. Valide Sultana's old cemetery was converted after the 1923 population exchange into the **Municipal Gardens**, across busy Koundouriótou street. The park's cool, melancholy paths seem haunted by discreet, slippered ghosts – except during Réthymnon's wine festival each July, when it overflows with jovial imbibers reviving ancient Dionysian rites.

Getting There

Thanks to a breakwater and lots of dredging, Réthymnon has a port and a **ferry** terminal. ANEK ferries sail to Piraeus 4 times a week in summer, 3 times a week, Nov–Mar. In summer there's also a boat to Santoríni 2 days a week, sailing at 7am and returning in the evening.

Olympic Airways buses run to Chaniá **airport** twice daily, from the local Olympic office.

Port authority, t 283 102 2276.

ANEK Lines, 250 Arkadíou, t 283 102 9874, *www.anek.gr.*

Olympic Airways, 5 Koumoundoúrou, t 283 102 2257.

Getting Around

The **bus** station, t 283 102 2212, is by the sea on the west side of town, near Igoum Gavriil. Buses run to all the main villages in the *nomós*, and those labelled 'El Greco-Skaleta' depart every 20min or so for the 10km stretch of hotels along the beaches east of town.

Tourist Information

EOT, E. Venizélou, t 283 105 6350. The official tourist office is on the town beach. Look for the monthly free English-language paper *Cretasummer*, full of things to do in and around town. *Open Mon–Fri 8–2.30.*

Tourist police, next to the EOT, t 283 102 8156.

Ellotia Tours, 161 Arkadíou, t 283 102 4533, f 283 105 1062, *elotia@ret.forthnet.gr*. A helpful agency able to organize tickets, excursions, accommodation and car or bike rental.

Festivals

Carnival Réthymnon hosts one of the biggest carnivals in Greece, a 3-day street party with a treasure hunt, masked ball and parade of thousands, with singing groups, theatre and no end of music, drinking and dancing.

21 May Commemoration of the Battle of Crete.

July–Sept Renaissance Festival, with classical music concerts, dance and theatre performances in the Venetian fortress. Information, t 283 105 0800.

21 June Klidónas Festival, Venetian harbour; dancing, singing and jumping over bonfires

Last 10 days of July Cretan Wine Festival and Handicrafts Exhibition, Municipal Gardens.

7–9 Nov Solemn commemoration of the explosion at Moní Arkádi.

Sports and Activities

A corny **Pirate Ship** (t 283 105 1643) makes daily excursions from the Venetian Harbour to Maráthi beach in Akrotíri (*see* p.118); its sister ship the **Popeye** sails to Balí (*see* p.170)

Hellas Bike Travel, 67 E. Venizélou, t 283 105 2764, *www.hellasbike.com*. Bikes for hire, and the help of a van, if you'd love to cycle down Mt Ida or the White Mountains but not up.

Paradise Dive Center, 51 Giamboudáki, t (mobile) 693 252 885. Initiation to scuba diving, courses and trips for certified divers.

Popeye Club, t 282 105 2803. The biggest watersport centre on Réthymnon beach: bananas, jet skis, parasailing and more.

The Happy Walker, 56 Tombázi, t 283 105 2920. Guided treks in western Crete.

Réthymnon Mountaineering Club, 12 Dimokratías, t 283 107 2398. Guided climbing tours and expert advice.

Along the Beaches

Many watersports operations are based in hotels in the resorts east of town.

Dolphin Diving Centre, t 283 107 1703, *dolphindc@usa.net*. Based at the Réthymno Mare Hotel on Skaléta beach, 11km east of Réthymnon town.

Kreta Watersports, Creta Palace Hotel, Misíria (*see* p.154), t 283 105 5181. Varied watersports, and courses in sailing and windsurfing.

Shopping

Réthymnon is made for browsing. Gold and jewellery, onyx and smart clothing shops line **Arkadíou** street; bazaar-like **Soúliou** is full of desirable arty stuff and crafts. Or soak up the sights and sounds of **Ethnikís Antistáseos**, where locals do much of their shopping. Thursday sees a big market off **Kazantzáki**.

Archaeological Receipts Fund, Arkadíou, t 283 105 3270. In the Venetian Loggia, this official shop has reproductions of Minoan artefacts and items from museums all around Greece.

International Press, 81 El. Venizélou, t 283 102 4111. English language papers and a vast range of guides and literature about Crete.

Kechimpari, 9 Soúliou, t 283 105 4729. Gold and silver by artists from around Greece.

Mourtzanos, 162 Arkadíou, t 283 102 2363. Historic shop with fine jewellery and gems.

Parthenis, 28 Salamínos, t 283 105 1290. Also in Athens, Mýkonos and Los Angeles, a Greek designer of classy women's clothes.

Traditional Cretan, 28 Souliou, t 283 102 4697. Spices, herbs, raki or honey, packaged to make attractive gifts.

Vasílis Psycharákis, 41 Ethnikís Antistáseos. A local institution: an old fashioned barber-shop that sells handmade Cretan knives.

Where to Stay

Réthymnon ✉ 74100

Luxury

Many of the most opulent modern hotels in the Réthymnon area are in Misíria, Skaléta and other resorts along the beaches to the east.

Artemis Palace, 30 Portaliou, t 283 105 3991, f 283 102 3785, thear.ho@otenet.gr (A). In the city, a large hotel with a resorty air and a courtyard pool that makes it one of the most popular places to stay in town. Big American breakfasts, too. Open April–Oct.

Porto Rethymno, 52A El. Venizélou, t 283 105 0432, f 283 102 7825 (A). Large seafront hotel with tasteful rooms, most of them with balconies and a sea view. Open April–Oct.

Veneto Suites, 4 Epimenidou, t 283 105 6634, f 283 105 6635, www.veneto.gr (A). Romantic 14th-century palazzo, handsomely converted with traditional Cretan decor, and a lovely restaurant (€20). Open all year.

Mythos Suites, 12 Plateía Karaóli, t 283 105 3917, f 283 105 1036, www.mythos-crete.gr (B). Ten suites furnished in traditional style, sleeping 2–5 people in a 16th-century house; all have air-con and there's a pool in the sunny patio.

Grecotel Creta Palace, Misíria, t 283 105 5181, f 283 105 4085, www.grecotel.gr (A). The most lavish hotel-villa complex in the area (4km from Réthymnon), with an indoor and two outdoor pools, tennis courts and more sports, especially for kids. Open April–Oct.

Expensive

Palazzo Rimondi, 21 Xanthoúdidou, t 283 105 1289, f 283 105 1013, rimondi@otenet.gr (A). 25 suites in a renovated mansion, around a courtyard with a pool. Open April–Oct.

Palazzo Vecchio, Plateía Iroon Politechniou, t 283 103 5352, f 283 102 5479, palazzovecchio@europe.gr. Charmingly restored Venetian building, in a quiet corner by the Fortezza, with a pool. Open April–Oct.

Veneto, 4 Epimenidou, t 283 105 6634, f 283 105 6635, www.veneto.gr (A). In a vaulted 14th-century monastery, a romantic hotel of suites with Cretan furnishings. Open all year.

Fortezza, 16 Melissínou, t 283 105 5551, f 283 105 4073, milodak@ret.forthnet.gr (B). Just under the castle walls: all rooms have balconies, and there's a garden courtyard and pool.

Macaris, 70 Stamathioudáki, t 283 102 0280, f 283 102 0284 (B). A garden hotel, a bit out of the way on the west of town, but with rooms overlooking its pools and lush garden.

Moderate

Brascos, at Ch. Daskaláki and Th. Moátsou, t 283 102 3721, f 283 102 3725, brascos@aias.gr (B). Slick, clean hotel. Open all year.

Leo, 2 Yáfe, t 283 102 6197. Charming bed and breakfast inn, in traditional Cretan style.

Ideon, Plateía Plastíra, t 283 102 8667, f 283 102 8670, ideon@otenet.gr (B). Enjoys a fine spot overlooking the harbour and has a small pool; very popular, so book early.

Garden House, 83 N. Foká, t 283 102 8586. Small but delightful rooms in a Venetian residence near the Fortezza, with a fountain; book well in advance.

Inexpensive

Achillion, 151 Arkadíou, t 283 102 2581 (E). Offers a hint of former elegance and harbour views from its balconies – and noise at night.

Katerina, Salaminós, t 283 102 8834. Three attractive studios in a traditional house, up a vertiginous spiral staircase.

Ralia Rooms, Salaminós and Athan. Niákou, t/f 283 105 0163. More atmospheric than most rooms places, with lots of wood.

Sea Front, 161 Arkadíou, t 283 105 1062. Run by Ellotia Tours next door; it has nice, pine-clad rooms, and the top-floor room has a terrace with a view.

Youth Hostel, 41 Tombázi, t 283 102 2848, *www.rethymno.com*. Pleasant, convenient and popular; hostel cards are not needed.

Elizabeth Camping, Misíria, t/f 283 102 8694, *www.sunshine-campings.gr*. One of the best campsites in the area, 4km east of town.

Eating Out

With its tiny fish restaurants, the **Venetian Harbour** is a great place to dine at night, but expect to pay at least €25–30 for the privilege. Scan the menus – some places offer lobster lunches for two for €35–55. Other popular places are on the Periferiakos, under the fortress, and Plateía Peticháki, while many of the eating places most favoured by locals are out of town, along the beaches or in the hills.

Avli, 22 Xanthoúdidou, t 283 102 4356 (*€30–35*). On different levels in a garden, the prettiest place to eat in town, serving some of the most flavoursome Cretan recipes and excellent desserts. Book ahead. *Closed Jan, Feb.*

Veneto, 4 Epiméndou, t 283 105 6634 (*€30–35*). In a hotel (*see* left), this wonderfully atmospheric restaurant has high-class Greek and Cretan dishes; excellent for a special meal. *Open April–Nov.*

Onirokritis, 16 Radamánthios, t 283 102 8440. Old Venetian setting and delicious Cretan cusine, with a piano and singer in the evening. In summer, also open for lunch.

Mouragio-Maria, Venetian Harbour, t 283 102 6475. Run by descendants of an old Venetian family, with meat dishes as well as fish.

Limonokipos, 100 Ethnikís Antistáseos, t 283 105 7078. In a cool inner courtyard filled with lemon trees, featuring reasonably priced New Cretan cuisine. *Open April–Oct.*

Caribbean, Pl. Peticháki, t 283 105 4345. Has Greek, Italian, Spanish and Latin American dishes, served up to live jazz.

Samaria, t 283 102 4681. Restaurants along the beach and Venizélou tend to the mediocre but this is an exception, despite plastic pictures on the menu: it has fine Greek cooking, with good *giovétsi* and *kléftiko*.

Sunset Taverna (**Heliovasilemata**), Periferiákos. On the west side of the Fortezza, offering basic local food and a splendid view; cranes (feathered ones) often prowl the shore.

Antonias Zoumas, P. Preveláki. Across from the bus station, this doesn't look much, but on Sunday afternoons it's packed with locals jawing through a four-hour lunch.

G.P. Chatziparaschos, 20 E. Vernardou, t 283 102 9488. Traditional bakery famous for its home-made filo pastry creations.

To Ktima tou Balasi, Giannoúdi, inland from Misíria, t 283 105 7668. Beautiful place for dinner, with homestyle Cretan cooking and lovely views. *Open Mar–Oct.*

Kosmikos Kentro Kontaros, on the Chaniá road, t 283 105 1366. Serves up excellent grilled food, barrelled wine and live Cretan music. There's always a chance that a Cretan wedding will be in full swing, complete with sozzled warriors firing rifles into the air – but not to worry, they seldom hit tourists.

Protohelidoni, Petrés (5km west), t 283 106 1577. A popular fish taverna serving up the day's catch, overlooking a lovely beach.

Entertainment and Nightlife

Réthymnon is no wall flower; in the evening crowd gather in the bars of Plateía Plastira before heading off for clubs.

Figaro, 21 E. Vernardou, t 283 102 9431. Popular rock'n'roll bar, with a touch of class.

Float Club, Arkadíou. Jumps on the dance music bandwagon.

Fortezza ,14 Nearchoú, t 283 105 5493. Attracts serious groovers with big dance beats and celebrity DJs.

T. N. Gounakis, 6 P. Koronaíou, t 283 102 8816. A fun old place summed up by its sign: 'Every day folk Cretan music with Gounakis Sons and their father gratis/free/for nothing and Cretan meal/dish/food/dinner thank you'.

Nafpigeio, Plateía Plastira. The trendiest music bar in town.

Oinodeio, 9 Melíssinou, t 283 105 6167. Classy venue for hearing live Cretan music, with occasional *rembétika* preformers.

Opera Club, Salamínas, t 283 105 1593. Réthymnon's biggest: DJs stick mainly to commercial dance music.

Cinema Asteria, Melissínou. Outdoor cinema showing a different film every night, usually in English with Greek subtitles.

From the Guóra Gate, **Ethnikís Antistáseos** street leads past the church of **San Francesco**, once part of the friary where Pétros Philágris, the Cretan who became Pope Alexander V (1409–10) began his religious career. He went on to become the first professor of Greek at the University of Paris in 1378, and a cardinal in 1406; when he was elected pontiff, he paid for the church's elaborate Corinthian-style portal. The building now belongs to the University of Crete, which is financing its restoration. Further down, Ethnikís Antistáseos forks: to the right is narrow **Soúliou**, a souk of a lane crowded with little tourist shops, and off to the left is the long narrow square of **Plateía T. Peticháki**, closed off to the north by the ornate lion-headed **Rimondi Fountain**, built in 1629 by another Venetian governor (you can guess his name) at the junction of several streets. All are now jam-packed with bars, perhaps fittingly, as the fountain was designed with a trough, to provide a watering hole for man and beast.

The fountain has been the heart of town ever since it was created, and all the finest buildings in Réthymnon are close by. The **Nerantzes Mosque** at the top of Plateía Peticháki by E. Vernárdou street retains a monumental rounded portal from its days as the Venetian church of Santa Maria. When it was made into a mosque in 1657, it was capped with three domes; today the city uses it as a concert hall. The tall, graceful rocket of a minaret was added in 1890; if it ever re-opens, climb up it for fine views. The **Historical and Folk Art Museum** is a little beyond the mosque at 30 E. Vernárdou (*t 283 102 3398; open Mon–Sat 10–2; adm*). It houses a delicious collection of traditional costumes, embroidery, photos, farming implements and pottery from a bygone age – which in Crete means only 40 years ago. On the ground floor is a historical section with manuscripts, documents, news articles and other items chronicling the last hundred years of changes in Réthymnon, although you need to read Greek to get much out of it. A block north of the museum on Arabatzóglou street, the little **Marine Museum** (*open Tues–Sat 10–2*) has shells, fossils and skeletons of sea creatures.

One more street north and just west of the Rimondi Fountain, at 25 Radamánthios, is the building that was once the city's principal *hammam* or **Turkish bath**. It was built in 1670 and is still intact, but off limits. In his *Tale of a Town*, Pandelís Prevelákis described its charismatic bath attendant, Madame Hortense from Provence, who in the first years of the 20th century was the favourite concubine of four admirals of the Great Powers – Potie (French), Cannavaro (Italian), Andreov (Russian) and Harris (British) – whose fleets were constantly patrolling around Crete at the time; Kazantzákis borrowed her for his old siren Bouboulina in *Zorba the Greek*. The real Madame Hortense, it appears, died a happier death than the Bouboulina in the story, and is still remembered fondly by the now very old people who knew her.

Snails Bourbouristi

If you're as fond of snails as the Cretans are, try one of the island's traditional recipes. Take 1kg of snails, preferably fed on pasta on the past few days, and boil them for half an hour. Rinse and clean well with cold water, and let them dry on a towel. When dry, sprinkle them well with salt, drench in flour and fry in hot olive oil, mouths facing down, for 3 minutes. Add a good helping of rosemary, stir, and cook for 2 more minutes. Pour a glass of dry white wine over the snails and serve.

To the east of the Rimondi Fountain, by Arkadíou street, is the 1550 **Venetian Loggia**, one of Crete's most beautiful Renaissance buildings. It was originally a club where the nobility and landowners of the region would meet and gamble, and from which proclamations were read to the populace. Nowadays it does duty as a museum shop. Continue from the Loggia along curving Neárchou street to get to Réthymnon's bijou little **Venetian Harbour**, lined cheek to cheek with seafood restaurants and patrolled by a small fleet of black and white swans. The long city beach extends to the east, lined with cafés and with a Tourist Information office. Just beyond the office a brief detour off the seafront will take you to the charming little **Kara Musa Pasa Mosque**, at the east end of Arkadíou near Plateía Iroon, and beneath its very own palm tree.

In the evening **Plateía Plastíra**, just west of the Venetian Harbour, is the magnet for the trendy young things of Réthymnon and foreign visitors looking for local streetlife. Makedonías street leads from the square to meet Chimáras street, where you'll find the **Centre of Contemporary Art-Kanákis Gallery** (*t 283 102 1847; open Tues–Sun 10–2 and 5–8*). This houses a permanent show of works by local painter Lefterís Kanákis and hosts often excellent exhibitions of Greek art from the last 200 years.

Archaeological Museum

t 283 105 4668; open Tues–Sun 8.30–3; adm

At the top of Makedonías Street, near the entrance to the Fortezza, the museum is housed in a pentagonal Turkish guard house and prison, beautifully rearranged to show off an ever-growing collection of finds from Réthymnon province. They are arranged by district; the oldest exhibits are chubby Neolithic figurines and handmade pots. There are fine Middle Minoan seals and pottery from Monastiráki, and hundreds of long-horned cattle and figures of worshippers with hands on their bosoms from the Minoan Peak Santuary at Vrýsinas (note the peculiar, two-headed push-me pull-you cow). The lovely strainer (1700 BC) in Case 6 was used for making perfumes. The most dazzling pieces hail from the Late Minoan cemetery at Arméni (*see* p.164): a boar-tooth helmet, bronze double axes, delicate vases, fragile remains of a loop-decorated basket from 1200 BC and *larnaxes*, including one painted with a wild goat and bull chase and a hunter holding a dog on a leash. A very late-period jug-eared goddess from Pagalochóri with upraised hands is little more than a personified cylinder. Post-Minoan finds include discs and mirrors from the Idaean Cave (although the famous shields are in Heráklion), pretty marble and glass jewellery boxes (*pyxides*), Graeco-Roman marble and bronze statues and an excellent coin collection.

The Fortezza

Open daily 9–4; adm

In ancient times, when Cretans were bitten by rabid dogs they would retire to the Temple of Artemis Roccaéa on Réthymnon's rocky acropolis, and take a cure of dog's liver or seahorse innards. All traces of this obviously interesting cult were obliterated in the 1570s, when the Venetians built, or rather forced the locals to build, the massive **Fortezza** on top of the remains of the temple.

The usually astute Venetians were guilty of some serious miscalculations with regard to Réthymnon. The local officials never quite hit the right note with the locals, and in June 1571, when Uluch Ali, the Bey of Algiers, showed up with his navy (as part of the general Ottoman-Venetian conflagration that culminated in the battle of Lepanto in October of that year) he found no one to fight; the Cretans, pressed into service under harsh conditions by the Venetians, had revolted, plundered and sacked the city, and headed into the hills in murderous pursuit of their overlords. Back in Venice, this led the Senate finally to vote to give their Réthymnon colonists the fort they had been asking for. The result is one of the best-preserved Venetian forts in Greece, designed with thick sloping walls to repel the lethal new artillery of the day. It was also one of the largest, with room for the entire population of Réthymnon and environs; however, the Cretans, after being compelled to build it, refused to move into it, preferring to stay in the surrounding town, and in 1645, after a bitter two-month siege, the defending Venetian garrison was forced to surrender it to the Turks. The Turks moved in, but by the 20th century everyone who could afford to move down to town had done so. It became a slum, and in the 1950s a den of ill repute.

In 1960 restorations were begun, enough to discourage the prostitutes but nothing too drastic. The **main gate** is still imposing, with its little watch tower on top and long vaulted passageway. Several of the old buildings have been converted into new uses for the city's cultural fêtes; the two-storey **Arsenale** is now an exhibition area, and the round, open-air **Erofili Theatre** has been built for the summer Renaissance Festival atop the Ag. Ilias Bastion. The Venetian church, converted into the **Mosque of Sultan Ibrahim**, is a strikingly austere cube with a spherical dome and painted *mihrab* that has been restored as a concert hall. Bits of the residence of the Venetian Rector are nearby, by the little 19th-century church of **Ag. Ekateríni**, now popular for weddings. The ruined two-storey building with an arch belonged to the Venetian Counsellors, and the funny little building with a pyramid roof was a powder magazine. The rest – old streets, workshops and buildings – have been left in dishevelled abandon; trees grow out of the ramparts, from where you can look down on the town.

Beaches around Réthymnon

Réthymnon has a 12km-strip of sandy beaches to its east, with well-organized facilities near the city and slightly quieter beaches further along at **Misíria**, **Plataniás** and **Skaléta**. With a scattering of large hotels, they can all be reached easily by bus and the Old National Road. For a change, though, consider heading west: quiet **Petrés**, 5km from town, is charming, with an excellent taverna; **Episkopí**, 10km west, has 3km of broad pale golden sand adjoining on the massive beach of Georgioúpolis (*see* p.142), and a choice of tavernas and beach bars to make a day of it. While there, you may want to venture inland to **Karotí**, just east of Episkopí, to visit the **Falkonás Enviromental Information Centre**, with an example of the rare Cretan evergreen plane tree and interesting displays on Crete's flora and fauna.

Nomós
Réthymnon

13

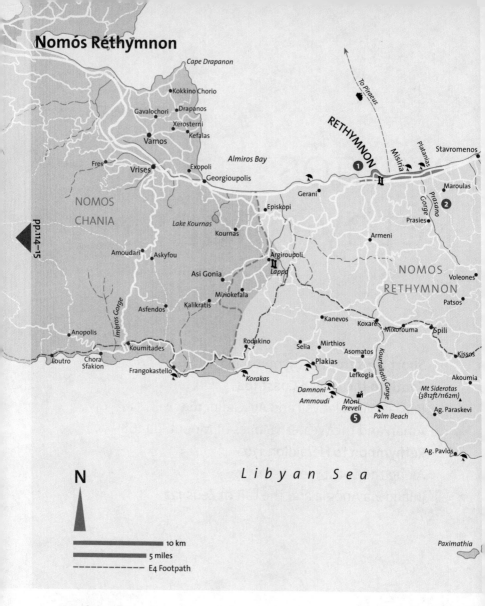

Nomós Réthymnon

Cape Drapanon
Kokkino Chorio
Gavalochori • Drapános
Xerosterni
Kefalás
Vamos
Fres
Vrises
Exopoli
Georgioupolis
Almiros Bay
NOMOS
CHANIA
Lake Kournas
Kournás
Amoudari
Askyfou
Asi Gonia
Lappa
Argiroupoli
Miriokefala
Asfendos
Kalikratis
Anopolis
Imbros Gorge
Koumitades
Loutro
Chora
Sfakion
Frangokastello
Korakas
Rodakino
Selia
Mirthios
Plakias
Damnoni
Ammoudi
Moni
Preveli
Palm Beach
Episkopi
Gerani
RÉTHYMNON
To Piraeus
Mísiria
Platanias
Stavromenos
Maroulas
Prasano Gorge
Prasies
Armeni
NOMOS
RÉTHYMNON
Voleones
Patsos
Kanevos
Koxare
Mixorouma
Spili
Kissos
Asomatos
Lefkogia
Akoumia
Kourtaliotis Gorge
Mt Siderotas
(3812ft/1162m)
Ag. Paraskevi
Ag. Pavlos
Ag. Pavlós

N

L i b y a n   S e a

Paximathia

10 km
5 miles
E4 Footpath

pp.114–15

Highlights

1 The Festival city of Réthymnon, with its fine long beach
  and Venetian-Turkish architecture
2 The botanical wonderland of the Prasanó Gorge
3 Anógia, heartland of Cretan traditional music, at the foot of Mount Ida
4 Old villages and cherry orchards in the peaceful Amári valleys
5 The monastery of Moní Préveli and the lush beaches below it
6 The lively beach village of Ag. Galíni, piled up above the Libyan Sea

Cretan Sea

Cape
Stavros

Panormos

Bali

Ag. Pelagia

Sises

Fodele

Palaiokastro

Ammoudara

Viranepiskopi

Melidoni
Cave

Perama

Savvathiana Convent

Skavidaras

HERAKLION

Amnatos
Eleftherna

Margarites

Axos

Tylisos

Tylisos

Moni
Arkadi

Axos
Sendoni Cave
Zoniana

Anogia

3

Gonies

Sklavokambos

Syvrito

Thronos

Apostoli
Ag. Fotini

Krousonas

Ag. Myronas

Meronas

Platania

Mt. Ida (Psiloritis)
(8057ft/2456m)

Dafnes

Monastiraki

Amari

Fourfouras

Idaean Cave

Venerato

Moni Paliani

4

Vizari

Nida Plateau

Ano Asitses

Ryzenia

Mt Kedros
(5829ft/1777m)

Ano Meros

Kouroutes

Kamares Cave

Rouvas Forest

Prinias

Nea Kria Vrisi

Apodoulou

Platanos

Kamares

Moni
Vrontisiou

Gergeri

Ag. Varvara

NOMOS

Melambes

Vorizia
Moni
Valsamonerou

Zaros

HERAKLION

Saktouria

Ag.
Georgios

Ag. Galini

Tymbaki

Ag. Deka

Kokkinos Pirgos

6

Ag. Triada

Vori
Moni
Kalyviani

Gortyn

Kalamaki

Phaistos

Mires

Geropotamos

Kommo

Sivas

Pitsidia

Cretan   Sea

Libyan   Sea

pp.198-9

Crete's smallest province, Réthymnon is also the most mountainous, wedged in between the island's highest peaks – the White Mountains to the west, and Zeus' own Mount Ida, or Psilorítis (8,057ft/2,456m), to the east. On the south coast there's one of Crete's most picturesque resorts at Ag. Galíni, Plakiás, low-key but growing fast, and Moní Préveli, in a lush and beautiful setting. The fortress-monastery of Arkádi, scene of a much-celebrated collective suicide in the name of Cretan freedom, is a popular day trip from Réthymnon, or you can venture under the shadow of Psilorítis into the haunting, lovely Amári valley, to find Crete at its most traditional. In the same spirit, a string of old mountain villages en route to Heráklion provide a good day's exploration, with superb views, ancient sites and three very special caves: Melidóni, another shrine of Cretan martyrdom; the Sendoni cave at Zoniá, with lovely stalactites; and the Idaean Cave itself, sacred shrine of Cretan Zeus.

Short Trips from Réthymnon

Moní Arkádi and Maroulás

Regular buses make it easy to get from Réthymnon to **Moní Arkádi** (*t 283 108 3076; open daily 8am–8pm; adm*), 23km southeast, Crete's holy shrine of freedom and a favourite destination for a day out. Founded in the 11th century on the lonesome flanks of Psilorítis, the monastery was mostly rebuilt in the 17th century; however, the lovely sun-ripened façade of its church, the *kathólikon*, Crete's finest essay in Venetian mannerism, dates from 1587. Arkádi was a major repository of ancient Greek manuscripts, spirited out of Constantinople before its fall to the Ottomans, and the monks performed important work in copying texts and disseminating them around Europe. When the Turks took Crete, they left the monastery alone, and in fact allowed it the unique privilege of keeping its bells, so that it was known as the *Tsanli* (bell) *Monastir*.

Arkádi resembles a small fort, which is one reason why Koronéos, at the head of the Revolutionary Committee of 1866, chose this remote spot for a base and a store for his powder magazine. When the Turks demanded that the abbot, Gabriel Marinákis, hand over the rebels, he refused; in response, 15,000 Turkish troops under Mustafa Pasha marched on Arkádi, as people from the surrounding villages took refuge inside the thick monastery walls in terror. On 7 November 1866 the Turks attacked, and after a two-day siege they breached the walls. Rather than surrender, the leader of the insurgents Konstantís Giampoudákis (or some say Abbot Gabriel himself) set fire to the powder magazines, blowing up 829 Turks and Greeks, many of them women and

Getting Around

There are four **buses** each day in the week, and three at weekends, to Moní Arkádi and back from the bus station in Réthymnon. To get there by **car**, follow the coast road eastwards as far as Plataniás, and then look for a turning south for Adele and Moní Arkádi.

To get to the **Prasanó Gorge**, take the early morning bus for Amari (which leaves Réthymnon bus station around 7–8am, but check current times the day before) as far as Prasiés, and then walk south out of the village as far as the first bend in the road to find the start of the gorge path.

children. Another 35 who had hidden in the Refectory were summarily massacred by the furious Turks. The suicidal explosion caused a furore in Europe, as Swinburne and Victor Hugo took up the cause of Cretan independence. Hugo's article on Arkádi reads soberingly enough like a commentary on Bosnia in the 1990s: 'Kings, a word would save this people. A word from Europe is quickly said. Say it. What are you good for, if not that? No. We are silent, and we want everyone else to be silent. It's forbidden to speak of Crete. Which is expedient. Six or seven Great Powers conspire against a little people. What is this conspiracy? The most cowardly of all. The conspiracy of silence.'

Besides the Gunpowder Room, where the blast left a gaping hole in the roof, you can visit the **Historical Museum** (*adm*), with the holey, holy banner and portraits of the heroes of 1866, the vestments of Abbot Gabriel, bits of the iconostasis, monkish embroideries and unlabelled icons. An old windmill was made into an ossuary, displaying a stack of skulls with holes blasted through them. There's a snack bar at Arkádi and a simple taverna on the road up at **Amnátos**, where the church has an ornate Venetian doorway (and a basketball hoop) on the side of the original building.

The surrounding rolling landscapes, wrapped in olive groves, are lovely. If you're driving an ideal halt on the way back to Réthymnon is hilltop **Maroúlas**, founded in the 13th century by a group of Venetian nobles. Protected from modern development, it's a pretty place to walk around, with two old Venetian towers, an ancient olive press, a handful of crafty boutiques and a spring famous for its excellent water.

The Gorge of Prasanó

Just east of Réthymnon is one of Crete's prettiest gorges, 'Green' **Prasanó**, formed by the torrential Plataniás river, which courteously dries up from mid-June to mid-October so you can walk down it. It's still not really easy going, so allow 4–5 hours for the full descent, wear sturdy shoes and take water. The track begins at the first bend in the road south of **Prasiés**, a handsome old village with several Venetian mansions. Walk up past a sheepfold, then bear to the left. A rich botanical wonderland, lined with plane trees – many of them contorted from the force of the river in winter – dates, olives, cypresses and rhododendrons, the gorge has three sets of narrow 'gates', where the walls climb up on either side to 500ft (150m). The gorge track brings you down to the coast by the old Réthymnon–Heráklion road near Misíria beach (*see* p.158), from where you can catch a bus back the last 5km to Réthymnon.

On the road up to Prasiés, the convent of **Ag. Iríni** is one of Crete's success stories; cut into the living rock like a citadel in the 14th century, it was abandoned after the revolt of 1866. Restoration work began in 1989, financed mostly by the needlework of its nimble-fingered nuns, and in 1995 its conservation won a Europa Nostra award.

South to the Libyan Coast

The *nomós* of Réthymnon encompasses the narrow 'neck' of Crete, and there's a good road that cuts between the mountains for the south, where Plakiás and Ag. Galíni are the main laying out-by-the-sea resorts, with Moní Préveli as a favourite day trip in between. North of Ag. Galíni await the lovely rural landscapes of the Amári valley, home of Crete's finest cherries and much much more.

Plakiás, Moní Préveli and Ag. Galíni

Directly south of Réthymnon (9km) on the Spíli-Ag. Galíni road, the sprawling village of **Arméni** took its name from Armenian soldiers granted land here by Nikephóros Phokás after the reconquest of Crete from the Arabs in 961. They were hardly the first to settle here: an unusually large, scarcely plundered **Late Minoan III cemetery** was discovered just north of the village (*signposted from the main road; t 283 102 9975; open Tues–Sun 8.30–3*). Some 200 chamber tombs from 1350–1200 BC fill seven acres, ranging from simple rock-cut depressions to elaborate underground or vaulted chambers reached by a *dromos* passage or steps (Tombs 159 and 200). Each tomb seemed to belong to a family and held a number of bodies, some in *larnaxes*, some not. The cemetery hints of an important Minoan town, but so far no one has found it, even though part of a paved road has been uncovered. Until then, you'll have to be content with the startling neo-Minoan house built by an archaeological enthusiast in Arméni.

Seven kilometres south of Arméni the road forks; both branches plunge along gorges, where vultures, hawks and eagles circle high overhead. The westerly road goes by way of **Kánevos** and the shorter **Kotsyfoú Gorge** to leave you west of Plakiás and go on to Frangokástello (*see* p.148), while the easterly road begins near **Koxaré** and cuts through the wild, steep-sided **Kourtaliótis Gorge**, so-named because of the sound the stones make when they tumble down in the wind. There's a place to pull over, where steps lead down to the chapel of **Ag. Nikólaos** and a waterfall spilling over a massive rock from five holes, made, they say, by St Nick himself as he laid his hand on the rock.

Plakiás (Πλακιάς) and Around

The Kourtaliótis road emerges at **Asómatos**, with rooms to rent and a restaurant-bar with magnificent views down to the sea. The village priest runs a fun little **Folklore Museum** (*open Mon–Sat 10–3*). Here the road forks for Préveli or Plakiás: if you head towards the latter you pass through **Lefkógia**, wrapped in olive groves, with 'rooms' places here and there and a path down to delightful **Ammoúdi Beach**. Lefkógia takes some of the overflow from **Plakiás**, framed by a brace of austere headlands.

A well-kept secret 20 years ago, Plakiás has boomed, blossomed or blistered, according to your point of view. Overall it's still pretty low key, and remains a good centre for walks and swimming, both on its own rather exposed grey sands and on the delicious sandy coves east of the headland at **Damnóni**. Here and there you'll see concrete pillboxes from the Second World War, when this stretch of coast was part of

Getting Around

There are 7 **buses** each day from Réthymnon to Plakiás, via Arméni, and from Plakiás there are two buses daily west along the coast to Chóra Sfakíon via Frangokástello, and two buses a day to Préveli.

From Réthymnon there are 5 buses daily to Ag. Galíni via Spíli. Ag. Galíni also has regular bus connections to Phaistós, Mátala, and Míres, and direct buses to and from Heráklion.

There are at least two buses daily from Réthymnon to Amári (departing in the early morning and late afternoon), stopping at Prasiés and all the other villages on route, but to tour the valleys around Mount Ida you really need to have a car.

In Plakiás in summer (April–Sept) there is a little open-sided 'tourist train' (actually trailers towed by a kind of tractor), the **Alianthos Express** (t 283 203 1851), that takes passengers around the beaches and villages of the area. From Plakiás and Damnóni the **Posidonia Fast Boat** makes regular trips to Lake Préveli Beach and back every day.

Tourist Information

It's still necessary to come prepared to Plakiás, as currently there are no banks or ATM cash machines in the town, although there is a private money-exchange office, and a post office. Ag. Galíni is bigger and better equipped, and has banks and ATMs.

Festivals

23 April and the **Friday after Easter**, Plakiás.
8 May Préveli.
27 May, 29 June *Panegýria* in Spíli.
June, first ten days Cherry Festival, Patsós
6 Aug *Panegýri*, Áno Méros

Where to Stay and Eat

Kánevos ✉ **74060**
Iliomanolis, t 283 205 1053. Taverna famous for its absolutely genuine Cretan homecooking, run by a wonderful couple who grow and produce most of their ingredients, down to the raki. *Closed Mon and Tues in Nov–Mar.*

an important Allied escape route to Egypt. East of Damnóni are two smaller but equally lovely coves with rocks to dive from; beyond them is Lefkógia's Ammoúdi Beach, and beyond that is **Schinaría**, sandy and sheltered, although the water is deep. Three km west of Plakiás you'll find a more sheltered beach, charming little **Soúda**, with grey shingle and tavernas. Late in the afternoon, head up to the old village of **Mírthios**, where the tavernas enjoy a superb sunset view over the sea.

West of Plakiás, **Selía** has more beautiful views from the church at the end of town. Upper and Lower **Rodákino**, further west again, hang over a ravine with a grey beach below; from here Patrick Leigh Fermor and the Resistance finally spirited General Kreipe off Crete to Egypt. After Rodákino it's 28km to Chóra Sfakíon (*see* p.145), passing by way of several quiet beaches, at **Korakás**, with a taverna and rooms (2km from Rodákino), and **Polyrízos**, sandy, shallow and safe for children.

Moní Préveli and its Beaches

This is the Paradise of Crete, and one of the best chosen places
to retire from the cares and responsibilities of life.
Captain Spratt, *Travels and Researches in Crete*

At the mouth of the Kourtaliótis Gorge is **Moní Préveli**, the beauty spot, main monument and centre of anti-Turkish resistance on the central south coast. The monastery, founded in 1594 and dedicated to St John the Baptist, has two parts to it. The road passes palm groves along the Megálopótamos (or Kourtaliótis) river, just

Plakiás ✉ 74060

Kalypso Cretan Village, Karavós, east of Plakiás, **t** 283 203 1296, **f** 283 202 3392, *kalypso1@otenet.gr* (*A, expensive*). In a lovely natural setting, with a delightful cove to itself, this former nudist colony has traditionally styled rooms, a pool and a well equipped diving centre. *Open April–Nov.*

Damnoni Bay, t 283 203 1373, **f** 283 203 1002 (*C, expensive*). Built in 1993, a cream-coloured complex that offers studio apartments, a pool, watersports and a seafood restaurant, and the plus of a view that doesn't include the larger Damnoni Bay resort.

Souda Bay Apartments, on the Soúda road west of Plakiás, **t** 283 203 1911 (*A, expensive–moderate*). Air-conditioned flats sleeping 2–4, with lovely views over the sea. *Open April–Oct.*

Alianthos Beach, t 283 203 1196, **f** 283 203 1197 (*C, moderate*). Popular 'neo-Minoan'-style family hotel on the edge of Plakiás, with green lawns and a swimming pool near the beach. *Open April–Oct.*

Livikon, t 283 203 1216, **f** 283 203 1216 (*C, moderate*). Next to Plakiás bus station, this is a good bet at the lower end of the moderate price range.

Lamon, t 283 203 1425, **f** 283 203 1424 (*B, moderate*). Pretty hotel in blue and white colours that's another good-value option with near-inexpensive level prices.

Pension Sokrates, t 283 203 1489. Inexpensive rooms near Damnóni Beach.

Youth Hostel, t 283 203 2118, *www.yhplakias.com*. A pleasant private hostel, set back in an olive grove.

Apollonia Camping, t 283 203 1318, **f** 283 203 1607. Plakiás' main campsite has a pool, laundry and mini-market. *Open April–Oct.*

Ariadni, Oniroú, **t** 283 203 1640 (€20). One of the most attractive local eating-places, with rare Greek and Cretan specialities such as *monastiráko* (pork with mushrooms, peas and prunes) and *erofilí* (lamb with artichokes and potatoes).

Sophia (€15). On the waterfront, with tables amid tiers of flowers and potted plants, where you can feast on a choice of 32

---

before a bridge from 1850 and the abandoned lower monastery, **Káto Préveli**. The monks here were in charge of agriculture; it's now abandoned and derelict, and only the church survives intact, with its roof. In the early 19th century, a few decades after Daskaloyánnis' aborted revolt in Sfakiá (*see* p.148), Abbot Melchisédek Tsoúderos began to collect arms and supplies for a new revolt; the Turks got wind of it, and in 1821, shortly before the War of Independence began on mainland Greece, came to destroy the monastery. Rather than resist Abbot Melchisédek welcomed the Turks with open arms, and got them so drunk they fell asleep, so the monks were able to flee. However, when the Turks woke up they sacked the monastery in rage.

The 'Back' monastery, **Píso Préveli**, is 3km further on, beautifully situated high on the coast overlooking exotic green vegetation (*t* 283 203 1246; *open daily 8–1 and 3–7; adm*). Its original Byzantine church was demolished by the monks in the 1830s, after the Turks kept refusing them permission to make repairs. They did, however, preserve the furnishings for the new church: the intricate gilt iconostasis, with 17th-century icons, and a miraculous piece of the True Cross that both the Turks and Germans tried to steal, without success; the story goes that the Germans tried to send it off in three different planes, only to find that their engines mysteriously died each time until they returned the precious titbit to the monks. Note the famous Byzantine palindrome ΝΙΨΟΝΑΝΟΜΗΜΑΤΑ ΜΗΜΟΝΑΝΟΨΙΝ ('Cleanse your sins, not only your face') on the fountain in the monastery's lower courtyard.

Throughout Crete's revolts in the 19th century Píso Préveli took in refugees who had abandoned their villages, and sheltered them until boats could ferry them to

different starters, pasta and meat or fish mains, irrigated with a long Cretan wine list. **Tasomanolis, t** 283 203 1129. Seafood taverna overlooking the sea on the road to Soúda Beach, owned by a fisherman who supplies the raw materials. *Open April–Nov.*
Galini, t 283 203 2103. Pretty little restaurant in the palms by Soúda Beach, serving traditional food backed by occasional live music.
Taverna Christos, t 283 203 1472. Under the tamarisks by Plakiás port, this taverna does a roaring trade with locals and has a few rooms to rent upstairs.
Kri Kri. Also on Plakiás waterfront, with good, classic, charcoal-grilled local cooking.

Spíli ✉ 74200
Other, smaller choices with rooms in the village are **Kefalovrisi, t** 283 202 2057, and **Heracles, t** 283 202 2411.
Green Hotel, t 283 202 2225 (*C, moderate*). Bedecked with flowers and plants, this village hotel makes a delightful refuge when the coasts are unbearably hot and crowded; book early in summer.

Kostas, t 283 202 2436. On the main road near the fountains, a taverna serving tasty Cretan mountain food which also has rooms for rent. *Open April–Oct.*

Ag. Pávlos ✉ 74056
Ag. Pavlos, t 283 107 1104 (*E, inexpensive*). One of a handful of places to sleep here, and with a phone, so at least you can ring ahead.

Ag. Galíni ✉ 74056
Although Ag. Galíni is stacked with all sorts of accommodation, don't arrive here without a reservation in summer, when package companies block-book nearly every hotel.
Sunningdale Bungalows, t 283 209 1161, f 283 209 1461 (*B, expensive–moderate*). Just 200 yards from the beach, next to the campsite, with simple but pleasant air-conditioned, self-contained rooms and a pool.
Galini Mare, t/f 283 209 1358 (*C, moderate*). Hotel with nice views and good facilities.
Areti, t 283 209 1240 (*D, moderate*). At the top of town, this is often your best chance if everything is full up.

independent Greece. In 1941, the monks maintained the tradition by sheltering hundreds of Allied troops from the Nazis until they could be evacuated to Egypt. In gratitude the British gave Préveli two silver candlesticks and a marble plaque, and one of the prize exhibits in the museum is a thank-you letter from the British army .

From the monastery it's a steep scramble down to the lovely sands at the mouth of the Kourtaliótis gorge, known as **Lake Préveli Beach**. These days the invaders it faces, on boats from Plakiás or Ag. Galíni, are mostly peaceful. Sunbeds and pedalos make the days when this was a famous hippy beach a dim memory, but a little way up the gorge above the beach the stream forms a little lake and delightful natural pools, just the right size for one or two people to lie in on a summer's day. If you're driving, take the road and new bridge before Káto Prevéli and follow it to **Palm Beach**, with a grove of rare Cretan palms and a place to park, and walk up the steps over the ridge.

Spíli and Ag. Galíni
The main road south from Réthymnon towards Ag. Galíni continues past the Plakiás turn off, by way of **Mixoroúma**, an age-old basket-weaving hamlet where seven weavers still ply their trade, and **Spíli** (Σπήλι), a charming farming village immersed in greenery. Spíli's old houses and churches have more character than most; the village centrepiece is a long fountain, where water splashes from a row of 17 Venetian lion-heads. If too many tour buses heave into sight, you can escape on any number of rural lanes through the olives. Further along the road are turn-offs over the **Sidérotas** ('Ironed') mountains for beaches: from **Akoúmia** a road leads down 10km to pristine

Minos, t 283 209 1218 (*D, moderate*). Nice views are this hotel's best asset.

Argiro's Studios and Rooms, t 283 209 1470 (*D, inexpensive*). Simple rooms that are not on any package company's list.

Manos, t 283 209 1394 (*D, inexpensive*). Near the bus station, with some of the cheapest rooms in town, some with en suite showers.

Camping No Problem. By the river, a brilliantly-named campsite with a pool and restaurant.

Madame Hortense, (€*20*). On a second floor over the waterfront, and lined with photographs of old Ag. Galíni, this long-standing favourite serves French and Greek dishes.

Kostas, t 283 209 1323. Has the prettiest and greenest setting of any restaurant in the village, by the beach, and offers delicately prepared fish dishes. *Open April–Oct.*

Ariston Taverna. Very good *stifádo, moussaka* and an excellent aubergine salad.

Onar. A popular old taverna, with excellent Cretan food cooked by Mother.

La Strada. In the centre of town, this modern place has a real pizza oven and serves its varied dishes up to jazz music.

Entertainment and Nightlife

Plakiás ✉ 74060

Entertainment after midnight is concentrated in the local dance spots: the modern, upmarket **Hexagon** in the centre, the air-conditioned **Blue Note** (which often has live music) or the **Meltemi Dancing Club**, a popular disco at the east end of the beach.

Nufaro/Joe's Bar. Popular late night, with an ecclectic music mix; Joe claims to be able to mix every cocktail in existence.

Ostraco. Music bar popular with a younger crowd, often playing a 70s–80s mix.

Ag. Galíni ✉ 74056

For working off the calories after midnight the **Jukebox**, **Paradise** and **Zorbas** clubs are Ag. Galíni's main standbys.

Hoi Polloi. In the centre of town is this friendly bar, where the guitar-playing owner plays live rock'n'roll and blues once a week.

Ag. **Paraskeví** Beach, while further east at **Néa Kría Vrísi** you can turn south for **Saktoúria** and lovely **Ag. Pávlos**, a sheltered sandy beach with a yoga centre to keep it company. The mountains here, the **Asiderótas** ('Unironed') fit their wrinkly name.

The road south ends up at **Ag. Galíni** (Αγία Γαλήνη), beneath an impressive backdrop of mountains. Once the port of ancient Syvrito (*see* opposite), this is the most photogenic resort on the south coast, its jumble of houses spilling prettily down the hill, peering over the shoulders of their neighbours. The beach is a bit puny for the number of bodies that try to squeeze on it, but there are plenty of watersports to be had, from jetskis to windsurfing. From the port, fishing excursions will take you out to try your luck for a few hours in the Mesara Gulf; other boats sail to nearby beaches, at Moní Préveli, Mátala, **Ag. Geórgios** (shingly, with three tavernas, 15 minutes from Ag. Galíni) and Ag. Pávlos (50mins), and to the pebble-beached islets called **Paximáthia**, thanks to their resemblance to the crunchy Greek rusks.

Amári and the Western Slopes of Mount Ida

Inland from Ag. Galíni, wedged between Mount Ida and the Kédros ridge, lie the two valleys of the ancient province of Amári, famed for its resistance in 1941–4, but also for its lush unspoiled charms, cherry orchards, olive groves and frescoed Byzantine churches. These valleys that time forgot are prime walking or touring territory, and a great place to look for wildflowers. Bring a picnic, though, as tavernas are scarce.

From Réthymnon the main road into the valleys runs south by way of Prasiés (*see* p.163), passing the Potámon dam. A turn right for **Voleónes** leads you into the cherry orchards of **Pantánassa** and **Patsós**; between them, in an enchanting shady gorge, is one of the province's 80 cave churches, dedicated to Ag. Antónios. Back on the bigger road, **Apóstoli** has grand views and a frescoed church, Ag. Nikólaos, dating from the 1300s; **Ag. Fotiní** just beyond marks the crossroads of the east and west valleys.

Nearly all the **west valley** villages were torched by the Germans, but were rebuilt pretty much as they were. The road twists up to **Méronas** and its restored Byzantine church of the Panagía, with a Venetian Gothic doorway and the arms of the Kallergis, one of the most prominent Byzantine families on Crete. Inside (*ask for the key across the road*) there are lovely early 14th-century frescoes that show the more naturalistic artistic trends from Constantinople. **Gerakári**, at the foot of Mt Kédros, is famous for its cherries, and has a shop selling local sweets and liqueurs. It's also the starting point for a stunning drive over the mountains to Spíli. Just south of Gerakári, the 14th-century church of Ag. Ioánnis (actually several single-roomed churches, built in stages) has austere, almost abstract frescoes. A similar old church at **Moní Kalodena**, above **Áno Méros**, sits in a lush setting among springs, looking across to Mount Ida.

However, if you have to choose one or the other, the **east valley** under Mount Ida itself is even lovelier, a proper Cretan Brigadoon. From Ag. Fotiní, follow the sign left for **Thrónos**, the sleepy heir to the ancient city of **Syvrito**, and the seat of a bishop (hence the name 'throne') until it was destroyed by the Saracens in 824. The setting, especially Syvrito's acropolis (a site known as *Kéfala*) is superb, even if the physical remains are underwhelming. In the centre of the village the mosaic carpet of the former cathedral, a three-aisled basilica, overflows from beneath the much smaller and simpler church of the Panagía, which, though, contains exceptional frescoes (late 13th and early 15th century). Two kilometres south, in the midst of a lovely valley, the medieval **Moní Asómati** has a fountain with cool water, and a pretty Venetian church rebuilt after its destruction by the Turks in 1682. In 1931 the monastery was converted into an agricultural college that specializes in the study of Cretan goats. Another kilometre leads to the bijou, pink-tile domed church of **Ag. Paraskeví**, where 13th-century murals decorate the tomb of Byzantine noble George Chorátzis.

Back on the main route – a historic road that in Minoan times linked Phaistos to the north coast – the University of Crete is excavating a **Minoan Proto-Palatial villa** of c. 1900 BC on a hill, a 5min walk from **Monastiráki**. After Chaniá, Monastiráki is the most important Minoan palace site yet discovered in western Crete, and was probably a dependency of Phaistos: it had abundant workshops and 50 storage rooms, where the *pithoi* when discovered still contained grape pips. The villa burned in about 1700 BC, around the same time as Knossos and Phaistos.

Amári (Αμάρι), 3km west and one-time capital of the province, is one of the loveliest villages in Crete, surrounded by enchanting views, especially from its Venetian tower. The church of **Ag. Ánna**, in a field outside the village, has the oldest dated frescoes in Crete, from 1225. South from Amári, near a small artificial lake at a spot called **Elliniká**, there's a 7th-century basilica made from Roman columns and reliefs; **Vizári**, 2km east, has Byzantine icons in its church of Ag. Nikólaos, and **Fourfourás** has 13th–14th-century frescoes in its Panagía tis Kardiotíssas. In Fourfourás you can pick up the E4 path to the summit of Mount Ida, although a more popular route is the driveable track from the next village south, **Kouroútes**, named after the famous noisemakers who concealed the cries of baby Zeus. A mostly paved, partially dirt road rises to the mountain refuge of **Toumpotós Prínos** (*t 283 102 3666*), at 4,921ft (1,500m). Lastly, **Apodoúlou**, on the road down to Ag. Galíni, has another Minoan villa and *tholos* tombs, and frescoes from the late 14th century in the church of Ag. Geórgios.

Réthymnon to Heráklion

East of Réthymnon is the province of Mylopótamos, famous for the best musicians in Crete and (the two may be related) for its *kouzouloi*, or true Cretans, who when confronted with a hopeless situation nevertheless strive to attain the impossible irrespective of all consequences to themselves, family or friends. The *kouzouloi* spirit expressed itself in Cretan resistance in the Second World War, when the struggle went on in the face of terrible German reprisals; today it continues far more peacefully, especially in the mountains, in efforts to maintain Crete's soul and traditions in spite of the cultural onslaught from mainland Greece, the EU and the global village.

Along the Coast

Between Réthymnon and Heráklion you have a choice of routes: the scenic, fast, coast-skirting E75 highway, passing a few small resorts squeezed under the mountains; or old, winding roads through a score of villages over the northern slopes of Mount Ida. The first road passes Réthymnon's beach sprawl and then, just before the coastal mountains block access to the sea, arrives at **Pánormos** (Πάνορμος), with a small sandy beach at the mouth of the Mylopótamos river. It's a pretty place, guarded by a fortress built by the Genoese in 1206; the ruins of a 5th-century basilica, the largest in Crete, suggest it was once a lot more important than it is now, although some rather unfortunate new building is trying to recapture that ancient rapture.

Further east, **Balí** (Μπαλί) has been transformed, in part thanks to the exotic cachet of its name, from a quiet, steep-stepped fishing village overlooking a trio of lovely coves into a jam-packed resort. However, the cove behind its port, **Paradise Beach**, is still well worth a swim (if you don't mind lots of company) and a stop for lunch. On the hill above town, the lovely, recently-restored 17th-century monastery of **Ag. Ioánnis Balí** is attractively built on several levels, and has a pretty Renaissance façade and fountain. To the east lies Ag. Pelagía, in Lassíthi (*see* p.201).

A Dip Inland: the Melidóni Cave

East of Balí the highway is rather dull, but an 8km detour up and over the mountains just south of Balí will take you to the **Melidóni cave** (*bring non-slip shoes; torches are on loan in the little chapel by the car park*). The access road cuts diagonally up the mountain flank, where the cave awaits just above a car park, its small mouth belying

Getting Around

There is abundant **bus** traffic along the north coast highway, and much less frequent services along the old road through Pérama. From Réthymnon there are around 2 buses each hour as far as Pánormos, and between Réthymnon and Heráklion there is at least one bus every hour, all stopping at Balí.

Sports and Activities

Hippocampos Dive Centre, Balí, t 283 409 4193, *balidive@otenet.gr*. Diving trips and training for beginners or the more advanced.
Lefteris Watersports, Balí Beach, t 283 409 4102. Everything you might want, including pedalos, jetskis, motorboats, parasailing and regular catamaran tours of local sea caves.

Where to Stay and Eat

Pánormos ✉ **74057**
Villa Kynthia, t 283 405 1148, in winter f 281 022 2970 (*A, luxury–expensive*). Provides luxury and romance on a small, individual scale, in a handful of air-conditioned rooms in a mansion from 1898, furnished with antiques; the bijou stone courtyard has a charming pool. *Open Mar–Oct.*
Panormos Beach, t 283 405 1321, f 283 405 1403 (*C, moderate*). A more conventional-style larger beach hotel.
Lucy's, t 283 405 1212 (*inexpensive*). Pleasant budget-level rooms.
Agyra, t 283 405 1002. On the harbourside, this taverna has the best seafood in town. *Open April–Oct.*
To Steki. Another enjoyable taverna, and especially good if you're sick of fish.

Balí ✉ **74057**
Most of these places are really only worth trying in the off-season.
Bali Village, t 283 409 4210, f 283 409 4252, *balibeach@her.forthnet.gr* (*B, expensive*). One of the first hotels here, and still the nicest.
Sophia, t 283 409 4202 (*moderate–inexpensive*). Good-value apartments, with pool, by a family-run taverna.
Ormos Atalia, t 283 409 4171, f 283 409 4400 (*C, expensive*). Fairly spacious 1970s apartments up on the hillside, with lovely sea views. *Open Mar–Oct.*
Delfina. A place to go for all the traditional Greek taverna treats.
Crazy Town Dancing Bar. Cranks up for a bop after midnight.

a vast and gloomy, unsettling gullet. The ceiling, ragged with stalactites, hangs 1,000ft overhead. The Minoans worshipped here, and just to the right of the entrance is a 3rd-century BC inscription to Hermes Talaios, who shared offerings here with Zeus Talaios and Talos (*see* p.35).

In 1824, when the Turks were doing their best to cut short Crete's participation in the Greek War of Independence, 324 women and children and 30 revolutionaries took refuge in the cave. When the Turks discovered their hideaway, the Greeks refused to surrender; the Turks tried to suffocate them by blocking up the entrance with stones, and when that failed they built a fire and, in one of the worst atrocities of the war, asphyxiated them all in the smoke. With its crumbling altar and broken ossuary it still seems haunted; curiously, the water that drips in the cave dries up between September and February – normally Crete's rainy season. Have a drink at the bar by the cave with Markos and Brenda Kyrmizakis, Cretans who went to Alabama and returned agiain to the old farming village of **Pérama**, just below Melidóni.

The **old road** between Pérama and Heráklion is pure rural Crete. In some villages just south of the road you may see fields dotted with large round piles of logs, smouldering away like overheated igloos; charcoal-burning is alive and well here, and has scarcely changed since the Middle Ages.

Inland via Anógia and the Lair of Zeus

A choice of roads skirts the north flanks of Psilorítis, and to see everything there is to see here involves some backtracking. From Réthymnon the easiest route inland is to follow the coast to **Stavroménos**, then take the Pérama road through **Viranepiskopí**, with two churches of interest: a 10th-century basilica near a Sanctuary of Artemis, and a 16th-century Venetian one. The old highway goes on to the Melidóni cave (*see* p.170), but a prettier road cuts 7km south to colourful **Margarítes**, home of a thriving pottery industry (pick up a 6ft Minoan-style *pithos*) and two frescoed churches, 14th-century Ag. Demétrios and 12th-century Ag. Ioánnis, with a stone iconostasis.

Another 4km south, modern **Eléftherna** (Ελεύθερνα) is just below ancient *Eleutherna*. Founded by the Dorians in the 8th century BC, this city survived into Byzantine times and along the way produced Diogenes the Physicist, a pupil of the Pre-Socratic philosopher Anaximenes of Miletus. As in most Dorian cities, the setting (on natural tiers, between two tributaries of the Mylopótamos river) and views are spectacular; any foe that came near had to pass mighty walls and a formidable **tower** (*Pýrgi*). According to historian Dio Cassius, Metellus Creticus was only able to capture Eleutherna for Rome after the tower was soaked in vinegar (!). Near it you can see a section of an aqueduct in the stone, leading to two massive Roman **cisterns** capable of holding 10,000 cubic metres of water. At the bottom of the glade, at the confluence of three brooks (reached by a dirt road from the village), there's also a Hellenistic bridge, with a striking pointed stone arch. Ongoing excavations here by the University of Crete have concentrated on the remains of a score of funeral pyres and their offerings from the Protogeometric to the Archaic period. A handsome Byzantine mosaic floor has been found, but the most beautiful treasures are four small ivory heads of exquisite workmanship. One dead notable of the 8th century BC was given not just the usual animal offerings, food and valuables, but a human sacrifice to take to the Underworld: archaeologists found the remains of a man trussed hand and foot, and somehow, even after 2,700 years, they could tell his throat had been cut.

Axós

Even higher and more precipitous, **Axós**, 30km east, was founded around 1100 BC by Minoans seeking refuge from Dorian invaders (it's believed to be the '*E-CO-SO*' on a Linear B inscription from Knossos). It was the only town on Crete to have a king of its own into the 7th century BC, and continued to thrive into the Byzantine period, when it counted 46 churches; today 11 survive. The far-scattered remains of ancient Axos reveal a huge town (whatever did they live on?, you may well ask). A sign in the village points up the ridge to the acropolis, scattered on terraces under 8th-century BC walls and the ruins of an Archaic sanctuary. Arrange to go up with Antonia Koutantou (**t** *283 406 1311*), who runs a weaving shop and has keys to the churches.

On the road east of Axós, a splendid panorama opens up over the hill towns of the Mylopótamos. Below the next one, **Zoniána**, is the cave of **Sendóni** (*open 8am–sunset; adm*), an old bandits' lair piercing a spur of Mount Ida; its 14 chambers contain one of Crete's most striking collections of stalactites, cave draperies and petrified waves.

They were discovered by a little girl, who according to locals was lured away by the fairies, or nereids; after an eight-day search she was found dead in the cave with a beatific smile on her face. Apparently she wasn't the only one lured here, for during the preparation of the cave for visitors skeletons of a man and woman were found.

Anógia (Ανώγεια) and the Idaean Cave

They have the feet of hares, the heart of lions, they have slim waists,
the trunks of cypress trees.
In days of old, when they had no knives, they fought the Turks with
the staffs in their hands...

Ioánnis Konstantinídis, 1867

The next village east is **Anógia**, 'the high place', at 2,428ft (740m), to which many of the inhabitants of ancient Axós moved in the Middle Ages, and where hints of their ancient dialect survived; even other Cretans sometimes have a hard time understanding the Anogeians. Famous for their free spirit, love of freedom and hospitality, they made their village such a stalwart resistance centre that it was burned by both Turks and Germans, the latter in reprisal for hiding the kidnapped General Kreipe, when all the men in the village were also rounded up and shot.

Anógia has since been attractively rebuilt. Stands and shops around **Plateía Livádi**, in the lower part of town, display bright examples of local weavings; brace yourself for a mugging by a score of little old ladies (including a few surviving widows of the martyrs) touting their wares. Social life is concentrated near the top, around the church of Ag. Geórgios (with 13th-century frescoes) and assymetrical **Plateía Meitani**, jammed full of plants and flowers and traditional *kafeneía*. The men of the village have their talents, too: the town is the capital of Cretan music and the cradle of some of its greatest musicians, including Níkos Xyloúris, 'the Nightingale of Crete' (*see* p.61).

Getting Around

Buses run through the mountain villages to Anógia twice daily from Réthymnon, but only Mon–Fri; for most of the year there are no services at weekends. Buses run more frequently from Heráklion, with 5 each way on most days, from Pórta Chanión bus terminal.

Where to Stay and Eat

Axós ✉ 74051
Yakinthos, *www.crete-hotels-rooms.com/ reservations/Yakinthos_Hotel* (*moderate*). Three pretty apartments and three studios in traditional Cretan style. The hospitable owners offer sound advice on the area, and good breakfasts are provided. *Open all year.*

Taverna Axós. A good taverna for lunch that hosts the occasional 'Greek Night'.

Anógia ✉ 74051
Pasparákis, t 283 403 1048 (*moderate–inexpensive*). Four flats near the main square, with basic furnishings. *Open all year.*
Aristea, t 283 403 1459 (*inexpensive*). In the upper town, a small, white, clean and bright pension, with good views.
Aris, t 283 403 1460. Another likeable modest pension.
Taverna Aetos, t 283 403 1262. Anógia prides itself on its lamb and *rakí*, and this place in the centre of the village, with an enormous grill, is a great place to tuck in. *Open all year.*
Michalis' Taverna, Sísarcha, between Anógia and Goniés, **t** 283 403 1696. Taverna in a very out-of-the-way village with simple rooms.

He was born in Plateía Meitani, and his sister runs a memorabilia-packed *kafeneíon* on the ground floor of the family house. The privately-run **Museum Grillios** displays sculptures and paintings by the late 'Grillios' (Alkiviadís Skoúlas), and some more recent artists from Heráklion have set up a glass workshop in the vilage, **Tarrha Glass**. At night you may well hear an impromptu concert in one of the cafés, and Anógia hosts two major summer festivals of Cretan music and other arts: the *Yakintheia*, in the first four days of July, and the *Anogéia* in early August (*see* p.91).

Just east of Anógia begins the 26km paved road to the beautiful **Nida Plateau**, carpeted with wild flowers in spring; in summer shepherds bring their flocks here, and a few still make their fresh *mýzithra* cheese the old-fashioned way, over an open fire in little stone huts (*mitata*). At the east end of the plateau, don't miss *Antartis*, a 100ft rock figure by Karina Rek. The road continues to the yawning maw of the **Idaean Cave** (Ιδαιον Ανδρον), at 5,050ft (1,540m). Back in Archaic times, the Idaean Cave took over the Diktean Cave's thunder, so to speak, in claiming to be the birthplace of Zeus. This was the ultimate Minoan cave sanctuary, ancient even to the ancients, and the Idaean cult preserved remnants of Minoan religion into Classical times – whatever the state religion said about 'immortal' Zeus, the Cretans remembered his origins as a vegetation spirit who had to die and be reborn every year. His cult at the cave was presided over by Idaean *Dactyls* or 'finger men'. Pythagoras' ancient biographer tells how he was inititiated by the Dactyls into the Orphic Mysteries of midnight Zagreus (Zeus fused with the mystic role of Dionysos, who was also killed as a child and reborn), the origin of his mystical theories on numbers and vegetarianism. A clue to what they got up to in the cave is preserved in a fragment of Euripides' lost play, *The Cretans*, in the confession of Cretan mystics in the palace of Minos:

> *My days have run, the servant*
> *I, Initiate of Idaean Jove;*
> *Where midnight Zagreus roves, I rove;*
> *I have endured his thunder-cry;*
> *Fulfilled his red and bleeding feasts;*
> *Held the Great Mother's mountain flame;*
> *I am Set Free and named by name*
> *A Bacchus of the Mailed Priests.*

The cave, previously known among locals as the 'cave of the Shepherdess', was identified in 1885, when bronze shields now in the Heráklion museum were found. More recent excavations have yielded roomfuls of votive offerings, dating from 3000 BC to the 5th century AD. A ski resort has opened nearby, and there's a marked track from the cave to the summit of **Mount Ida**, Crete's highest peak (8,057ft/2,456m), a trek of about 7 hours' round trip (12 hours from Anógia) for a reasonably well-prepared hiker. Beware that snow falls as late as June (storms are an unforgettable experience on the summit). A guide is helpful to find the most direct route to the top, marked by a shelter and the chapel of **Tímios Stavrós** (where an Irish girl robbed young Níkos Kazantzákis of his virginity, at least according to his *Report to Greco*). If you have very warm sleeping bags, water and food, consider spending the night.

Heráklion

14

Heráklion

Rocco al Mare

Venetian Harbour

Ferry Terminal

S. VENIZELOU

Historical Museum

KALOKAIRINOU

KOUNDOURIOTOU

Catholic Church

Arsenali

K. PALEOLOGOU

THEOTOKOPOULOU

VIRONOS

EPIMENIDOU

E

C

25 AVGOUSTOU

P. ANTONIOU

C

D

SKORDILON

PLATEIA NEARCHOU

CHANDAKOS

1878

MINOTAVROU

MALIKOUTI

SFAKION

KAZANTZAKI

KORONEOU

El Greco Park

Morosini Fountain

Ag. Titos

AGIOU TITOU

MIRABELOU

Battle of Crete and Resistance Museum

BOFOR

MIRIONOU

MICHELIDAKI

PSAROMILIGON

CHANDAKOS

PLATEIA VENIZELOU

Loggia (City Hall)

ANDROGEO

KORAI

IDOMENEOS

XANTHOUDIDOU

HATZIDAKI

Archaeology Museum

DOUKOS

IKAROU

KALOKERINOU

G

Ag. Markos

DAEDALOU

To **A** and **B**

PLATEIA EKATERINIS

ZAMPELIOU

GRAMVOUSAS

ARGIRAKI

IDIS

DIKEOSINIS

PLATEIA ELEFTHERIAS

AGIOU MINA

Ag. Mina

Ag. Ekaterina

KATEHAKI

1821

Market

POL

M

GIANARI

TRIS KAMARES

MONIS KARDIOTISIS

Cathedral

PLATEIA FEREOU

KARTEROU

1866

ZOGRAFOU

PLATEIA ARKADIOU

EVANS

PEDIADOS

DIMOKRATIAS

MARKOPOULOU

THESSALONIKIS

VIKELA

PLATEIA KORNAROU

Bembo Fountain

AVEROF

OTHONOS

TOBAZI

GIANNIKOU

M. MOUSOUROU

TRIFISTOU

SPINALOGAS

K. GIABOUDI

P. NIKOUSIOU

VIANON

EVANS

PLATEIA KIPROU

CHRYSOSTOMOU

KOMENO BENTENI

NIKOLAOU PLASTIRA

KENOURIA PORTA

F

To the Natural History Museum

Tomb of Níkos Kazantzákis

MARTINENGO BASTION

E. PAPANDREOU

N

Bus Departures

A Airport–Amnissos, No 1
B Mátala–Phaistos
C Knossos, No 2
D Malia–Ag. Nikolaos–Ierapetra–Sitia
E Rethymnon–Chania
F Kastelli–Viannos
G Archanes

200 metres
200 yards

Hustling, bustling Heráklion (HPAKΛEIO in Greek, and also Iraklion, Iraklio, Herákleon and other spellings in English) is Crete's capital, the principal seat of its university and the fourth largest city in the whole of Greece, with a population of 127,000 – and so the kind of place that most people go on holiday to escape, a busy, noisy place with more than its share of crowds and traffic. As Crete's main transport hub, however, it's hard to avoid, and, above all, it can boast of the island's two top attractions: the world's greatest collection of Minoan art in the city's Archaeological Museum, and the extraordinary palace of Knossós, just outside the city amid its modern southern suburbs. Henry Miller spent several months here on the eve of the Second World War, having come to Crete to escape the war clouds gathering in the rest of Europe, and left a memorable description of the city in his 1941 travel book *The Colossus of Maroussi*. On the one hand, he was in no way complementary: Miller described Heráklion as 'a confused, nightmarish town', a strong-smelling place 'suspended in a void between Europe and Africa' and related to Minoan Crete only 'in the way that Walt Disney's creations are American'; on the other, though, and in spite of all the noise and stinks, the great sensualist also declared with real enthusiasm that 'every inch of Heráklion is paintable'.

History

Heráklion has gone through as many name changes as Elizabeth Taylor. It began modestly as *Katsamba*, the smaller of Knossos' two ports, and took on its current name in the Classical period. In the 800s AD the Saracens saw the potential of the site and built their chief town and pirates' base here, naming it *Kandak* ('the moats'), because of the trench they dug around its walls. By the time Crete was reconquered for Byzantium by Nikephóros Phokás in the 960s, Kandak had become the leading slave market in the Mediterranean. Another three centuries later, the Venetians in turn saw the value of Kandak and kept it as the capital of Crete, renaming it *Candia*, or Candy, although the mighty walls they built around it so impressed the Cretans that they decided to call it *Megálo Kástro*, the 'Big Castle'. The Turks, when they finally took Candia after their long long siege (*see* p.182), kept the city as their seat of government until 1850, when they transferred the administration to Chaniá. When Crete became autonomous and then part of Greece the classical name Heráklion was revived, and it subsequently took back its role as island capital in 1971.

Venetian Heráklion

When Crete won its autonomy in 1898, Arthur Evans (*see* p.193), already a local hero for filing news reports in Britain on Turkish atrocities, was instrumental in persuading the Cretans to safeguard their Venetian walls and monuments, and it's a good thing he did, because Heráklion would be a landmark-less mess without them. The old front door, the **Venetian Harbour**, is now a couple of hundred yards west of the modern arrival points at the ferry docks and main bus depots, but still offers the best introduction to the city. Two monuments recall the Venetians' ability to supply Heráklion during its 21-year siege by the Turks (*see* p.182). Out on the harbour mole, the over-restored 16th-century fortress of **Rocco al Mare** is guarded by a fierce lion of St Mark

Getting There

By Air

Heráklion's **airport** is 4km east of the city towards Amnísos. It's linked to town by local bus **no. 1**, which begins at Pórta Chaníon (**A**, on the map on p.176) and passes through the centre of town and Plateía Eleftherías, and by Olympic Airways buses that connect to all Olympic flights from Plateía Eleftherías. A **taxi** to Heráklion from the airport costs around €8.

Airport information, t 281 024 5644.

Aegean Airlines, 11 Dimokratías, **t** 281 034 4324; airport office, **t** 281 022 2217.

Olympic Airways, Plateía Eleftherías, **t** 281 022 3400/**t** 281 022 9191.

By Sea

The **ferry terminal** for ships from mainland Greece is on the east side of the port. Travel agents selling ferry tickets line 25 Avgoustou street, the main route up into the city from the Venetian Harbour. **ANEK Lines** and **Minoan Lines** both have daily ferries to and from Piraeus, and Minoan also sails direct to and from Thessaloníki, via Rhodes.

Port authority, t 281 024 4956.

ANEK Lines, no. 33, 25 Avgoustou, **t** 281 022 2481, **f** 281 034 6379.

Minoan Lines, no. 78, 25 Avgoustou, **t** 281 022 9602, **f** 281 033 0855, *www.minoan.gr*.

Paleologos Shipping, no.5, 25 Avgoustou, **t** 281 034 6185, **f** 281 034 6208, *info@greekislands.gr*.

By Bus

Heráklion has several bus depots (indicated by **letters** on the town plan on p.176). Three of them are clustered on Koundouriotou, east of the Venetian Harbour (an area sometimes referred to by local agents as Bus Station A); the other main bus-departure point is by Pórta Chaníon, over on the west side of town.

For destinations east of Heráklion, including Mália, Ag. Nikólaos and Lassíthi: from the station on the land-side of Koundouriotou (**D, t** 281 024 50170). Buses are very frequent on the Heráklion–Ag. Nikólaos route, some of them the KTEL's new double-deckers.

For main points west of Heráklion (Réthymnon, Chaniá): across the street on the seaward side (**E, t** 281 022 1765).

For buses heading southwest, to the south coast and the mountains (Ag. Galíni, Anógia, Týlisos, Gortyn, Phaistos, the Mátala coast): from Pórta Chaníon (**B, t** 281 025 5965).

For the southeast (Thrapsanó, Áno Viánnos, Mýrtos): from outside Plateía Kíprou (**F**).

For Archánes: buses leave from the east bus depot (**D**), stopping in Plateía Venizélou (**G**).

Getting Around

Main hubs for city **bus** routes are on Koundouriotou, by the main bus depots, and Plateía Eleftherías. For **Knossos** take bus **no. 2** from outside the east bus station (**C**). The best local buses to nearby beaches leave from Plateía Eleftherías: **no. 6**, for Ammoudára and Ag. Pelagía to the west, and **no. 7**, for Amnisós and beaches to the east (via Pórta Chaníon).

There are **taxi** ranks in Plateía Eleftherías and Plateía Venizélou, and you can call for a cab on **t** 281 021 0102.

Car and Bike Hire

There are any number of car rental agencies along 25 Avgoustou and on Doukós Bofór, near the main bus depots. Rates are usually reasonable, but be ready to haggle: try **Mike Tours**, 76 Ikarou, **t** 281 024 1362, *www.miketours.gr*, or **Blue Sea Car & Bike Rental**, 5–7 Kósma Zotoú (off 25 Avgoustou), **t** 281 024 1097, which also has bikes and scooters.

Tourist Information

Hospitals: Panelisteimiako, **t** 281 039 2111; Venizélou, **t** 281 036 8001.

Internet access: **Istos Cybercafé**, 2 Malikouti, **t** 281 022 2120, is quite handily located near the Archaeological Museum; **Netc@fé**, 4 1821 street, **t** 281 022 9569, and **5 Korai**, 5 Korai street, are both centrally-located cybercafés.

Left luggage: there are facilities in the east (**D**) and southwest (**B**) bus stations (*both open 8am–8pm*), and at the airport (*open 24hrs*).

Tourist police: 10 Dikeosínis, **t** 281 028 3190.

Post office: Plateía Daskaloyiánnis, **t** 281 028 2276. Not far from Plateía Eleftherías.

Festivals

2–6 June: Heráklion flower festival.

June–Sept: **Irakleio Summer Festival**, a major arts fest that brings in big-league theatre, ballet, opera and traditional music; information t 281 024 2977.

11–19 Sept: Heráklion's grape festival.

11 Nov: huge *panegýri* for the city's patron, Ag. Minás.

Sports and Activities

Heráklion has Crete's most important soccer team, **OFI**, whose stadium, on the west side of town near the Pórta Chaníon gate, is slated to host some of the football games in the 2004 Olympics.

Anopolis Water City, t 281 078 1316. Located a little south of Heráklion airport, this water park has a huge range of slides.

Bowling Centre, Ethníkis Antistáseos, Supermodern complex in Heráklion's new town, with 10-pin bowling, billiards and a Net café.

Happy Train. Sightseeing tours of the town in the usual jolly, open-sided trailers leave hourly from outside the Archaeological Museum and the Venetian Harbour, and follow a circular route around town.

Poseidon Dive, Ammoudára, t (mobile) 697 773 2030. Diving instruction for all levels and guided dives for experienced divers.

Shopping

Heráklion's stores are mostly for local consumption, but the **Market** in 1866 street is a good bet for edible souvenirs and spices, and tourist tat. **1821 street** and pedestrianized **Daedálou** and the streets around it make up Heráklion's main shopping districts, with most of the city's fashion stores including plenty of well-known international names (Hugo Boss, Zara and so on).

Aerákis, 34 Daedálou. An engaging mix of Cretan products, traditional and modern: music, honey and herbs, too.

Cretaphone, 6–10, 1821 street. An excellent choice of old and new Cretan music.

Kastrinogianni, Plateía Eleftherias, t 281 022 6186. Probably the best shop in Heráklion for traditional Cretan crafts, as well as copies of the Minoan artefacts displayed in the Archaeological Museum across the square.

Lexis, Evans street. A good bookshop for English speakers.

Lyrarakis, 94 G. Papandréou, t 281 028 4614. An attractive old shop with a wide choice of Cretan wines.

Planet International, corner of Chándakos and Kydonias. Another shop with a wide choice of books in English.

Where to Stay

Heráklion ✉ 71500

Be sure to book ahead in summer, when millions pass through Heráklion, even if only for one night at a time. If you haven't reserved a room and can't find a place to stay, try the **Hotel Managers' Union**, 19 Giannitóson, t 281 028 1492, or the **Room Renters' Union**, 1 Gamaláki, t 281 022 4260, both of which have booking services.

Many visitors prefer to get a room in one of the beach hotels in the resorts either side of Heráklion, such as Ammoudára and Amnísos, and take day trips into town, rather than stay in the city itself; for these beach resorts, *see* pp.201–4,

Luxury

Atlantis, 2 Ighías, t 281 022 9103, f 281 022 6265, *www.grandhotel.gr* (A). Near the Archaeological Museum, this is Heráklion's traditional première hotel; it offers luxurious air-conditioned rooms (some with disabled access), a small indoor pool, a fitness club, two restaurants, satellite TV and a very pretty roof garden. *Open all year.*

Astoria Capsis, Plateía Eleftherías, t 281 034 3080, f 281 022 9078, *www.astoria-capsis.gr* (A). A similarly priced upscale hotel, also very central and just as smart as the Atlantis, with the impressively seductive extra of a rooftop pool and bar, plus a cinema next door. *Open all year.*

Galaxy, 67 Dimokratías, t 281 023 8812, f 281 021 1211, *galaxy@galaxy_hotels.com* (A). Just outside the city walls to the southeast, this stylish modern hotel offers contemporary serenity in its recently renovated rooms, all with full air-conditioning. The best rooms are the ones overlooking the pool and the sun terrace.

Expensive

Lato, 15 Epimenídou, t 281 022 8103, f 281 024 0350, *www.lato.gr* (*A*). A family-owned establishment that's well laid out as a boutique hotel following a major overhaul in 2001. Its contemporary-style rooms have internet hook ups throughout, and there are lovely sea views from all the balconies. An attractive option. *Open all year.*

Kastro, 22 Theotokópoulou, t 281 028 5020 (*B*). A more conventional city hotel near the El Greco park, but still with recently brightened-up rooms, each one with an internet port and air-conditioning.

Moderate

Many of Heráklion's mid-range hotels are located near the port and the bus stations.

Ilaira, 1 Ariádnis, t 281 022 7103, f 281 024 2367 (*C*). Traditionally decorated rooms with balcony and a cafeteria roof terrace; Ariádnis street is just south of Malikoúti, not far from the Archaeological Museum.

Daedalos, 15 Daedálou, t 281 024 4812, f 281 022 4391 (*C*). Also convenient for the museum and other sights in the centre of the city, and located on Heráklion's favourite pedestrian-only shopping street. Paintings by local artists are in the lobby, but otherwise it's plain and modern.

Kris, 2 Doukós Bofór, t 281 022 3211 (*C*). A friendly hotel near the ferry dock and the main bus depots, with a cheerful blue-and-red colour scheme and well-positioned rooms with fridges, a big plus in summer.

Inexpensive

Rea, 1 Kalimeráki, t 281 022 3638, f 281 024 2189 (*D*). One of the most pleasant cheap choices, near the sea at Plateía Neárchou, and quiet.

Atlas, 6 Kandanoléontos, t 281 028 8989 (*E*). A touch of streamlined Art Deco on a noisy pedestrianized street near the centre, although the rooms don't all live up to the promise of the exterior. *Open April–Oct.*

Youth Hostel, 5 Víronos, t 281 028 6281. Conveniently placed, and usually with a dorm bed to spare.

Rent Rooms Hellas, 24 Chandákos, t 281 028 0858. In the former youth hostel building, Hellas has all sorts of accommodation available at low prices.

Lena, 10 Lachaná, t 281 022 3280, f 281 024 2826 (*E*). Clean, simple rooms on a quiet street west of 25 Avgoustou.

Hellas, 11 Kandanoléontos, t 281 022 5121. Pleasant, friendly and has a courtyard.

Idaeon Andron, 1 Perdikári, t 281 028 1795. Behind the Venetian Loggia, this pension has pleasant small rooms and a tiny courtyard.

Eating Out

Trendies in Heráklion have created a quiet, car-free haven for themselves in the narrow streets between Daedálou and Ag. Titos, more or less around the Venetian Loggia; buildings have been cleaned up and restored, and the city's most charming little restaurants, tavernas, pizzerias and bars have appeared on cue to fill them up. Prices tend to be a bit over the odds by normal Cretan standards, but the food is often more imaginative than the local norm, too.

Loukoulous, 5 Korái, t 281 022 4435 (€*25–30*). An elegant restaurant in a beautifully restored old mansion, specializing in new-style Mediterranean dishes with Cretan and Italian touches, many of them prepared in a wood-fired oven. It's famous for its steaks, but you can get delicious pizza here as well. *Closed Sun lunch.*

Giovanni, Korái, t 281 034 6338 (€*20–25*). Just opposite the Loukoulous, this one offers tasty Italian cuisine, including the likes of mushroom risotto, a wonderful choice of pasta dishes and fresh fish served Italian-style, all topped off with rich Italian desserts. There's a choice of fixed-price menus for two, centred on fish, Italian, Greek and vege-tarian dishes, and an extensive wine list from Crete and the rest of Greece

Merastri, 17 Chrysóstomou, t 281 022 1910 (€*20*). A great new restaurant located in a charming old stone villa and serving some of the best Cretan food on the island, prepared in a traditional wood oven; high-lights are the delicious homemade bread, and roast lamb that will melt in your mouth. Chrysóstomou is the broad street that runs away southwards through new Heráklion from Plateía Kiproú and the Kenoúria gate. *Open June–Sept, eves only exc Sun.*

Odion, Mirampélou and Ariádnis, t 281 022 3393 (€20). Housed in the former music conservatory, behind the Atlantis hotel, the Odion offers elegant dining on Mediterranean and international classics, with a fine array of seafood dishes, accompanied by a huge choice of wine from the cellar. *Open eves only, exc Mon.*

Pagopolio, Plateía Ag. Títos, t 281 034 6028 (€20). Modern but welcoming place overlooking the lovely square of Ag. Títos, serving a range of international and Greek classics – often with a Cretan touch – as well as some of the chef's own creations.

Embolo, 7 Milara and Evans, t 281 028 4244 (€18). Come here for a dose of traditional food, firy *raki* and Cretan music; its owners, the Stavarkákis brothers, are both traditional musicians, and you can hear live music here every Tuesday, Friday and Saturday. *Open evenings only.*

Tazédikdo, 55 Dimokratías, t 281 024 5224. A restaurant of character, serving imaginative modern Greek cuisine using organic ingredients, including a good selection of tempting mezédes. *Open all year, eves only in summer.*

Kyriakos, 53 Dimokratías, t 281 022 4649. Next to the Tazédikdo, but much more traditional, this Heráklion institution serves the classics on white tablecloths, and is ever-popular with locals for its delicious homecooked dishes in big portions. *Closed Sun.*

Ionia, Evans, t 281 028 3213. The oldest *magirio* (old-fashioned Greek cookshop) in Heráklion, serving up some unusual mountain dishes such as goat with chestnuts or liver with rosemary. *Closed Sat and Sun eves*

Karavolas, 108 S Venizélou, t 281 025 5449. A bit away from the town centre and not much more than a shed by the sea, but it serves generous doses of cheap but perfectly prepared seafood every lunch time (and in evenings, too, July–Aug).

Curry House, Daedálou, by Perdikári, t 281 022 4274. For a change from the local fare, this restaurant Indian offers a classic curry mix.

Kirkor, Plateía El. Venizélou. The place to come to for local pies and *bougátsa* (sweet pies filled with creamy custard).

Themis, corner of Plateía Nikoforou Fóka and Dikeosínis. Famous for the best ice cream in town, as well as for traditional sweets.

Entertainment and Nightlife

El Greco (or more properly, Theotokopoúlos) **Park** is the place to head to for a shot of *raki* or *ouzo* to soften the day, before heading out to dinner. Each summer the clubs and discos by the beach to the west in **Ammoudára** are especially popular with young boppers, but if you'd rather stay in town, stroll down Doukós Bofór street or along the seafront to find the city's main clubs, and keep a look out for posters and fliers.

Heráklion attracts quite a few Greek and occasionally foreign bands on the concert circuit; in the summer, too, occasional performances are presented in the **Rocco al Mare** citadel on the Venetian Harbour, especially as part of the Irakleio Festival.

Café Veneto, 9 Epimenídou, t 281 022 3686. One of the city's most sophisticated venues: this elegant day- and nightspot, not far from 25 Avgoustou, has an alluring roof terrace overlooking the port.

Idaeon Andron, Korai and Perdikari, t 281 024 2041. A cool and trendy late-night bar – near the pension of the same name – that's excellent for quiet backgammon and drinks or rounding off an intimate evening, with a mellow jazz background.

Kastro, Doukós Bofór. A much more traditional, very locally oriented night out, with Cretan music and dancing presented in time-honoured Greek style.

Portside Club. On the seafront, this buzzy disco-bar is extremely popular with young Greeks, who knock back drinks around the cross-shaped bar.

Limeniko Café, S. Venizélou. On the seafront just west of the Venetian Harbour, and mercifully isolated from the traffic, this club-bar has an eclectic soundtrack of international pop-rock as well as traditional Greek music.

Loft Club, S. Venizélou. Next door to the Limeniko, this classic disco-club opens its doors to the masses at midnight and keeps buzzing until daylight.

Privilege, 7 Doukós Bofór, t 281 034 3500. Another essential port of call for those who are still full of beans late at night.

and enjoys splendid views of the city (*t 281 028 9935; open Tues–Sat 8.30–3, Sun 10–3; adm*). The looming arches of the Venetian **Arsenali**, or shipyards, have been partially obscured by the street, and although less impressive today than the fortress they too were vital in maintaining the sea links that allowed the city to hold out for so long.

The main street ascending into town from the Venetian Harbour, **25 Ávgoustou** street (the former Venetian *Ruga Maistra*) has several stately neoclassical buildings, housing shipping agents, car hire shops and banks; in the 1900s it was nicknamed 'Street of Misconceptions', because its relative grandeur hid the slums on either side. Halfway up, handsomely set back in its own square, is the Byzantine church of **Ag. Títos**, which owes its stately cubic form to the Turks, who used it as a mosque and rebuilt it after various earthquakes, lastly in 1869; note the base of the minaret on the side of the narthex. The chapel to the left of the narthex houses the island's most precious relic, the head of St Titus, a favourite disciple of St Paul and first bishop of Crete, who died in Górtyn *c.* AD 96. When forced to give up Crete the Venetians made off with Titus' skull, and only returned it when Pope Paul VI obliged them to, in 1966.

It takes a bit of imagination to reconstruct it, but homesick Venetians designed what is now **Plateía Venizélou**, at the top of 25 Ávgoustou, as a miniature Piazza San Marco. Heráklion's City Hall now occupies the handsome, Palladian-influenced **Venetian Loggia** (1628), the fourth in a series, built by the city's 'General Provisioner' or *Provveditor* Francesco Morosini as a meeting place for the Venetian and Cretan nobility. The inner *exedra* is covered with fine Renaissance reliefs of weapons and frowning bookworm lions (actually copies, as the damaged originals are in the

The Siege of Heráklion: 1648–69

After the Turks took Réthymnon in 1646, their battle plan was to capture the rest of Crete and so isolate Heráklion behind its beetling walls. Although the Venetians and Cretans put up a brave resistance, by 1648 the whole of the island except for Heráklion and the island fortresses at Gramvoúsa, Soúda and Spinalónga had fallen. These were desperate times; although the Turks won points with the locals by promising early on to remove all Latin bishops from Crete and restore the Orthodox hierarchy to its pre-eminent position, one account says that in one year alone (1657) some 60,000 Cretans, their homes destroyed in the battles, converted to Islam to avoid the crippling taxes levied on non-Muslims.

The siege of Heráklion began in May 1648, when the Turks under their commander Deli Hussein cut off the aqueduct from Archánes and surrounded and bombarded the walls. Sixteen years later, they were in exactly the same spot, although by this point the Turks had become convinced that the citadel was somehow enchanted; the frustrated Sultan refused to hear its name mentioned in his presence. The Cretans owed much of their staying power to Francesco Morosini, admiral of Venice's Aegean fleet (from the same family as the *Provveditor* Morosini, and uncle of the Francesco who blew the top off the Parthenon), who kept close tabs on the Turkish navy and thwarted all attempts to cut off the city by sea. But mostly the Turks found their war with the Holy Roman Empire more pressing than conquering Crete.

Historical Museum); the upper freize, which was never completed, once supported an array of rooftop statues. Under the Turks the building became the seat of the finance officer, the *Tefterdar*, and the secretary in charge of Christian affairs; subsequently it has suffered an earthquake and other troubles, but in 1987 it was awarded a Europa Nostra prize for its restoration. Also near the square is **San Marco (Ag. Márkos)**, the first Venetian church on Crete (1239). Twice rebuilt after earthquakes, stripped of its lofty campanile and converted into a mosque, it has been restored for use as a concert hall and exhibition centre. Water dribbles (usually) from the mouths of the lions of the **Morosini Fountain**, commissioned in 1626 by Francesco Morosini, who brought water in from Mount Júktas to replace the old wells and cisterns. Although minus its figure of Neptune, the sculptural decoration of sea nymphs and mermen riding sea monsters, dolphins and bulls is some of the finest Venetian work on Crete; the 14th-century lions were filched from an older fountain.

South of Plateía Venizélou, the city's outdoor **market** down 1866 street resembles a bazaar, a permanent display of Crete's extraordinary fecundity. Several stalls sell dried Cretan wedding cakes – golden wreaths decorated with scrolls and rosettes. Similar forays into the Baroque can be seen at the south end of the market in **Plateía Kornárou**, in carvings adorning the **Bembo Fountain** (1588), which was put together by the Venetians from ancient fragments, including a headless Roman statue brought from Ierápetra; the Turks added the charming kiosk-fountain, or **Koúbes**, now a café, and the Cretans added the modern sculptures of Erotókritos and Arethoúsa, the hero and heroine of their national epic poem. To the east, the great hemicycle of **Plateía**

The turning point came in 1664, when the treaty of Vasvar freed up Ottoman troops to make a concerted effort on Crete. In 1666 Deli Hussein was recalled to Istanbul, beheaded and replaced by the Grand Vizir Ahmet Köprülü, victor over the Austrians, who staked his reputation on being able to take the city. In response Venice, which had implored other European powers to help defend the last Christian outpost in the eastern Mediterranean, sent reinforcements under their gallant Francesco Morosini.

The arrival of Köprülü outside the walls of Heráklion with 40,000 fresh Ottoman troops finally nudged the Europeans into action, but they arrived only to quarrel, and their troops and supplies were all too little, too late. In 1667, the defenders suffered a grave setback when the Greek colonel Andreas Barótsis deserted to the Turks and betrayed all the weak spots on the walls (Köprülü made it known he had a fortune to offer anyone who changed sides). Still the walls held out, and in May 1669 the last reinforcements arrived, 6,000 French troops under the Duke of Beaufort, who gave his name to the street Doukós Bofór, above the harbour, and died shortly afterwards with 500 of his men in a hopeless foray which led to the French pulling out altogether. Seeing that his men could only hold out a few more days, Morosini secretly negotiated the city's surrender on 5 September, and with 20 days of safe conduct sailed away with nearly all the Christian inhabitants of Heráklion, all the possessions they could carry and the city's archives (in the belief that Venice would some day regain Crete), a result bought with the lives of 30,000 Christians and 137,000 Turks.

Eleftherías, a major traffic and transport hub of modern Heráklion, is dotted with monuments to the Unknown Soldier and to great Cretans with equally great moustaches, surrounded by cafés and sweet shops that haven't changed since the 1970s.

The Archaeological Museum

t 281 022 6092; open April–Oct, Tues–Sun 8am–7pm, Mon noon–7pm; Nov–Mar, Tues–Sun 8am–5pm, Mon noon–5pm; adm. To avoid the endless tour groups, arrive early; note that your ticket is valid for the whole day, so if you get overwhelmed you can go out for a drink or lunch and re-enter later.

Heráklion's Archaeological Museum, a short walk north of Plateía Eleftherías, is an ungainly, somewhat airless coffer that holds the greatest treasures of Minoan civilization. Thanks to Cretan archaeologist Joseph Hadzidákis, a law was passed in the early days of Crete's autonomy which decreed that every important antiquity found on the island belongs to the museum. The resulting collection – arranged in chronological order – is dazzling, delightful and entirely too much to digest in one visit.

Neolithic to the Old Palace Period: Rooms I–III

Room I begins with artefacts from the Neolithic (from 5000 BC) and Pre-Palatial periods (2600–2000 BC); the fine craftsmanship that would characterize Minoan art is already apparent in delicate golden leaf pendants, polished stone vessels, boldly shaped red and black Vasilikí pottery and carved sealstones (especially the unique 16-sided hieroglyphic seal from Archánes, in Case 11). Crete's future obsession with bulls is revealed in three tiny noodly clay men clinging to the head of a bull; early Cycladic idols and Egyptian seals from tombs of the Mesará plain point to a precocious trade network. **Rooms II** and **III** are devoted to the Old Palace era (2000–1700 BC), when the Minoans made their first polychromatic Kamáres ware, anticipating the aims of Art Nouveau: each work was individually crafted, marrying form and decoration, using stylized natural motifs. The extraordinary virtuosity of Minoan potters 3,500 years ago is especially striking in their delicate 'eggshell ware' cups. One case displays the famed **Knossos Town Mosaic**: faïence plaques, each shaped and painted like a miniature Minoan house, used by Arthur Evans as a guide in his reconstructions at Knossos.

Phaistos in particular flourished in Old Palace times. The Kamáres vases found there reached a dizzying peak of decorative richness, studded with high-relief flowers and scalloped edgings, evidence that the multi-talented Minoans may also have been the first to wander into kitsch. The mysterious clay **Phaistos Disc** (*c.* 1700 BC), in the centre of Room III, is the earliest known example of moveable type: 45 different symbols are stamped on both sides in a spiral. The theory that the disc is a forgery has been disproved by the discovery of seals with similar pictures and/or ideograms. At least a dozen translations have been attempted, but none has been taken seriously.

The New Palace Period: Rooms IV–IX

The vast majority of exhibits date from the Minoans' Golden Age, the New Palace period (1700–1450 BC), arranged more or less geographically in **Rooms IV–IX**. Potters

A Fresh Look at the Frescoes

What should be a major controversy over artistic restoration has still not really got underway. Yet, look closely at the Minoan frescoes in Heráklion's Archaeological Museum (*see* p.187). On most there's a stark difference between what you think are the frescoes, and certain dark crumbly bits that seem to deface the figures. Most people are amazed to discover that these crumbly bits are in fact all that survives of the originals, and the rest – 90 per cent in some cases – is entirely the work of Arthur Evans' restorers, notably Edmund Gillérion. The famous *La Parisienne* is one of the very few frescoes in which the face was entirely intact.

Some archaeologists deride their work as completely fanciful, too close to the Art Nouveau popular in Evans' time. This is very unfair, but perhaps typical of the urge among many scientific-minded types to deny the existence of what they cannot explain. In fact, the restorers did a masterful job, and on the whole an honest one. But many of their interpretations can still be questioned, as in the *Fresco of Women* from the East Wing at Knossos, where faces, poses, and most decorative detail were inferred from other works, or even invented. These frescoes just happens to be among the greatest artistic achievements of all time – and maybe there should be a bit of controversy, if doubt exists about the way they are presented to us. One might complain, for example, that the precise draughtsmanship of the restorers distorts the feeling of the originals, done in looser, more casual brushstrokes.

The problem with this kind of controversy is one of divided interests. Full-time archaeologists often have little artistic understanding, but know the details of how such frescoes are reassembled, how surfaces and pigments react over time, and so on. Art historians have been slow to take on this subject, perhaps for fear of stepping on archaeologists' toes. Maybe the two should get together; the Knossos restorations make lovely and familiar images, but it may be time to take a closer look.

turned to even freer, more naturalistic designs, with floral and marine motifs. Stone vases and *rhytons* (ritual pouring vessels) became ever more rarefied as the Minoans sought the hardest and rarest marbles, porphyrys and semi-precious stones to carve and polish, bringing out their swirling grain. **Room IV** contains several masterpieces: a magnificent bull's head *rhyton* in black steatite, with eyes of rock crystal and jasper (and modern gilt wooden horns), found in the Little Palace at Knossos; the leopard axe from Mália; and, from the main palace at Knossos, the bare-breasted snake goddess statuettes; a draughtsboard in ivory, rock crystal, blue glass paste and gold and silver leaf, complete with four gaming pieces; and the ivory bull leaper, the oldest known statue of a freely moving human figure. Muscles and tendons are exquisitely carved, especially in the hand. Fragments of two other figures suggest that the bull leaper formed part of a composition, not unlike the one shown in the *Toreador* fresco.

In **Room V** are finds from Knossos that just pre-date its destruction in 1450 BC, when the Linear A and Linear B clay tablets in Case 69 were baked in the conflagration. **Room VI** has finds from cemeteries at Knossos, Archánes and Phaistos (New Palace and Post-Palace, 1450–1300 BC). Miniature sculptures offer clues about Minoan funerary practices, banquets and dances; an ivory *pyxis* (jewellery box) shows a band of men hunting a bull. Gold-working reached its height in this period; note especially the Isopata seal ring, showing four ladies ecstatically dancing. Another in a similar style is believed to show tree-worship, as does the famous *Ring of Minos*, a gold ring found by a young boy at Knossos in 1928. It was long believed to be lost, after the boy's father confided it to a priest who demanded a fortune for it, but one of the priest's heirs recently turned it over to the museum. Several works in this room show the influence of the Mycenaeans (the ivory plaques with warriors' heads), who are also made to answer for weapons that made an appearance on Crete – boar tusk and bronze helmets and 'gold-nailed swords' as described by Homer. The pot of carefully arranged horse bones is a sacrifice from the Mycenaean/Minoan tomb at Archánes.

Items found in the luxurious country villas of central Crete fill **Room VII**. The show-stoppers here are the gold jewellery pieces, particularly the exquisite pendant of two bees depositing a drop of honey in a comb and the three black steatite vessels from Ag. Triáda, with beautifully executed low reliefs. The *Harvesters' Vase* shows a band of men with winnowing rods, accompanied by what looks like a priest and band of singers. On the *Cup of the Chieftain* a young man with a sword over his shoulder reports to a long-haired chieftain clad in boots, loincloth and a necklace; a *rhyton* has four zones depicting lively athletic scenes: boxing, wrestling and bull sports.

The New Palace period contents of **Room VIII** are from Zákros, the only large palace to escape ancient plunderers. The floral and marine pottery is delightful, and the stone vases include a little rock-crystal amphora with a handle of crystal beads and a green stone *rhyton* with a scene of a Minoan peak sanctuary, in which springing wild goats and birds presumably represent an epiphany of the goddess. **Room IX** has items from ordinary Minoan houses of the era. The collection of seals is exceptional; no two are alike, although many repeat motifs, in natural or religious scenes. Minoan engravers achieved an astounding technique; suspicions they must have used lenses to do such work were confirmed when one of rock crystal was found at Knossos.

Post-Palace and Later: Rooms X–XIII

The Post-Palace period artefacts in **Room X** (1450–1100 BC) show a gradual decline in inspiration, a coarsening, and ever-heavier Mycenaean influences. Pottery decoration is increasingly limited to strict bands of patterns. Figures lose their grace and *joie de vivre*; the clay goddess statuettes are stiff and stylized, their flouncy skirts reduced to smooth bells, their breasts to nubs, their arms invariably lifted, as if imploring the fickle heavens. A terracotta group of women seem to perform a modern Cretan dance. One goddess has opium poppies sprouting from her hat; Minoan religion and artistic creation may well have involved the use of opium and alcohol (this may also explain their apparent lack of aggression compared to other 'cradles of civilization').

The Dorian invasion or immigration heralded an artistic dark age, evident in the Sub-Minoan and Early Geometric periods of **Room XI** (1100–900 BC); the quality of the work is poor all round, and generally limited to simple, abstract linear decoration, whether made by tenacious pockets of Minoan refugees or by the invaders; among the finer pieces are the votive offerings dedicated to Eileithyia, the protectress of childbirth, from the cave of Inatos, and a *rhyton* in the form of an ox-drawn chariot.

Room XII shows an improvement in life and art in the Mature Geometric and Orientalizing periods (900–650 BC), when Crete was probably the richest place in Greece. Familiar Greek gods make an appearance: Zeus holding an eagle and three thunderbolts on a pot lid, Hermes with sheep and goats on a bronze votive plaque. Huge Geometric vases are decorated with polychromatic patterns; Orientalizing pottery, with its griffon, sphinx and lion motifs, shows the eastern influences that dominated Greek civilization in the 8th–7th centuries. One vase, in Case 163, shows a pair of lovers, naturally presumed to be Theseus and Ariadne. Bronze offerings found in the Idaean Cave are especially intriguing, notably a couple in a boat. Some fine gold work has survived, as well as a terracotta model of a tree covered with doves.

At the foot of the stairs, **Room XIII** contains Minoan *larnaxes*, or terracotta sarcophagi. Minoans were buried in a foetal position, so their tombs are quite small; in the Old Palace days they were made of wood, and the changeover to clay suggests the Minoans may have over-exploited their forests. The belief that living Minoans used their *larnaxes* for bathtubs before they died seems absurd but widely held, perhaps because it supports Evans' designation of the Queen's bathroom at Knossos.

Second Floor: The Frescoes

Yet another art the Minoans excelled at was fresco, displayed upstairs in **Rooms XIV–XVI**. Almost as fascinating as the paintings themselves is the work that went into their reconstruction by the Swiss father-and-son team hired by Evans. In painting the Cretans followed Egyptian conventions in colour: women are white, men are red, monkeys are blue, a revelation that led to the re-restoration of *The Saffron Gatherers*, one of the oldest frescoes, originally restored to show a boy and now reconstructed as a monkey picking crocuses, after a similar subject was found at the Minoan colony on Santoríni. The first room contains the larger frescoes from the palace of Knossos, such as the nearly completely intact *Cup-Bearer* from the *Procession* fresco, which once lined the Corridor of the Procession and great Propylon and is believed to have shown 350 figures altogether. Here too are *The Dolphins*, *The Prince of the Lilies*, *The Shields*, and the charming *Partridges* found in the 'Caravanserai' near Knossos, and the *Lilies* from Amnísos. The 'miniature frescoes' in the other two rooms include the celebrated *Parisienne*, as she was dubbed by her discoverers in 1903, with her eye-paint, lipstick and 'sacral knot' jauntily tied at the back; others, full of tiny figures, show a ceremonial dance and a tripartite shrine ritual. Then take a good look at the most famous fresco of all, *The Bull Leapers* (or *Toreadors*, see p.188)

The Ag. Triáda Sarcophagus

In pride of place in the centre of the upper floor, this sarcophagus is the only stone *larnax* found on Crete. However, what really sets it apart is its layer of plaster painted so elaborately that it strongly suggests the sarcophagus held the remains of a VIP before it was re-used in an insignificant tomb in Ag. Triáda. The subject is a Minoan ritual: on one side a bull is sacrificed, blood pouring from its neck caught in a vase. A woman makes an offering on an altar, next to a sacred tree with a bird in its branches, the epiphany of the goddess; a man plays a flute as three other women enter in procession. On the other long side of the tomb two women, to the left, are bearing buckets, perhaps of bull's blood, which are emptied into a larger pot between pillars topped by birds and double axes. They are accompanied by a man in female dress, playing a lyre. On the right three men carry animals and a model boat, which they offer to an armless, legless figure, either a dead man, wrapped like a mummy, or an idol or *xoanan*, as worshipped at Archánes (*see* p.204). On the narrow sides of the sarcophagus, pairs of women ride in chariots pulled by griffons and a horse.

The Bull in the Calendar

... there too is Knossos, a mighty city, where Minos was king for nine years,
a familiar of mighty Zeus.

Odyssey, book XIX, translated by Robert Fitzgerald

The so-called 'Toreador Fresco' found at Knossos is one of the most compelling icons of the lost world of ancient Crete. The slender, sensual, bare-breasted maidens who seem to be controlling the action are painted white, the moon's colour, as in all Cretan frescoes, while the athlete vaulting through the bull's horns appears, like all males, in red, colour of the sun. Mythology and archaeology begin to agree, and the roots of the story of Theseus, Ariadne and the Minotaur seem tantalizingly close.

Note the border – four striped bands and a row of multicoloured lunettes. Neither Arthur Evans nor other archaeologists noticed anything unusual about it. An English professor from Maine named Charles F. Herberger (*The Thread of Ariadne*, 1972) was the first to see that this border is in fact a complex ritual calendar, the key to the myth of Theseus in the Labyrinth and much else. The pairs of stripes on the tracks, alternately dark and light, for day and night, count on average 29 through each cycle of five-coloured lunettes, representing the phases of the moon – this is the number of days in a lunar month. By counting the stripes on the four tracks, Herberger found that each track gives roughly the number of days in a year; the whole, when doubled, totals exactly the number of days in an eight-year cycle of 99 lunar months, a period in which the solar and lunar years coincide – the marriage of sun and moon.

To decipher the calendar, you can't simply count in circuits around the border; there are regular diagonal jumps to a new row, giving the course of the eight-year cycle the form of a rectangle with an 'x' in it. The box with the 'x' is intriguing, a motif in the art of the Cretans and other ancient peoples as far afield as the Urartians of eastern Anatolia. A Cretan seal shows a bull apparently diving into a crossed rectangle of this sort, while a human figure vaults through his horns. Similar in form is the most common and most enigmatic of all Cretan symbols, the double axe or *labrys*. The form is echoed further in a number of seals that show the x-shaped cross between the horns of a bull, or between what appear to be a pair of crescent moons.

The home of the *labrys*, the axe that cuts two ways, is the labyrinth. Arthur Evans believed the rambling palace of Knossos itself to be the labyrinth, a pile so confusing even a Greek hero would have needed Ariadne's golden thread to find his way through it. In the early days of archaeology, men could read myths so literally as to think there was a tangible labyrinth, and perhaps even a Minotaur. Now, it seems

Near the sarcophagus is a fine model of Knossos, and the **Giamalakis collection** (**Room XVII**), with unique items from all the Cretan periods, from a finely worked Neolithic goddess, unusually seated in a lotus position, to a curious model of a round shrine from the Proto-Geometric era. Two figures on the roof peer down through a light-well at the goddess (with uplifted arms), revealed through a detachable door.

Downstairs again, there are products of ancient Crete's last great breath of artistic inspiration, the bold, severe 'Daedalic style' of the Archaic period (700–650 BC),

more likely the labyrinth was the calendar itself, the twisting path that a *Minos*, a generic name for Cretan priest-kings, representing the sun, followed in his eight-year reign before his inevitable rendezvous with the great goddess. This meeting may originally have meant his death (in a bull mask perhaps) and replacement by another Theseus; later it may have been simply a ceremony of remarriage to the priestess who stood in the transcendent goddess's place, celebrated with a bull-vaulting ritual. It has been claimed the occasion was also accompanied by dancing, following the shape of the labyrinth, where dancers proceeded in a line holding a cord – Ariadne's thread. Homer said 'nine years', and other sources give nine years as the period after which the Athenians had to send captives to Crete to be devoured by the Minotaur – it's a common ancient confusion, really meaning 'until the ninth', in the way the French still call the interval of a week *huit jours*. Whatever this climax of the Cretan cycle was, it occurred with astronomical precision following the calendar, and a rich, many-layered symbolism difficult for us scoffing moderns ever to comprehend.

That the Cretans had such a complex calendar should be no surprise – a people who managed plumbing and three-storey apartment blocks, and still found time to rule the Mediterranean seas. The real attraction lies not just in the intricacies of the calendar, but in the scene in the middle, where the diagonals cross and the ancient science translates into celebration, into dance. Cretan art speaks to everyone, with a colour, beauty and immediacy never before seen in art, and all too lacking in our own time. No other art of antiquity displays such an irresistible grace and joy, qualities which must have come from a profound appreciation of the beauties and rhythms of nature – the rhythms captured and framed in the ancient calendar.

contained in **Rooms XVIII** and **XIX**. Among the terracotta votives from Gortyn note the figure of Athena, with a face like an African mask and a helmet that looks like a fish hook. There is a striking frieze of warriors from Ryzenia and bronze votive shields and cymbals from the Idaean Cave, one showing Zeus holding a lion over his head while the *Kouretes* bang their shields; stylistically they seem Syrian or Phoenician, and chances are they were made by craftsmen from the Middle East who came to work on Crete. The figures in hammered bronze of Apollo, Artemis and Leto, from the 8th-century BC Temple of Apollo at Dreros, are other key Daedalic works, and the oldest surviving cult images in Greece. The bronze goddesses, mother and daughter, are here reduced to anthropomorphic pillars, their once dancing arms now glued to their sides, their outlandish hats, jewels and flounced topless skirts reduced to something approaching a nun's habit. They could be a salt and pepper set. Yet the real anticlimax is reserved for **Room XX**, on Classical Greece and the Graeco-Roman period, when Crete, one of the cradles of the 'Greek miracle', was left an insignificant backwater.

The Cathedral and the Byzantine Museum

Across on the other side of the old city, west of Plateía Venizélou and south of Kalokerinoú, is the overblown cathedral dedicated to Heráklion's patron **Ag. Miná** (1895), which dwarfs its convivial little predecessor next door. The interior, able to hold 5,000 parishioners and with a special women's section, is pure Byzantine revival, illuminated by an insanely over-decorated chandelier, the domes and vaults frescoed throughout with stern and sad saints and a ferocious *Pantokrator*; the clock, from Smyrna, has Arabic numerals, rarely seen in a Greek church. **Old Ag. Miná**, in contrast, has a beautiful gilt iconostasis with fine icons; one of St. Minas on his white horse has long been the special protector of Heráklion (Orthodox martyrology claims that Minas was a 3rd-century Egyptian soldier, but you can't help wondering if his name had something to do with his special veneration here in the old port of Knossos).

On the same square is sun-bleached **Ag. Ekaterína** (1555), in its day an important school linked to the Monastery of St Catherine on Mount Sinai. One subject taught here was icon painting – El Greco studied here before leaving for Venice – and today the church appropriately holds a **Museum of Byzantine Icons** (*t 281 028 8825; open Mon, Wed, Sat 9.30–2.30; Tues, Thurs, Fri 9.30–2.30 and 4.30–6.30; adm*). The pride of the museum is six icons by Micháil Damáskinos, the contemporary of El Greco who also went to Venice but returned to Crete to adorn his motherland with Renaissance-inspired icons; the use of a gold background and Greek letters are the only Byzantine elements in his delightful masterpiece, *The Adoration of the Magi*. In his *Last Supper*, Damáskinos set a Byzantine Jesus in a setting copied from an Italian engraving – a bizarre effect heightened by the fact that Christ seems to be holding a hamburger.

Other Museums in Heráklion

Behind the Archaeological Museum, on the corner of Doukós Bófor and Hatzidáki, is the **Battle of Crete and Resistance Museum** (*t 281 034 6554; open Mon–Fri 8–3*), a collection of weapons, photos and uniforms giving a full account of the fierce Cretan struggle in 1941–4. Across the street, note the uprooted stacks of Turkish tombstones.

The **Historical Museum of Crete** (*t 281 022 8708; open Mon–Fri 9–5, Sat 9–2; adm*) is across town at 7 Kalokairinoú, near the seafront and the ruined Venetian church of San Pietro. Housed in the neoclassical mansion of its founder, Andréas Kalokairinós, and a newer annex, this fine collection picks up the thread where the Archaeological Museum leaves off, beginning with artefacts from Early Christian times. There are delightful 18th-century Turkish frescoes of imaginary towns, pretty odds and ends from Venetian churches, a 12th-century marble well carved with hunting scenes, Venetian and Turkish tombs, coats-of arms, the original carvings from the Loggia, a delightful Venetian wall fountain made of tiny jutting ships' prows, ships' figure-heads, sultans' *firmans*, portraits of Cretan revolutionaries and their 'Freedom or Death' flag, a large coin collection, icons, more religious relics and excellent 14th-century wall paintings, by Kardoulianó Pediádos. In a little room all to itself hangs the *Imaginary View of Mount Sinai and the Monastery of St Catherine* (*c*. 1576) by Doménikos Theotokópoulos (El Greco), his only known painting on Crete. It is also one of his few landscapes – in Italy and Spain, where he spent the rest of his life, they weren't very marketable. Although the painting is still very post-Byzantine in style, the mountains foreshadow a little of the magic of his *View of Toledo*. There are also photographs of Cretan *kapetános*, each one bristling with bigger moustaches and more weapons in his bandolier than the last. They make a striking contrast with the reconstructed libraries of famous locals who lived by the pen, Níkos Kazantzákis and Emmanuél Tsouderós, once prime minister of Greece. Other rooms contain a sump-tuous array of traditional crafts, such as intricate red embroideries and weavings from Ottoman Crete; some 700 traditional patterns have been recorded.

The **Natural History Museum of Crete** (*t 281 032 4711; open daily 9–7; adm*), outside the walls southwest of town at 157 Knossóu, is a recently-opened venture run by the University of Crete. It takes a serious look at the island's flora and fauna, with special sections on endangered animals, life in caves, and how human settlements have used and adapted the island's natural resources. Outside it is a botanical garden with plants endemic to Crete – including its now rare magic herb, dittany (*see* p.228).

The Venetian Walls and the Tomb of Kazantzákis

Michele Sammicheli, the greatest military architect of the 16th century, designed the 4 kilometres of walls and 12 fort-like bastions around Heráklion's historic centre so well that it took the Turks 21 years to get inside. Brilliantly restored, the walls are nearly as vexing to get on top of today as they were for 1660s besiegers; in places they stand 46ft thick. Tunnels have been pierced through the old gates, but the **Chaniá Gate** (**Pórta Chaníon**) at the western end of Kalokerinoú preserves much of its original appearance. At the southern end of the walls, a side street leads up from N. Plastirá street to the **Martinengo Bastion**, largest strongpoint in the walls and the highest point in the city. Inside it there is a stadium and the simple **tomb of Níkos Kazantzákis**. Heráklion's great writer, who died in 1957, chose his own epitaph: 'I believe in nothing, I hope for nothing, I am free.' Sometimes you'll see offerings of fruit, which he requested just before he died; the pious have erected a simple wooden cross. In the distance you can see the striking form of Mount Júktas (*see* p.208).

Knossos (ΚΝΩΣΟΣ)

City bus no.2 departs for Knossos every 10 minutes from near the Lassíthi bus station in Heráklion (C on map, p.176), with a stop in Plateía Venizélou.
The site (t 281 023 1940) is open daily 8–7, except for important holidays; adm exp. To avoid the crowds, arrive as the gate opens or come late in the day. The free car park fills up fast, but private ones have opened up along the road.

The weird dream-image has come down through the ages: Knossos, the House of the Double Axe, the Labyrinth of King Minos. The audacious bull dances, secret mysteries and Jungian archetypes evoke a deep, mythopœic resonance few places in Europe can equal. Thanks in good part to Arthur Evans' imaginative if controversial reconstructions, brightly painted in primary colours and rising up two storeys against the hill-girded plain, Knossós has become the second most visited place in Greece after the Acropolis. Plus, tall cypresses and views of the jagged hills and olive groves to the east and vineyards to the south make Knossos something of a garden ruin.

History

The first Neolithic houses on the hill next to the Kairatos river, which may then have been navigable, date from the 7th millennium BC, or perhaps earlier; few Neolithic sites in Europe were so deeply rooted in the earth. In the 3rd millennium an Early Minoan settlement was built over the Neolithic houses, and *c.* 1950 BC the first palace on Crete was erected on top. It collapsed in the earthquake of 1700 and a new, even grander palace, the Labyrinth, was built on its ruins. 'Labyrinth' derives from *labrys*, or 'Double Axe', a potent symbol that suggests the killing of both victim and slayer; you'll see them etched on pillars and walls throughout Knossos. For the next 300 years new buildings went up all around the palace; vast cemeteries, stretching all the way to Heráklion's modern cemetery of Ag. Konstantínos, attest to a large population. In 1450 BC (give or take a century or two) Knossos was again destroyed by a huge fire but, unlike the other palaces, it was repaired once more, probably by Mycenaeans, and survived at least until 1380 BC. After a final destruction, the site was never built on again; it was considered evil, cursed in some way. Evans noted during his excavations that the guardians he hired to watch the site heard ghosts moaning in the night.

In the Geometric era a community near Knossos adopted its name, and by the 3rd century BC was one of Crete's leading cities, although later it lost its supremacy to Gortyn. The Romans built a city here that survived into the Byzantine era. Meanwhile the ruined palace was slowly buried, but not forgotten; unlike Troy and Mycenae, the site was always known. Cretans went there to gather *galopetres* – 'milkstones' – Minoan sealstones, which nursing mothers prized as amulets to increase their milk.

The Labyrinth lay quietly through the centuries until the great German self-taught archaeologist Heinrich Schliemann's excavations of Troy and Mycenae electrified the world. In 1878 a merchant from Heráklion, appropriately named Mínos Kalokairinós, dug the first trenches into the palace of his namesake, at once finding walls, enormous *pithoi* and the first Linear B tablet. Schliemann heard the news and in 1882, when he met a young English Classics scholar named Arthur Evans, confided to him

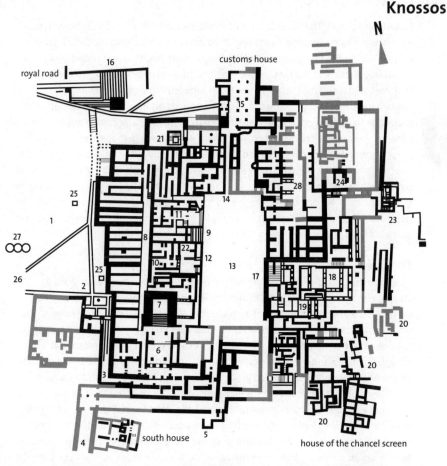

Knossos

N

royal road | 16

customs house

15

21

28

24

14

25

1

23

27

8

11

9

25

22

12

26

2

10

13

17

18

7

19

20

3

20

6

20

4

south house · 5

house of the chancel screen

1	West Court	11	Throne Room	21	north lustral basin
2	west porch	12	Tripartite Shrine	22	temple repositories
3	Corridor of the Procession	13	Central Court	23	east bastion
4	stepped porch	14	north entrance passage	24	store rooms of giant pithoi
5	south entrance	15	North Pillar Hall	25	altar
6	south Propylon	16	theatre	26	bust of Arthur Evans
7	Grand Stair	17	Grand Staircase	27	storage silos
8	store room corridor	18	Hall of the Double Axes	28	Corridor of the
9	stair	19	Queen's Megaron		Draughtboard
10	pillar crypts	20	southeast house		

his plans to excavate Knossós one day. Five years later Schliemann arrived on Crete and negotiated the purchase of the site, but the Turkish owners were impossible to deal with and asked for too much money. He left in despair, and in 1890 he died.

The field thus cleared, Evans, by then curator of the Ashmolean Museum in Oxford, arrived in Crete in 1894. A keen student of early forms of writing, he was especially fascinated by the mysterious script on Cretan sealstones and the Linear B tablet shown him by Kalokairinós. He spent the next five years purchasing the property with the help of Cretan archaeologist Joseph Hadzadákis, while sending home reports of

Turkish oppression. The purchase of Knossos coincided happily with Cretan independence, and on 23 March 1900 Evans began excavations jointly with the British School at Athens. Within the first three weeks the throne room had been excavated, along with fresco fragments and the first Linear A tablets, apparently belonging to a civilization that predated the Mycenaeans, which Evans labelled 'Minoan' for ever after.

When his father and uncle died in 1908, Evans used his inheritance to embark on a project he had dreamed of, to 'reconstitute' part of Minos' palace. Scholars dispute the wisdom and accuracy of his reconstructions; they disagree perhaps even more on the purposes and names Evans assigned the different rooms of the palace, along with his interpretation of the Minoans as peaceful, flower-loving sophisticates. Evans' Queen's bathroom, for instance, may have been a basin where dead bodies were pickled before mummification. No one conjecture seems to cover all the evidence, all the myths; the true meaning and use of Knossos may only lie in an epiphany of the imagination. The Cretans of 4,000 years ago saw a different world through different eyes.

The Site

Despite the controversy, Evans' reconstructions result from guesses as good as anyone else's, and succeed in his goal of making Knossos come alive for the casual visitor. They evoke the grandeur of a 1,500-room Minoan palace in a way none of the unreconstructed sites can match; a visit here makes Phaistos, Mália and Zákros easier to understand. Detailed guides are on sale, but tours go through so often that it's easy to tag along and overhear explanations. A first stop is the Bust of Evans, erected by the British School and unveiled in 1935, occasioning Evans' last visit to Knossos.

Unlike most of their ancient contemporaries, Minoans oriented their palaces to the west, not east, and the modern entrance is still the **West Court**. The three large holes were grain silos, originally protected by domes; later residents used them for rubbish. To the right a porch leads to the **Corridor of the Procession**, named after the fresco in the Heráklion museum, and the **Propylon** or south entrance. Steps lead from there to an upper floor that Evans, inspired by Venetian palaces, called the '**Piano Nobile**'. Of all his reconstructions, this is considered the most fanciful. The **Tripartite Shrine**, with its three columns, is typical of Minoan palaces and may have been used to worship the Goddess in her three aspects of mistress of heaven, earth and the underworld.

A narrower staircase descends to the **Central Court**, measuring 196ft by 98ft (60m by 30m). This was once closed in by tall buildings, which among other things may have provided seats to view the bull leaping (although leading bulls in through the Labyrinth would have been problematical; in another theory the court was 'Ariadne's dancing floor'). The monumental **Horns of Consecration** of porous stone that decorate the cornices and altars are perhaps the most universal Minoan symbol. Knossos was littered with horns of all sizes (one pair, found in fragments, was once 4ft high).

From here enter the lower levels of the **West Wing**, site of the **Antechamber** and the surprisingly tiny, shadowy **Throne Room**, where Evans uncovered a scallop-edged alabaster throne, still in place after thousands of years. Wear and tear by visitors has made it necessary to block off the room so that you can no longer sit where Minos, or a Minoan priestess, or Knossos' Mycenaean-era boss sat. On each side are gypsum benches and frescoes of heraldic griffons, in Mycenaean style; the **Lustral Basin**, like others at Knossos, may have held water used in rituals, or served to reflect light that descended in light wells into the poky rooms, or both. Evans found evidence here of a possible last-ditch effort to placate the gods as disaster swept through Knossos.

The stair south of the Antechamber ascends to an upper floor, used in part for storage, as in the **Room of the Tall *Pithos*** and **Temple Repositories**, where the famous snake goddess statuette was found. Note the pillars that thicken near the top, a feature unique to Minoan architecture and distinctly similar to the trunk of the 'horizontal' cypress native to the Gorge of Samariá. The Minoans may have hoped the form would be earthquake-resistant. Returning to the Central Court, note the high relief fresco copy of the *Prince of the Lilies* at the end of the Corridor of the Procession.

Evans, who grew up taking monarchies for granted, had no doubt that the more elaborate **East Wing** of the palace contained the '**Royal Apartments**'. Here are the Minoans' most dazzling architectural *tour de force*, the **Grand Staircase** and **Central Light Well**; almost five flights of broad gypsum steps are preserved. However, when you descend to the two lower floors (which were found intact) it's hard to imagine that any royal family would choose to live buried so deep, with little in the way of light and air in spite of all the Minoans' clever architectural devices; the near prox-imity of the 'Royal Workshops' would have made them noisy as well. The rooms did have something modern royals couldn't live without: plumbing. The excellent water and sewer system of Knossos is visible under the floor in the **Queen's Megaron** and its bathroom, complete with a clay bathtub, fill-up bucket and flush toilet – amenities Versailles could scarcely manage. The **King's Megaron**, also known as **Hall of the Double Axes** for the many carvings of the symbol on the walls, opens onto the **Hall of the Royal Guard**, with a copy of the fresco of large, cowhide figure-of-eight shields.

North of the royal apartments, the long **Corridor of the Draughtboard** is where the superb gameboard in the Heráklion Museum was found, and where you can see clay pipes used to bring water from the Mount Júktas aqueduct. The **Magazines of Giant**

Reconstruction of Knossos' State Apartments, on the west side of the Central Court: on the right, entrance to the Throne Room; to the left of it, stepped porch leading to the Central Hall; further left again, the main shrine of the palace, with crenellated roof.

Pithoi to the east bring to mind the myth of Minos' young son Glaukos: wandering in the Labyrinth, the boy climbed into a *pithos* of honey to steal a taste, but fell in and drowned. The anxious father located his body thanks to his prophet Polyidos, and in grief Minos locked him in a room with Glaukos' body with orders to bring him back to life. As Polyidos despaired, a snake came out of a hole in the wall: he killed it, but watched in amazement as another snake appeared with a herb in its mouth, which it rubbed against its dead fellow to revive it. Polyidos tried the same on Glaukos and resuscitated the boy, but Minos, rather than reward Polyidos, ordered him to teach Glaukos the art of prophecy. The prophet obeyed, but as he sailed away from Crete he told the boy to spit in Polyidos' mouth, so that Glaukos forgot all he had learned.

As you leave, going north, there's a relief copy of the bull fresco, and near it the '**Customs House**', supported by eight pillars, which was possibly used for handling imports and exports. Below is the oldest paved road in Europe, or **Royal Road**, ending abruptly at the modern road; originally it continued to the Little Palace and beyond. The road ends at the '**Theatre**' (looking more like a large stairway), where 500 people could stand or sit to view religious processions or dances, as pictured in the frescoes.

Around Knossos

Some highly intriguing Minoan buildings have been excavated outside the palace. Nearest are the reconstructed three-storey **South House**, complete with a bathroom and latrine, the **Southeast House** and the **House of the Chancel Screen**, both believed to have been the residences of VIPs – the last has a dais for a throne or altar. Other constructions, outside the palace grounds, require special permission to visit, such as the **Royal Villa**, with its throne and beautifully preserved Pillar Crypt, where channels and two depressions around the square pillar received libations to the god. The **Little Palace**, just across the modern Heráklion road, had three pillar crypts and was used after the Minoans as a shrine; the magnificent bull's head *rhyton* was found here.

To the south, a sign on the main road points to the **Caravanserai**, as Evans named it, believing weary travellers paused here to wash the dust from their feet in the stone trough. The walls have a copy of the lovely *Partridge* fresco. Further south are four pillars of the Minoan **aqueduct** that carried water over a stream, and south of that the unique **Royal Temple Tomb**, where the natural rock ceiling was painted blue and a stair leads up to a temple on top. One especially controversial find was Peter Warren's 1980 unearthing of the **House of the Sacrificed Children**, 330ft from the Little Palace, a typical Minoan house that was found to contain a large cache of children's bones bearing the marks of knives, as if they had been carved up for supper. The Minoans, having been found guilty of human sacrifice in the Anemospiliá shrine at Archánes (*see* p.207), now had cannibalism to answer for. Many historians believe the children had died of natural causes and their bones were stripped of any last flesh before re-burial – a custom that survived in parts of Greece into the 19th century.

Lastly, you can pay your respects to the exterior of the **Villa Ariadne**, the house that Evans built for himself; it is set back in a garden just up the road to Heráklion (take the first left). After the Battle of Crete it was selected by General Kreipe as his head-quarters, and it later saw the signing of the German surrender on Crete.

Nomós Heráklion

Nomós Heráklion

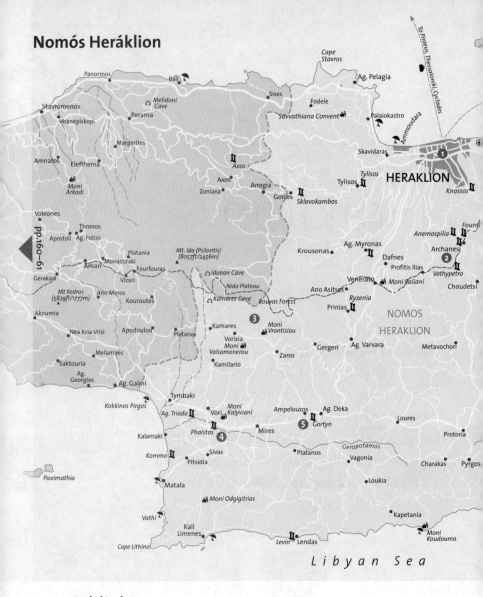

Highlights

1 Heráklion: the wonders of the Archaeological Museum and the Palace of Knossos
2 Archánes, under Mount Júktas, the Holy Mountain of the Minoans
3 Crete's last big oak forest at Rouvas, and the lovely lake and gorge at Záros
4 The great Minoan palace of Phaistos and the 'summer villa' of Ag. Triáda,
   in beautiful settings
5 The ruins of Gortyn, Roman capital of Crete and Libya
6 Remote beaches of the south coast, at Keratókambos and Árvi

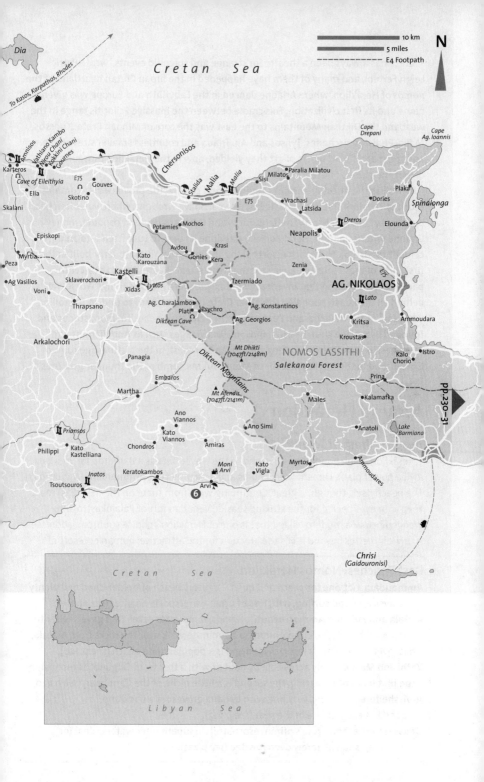

Map Labels

Legend
- 10 km
- 5 miles
- E4 Footpath

N

Dia

To Kasos, Karpathos, Rhodes

Cretan Sea

Cape Drepani

Cape Ag. Ioannis

Annisos
Karteros
Vathiano Kambo
Gyrou Chani
Kokkini Chani
Gournes
Cave of Eileithyia
Elia
Skalani
Episkopi
Myrtia
Peza
Ag Vasilios
Voni
Sklaverochori
Thrapsano
Kastelli
Xidas
Lyttos

E75

Gouves
Skotino

Chersonisos

Stalida
Malia
Malia

Sisi
Milatos
Paralia Milatou
Vrachasi
Latsida

Plaka
Dories
Spinalonga
Elounda

Potamies
Mochos
Avdou
Krasi
Kato Karouzana
Gonies
Kera

Dreros

Neapolis

Zenia

AG. NIKOLAOS

Lato

Tzermiado

Ammoudara

Ag. Charalambo
Plati
Psychro
Diktean Cave
Ag. Georgios
Ag. Konstantinos
Ag. Georgios

Kritsa
Kroustas

Kalo Chorio
Istro

Arkalochori

Panagia

Embaros

Martha

Dktean Mountains

Mt Dhikti
(7047ft/2148m)

NOMOS LASSITHI

Salekanou Forest

Prina

Males
Kalamafka

PP.230–31

Ano Viannos
Kato Viannos
Chondros
Amiras

Mt Afendis
(7047ft/2141m)

Ano Simi

Anatoli

Lake Barmiana

Priansos
Philippi
Kato Kastelliana

Inatos
Tsoutsouros
Keratokambos

Moni Arvi
Arvi

Kato Vigla

Myrtos

Ammoudares

⑥

Chrisi (Gaidouronisi)

Cretan Sea

Libyan Sea

'Crete has always been a theatre for strange and splendid events,' wrote Patrick Leigh Fermor, and many of them have happened in the broad Cretan heartland of the *nomós* of Heráklion, where Ariadne danced in the Labyrinth and Europe was given a name and its first civilization. This cradle between the massive Psilorítis range in the west and the Diktean Mountains to the east was the core of Minoan Crete: Knossos, Mália, Phaistos, Archánes, Týlisos and Ag. Triáda and countless smaller sites are here, and the magnificent works of art they yielded, now in the Heráklion museum, are one of the glories of Greece.

As well as the finest in ancient Cretan art and culture, the province also contains much of the dark side of what the last 40 years have wrought, where you often hear people say that what the Venetians, Turks and Germans couldn't conquer, money has undone without a fight. Heráklion city has done its best to turn itself into an ugly cement toadstool. The beach resorts along the lovely north coast, jerry-built in the first flush of mass tourism, are a scar that won't heal, illustrating a 20th-century paradox on the island that invented paradox: prosperity makes things worse. Yet behind all the beach boogaloo the other Crete isn't at all hard to find, in the rolling vineyards of the Malevízi and Péza valleys, in a clutch of beautiful monasteries and frescoed Byzantine churches, in handsome old villages such as Áno Viánnos and Archánes, in secret beaches along the Libyan Sea coast, in the picturesque ruins of Gortyn, and in the mighty menhir of Mount Júktas, tomb of the thunder-god Zeus.

Around Heráklion

Beaches West of Town

Heráklion is surrounded by sand, and to the west offers as a backdrop for your beach idyll a power plant, cement works, clubs and apartments at **Ammoudára** (Αμμουδάρα). The beach itself, though, is great. Continuing west from there on the new (E75) road, keep your eyes peeled for the striking seaside Venetian fort of **Palaiókastro** and, wedged below, a modern village that is one of Heráklion's choice suburban addresses. A few kilometres beyond it lies the junction for the attractive, upmarket resort of

---

Best Beaches: Nomós Heráklion

Ammoudára: not one for peace and quiet – a resort beach of golden sand and plenty of waves for good surfing, with lots of other watersports on offer (*see* above).

Mátala and **Kókkino Ámmos:** beautiful sands, famous for caves that gave shelter to hippies in the 70's; Kókkino Ámmos, a 20-minute walk over the rocks from Mátala, has lovely pink sand, is less crowded and is a popular nude beach (see p.220).

Vathí and **Marsaló:** only accessible by boat or with a trek from Odgigitrias monastery: the first has a fjord setting, the second is a little niche of the Caribbean (*see* p.220).

Arví: sheltered and very, very hot, with banana groves for a backdrop; a good bet early or late in the year (*see* p.223).

Goúves: the best on Crete's prime resort-stretch: superb clear waters, ideal for snorkelling and still rarely overcrowded (*see* p.223).

Getting Around

City **bus** no.6 runs from Plateía Eleftherías in Heráklion west along the coast road up as far as Ag. Pelagía, stopping in Ammoudára and Palaiókastro and other points en route.

Where to Stay and Eat

Ammoudára ✉ 71500

Candia Maris, t 281 031 4632, f 281 025 0669, *www.maris.gr (L, luxury)*. Plush rooms and bungalows in a seaside garden give all-inclusive comfort, including a new thalassotherapy centre. *Open all year.*

Grecotel Agapi Beach, t 281 031 1084, f 281 025 8731, *www.grecotel.gr (A, luxury)*. Right on the beach, with three pools, the Agapi Beach offers all the fancy beach accessories you could desire. *Open April–Oct.*

Dolphin Bay, t 281 082 1276, f 281 082 1312 (*A, expensive*). A huge, classic resort hotel with all the facilities you'd expect.

Camping Heráklion, t 281 025 0986. Right by the beach, this big A-class campsite has very modern facilities.

Delfini, Linoperámata, just west of Ammoudára, t 281 084 1361 (*€20*). Head past the delightful cement works to sit yourself down at one of the best seafood restaurants on the coast. *Open evenings only, and weekends only Nov–Feb.*

Ag. Pelagía ✉ 71500

For traditional Cretan food, try the clutch of several tavernas up in **Rodiá**, between Ammoudára and Ag. Pelagía.

Capsis Beach Resort, t 281 081 1212, f 281 081 1076, *www.capsis.gr (A, luxury)*. Big hotel and villa complex with about every luxury you could think of and three beaches, several pools, a watersports school and a 'New Minoan' conference centre. *Open all year.*

Peninsula, t 281 081 1313, f 281 081 1291, *www.peninsula.gr (A, luxury)*. Perched on the rocks, with a lovely terrace overlooking the beach, this is another one that offers a long list of leisure activities: a playground and paddling pool for kids, watersports, tennis courts, a disco and more.

Alexander House, t 281 081 1303, f 281 081 1381, *alexhh@iraklio.hellasnet.gr (A, expensive–moderate)*. A smaller, newer hotel, with comfortable air-conditioned rooms, still with satellite TV, minibars and balconies with views of the pool and the sea.

Panorama, t 281 081 1002, f 281 081 1273 (*B, moderate*). Comfortable mid-range resort hotel with a pool, watersports and tennis.

Amazona, t 281 081 1169 (*D, moderate*). One of the town's nicer, less-expensive choices.

Muragio, t 281 081 1070. A waterfront taverna with delicious fish dishes.

Valentino, t 281 081 1106. More seafood, but also pizzas made in a real Italian *forno*.

Nightlife

Prime Club, Ammoudára. Huge outdoor venue where Heráklion struts its stuff in summer.

Anagennisi, coast road near Ammoudára. Big traditional music club where Cretans come to hear *lýra* wizards do their stuff.

Nanu and **Paradise**, Ag. Pelagía. Two modern seafront cafés that liven up in the evening.

Ag. Pelagía (Αγ. Πελαγία), strewn like chunks of coconut over the headland that marks the outer gate of the Bay of Heráklion. A 3km road descends to quiet coves and a protected, if narrow, sandy beach, endowed with upmarket hotels. Remnants of a Minoan harbour town, *Kytaiton*, were found on the edge of a cliff on the west side of the bay. If it all seems too busy, look out for a sign for the quieter beaches further west, at the pretty bay of **Made** (pronounced 'Mathay') by the Athina Palace Hotel.

Between the new and old coast roads south of Ag. Pelagía there are a couple of possible detours. One is to the beautiful **Convent of Savvathiana** above Rodiá, surrounded by huge trees and with lovely views. It has two main churches or *katholikóns*, linked by a path and a little stone bridge over a brook, dated 1596. During the siege of Heráklion the monastery was destroyed, and the monks taken as slaves to

When Saints Burst into Flames

Instead of making people pray, you make them admire.
Beauty inserts itself as an obstacle between our souls and God.

Grand Inquisitor Cardinal Guevara, to El Greco

Born in 1541 (apologies to Fódele, but the archives and recent research all say in Heráklion), Doménikos Theotokópoulos spent all his early life on Crete, but the details of his youth are obscure. It is known that his first training was as an icon painter, perhaps studying alongside Micháil Damáskinos, his contemporary. Only one painting by a young Theotokópoulos survives on Crete, in Heráklion's Historical Museum (*see* p.191), although a surviving Cretan document of 1566 refers to him as 'master painter'. Soon after this date, however, he was in Titian's workshop in Venice, although the elongated, linear, mystical style of another Venetian, Tintoretto, proved a greater influence. He studied the works of Correggio and Parmigianino in Parma on his way to Rome in 1570, where he discovered the work of Michelangelo and the Central Italian Mannerists (Pontormo, Rosso Fiorentino) and their startling colours, unrealistic perspectives and exaggerated, often tortured poses.

Like a true Cretan, Theotokópoulos had a proud, passionate nature. During his stay in Rome, when Pius V was casting about for an artist to paint clothes on the figures of Michelangelo's *Last Judgement*, the Cretan suggested the Pope would be better off destroying the fresco altogether, because he could paint a better one that was chaste to boot. 'Michelangelo is a good man, but he didn't know how to paint,' he said. The Romans were so astounded by his audacity that they ran him out of town.

Africa; the Patriarchate managed to raise money to free them, and when they returned they carried on fighting the Turks. The graves of the heroic monk-fighters are near the *katholikón* of the Theotokos. Since 1945 the monks have been replaced by nuns, and in 1991 they found an icon, blackened with age, and sent it to be cleaned; it turned out to be a documented but long-believed-lost version of the *Great art thou, O Lord icon* by 18th-century master Ioánnis Kornaros, similar to one at Toploú in Lassíthi (*see* p.258). Further west, orange groves surround **Fódele** (Φόδελε). According to an old tradition, this sleepy village with its pretty Byzantine church of the Panagía (1383) was the birthplace of Doménikos Theotokópoulos, better known as El Greco (*see* above). A plaque was erected in his honour by the University of Toledo in 1934, and the restored **House of El Greco** (*open Tues–Sun 9–5*) has been opened to visitors.

Beaches East of Town

East of Heráklion, the airport features in the beach backdrop. The bus from the city crawls through the suburbs of **Póros** and **Néa Alikárnassos**, both populated in the 1920s by refugees from Asia Minor, to the not exceptionally attractive main city beach at **Karterós** (7km) and beyond that to **Amnisós** (Αμνισός), the first of the long string of resorts east of Heráklion. It overlooks the islet of **Día** (Zeus), which played a significant role in Minoan religion: in the oldest-known version of the Ariadne story she was kidnapped from Knossos, brought to Día and killed. Today the island is a

Fortunately, he had a place to go. In Rome, he had met Diego de Castilla, Dean of Canons of Toledo Cathedral, who gave him his first major commission: the altarpiece of Toledo's Santo Domingo el Antiguo (1577; now in the Art Institute of Chicago). It was with this painting that he perfected his unique, uncanny, highly personal style, shot full of tension – the intense, vibrant, lightning colours that seem to flicker on the canvas, the nervous line and figures that rise up like flames, all perceptions heightened to a fervent rapture and honed to the spiritual essence of truth. For all that, *El Greco*, the Greek, as he became known, never found favour with the religious, art-loving Philip II, who panicked at the unveiling of the *Martyrdom of San Mauricio* that he painted for the Escorial in 1587. The painter refused all hints from the royal advisors that supplication or an offer to soften the colours might win him the king's approval, but in a huff took his brushes off to the holy city of Toledo, where he spent his last 37 years with his common-law wife, Jerónima de las Cuevas. Incapable of doing anything halfway, he lived like a lord, buying a 24-room palace in Toledo's abandoned Jewish quarter, accumulating an important humanist library and employing a lutanist and guitarist to accompany his every meal. Although he never lacked for commissions from the Church or for private portraits (usually of clergymen), after his death all his worldly possessions fitted into a single trunk.

The poet Hortensio Paravicino told him, 'You make snow itself burst into flame. You have overstepped nature, and the soul remains undecided in its wonder which of the two, God's creatures or yours, deserves to live.' Although he never returned to his native island, Theotokópoulos never forgot his origins, and always signed his paintings with his Greek name in Greek letters, often followed by *KRES*, or *CRETAN*.

sanctuary for Crete's endangered ibexes, or *kri-kri*, and for the world's largest colony of Eleonora's falcons. Both species have somehow learned to cope with charter flights swooping overhead every five minutes.

But Amnisós has been a busy place since Neolithic times. It was a port of Knossos, and it was from here that Idomeneus and his 90 ships sailed for Troy; here the ship of Odysseus, at least in one of his lying stories, was long prevented from sailing by the north wind. The Minoans must have often encountered the same problem, and got around it by loading and unloading at a south-facing port on Día. Minoan Amnisós had two harbours, on either side of a hard-scramble hill topped by the ruins of a Venetian village. At its east end is the fenced-off **villa** of 1600 BC that yielded the lovely *Fresco of the Lilies* in the Heráklion museum; on the northwest side is an Archaic Sanctuary of Zeus Thenatas. In the 1930s, while excavating Amnisós' Minoan 'Harbour Master's Office', Spyridon Marinátos discovered a layer of pumice, the physical evidence he needed to support his theory that Minoan civilization had been devastated in its prime by ash flung by a cataclysmic eruption on Santoríni.

One kilometre inland from Amnisós, up the road to Elia, is the atmospheric **Cave of Eileithyia**, goddess of fertility and childbirth, daughter of Zeus and Hera and mother of Eros (*get the caretaker's address at the Heráklion tourist office*). Few divinities have enjoyed Eileithyia's staying power: her cave, which was also mentioned by Homer, attracted women far and wide from the Neolithic era to the 5th century AD.

Getting Around

Heráklion city **bus** no.7 runs from Plateía Eleftherías all along the coast road through Karterós, Amnisós and other towns as far as Gournés. Many longer-distance buses to Lassíthi stop at several destinations, too.

Where to Stay and Eat

Karterós and Amnisós ✉ **71500**
Minoa Palace, t 281 038 0404, **f** 281 038 0422, *minoapalace@akashotels.com (A, expensive)*.

A smart beachside complex in the middle of Amnisós' seafront, with a pool, a floodlit tennis court, attractive bars and restaurants and a score of activities and sports for all ages. *Open April–Oct.*
Exanatas, t 281 022 0474 *(€20)*. By the beach in Póros, not far from the city, this is a favourite place for a long, lazy meal of endless tasty titbits or *mezédes*, both seafood and vegetarian, served in a shady courtyard and washed down by local wine. *Closed Sun.*
Toumbrouk, Karterós. Another excellent beachside fish taverna, a spot that makes a visit to Karterós worthwhile.

Stalagmites, resembling a mother and her children (the latter are hard to make out) were the main focus of worship; pregnant women would rub their bellies against a third one, which resembles a pregnant belly complete with a navel. The rock-cut platform at the cave's mouth, the **Square of the Altars**, is named after the large cubes of living rock that may have been used in ancient ceremonies.

Back on the beach road, next along is **Vathianó Kambó**, a medium-sized resort. By the Hotel Demetra is **Nírou Cháni** (*t 289 707 6110; open Tues–Sun 8.30–3; adm*), a well-preserved Minoan villa known as the House of the High Priest, where a trove of 40 tripods and enormous double axes was found. It has two paved courts and benches, perhaps used for specific ceremonies. For Mália and resorts further east, *see p.223.*

South from Knossos: Archánes and Myrtiá

One of the ancient proofs of Epimenides' paradox 'All Cretans are liars' was the fact that Zeus the immortal was born and buried on Crete, the profile of his bearded face easily discerned in the lines of **Mount Júktas**, visible on the road south of Knossos. This road was a main Minoan thoroughfare, and saw some modern history as well: at the turn-off for Archánes a band of Cretan Resistance fighters, led by Major Patrick Leigh Fermor and Captain W. S. Moss, dressed in German uniforms, kidnapped General Kreipe on 26 April 1943 as he was being driven from Archánes to his residence at Villa Ariadne (as told in Captain Moss' *Ill Met by Moonlight*). The General was marched up to Anógia on Mount Ida, while the car was abandoned on Pánormos Beach with a note saying that this was the work of British commandos and any local reprisals would be against international law. But the Germans were convinced Kreipe was still on Crete and launched a massive search for him, with dire consequences for Anógia (*see* p.173), which they suspected of sheltering the raiders. The privately-run **Cretan Historical and Folklore Museum** (*t 281 075 1853; open Wed–Mon 9.30–2; adm*), signposted 3km from Archánes, has a vast collection of memorabilia from the Battle of Crete, personal belongings of Kreipe and displays on the abduction.

Thanks to a dynamic mayor and EU funds, the village of **Archánes** (Αρχάνες) is one of the most attractive in Crete, the winner of European accolades for its development projects. Civic pride is tangible here; flowers spill over balconies, the walls of old manor houses are painted in warm colours and the streets, many off-limits to cars, have been re-paved with stones and are lit by old-fashioned street lamps. In 1989 the Municipality of Archánes founded the organization that is now the Development Agency of Heráklion, dedicated to promoting sustainable tourism.

With its abundant sources of water, Archánes has often been called on to supply the north; the Minoan aqueduct to Knossos began here, as did the **Venetian aqueduct**, built in 1628 and ending in Morosini's fountain in Heráklion (parts of it can still be seen in the Archaniótiko Gorge, by the road to Silamós). A third, Egyptian, aqueduct, an impressive work of the 1830s, still humps across the road south of Knossos. Besides water, Archánes is a major producer of wine (Archánes and Armanti) and table grapes called *rozáki*. These were in such demand in the 1900s that Archánes was said to have the highest per capita income in Greece – witnessed by the grand neoclassical school, the **Diaktirio** (1901). In the centre, surrounded by cafés and tavernas, the church of the **Panagía** (*open mornings*) has a bell-tower decorated with stone heads and an exceptional collection of 16th–19th-century icons, amassed by the priest.

From the 15th century on visitors would come up to Archánes, intrigued by the story of Zeus' tomb, but the first hint that there was something more than stories had to wait until the 1900s, when a fine alabaster ladle inscribed with Linear A was found on the outskirts of town. In 1922 Evans noted the 'palatial character' of walls uncovered on a building site, and surmised the existence of a 'summer palace' in Archánes. Then, in 1964, Ioánnis and Éfi Sakellarákis began excavating what was to become, after Zákros, the biggest of all recent Minoan discoveries. **Archánes' palace**, rather unfortunately for them, is in the centre of the old Turkish quarter of the village, on a site inhabited continuously since 2000 BC, limiting the area they could attack with their

Getting Around

Buses run every hour to Archánes Mon–Fri, and slightly less frequently at weekends, from the east bus depot and Plateía Venizélou in Heráklion: get off at Epáno or Áno Archánes.

Festivals

July: Archánes International Guitar Competition.

Where to Stay and Eat

Archánes ✉ 70100

The charming outdoor **Cine Paradise**, in the centre of Archánes, shows films in English.
Villa Archanes. Áno Archánes, t 281 039 0770, f 281 039 0778, *www.maris.gr* (*luxury*). In a renovated house from 1890, and opened in 2001, with six beautiful apartments in traditional style, complete with handwoven fabrics. Plus a serene setting and rigorously authentic Cretan cooking in the café, using only organic ingredients. *Open all year.*
Orestes Rent Rooms, t 281 075 1619 (*inexpensive*). Simple, and just outside the centre.
Spitiko, t 281 075 1591. Taverna with good stews and grilled meats, in the main square.
Lykastos, t 281 075 2433. Also in Archánes main square, with excellent Cretan food, especially meats and meat pies, cooked in a wood-fired oven.
Oistros Wine Bar, t 281 075 2633. A café with occasional live music.

Skaláni, north of Myrtiá ✉ 71500
Taverna Marazakis, t 281 073 1435. A great place for lunch or dinner after visiting the vineyards and Kazantzákis museum, with local dishes and a choice of Péza wines.

spades. The largest visible section is between the modern buildings along Mákri Sokáki and Ierolóchiton streets; dating from the New Palace period (*c.* 1700–1450 BC), the walls that have been preserved were up to 6ft in height and very thick, to support one or more storeys; only in Knossos and Phaistos were similar coloured marbles, gypsum and other luxury materials used. It had elaborate frescoes, a drainage system and a large cistern built over a spring (a skull found here may belong to a victim of the earthquake that knocked down the palace). A 'theatrical area', a small exedra and Horns of Consecration were found near the church of Ag. Nikólaos; an archive yielding Linear A tablets was unearthed on Kapetanáki street. Some finds are in the small but informative **Archaeological Museum** nearby (*open Wed–Mon 9–1.30 and 5–8*).

Just south of Archánes is the lovely church of the **Asómatos** (the 'Bodyless One', an Orthodox attribute for St Michael), with fine frescoes donated by Michail Patsidiótis, dated 1315: *The Battle of Jericho, The Sacrifice of Abraham* and the *Punishment of the Damned* are especially good (ask the priest at the Panagía for the key).

The Minoan Cemetary of Fourní

In Minoan times, a paved road from the palace led to the **Necropolis of Fourní** (*t 281 075 1907; open daily 8–2.30*) set atop a rocky ridge 1.5km to the northeast; it still exists as a track, a steep walk up from the road, but nowadays you can get there by car up a road from **Káto Archánes**. This five-acre site has proved to be one of the most important prehistoric cemeteries in the Aegean, in use for 1,250 years (2500–1250 BC). Near the guardian's hut, note the building identified as a **kósmiko**, where craftsmen made votives and other items used in burials. Most spectacular of all are three *tholos* tombs, especially **Tholos A**, which was long used as a farmer's hut, and as a hiding place in the Second World War. Debris and rocks (and a Venetian coin, perhaps left by someone hunting for the grave of Zeus) filled the bottom floor, while below, tucked in a side chamber behind a false wall, lay a priestess or royal lady from the 14th century BC, buried in an ankle-length gold-trimmed gown and surrounded by grave offerings: 140 pieces of gold and ivory jewellery, a footstool elaborately decorated with ivory and the remains of a sacrificed horse and bull, the bones carefully carved. The *dromos* or ceremonial path leading to the entrance is the longest on Crete. The lower layer of the collective burials in **Tholos C** goes back to 2500 BC, and yielded a large cache of marble Cycladic figurines and jewellery, in the same style as the Treasure of Priam that Schliemann found at Troy. The **Mycenaean Grave** enclosure with seven shaft tombs and three stelae is unique on Crete; its libation pit or *bothros* had been so saturated with milk and wine offerings to the dead thousands of years ago that when the Sakellarákis team dug into it they were overwhelmed by 'the unbearable stench'.

The Bloodstained Shrine of Anemospiliá

Five kilometres northwest of Archánes, above the town dump, on the panoramic, windswept promontory of **Anemospiliá**, the Sakellarákises discovered an isolated **tripartite shrine** in 1979, which is now not fully open to visitors but is visible from the road. Such shrines were often depicted in Minoan art, but this was the first one to be found that matched the pictures. In the middle room, the most fascinating discovery

The Father of Zorba

Born in Heráklion in 1883, Níkos Kazantzákis was the son of Captain Michélis, a storekeeper and revolutionary from Myrtiá, and grandson of a Saracen pirate (the old name of Myrtiá was *Varvari*, 'barbarians', because of the many Saracens who settled there). One of Kazantzákis' first memories was of his father lifting him up to a gallows to kiss the feet of Cretan rebels hanged by the Turks. Although Níkos paid tribute to his father in one of his best novels, *Freedom or Death* (*Kapetanos Michelis* in Greek), his Cretan fighting spirit expressed itself in a lifelong battle of ideas, leaving him ultimately unclassifiable; like Epimenides the Cretan Sage he relished paradox, and the Minoan double axe was the symbol on his letterhead. He seemed to fit several lifetimes into his 74 years, intellectually flirting with Nietzsche, Lenin, Bergson, Christ, St Francis, Buddha and Homer while his travels took him around the world: he served in the Greek Ministry of Education, in the Balkan Wars, and helped resettle Greek refugees from the Caucasus in 1919; in the 20s he was involved in Communism. He translated everything from the *Iliad* to the *Petit Larousse* into modern Greek, wrote travel critiques on Spain, Russia, China and England, and began the work he considered his masterpiece, the *Odyssey*, 33,333 verses long. The public, however (as the translations in the Myrtiá museum show, *see* p.209) has always preferred his novel inspired by a Macedonian miner and skirt-chaser named George Zórbas, with whom Kazantzákis operated a lignite mine during the First World War.

In 1930 Kazantzákis went on trial for atheism, and was later excommunicated from the Orthodox Church. He spent the last ten years of his life in Antibes; perhaps, like

was a pair of large clay feet from a *xoanon*, an idol made from wood and other perishable materials worshipped in Greece since Neolithic times; according to Pausanius, the Greeks believed they were first made by Daedalus on Crete. The eastern room was apparently used for bloodless sacrifices; the western room, however, produced perhaps the most controversial finds in a century of Minoan archaeology. In it were the remains of three people caught in the sanctuary as the massive earthquake struck *c.* 1700 BC. The skeleton of a 17-year-old boy was bound on an altar, next to a dagger; an autopsy by the Medical School of the University of Manchester (which has made a speciality of doing coroner's reports on prehistoric stiffs) showed that the blood had been drained from his upper body, and that he had probably had his throat cut. The other skeletons belonged to a man wearing a ring of (then rare) iron, and a woman who carried sickle cell anaemia: people of fine breeding, perhaps a priest and priestess. A fourth skeleton, of indeterminate sex, was caught by falling masonry in the antechamber. A precious Kamáres ware vase was found near the body; it may have been full of the boy's blood, an offering with which the Minoans attempted to appease a furious god, possibly Poseidon the Earth-shaker.

The gruesome findings came as a shock. The graceful, arty people evoked by Evans seemed too sophisticated for such barbarities, despite hints of human sacrifice in Cretan mythology – besides the tribute of Athenian youths to the Minotaur, another account tells how the half-legendary shaman Epimenides went to Athens to deliver fellow Cretan Míkis Theodorákis, he found it easier to imagine and be inspired by Crete from far away. During this time he wrote the *Fraticides, Freedom or Death*, his semi-autobiographical *Report to Greco* and the controversial *Last Temptation of Christ*, which made the Pope's Index when it was published in 1954, causing a furore similar to the one provoked by Martin Scorsese's film of the novel many years later. Kazantzákis was 74 when he was nominated one last time for the Nobel Literature Prize (the Church actively lobbied against him, and he lost by one vote to Albert Camus) and he died shortly afterwards, in October 1957, from hepatitis contracted from a vaccination needle. The museum has photos of his funeral in Heráklion, attended by throngs of dignitaries. The Church sent only one priest, at the insistence of the government – normally a hundred or so would officiate at the funeral of a great man – but forbade him to say any prayers.

If nothing else Kazantzákis was the ultimate Cretan writer, who powerfully evoked the island's fierce spirit of independence, its love of freedom and its spiritual preoccupations, its capacity to create and kill its own gods. 'There is something in Crete like a flame,' he wrote. 'Call it a soul, something beyond death that isn't easy to define, made of pride, stubbornness, valour, disdain, and of that inexpressible, immeasurable element that makes you happy to be a Cretan.' In his best writing he re-enchants day-to-day existence, his philosophy compressed in the character of Zorba, who never loses his wonder at life. In his *Odyssey*, his Odysseus tells of the ultimate goal, of being 'delivered from deliverance'; for Kazantzákis it isn't God who saves humanity, but humanity which must save God.

the city from the curse of Kylon, by means of human sacrifices. But such extreme acts were probably only resorted to in extraordinary situations, when the sacrifice of one was made in the hope of saving many, in this case from violent earth tremors. Even then, the practice was not done in public, but behind the doors of the shrine.

Beyond Archánes: Vathýpetro and Mount Júktas

Two kilometres south of Archánes, just off the main road, a short path leads to the Minoan villa complex of **Vathýpetro**, spectacularly set high on a spur facing Mount Júktas over a rolling patchwork of olives and vineyards. In plan it resembles a baby palace of Knossos: it has a small west court and larger central one, a tripartite shrine, and a three-columned portico with a small courtyard to its east, closed off by a fancy structure found nowhere else, recessed in the centre and supported by symmetrical square plinths. First built *c.* 1580 BC, Vathýpetro was shattered, probably by an earthquake, *c.* 1550. It seems to have been rebuilt as a rural craft centre; clay loom weights and potters' wheels were found, and the oldest-known wine press in Greece. The cool cellars suggest that Minoans were already refined winemakers 3,500 years ago.

To this day the vintners in the area repeat a ritual that may be as old as Vathýpetro itself: every 6 August the first fruits of the harvest are ritually offered to the deity on the 2,660ft (810m) summit of **Mount Júktas**, the sacred mountain of the Minoans. A good dirt road just before Vathýpetro leads up to the summit and the church where it all happens, while the original Minoan peak sanctuary of **Psilí Korfí** is just to the north (it's fenced off, but many people slip through a hole in the fence for the stunning view). This has yielded large quantities of votive gifts and bronze double axes, and also served as a navigational landmark for Minoan sailors; a young Poseidon was one of the gods worshipped here. Griffon vultures nest on Júktas' western slopes and the mountain meadows produce an exceptional array of orchids each spring.

The broad road south of Vathýpetro continues to **Ag. Vasílios** and **Moní Spiliótissa**, a convent with a frescoed church built into a dim cave, hidden in a lush grove of plane trees; the spring water bubbling out of its foundations is known for its healing properties, and was piped into Heráklion by the pashas. It's a pretty walk of a few hundred yards to the simple church of **Ag. Ioánnis**, with frescoes dated 1291, 'in the reign of Andronicus Paleológos'. Just south of here a dirt road west allows you to circle back to the north around the back of Mount Júktas by way of **Kanlí Kastélli**, or the Bloody Fortress, built by Niképhoros Phókas when he liberated Crete from the Saracens in 961.

Folk music fans may prefer to head south of Archánes to **Choudétsi**, where Irish musician Ross Daly, who has lived on Crete for 20 years and made several recordings with local musicians, has set up a Musical Center and museum of folk instruments.

Myrtiá and Níkos Kazantzákis

Alternatively, and just as scenically, you can circle back from Ag. Vasílios to Heráklion to the east, by way of Crete's most prestigious wine region, **Pezá**; in Pezá village, the **Minos Winery** welcomes visitors with a video, tour and tastings (*t 281 074 1213, www. minoswines.gr*). Another Pezá village, **Myrtiá**, sits nearby high on a ridge over a sweeping landscape of vineyards. Besides the views, the main reason to visit here is the **Kazantzákis Museum** (*t 281 0741 689; open Mon, Wed, Sat and Sun 9–1 and 4–8, Tues and Fri 9–1; closed Thurs; adm*), in the house where the father of Crete's great novelist was born; photos, documents, dioramas and memorabilia evoke the writer's life.

Southwest of Heráklion

The Minoan Villas of Týlisos (Τύλισος)

t 281 022 6092; open daily 8.30–3; adm; park in the village and walk up or subject yourself to the embroidery ladies who run the 'Free Parking' next door.

Týlisos, like many villages in these parts, enjoys a lovely setting, surrounded by mountains and swathed in olives and vineyards, but it has something else, too: three large Minoan villas (**A**, **B** and **C**) unearthed in the early days of Minoan archaeology, between 1902 and 1913. Built in the New Palace period and destroyed *c.* 1450 BC, the villas stood two or perhaps even three storeys high. They contained small apartments and extensive storage facilities; palatial elements such as light wells, lustral basins, colonnaded courts and cult shrines are reproduced here in miniature. The typical Minoan love of twisting little corridors is further complicated here by the fact that the Dorians founded a town on the site, re-using many walls. Rectangular Villa B, nearest the entrance, is the oldest and least preserved; Villas A and C are extremely

Týlisos

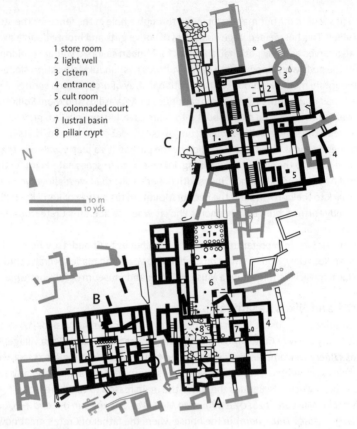

1 store room
2 light well
3 cistern
4 entrance
5 cult room
6 colonnaded court
7 lustral basin
8 pillar crypt

N

10 m
10 yds

C

B

A

well built of finely dressed stone: door jambs, walls (some up to 6ft high), stairs, pillars and the drainage system survive. Water was pumped from 2km away by aqueduct. Villa C was rebuilt in the Post-Palace period, when its round cistern was added.

The road west of Týlisos continues to **Sklavokámbos**, where a Minoan villa went up in flames so intense that its limestone walls were baked as if in a kiln. The presence of such elaborate villas seems to suggest that the Minoan nobility took time off in the country, but the fact they stand along the road from Knossos to the sacred Idaean Cave may be a key to their purpose. Further west towards Anógia, **Goniés**, in a giant bowl under Mount Ida, is the entrance to the **Malevízi**, the grape-growing region that gave its name to *malvasia* or malmsey, a favourite wine in medieval England.

Dáfnes, Veneráto and Ag. Varvára

The main road southwest of Heráklion to Gortyn, Phaistos and Mátala passes through low hills and dense vineyards, especially around **Dáfnes**, where the grapes are made into a respectable red local wine (or VDQS). The handsome village of **Veneráto** ('respected') offers the main reason to stop, with a 2km detour to the convent of **Palianí**, home to 50 nuns. It is one of the oldest on Crete, mentioned in documents going back to the 7th century; as an imperial Byzantine convent it was claimed by the

Doge himself in 1212, reckoning himself heir to all the emperor's possessions on Crete. Besides early Byzantine capitals and 13th-century frescoes, the surest sign of Paliani's great age is its venerable **Holy Myrtle**, reckoned to be 1,000 years old and worshipped in yet another remarkable example of atavism that ultimately goes back to the Minoans. The nuns claim their icon of the *Panagía Myrtidiotissa* was found by the roots, and that there's another icon in the heart of the tree. Next to it, a pair of ancient capitals are used as altar tables for the consecration of bread offerings every 23 September; any myrtle twig that dares to sprout within reach is plucked by the faithful for good luck. The nuns have a shop selling their lace and embroideries.

The lush green valleys west of here are seldom visited. The biggest village is **Ag. Mýronas**, with a 13th-century Venetian church, and the scanty ruins of ancient **Rafkos** just north. South, on the cool slopes of Psilorítis above **Áno Asítses**, is the whitewashed **Monastery of Gorgolaïni**, probably founded in the 16th century, when the Venetians allowed the establishment of new Orthodox religious houses. It was destroyed in 1821 by the Turks, rebuilt, and continued to be a nest of revolt; the statue of *Kapetanos* Frangiás Mastrachás in the courtyard commemorates his death in battle here in 1868. Today, two monks remain at the monastery. Until it was stolen in 1991, Gorgolaïni's pride was a fine 16th-century lion's-mouth fountain. You can pick up the E4 long-distance path from the monastery to Mount Ida; the Greek Mountaineering Federation runs a shelter further up at **Prinos** (*t 281 022 7609*), at 3,609ft/1,100m.

Getting Around

There are four **buses** daily to Týlisos from Heráklion, from Pórta Chaníon depot; several buses daily also run from the same depot on the road through Veneráto and Ag. Várvara, of which one or two turn off for Kamáres.

Where to Stay and Eat

Týlisos ✉ 71500

Hotel Arolithos, t 281 082 1050, **f** 281 082 1051 (*A, expensive*). A few km west of Týlisos, rooms in stone houses in an 'authentic Cretan village' from 1988, with a folklore museum. *Open all year.*

Ag. Mýronas and Area ✉ 70013

Agioklima, Petrokéfalo, 3km north of Ag. Mýronas, **t** 281 022 3861, **f** 281 022 3861, *users.forthnet.gr/her/agioklima* (*A, expensive–moderate*). A somewhat more authentic experience: three stone houses in a hilltop village, with fireplaces and gorgeous views of Mount Ida. Each sleeps up to 4 and has lovely traditional fittings. *Open all year.*

Viglatoras, Sárchos, 2km south of Ag. Mýronas, **t** 281 071 1332, **f** 281 025 2581, *www.iliatoras.gr* (*expensive–moderate*). Traditional cottages sleeping 2–4 on a 7-acre farm, in a lovely setting. The main house is used as a restaurant and for a variety of activities – weaving and cooking lessons – and guests can pick fruit and vegetables from the garden; the coffee shops features mountain teas, Greek coffee slowly boiled in ashes and the ultimate in Cretan tradition – hookahs. The owners also rent out a larger villa. *Open all year.*

Zarós ✉ 70002

Idi Hotel, t 289 403 1302, **f** 289 403 1511 (*C, moderate*). One of the nicest mountain hotels on Crete, with lovely views of the valley and a verdant garden surrounding pools and a 400-year old water mill.

Taverna Votomos, t 289 403 1666 (€15). Shares the view. Fresh salmon and trout hold pride of place on the menu, and some evenings are given over to Cretan music and dancing.

Limni, t 289 403 1338. In the Tourist Pavilion by the lake, this offers solid Cretan cooking and trout, too. *Open all year.*

Further south again, the large, straggling village of **Ag. Varvára** stands amid cherry orchards at approximately the geographical centre of the island; a chapel dedicated to Prophet Elijah sits atop a large rock known as the '*omphalos*', or navel, of Crete. The weather here can be dramatic: at **Mégali Vríssi**, to the east, Crete's first 'Aeolian park' harnesses the cross-island winds with windmills, the biggest and strongest in Greece. Today the island leads all the regions of Greece in its use of renewable energy sources, which supply ten per cent of the demand, while the declared goal is to up this figure to 20 per cent by 2010. Environmentalists believe Crete could do much more with its wind and solar potential to meet an ever-growing need for power on an island stretched to the limits in summer, between the demands of agriculture and tourism.

Just south, in the afternoon shadow of Mount Ida, **Priniás** has a pair of cave tombs and, 3.5km east, the hilltop ruins of **Ryzenia** (1600–200 BC). This Minoan town controlled the main road between Knossos and Phaistos, and later the route to Gortyn. On its acropolis you can see two ruined Archaic temples, one dedicated to Rhea (origin of the striking Daedalic frieze and some of the best Archaic sculpture in the Heráklion museum) and a Hellenistic fort; a Geometric-era cemetery has been found below. The picturesque rotunda of the church of **Ag. Geórgios tou Chostou** stands strikingly in a ravine near the hamlet of **Pirouniana**, just northwest.

The South Slopes of Mount Ida: Gérgeri, Zarós and Kamáres

A lovely, winding road west of Ag. Varvára skirts the olive groves and rich orchards on the south flanks of Mount Ida. Nearly all the villages here began as Minoan farming communities. **Gérgeri** (Γέργερι) has been famous since antiquity for its fresh springs, and today local women run an agricultural cooperative to market their artichokes, cherries and other garden products. The hills above the village have paths into the beautiful **forest of Rouvas**, Crete's oldest oak forest, rich with endemic flora, and now an officially protected area.

Further west, **Zarós** (Ζαρός) is a local beauty spot by a spring-fed artificial lake, complete with swans and little wooden bridges. It's the source of an excellent bottled mineral water; the Romans, antiquity's most obsessive water connoisseurs, built an aqueduct from here to Gortyn so they wouldn't have to drink anything else. The steep path up into the lovely gorge of Zarós starts just behind the lake tourist pavilion, and is a good place to bring a picnic, and to find dittany (*see* p.228). The gorge is deep and green, but has bridges over the tricky places, with fine views of Psilorítis on the way.

Some of the finest art in Crete was created for the two monasteries west of Zarós. **Moní Vrontísiou**, among centuries-old plane trees, was burned by the Turks in 1821 for its revolutionary activities, but still has a pretty gate and 15th-century Venetian fountain, decorated with reliefs of Adam and Eve and the rivers of the Garden of Eden. A massive tree, its core blasted hollow by lightning, houses the kitchen of the *moní*'s café. The 14th-century frescoes in its double-aisled church are only a pale shadow of the treasures Vrontísiou once had – in 1800, after a premonition of its sacking, the abbot sent six panels by Micháil Damáskinos to Ag. Ekateróna in Heráklion, where they remain (*see* p.190). They were painted during Vrontísiou's golden age, when it was the principal intellectual centre in central Crete; now it has but two monks.

Five kilometres west, **Moní Valsamonérou** is reached by a 3km dirt track from **Vorízia**, another village rebuilt after being obliterated by the Nazis (*the guardian lives here, although he's usually at the church on weekday mornings*). Of the monastery little remains beyond the enchanting assymetrical church dedicated to Ag. Fanoúrios, with two naves and a third, transverse aisle added like an afterthought around the corner. The fine frescoes in the north aisle, dedicated to the Virgin, are by 14th-century master KonstantínosRíkos, and the church has a beautiul 16th-century iconostasis.

The road continues to **Kamáres**, the base for the 3–4-hour path (there's also a very winding road, but with no place to stop) up the flank of Mount Ida to the **Kamáres Cave** at 5,000ft/1,525m, an important cave sanctuary where it is thought the Minoans worshipped Eileithyia, goddess of childbirth. Its gaping mouth, 65ft high and 130ft wide, is visible from Phaistos; pilgrims from the palace brought their offerings in the refined pottery first discovered here – hence Kamáres ware (*see* p.55) – and made in Phaistos' workshops. Their discovery by Italian archaeologists in 1893 was a major influence on Evans' decision to come to Crete. Experienced walkers only should attempt the 5–6-hour path up to the summit of Mount Ida, beginning near Kamáres.

Down to Phaistos and the South Coast

Ancient Sites of the Mesará Plain

Tucked below the southern flanks of Mount Ida, the long Mesará Plain has been the breadbasket of Crete and one of its most densely populated areas ever since the time of the first Minoans. Because of this it contains a spectacular concentration of ancient sites: Minoan Phaistos and Ag. Triáda, and the capital of Roman Crete, Gortyn.

Gortyn (Γόρτγνα) and Míres (Μοίρες)

t 289 203 1144; open daily 8–7; adm. If you arrive by bus, get off at the Gortyn site entrance and then, when leaving, make your way back towards the village of Ag. Déka to find the northbound bus stop.

The Geropótamos river and its tributary the Lethaios water the plain, and the city of **Gortyn** (or Gortys, Gortyna). Strategically located on both banks of the Lethaios, and with ports at Mátala and Levín, it grew most with the arrival of the Dorians. Founded according to legend by either King Minos or colonists from Sparta, Gortyn supplanted Phaistos to become 'the second city of Crete' by the time of the *Iliad*; in early Classical

---

Getting Around

There are at least 12 buses daily between Heráklion and Míres, passing Gortyn, and 8 daily Mon–Fri direct to and from Phaistos (9 at weekends). All services to this area run from the Pórta Chaníon depot in Heráklion.

There are also 4 buses each day to Phaistos from both Ag. Galíni and Mátala, and more between Ag. Galíni and Míres. Many other destinations can be reached with a change at Míres; buses on the Míres or Phaistos–Ag. Galíni routes pass near to Ag. Triáda, but be ready to walk about 1km from the main road.

times it replaced arch-rival Knossos as the ruling city of the island. Hannibal's brief sojourn here in 189 BC after his defeat by Rome may have given its inhabitants some insight into the Big Noise from Italy, for they helped the Romans capture Crete; in reward Rome made Gortyn capital of both Crete and the province of Cyrenaica, including much of North Africa. In 828 AD the Saracens wiped it off the map.

In its prime Gortyn had a population of 300,000, and its ruins are scattered through a mile of olive groves – only the basilica and odeon are fenced in. The apse is all that survives of the tremendous 6th-century AD **Basilica of Ag. Títos**, once one of the most important in Greece but now a roost for local birds. Titus, originally buried here, was one of St Paul's favourite disciples, sent to convert Gortyn and be Crete's first bishop. Nearby, built into the walls of the elegant Roman **Odeon** (rebuilt by Trajan in AD 100), is Gortyn's great prize, the **Law Code of Gortyn**, covered by a shelter (*see* opposite).

Just up and behind the Law Code is the famous **plane tree** of Gortyn, by the Lethaios river. It's not apparent in summer, but this is one of a rare Cretan evergreen species; the story goes that it has kept its leaves for modesty's sake ever since Zeus in his bull disguise brought the Phoenician princess Europa into its shade and had his evil way with her, resulting in the birth of Minos, Rhadamanthys and Sarpedon (*see* p.30). Statues found during the excavations are displayed in the **Loggia**, next to a snack bar.

The rest of Gortyn is outside the enclosed area. If it's not too hot, climb the **Acropolis** on the other bank of the Lethaios. This has remains of an early (8th- or 7th-century BC) **temple** with three chambers, a long sacrificial altar and a sacrificial pit. The large

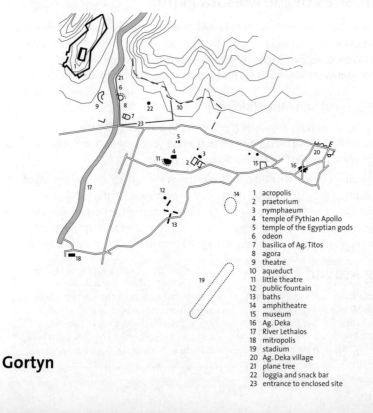

1 acropolis
2 praetorium
3 nymphaeum
4 temple of Pythian Apollo
5 temple of the Egyptian gods
6 odeon
7 basilica of Ag. Titos
8 agora
9 theatre
10 aqueduct
11 little theatre
12 public fountain
13 baths
14 amphitheatre
15 museum
16 Ag. Deka
17 River Lethaios
18 mitropolis
19 stadium
20 Ag. Deka village
21 plane tree
22 loggia and snack bar
23 entrance to enclosed site

Gortyn

Human Rights, Dorian-style: The Code of Gortyn

The first block of engraved limestone, accidentally discovered in a mill stream in 1857, was acquired by the Louvre. It attracted a good deal of attention. At the time no one had ever seen a Greek inscription so ancient, and it wasn't until 1878 that the inscriptions on this first block, dealing with adoption, were translated, using the writing on ancient coins as a study guide. No one suspected there was any more to it until one summer day in 1884 when Halbherr, the Italian archaeologist who would later excavate Phaistos, noticed a submerged building – the Odeon – while cooling his feet in the same mill stream, shallower than usual because of a drought. The rest of the inscription, over 600 lines divided in 12 blocks, was found soon after in a farmer's field; only the tops of blocks X and XII and a piece of block IX are missing.

Gortyn was famous for laws long before anyone knew the code existed. Crete, after all, was ruled by Minos, who 'every nine years received the laws of Zeus' and was later made one of the three judges in Hades. In Classical times Crete was universally recognized as the first place to codify laws, and even older legal inscriptions were subsequently found at Dreros (*see* p.239). Ancient sources such as Aristotle wrote of a certain Thaletas from Gortyn, who in the 8th century BC composed paeans (hymns) to Apollo, migrated to Sparta and introduced his paeans there; he was also said to be a lawgiver, the predecessor of the Spartan Lycurgus, and sang odes that encouraged obedience (which the Spartans continued to do on annual basis into historical times).

If the Spartans were content to sing their laws, the Gortynians preferred to write them down, in *boustrophedon*, 'as the ox ploughs' – from left to right, then right to left – in the Dorian dialect of *c*. 500 BC; the laws themselves are believed to predate their writing by 200 years. The Code is the longest such inscription to survive from antiquity, and because of it the civil laws of Archaic Crete are better known in their precise detail than Roman law. Significantly, the code was made for public display, and in spite of the inequalities of the ancient class system, which had a different set of rules for free men and serfs or *klerotai* (the native Minoans), the Gortyn Code is liberal in many ways. It gave women property rights they lacked in ancient Athens and in much more recent systems (the Code Napoléon, for one); if divorced, a wife kept all the property she brought to the marriage, along with half the produce derived from it. If she married beneath her station, the mariage was given special recognition. Debtors were punished but not enslaved (as elsewhere), the *klerotai* had recourse against cruel masters and there was a presumption of innocence until proven guilty long before it became the core of Anglo-American law.

stone reliefs that decorated it lent credence to the existence of the semi-legendary Daedelus, the reputed earliest 'Greek' sculptor, who had connections to the place (his wife was said to be from Gortyn). Lofty Roman walls defended the hill, and there's a well-preserved **fort**, perhaps built at the expense of the city's largest theatre, largely chewed away in the hillside below. A few minutes' walk down towards **Mitrópoli** reveals an Early Byzantine church with a mosaic floor, cut in two by the village road.

Signs from the main road point to paths in the olive groves where you can spend an hour or two wandering, nine times out of ten without another soul in sight; the lack of labels, the ground littered with pot sherds and broken tiles, and the half-hearted fences make it seem as if you were intruding into a 19th-century romantic engraving of ancient ruins. There's a small **Temple of Isis and Serapis**, the Egyptian gods who became popular in the late Roman Empire, and the more elaborate **Temple of Pythian Apollo**, the most important in Gortyn and often rebuilt since Archaic times; the inscription is another segment of Gortyn's Law Code, written in an even older dialect.

Most imposing of all is the 2nd-century AD **Praetorium**, seat of the Roman governor charged with ruling Crete and North Africa. Even after the Saracens roared through, it continued in use as a monastery, at least until Venetian times. Part of the complex is the fountain or **nymphaeum**, where the waters from the Zarós aqueduct flowed into the city. Further south are the massive ruins of the **gate**, an **amphitheatre**, **stadium** and **cemetery**, while the main path leads to the village of **Ag. Déka**, named after ten churchmen martyred here c. AD 250 on the order of Emperor Decius, for their refusal to take part in a temple dedication. The block on which they were beheaded is kept in the church, and their tombs in the new chapel at the west end of the village are the subject of much Cretan devotion. If you feel like some clambering, head 2km west to **Ampeloúzos**, where you can visit Crete's other 'labyrinth' – Gortyn's ancient quarry.

Míres, 9km to the west, is a lively, workaday agricultural town that has taken over Gortyn's old role as the commercial centre of the Mesará plain. On Saturday it hosts a big market. If you're relying on buses, count on spending some time here, waiting for changes for Phaistos, Mátala, Ag. Galíni, the Amári valley or Réthymnon. About 3km west of town up a minor road is the convent of **Moní Kalyvianí**, which was founded by the 14th century (the date of the oldest church and its frescoes), but was abandoned when the Turks occupied the island. In 1865 an icon of the Virgin was discovered in a neglected corner of the church, then used as a stable by Turkish farmers. Believed to be miraculous, it ignited a huge controversy on Crete, where revolt already crackled in the air: the Turks were adamantly against letting Christians gather here to be cured, and the Christians insisted on standing outside the church in the hot sun until they gave in. The case eventually went to the judgement of the 'Powers', who ruled in favour of the Christians. As the number of pilgrims swelled, a new church was built to house the icon, and since 1957 a new convent here has filled with nuns, who run an orphanage, a retirement home, a museum of popular and religious art and a shop selling their needlework. Apparently the miraculous icon is still at it; it wept in 1974, just before the Cyprus calamity, and again in November 1994, but no one knows why.

Phaistos (Φαιστός)

t 289 204 2315; Palace open daily 8–7; adm. Try to arrive early or late to avoid the crowds; a tourist pavilion at the site has a café and guest rooms (t 289 204 2360).

Superbly situated halfway up a high hill overlooking the lush Mesará plain and Mount Ida, **Phaistos** was one of the oldest cities in Crete, second only to Knossos in importance in Minoan times. It was the fief of Minos' brother Rhadamanthys and the birthplace of Epimenides, one of the Seven Sages of ancient Greece. The first palace was built around 2000 BC, and destroyed in an earthquake in 1700 BC; the second was built on top of the first and destroyed *c.* 1450 BC. Like Knossos but on a smaller scale, it was finely built of luxurious alabaster and gypsum, with a similar elaborate drainage system; masons' marks suggest the two palaces were the work of the same builders. Phaistos' workshops produced exquisite art, and yet, unlike at Knossos, no frescoes have been found. Below the palace 50,000 people lived and worked; villages dependent on the palace were scattered across the Mesará. Until Hellenistic times Phaistos remained an independent city-state, warring with Gortyn, until the latter crushed it once and for all in the 3rd century BC. Excavations, led by the flamboyant Italian Federico Halbherr, began in 1900, just after Evans began digging at Knossos.

Archaeological purists dismayed by Evans' reconstructions at Knossos breathe a sigh of relief at Phaistos, where only your mind's eye will reconstruct the original three-storey palace from the low, complicated walls and foundations; the fact that the second palace was built over the first means that you need an especially good imagination to evoke what one or the other may have looked like. Visits begin in the northwest, in the paved **Upper Court** with its raised **Processional Way**. This takes you down steps into the **West Court**, originally part of the Old Palace – the only section that the architects of the New Palace re-used after the earthquake, when the lines of the building were otherwise completely reorientated; the lower façade of the Old Palace survives just before the Grand Stairway. The West Court has eight straight tiers

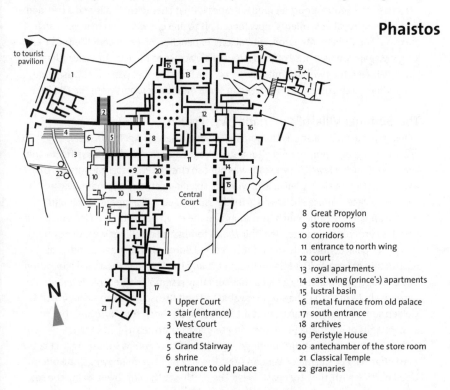

Phaistos

to tourist pavilion

Central Court

N

1 Upper Court
2 stair (entrance)
3 West Court
4 theatre
5 Grand Stairway
6 shrine
7 entrance to old palace
8 Great Propylon
9 store rooms
10 corridors
11 entrance to north wing
12 court
13 royal apartments
14 east wing (prince's) apartments
15 lustral basin
16 metal furnace from old palace
17 south entrance
18 archives
19 Peristyle House
20 antechamber of the store room
21 Classical Temple
22 granaries

known as the **theatre**, where people may have watched dances or other performances, and two stone-lined **granaries** or silos, originally protected by domed roofs.

The **Grand Stairway** was carved with special care, part from stone and part from the
living rock; the steps are slightly convex, to let rainwater run off. At the top, the **Great
Propylon**, the main entrance to the West Wing, stands just before a light well with
three columns. Another stair descends to the **Antechamber of the Store Rooms**,
where Halbherr found a huge cache of sealstones, and beyond it the **store rooms**; one,
with a roof, still has its giant *pithoi*, along with a stone stool for standing on to scoop
out the contents and a built-in vessel in the floor to collect wine or oil run-offs. A
corridor separated the storage areas from the main **shrine**, lined with stone benches.

From the Antechamber of the Store Rooms opens the **Central Court**, its long sides
originally sheltered by porticoes; buildings on all sides would have hidden the
tremendous views it enjoys today. A stepped block in the northwest corner may have
been the platform used by bull dancers as a springboard for 'diving leaps'. To the
southwest are a series of rooms fenced off and mingled with bits of the Old Palace,
and the foundations of a Classical-era temple. Landslides have swept away much of
the once residential **East Wing**, but the small chamber on its north side, a bathroom,
and a gypsum-paved lustral basin with stairs have earned it the name of '**Prince's
Apartments**'. A horseshoe-shaped **forge**, built in the Old Palace era for smelting
metals and the earliest one found in Greece, is at the end of the corridor to the north.

North of the Central Court a grand entrance with niches in the walls and a corridor
lead to more '**royal apartments**', now fenced off to prevent wear and tear; you can just
make out the **Queen's Megaron**, with alabaster benches. An open peristyle tops the
King's Megaron, which once offered a royal view across to the Kamáres cave (the dark
patch between the twin summits, *see* p.213). The Phaistos Disc (*see* p.184) was found
east of here, with pottery from 1700 BC, in some mud-brick rooms from the Old Palace.

The 'Summer Villa' of Ag. Triáda (Αγ. Τριάδα)

Only 3km east of Phaistos is the smaller Minoan palace of **Ag. Triáda** (*t 289 209 1360;
open daily 8.30–3; adm*), named after a small Venetian-era church on the site. No one
knows why such a lavish little estate was built so close to Phaistos: guesses are that
a wealthy Minoan simply fell in love with the splendid setting, or it may have been a
summer palace – unlike Phaistos, Ag. Triáda usually gets a sea breeze. In Minoan times
the sea apparently came much further in, and the ramp below the villa led down to a
port. It's certainly an old site; Neolithic *tholos* tombs and dwellings were discovered
under the 'palace', first built around 1600 BC and burned in the great island-wide
destruction of 1450 BC. The Minoans rebuilt it, and the Mycenaeans added a *megaron*
and a village, dominated by an area that curiously resembles a Hellenistic *agora*, with
a row of shops in a *stoa*. The site, excavated by the Italians off and on since 1902, has
yielded some of the Minoans' finest art, including the *Harvesters' Vase* and the
sarcophagus of Ag. Triáda (from the cemetery to the northeast).

The intimate scale and surroundings – and lack of tour groups – make Ag. Tríada the
most charming of the major Minoan sites. The villa had two main wings, one orientated north–south, the other east–west. The north–south wing, overlooking the sea,

1 Late Minoan/Mycenaean-era town
2 market
3 entrance
4 shrine
5 South Court
6 Mycenaean megaron
7 Ag. Georgios
8 store rooms
9 Hall of Archives
10 ramp
11 North Court

was the most elaborate, with flagstoned floors, gypsum and alabaster walls and benches. One room had built-in closets. The drainage system was excellent, and *pithoi* still stand intact in the store rooms. At the entrance to the excavations is the church of **Ag. Geórgios Galatás** (1302), with fine frescoes (*ask the site guardian for the key*).

As an aside, the room with the built-in closets was also decorated with the fresco of the *Stalking Cat*, evidence that the Minoans had cats, perhaps having acquired them, like so many other things, from Egypt. Curiously, for centuries the outback of Crete was famous for its wild 'ghost cats', the *fourokátos*; two pelts purchased in 1905 by an English member of a scientific expedition were the only evidence that such creatures existed until April 1996, when an Italian expedition from the University of Perugia caught one in a trap. Studies are underway to determine whether the wild cat existed on Crete prior to the island's separation from the mainland, or if the domesticated animal was brought to Crete, perhaps by the Minoans, and later took to the hills.

Around the South Coast: Mátala to Árvi

This corner of Crete offers more than the fossils of long-lost civilizations. Just to the north of Phaistos the old village of **Vóri**, on the road to Ag. Galíni (*see* p.167), hopes to waylay you with its superb **Museum of Cretan Ethnology** (*t 289 209 1394; open daily 10–6; adm*). This is the best place to learn about traditional country life in Crete – a civilization not yet lost, if in danger of extinction – with excellent descriptions in

English to go with its array of pottery, musical instruments, furniture and costumes. Charmless **Tymbáki**, 3km west, combines tomatoes under plastic with some dogged tourism, thanks to its long sandy beach, **Kókkinos Pírgos**, 'Red Tower', a name that predates its career as the Ketchup Coast. In spring and autumn migratory birds stop over at the wetlands at the end of the beach, at the mouth of the Geropótamos river.

Mátala (Μάταλα) and Kómmo (Κόμμος)

To the south and east, this is a wild, rockbound coast, which only here and there permits tortuous roads to descend to the sea. The main one leads to **Mátala**, with its lovely and once notorious beach under sandstone cliffs. The cliffs are riddled with cave tombs (*open 8–3*) from the 1st–2nd centuries AD, which over centuries the locals enlarged into cosy little rooms. In the 1960s, Americans bumming round Europe found they made a perfect (and free) place to crash in winter, and they were joined by a sizeable international hippy colony. In the killjoy 1990s hippies were banished, but if you stay overnight some of their spirit lingers on in Mátala's laid-back atmosphere, although grannies hawking rugs may be your strongest memory if you just stop by.

If the town beach is a massive body jam, a scramble over the rocks will take you in about 20 minutes to Mátala's second beach, beautiful **Kókkinos Ámmos**, 'red sand', with caves (inhabited, this time), clothes optional. Excursion boats sail to other small beaches at **Ag. Farágo** (at the end of a rocky gorge), **Marsalo** (very pretty, with palm trees) and, perhaps best of all, **Vathí** (in a little fjord): all three can also be reached by paths from Odgigitrías Monastery (*see* below). All these sands are also nesting grounds for loggerhead turtles, so avoid walking on the beaches on summer nights.

Mátala has been a midwife of tourism for nearby **Pitsídia**, along the main road, and **Kalamáki**, a cement resort on the long beach to the north. At the south end of this

Getting Around

There are **6 buses** daily between Heráklion and Mátala, and 12 daily to Míres, all from the Pórta Chaníon depot in Heráklion; there is also one bus a day to Léndas (1pm, Mon–Fri only). Other local services run from Míres.

Some buses from Heráklion to the Áno Viánnos area operate from Pórta Chaníon, but others leave from Plateía Kíprou. There are only a few direct services each day.

Where to Stay and Eat

Mátala and Area ✉ 70200

Mátala closes shop at the end of October, but by Easter it's hard to find a room, as many Greeks flock down for their first swim of the year. There are also several places offering simple budget rooms in Kalamáki and Pitsídia.

Armonia, t 289 204 5735, f 289 204 5758 (*B, expensive*). Quiet, small hotel 500m from the beach, with a pool and useful mosquito netting in every room. *Open April–Oct.*

Valley Village, t 289 204 5776, f 289 204 5445 (*B, moderate*). On the edge of Mátala village, with a pool, Greek dancing shows and barbecue nights. *Open April–Oct.*

Zafiria II, t 289 204 5112, f 289 204 5725 (*C, moderate*). Handy for town and beach, and reasonably priced, but completely booked by operators in season. *Open Mar–Oct.*

Nikos, t 289 204 2375, f 289 204 2120 (*E, inexpensive*). Pleasant place just outside Mátala, with a play area for kids. *Open April–Oct.*

Sofia, t 289 204 2134, f 289 204 5743 (*E, inexpensive*). A good-value option on a lane full of rooms to rent.

Mátala Camping, t 289 204 2720, f 289 204 2340. Just behind the beach is this cool campsite in the shade, with low prices.

beach is Minoan **Kómmo**, once the port of Phaistos. Recent excavations have revealed substantial remains – the largest Minoan port as yet known on the south coast. It's not officially open, but you can stroll along the beach and see what's been revealed: a massive building of dressed stone (probably a warehouse), dry docks, houses (one with a wine press) and a strip of road with wheel-ruts that probably lead to Phaistos. Near the beach was a sanctuary, sacred long after the Minoans: the 10th-century BC Dorians built a temple here, as did the Phoenicians and Classical Greeks.

Gortyn's Ports: Kalí Liménes (Καλοί Λιμένες) and Léndas (Λέντας)

Phaistos' rival Gortyn had several ports to the east, but the rugged coastal mountains preclude any seaside drive; on public transport you often have to go by way of Míres to catch the few buses each day. **Kalí Liménes** can be reached from Phaistos with a steep winding drive past the 16th-century **Moní Odgigitrías**, still defended by a tower with its 'killer' – a hole over the gateway for pouring boiling oil on intruders. Gortyn's main harbour, Kalí Liménes, the 'Fair Havens', is where the storm-tossed ship carrying St Paul put in on its way to be wrecked off Malta. Winters are so mild here that swallows don't migrate to Africa – locals say they're the souls of the anchorites who lived in these hills. Unlike its neighbours, though, Kalí Liménes has kept pace with the times; instead of saints, it now hosts oil tankers. If you don't mind them, there are beaches under the cliffs, a few cafés and some (albeit scant) Roman ruins and Minoan *tholos* tombs as proof of its antique authenticity, just east at **Lasaia**.

Ruins of another of Górtyn's harbours, **Levín** (or Lebena), are near the ramshackle fishing village-resort of **Léndas**. From Kalí Liménes you can get there via a rough but passable coast road and several small beaches, or you can take a new road from Gortyn; the sheltered shingle beach attracts hordes of Greeks on summer weekends.

Camping Kommos, t 289 204 2596. Near the Kommos ruins, with a pool.

Syrtaki. Has centre spot in Mátala's row of seaside tavernas, and serves all the Greek favourites at reasonable prices.

Zeus Beach Taverna. On the beach: moussaka, stuffed tomatoes and other tasty dishes made by mama.

Alexis Zorba. Also a taverna on the beach, and with good fresh soup.

Bodikos, Pitsídia, t 289 204 2438. For a change, with Italian and vegetarian dishes.

Kivotos, Sivas, t 289 204 2744. Delicious oven-baked dishes and live music daily in summer.

Tommy's Music Bar. By the beach, with cocktails to go with Mátala's famous sunsets.

Léndas ✉ **70200**
Studios Galini, t 289 209 5369 (*A, moderate*). Small tidy complex on the hill, overlooking the beach. *Open April–Oct.*

Keratókambos ✉ **70004**
Komis Studios, t 289 505 1390 (winter t 210 211 2138), f 289 505 1393, *www.komisstudios.gr* (*A, expensive–moderate*). On the seafront, a welcoming place with 15 traditionally-styled, ecologically sound studios in a garden, with a bar-restaurant. *Open May–Oct.*

Doriakis Apartments, t 289 505 1359 (*moderate*). Just behind Komis, in two buildings: flats in the newer one have air-con, but the older ones aren't bad either.

Áno Viánnos ✉ **70004**
Taverna Lefkes, t 289 502 2719. In the square, the best place for local dishes, prepared by a dab hand in the kitchen. *Open April–Nov.*

Árvi ✉ **70004**
Ariadne, t 289 507 1300 (*C, moderate*). The biggest hotel here, but there are a number of rooms places, too. *Open April–Oct.*

Hot springs just to the east led in the 4th century BC to the building of an **Asklepeion**, a sanctuary of the god of healing. There are mosaics, bits of a temple, and a pool amid the tamarisks where patients still wallowed in the waters until a few decades ago, but these are now pumped elsewhere. Most wallowing in Léndas these days happens at **Yerókambos**, a long sandy beach where clothes are an option few take up.

East of Gortyn to the Diktean Mountains

The region east of Gortyn towards Ierápetra has no major attractions, no easy-to-reach beaches, no Minoan palaces and not many tourists, in part thanks to the difficulties in reaching the sea through the austere **Asterousia** mountains. There are two ways of reaching **Pýrgos**, largest of its villages: the main road, which is scenic enough, or a more rugged route (four-wheel-drive recommended) south of Gortyn by way of **Vagoniá** and **Loúkia**. This passes through once-abandoned **Kapetaniá**, given a new lease of life by some Austrians who have restored its houses and set up a climbing centre (*t 289 304 1440*). Further east a track descends to **Moní Koudoumá**, on a lovely pine-clad cove. Partly built in a cave, the monastery was founded in 1870 by two saintly Cretan monks, although old churches and abandoned hermitages along the shore show they were hardly the first holy men to settle here. There are simple cells, if you want to spend a night. The easiest way to Koudoumá is by boat from Léntas; a path from the monastery leads up to the 4,038ft (1,230m) summit of **Korfí**.

Phílippi, east of Pýrgos, is dominated by the Byzantine fortress of **Castel Belvedere**, renovated by the Genoese during their brief tenure of the island. It gave a name, Kastélliana, to the surrounding hamlets and the fishing village of **Tsoútsouros**, with a rather crowded beach now smartened up with a marina. This was the site of **Inatos**, port of ancient **Priansos**, of which a few remains can be seen above **Káto Kastélliana**.

At **Mártha** the road joins the one from Chersónisos (*see* p.224). At **Káto Viánnos**, another 7km east, a good road descends to the sea by way of pretty **Chóndros**. Above it rise the twin peaks of the hill of Kefala; a path at a sharp bend of the road leads up to a rare **Late Minoan settlement**, built in this remote area after the collapse of the great palaces. Its houses had very thick walls and stone benches, and good views. The road carries on down to **Keratókambos**, a fishing village that was especially well defended: this was the beach where the Saracens landed in their invasion of Crete in 823, and to make sure it wouldn't happen again the Venetians built a fort by the sea and another one a kilometre east, known as **Kastrí**. Locals, and hundreds of Athenians in August, come here to swim on the huge sandy beach, but so far there are only a handful of places to stay and a few tavernas – although this looks as if it may change.

Áno Viánnos (Ἄνο Βιάννος) and Árvi (Ἄρβη)

Áno Viánnos, historically the most important village in these parts, hangs on the southwest flanks of Mount Díkti. It has been inhabited since early Minoan times, and in the Archaic era its people founded a colony on the River Rhône, on the route to the tin mines of the British Isles, which still bears its Cretan name, *Vienne*. It was a citadel of resistance against the Turks (who flattened it twice, in 1822 and 1866) and the Germans, who executed 820 people in the area. On the acropolis of Áno Viánnos are the ruins of a Venetian castle and a Turkish tower; in the Pláka district below don't miss the little churches of **Ag. Pelagía**, with frescoes by Emmánouil Fókas from 1360, and **Ag. Geórgios**. The latter is near an incredible plane tree that's believed to be the oldest in Greece after the granddaddy of them all, Hippocrates' plane tree on Kos.

East of Áno Viánnos, at the Amirás crossroads, a memorial remembers 400 men, women and children massacred here by the Nazis on a single day, 14 September 1943. The road descends past greenhouses to **Árvi**, enclosed in its own toasty little world, at the head of a valley of banana plants flourishing in the red soil. It has a pebble beach, good for a swim early or late in the year, and a picturesque monastery, **Ag. Antónios**. Other beaches are tucked along a track to the east, especially at **Akrotíri Sidonía**.

Meanwhile, if you continue east on the main road you'll see a sign north to **Áno Sími** (Άνο Σύμη). From this tiny hamlet a bumpy dirt road leads a few kilometres up into a plane tree forest, where three jumbly stone terraces and an outdoor altar of a **Temple to Aphrodite and Hermes** remained in business from 1600 BC to AD 300. Brave souls can continue walking up to the lunar landscapes of the high mountain plateau.

East of Heráklion: Crete's Holiday Costa

Gouvés, Chersónisos and Mália

East of Vathianó Kambó (*see* p.204), Europa, once raped on the island by Cretan Zeus in the form of a bull, gets her revenge. Here bullish developers have raped the lovely, sandy coast to pander to the yearning of cold Europa to soak up ultraviolet rays and cheap drink. This is the place to cocoon yourself in compounds full of sunburnt people of your own nationality, gather in 'pubs' to watch the football scores, and party the night away till you keel over. But what goes around comes around. The Dorians, pioneer cultural polluters who swamped these shores back in 1100 BC with heavy metal swords, were probably just as silly and tippled even worse. Yet the beaches are so big, and so close to Heráklion airport (you can be nursing a cocktail on the sands in about an hour of landing), that both Chersónisos and Mália also host some of the island's biggest and fanciest resort complexes, as well as Crete's first golf course.

Even if you aren't looking for thalassotherapy or a cup of REAL ENGLIHS (sic) TEA, you may find a reason or two to put on the brakes in holiday land. The beaches east of Heráklion are at their best (and sanest) at **Gouvés**, with beautiful rockpools where you can find starfish, crabs and scores of tiny shrimps, and a lovely shingle beach where the snorkelling is so good it may inspire you to try a little diving. Inland, signs point to **Skotinó** village and beyond it the enormous **Cave of Skotinó**. It has several chambers, the first a stunning lofty ballroom with a stalagmite mass in the centre lit by sun pouring through the cave's mouth. A huge amount of Minoan cult activity took place in the low-ceilinged chambers at the back, around curious rock formations (one looks like the bearded head of Zeus) and natural rock altars; it has even been suggested this cave, not Knossos, was the real labyrinth of the double axe.

Just 10km east is **Chersónisos** (Χερσόνισος), more properly Liménas Chersonísou, a synthetic tourist ghetto from end to end, complete with a Cretan museum village, the **Lychnostatis Museum** (*t 289 702 3660; open Sun–Fri 9.30–2; adm*). In the old times, Chersónisos was the port of ancient Lyttos, and had a famous Temple to Britomartis and Artemis. Little remains of these ancient glories: a reconstructed Roman fountain by the beach, bits of harbour installations, and a Roman **aqueduct**, at Xerokámares on the road to Lassíthi. On the west side of town, overlooking the harbour, are the ruins of a 5th-century basilica with three aisles, believed to be the seat of one of Crete's first bishoprics; a second basilica, from the next century, can be seen at the east end of town near the church of Ag. Nikólaos. If all the fun in the sun gets too intense, there are traditional villages just above – **Áno Chersónisos** and **Koutouloufári** – where you can catch your breath. East of Chersónisos are mellower **Stalída** and, in the centre of a 6km sandy bay, Crete's biggest resort town of all, **Mália** (Μάλια), which has a better beach than Chersónisos and has done its best to take over as the noisiest, rowdiest,

Getting Around

Buses run every 20mins between Heráklion and Chersónisos and Mália, 6.30am–10pm daily. At least 2 buses hourly continue to Ag. Nikólaos, all passing Mália ruins.

Sports and Activities

Crete Golf Club, 6.5km from Chersónisos; for info contact the **Creta Maris** hotel (*see* below) or *www.golfers.gr/crete_golf1.html*. Brand new 18-hole course.

Big Blue Diving School, Hotel Afroditi, Gouvés, t 289 704 2363. Fully-equipped diving centre.

AquaSplash Waterpark, by old Chersónisos, t 289 702 4950, *www.aquasplash.com*. The newest attraction for kids (and elders), with all sorts of water-based mayhem.

Horse Riding Centre, Star Beach, Chersónisos, t 289 702 3555. Guided rides on the beach.

Dolphin Water Sports, Mália, t 298 703 2250, *www.water-sports.gr*. Another centre offering the full range of dives and training.

Where to Stay and Eat

Gouvés ✉ 70014

Creta Sun Club, t 289 704 1103, f 289 704 1113, *www.grecotel.gr* (*A, luxury*). Hotel and bungalows with every comfort, extending along the beach; a big range of water sports make it ideal for families. *Open all year.*

Pantheon Palace, t 289 704 2025, f 289 704 2025 (*A, luxury–expensive*). Self-contained bungalows by the sea in a villagey setting. *Open April–Oct.*

Camping Creta, t 289 704 1400, f 289 704 1792. Large, well-organized site. *Open Mar–Nov.*

Taverna Anissara. Delicious Cretan specialities served up in a tranquil garden setting.

Chersónisos ✉ 70014

It's hard to find cheap rooms here, although local travel agencies do their best to help.

Royal Mare Village, t 289 702 5025, f 289 702 1664, *www.aldemarhotels.com* (*L, luxury*). An opulent compound with big rooms in bungalows among gardens, and Greece's largest thalassotherapy centre. The sophisticated restaurants have beautiful views, for a price (*around €55*). *Open Mar–Nov.*

Knossos Royal Village, t 289 702 3375, f 289 702 3150, *www.aldemarhotels.gr* (*L, luxury*). Glossier than ever since renovation in 2002, with vast outdoor and indoor pools, a water slide, very elegant dining in its restaurant, Fontana Amorosa (*€40*). *Open Mar–Nov.*

Creta Maris, t 289 702 2115, f 289 702 2130, *www.maris.gr* (*L, luxury*). Recently redecorated Aegean-style, six bars, free nursery, and peaceful rooms, all with a veranda or door to the garden. *Open Mar–Nov.*

Katrin, Stalída, t 289 703 2137, f 289 703 2136, *katrin@hrs.forthnet.gr* (*B, moderate*) The pick of this category in the locality, with three pools, but book well in advance.

most party-driven tentacle of the holiday sprawl east of Heráklion: at night, the bars lining the beach road thump and grind away with more decibels than sense.

Ancient Mália

There is an older, wiser Mália inland and, oldest of all, the **Minoan Palace of Mália** (*t 289 703 159; open Tues–Sun 8.30–3; adm*), near a quiet beach 3km to the east. In myth the fief of Minos' younger brother Sarpedon, Mália controlled the fertile coastal plain under the Lassíthi mountains, now given over to banana plantations. Its history follows the same pattern as Knossos: the site was inhabited from the Neolithic era (*c.* 6000 BC), and the first palace was built in 1900 BC. When this was devastated by the earthquake 200 years later, another palace was built over the first, then ruined in the catastrophe of *c.* 1450 BC. Compared to Knossos and Phaistos, Mália is 'provincial', built of local stone rather than alabaster or gypsum, and apparently without frescoes. On the other hand, the lack of later building makes it easy to understand the plan.

Selena, 13 Maragáki, t 289 7022 412 (*moderate*). Good value, with kitchenettes in rooms.

Youth Hostel, El. Venizélou, t 289 702 3521 (*inexpensive*). Well-run hostel with the cheapest beds in town.

Caravan Camping, t 289 702 2025. Well-shaded camp site.

Ta Petrina, Áno Chersónisos, t 289 702 1976 (€20). A courtyard setting, tasty meats and enjoyable vegetarian dishes. *Open all year.*

Tria Adelfia, Áno Chersónisos, t 289 702 2029 (€15). Above-average Cretan food – starters are especially tasty. *Open all year.*

Artemis, Stalída, t 289 703 2131. Beach taverna that's one of the area's best.

Mália ✉ 70007

Away from the beach, in Mália 'proper', it's easy to find smaller, cheaper hotels.

Ikaros Village, t 289 703 1267, f 289 703 1341, *Ikaros@hrs.forthnet.gr* (*A, expensive*). Lavish hotel complex designed as a traditional Cretan village. *Open April–Oct.*

Grecotel Mália Park, t 289 703 1461, f 289 703 1460, *www.grecotel.gr* (*A, luxury*). Plush bungalows near the beaches and Mália ruins, in a palm grove, with watersports and a mountain-bike centre. *Open April–Oct.*

Sirens Beach Hotel and Village, t 289 703 1321, f 289 703 1325, *www.sirensbeach.gr*. (*A, expensive–moderate*). The oldest hotel complex in Mália, built in the 1970s but constantly updated; beautiful gardens, and the area's prettiest views. *Open April–Nov.*

Helen, t 289 703 1545 (*C, moderate*). A kilometre from the beach, a mid-range option popular with British tour operators.

Ermioni, t 289 703 1093 (*E, inexpensive*). One of the best budget choices in town.

Ibiscus, t 289 703 1313, f 289 703 2042 (*E, inexpensive*). Near the main road, this has the asset (in a budget hotel) of a pool.

Youth Hostel, t 289 703 1555. Just east of town, the hostel is new and nice, but fills up fast.

Kalesma, 8 Omirou, t 289 703 3125. Handsome stone house containing Mália's best place to eat, with a big range of *mezédes* to go with wine from the barrel. *Open Mar–Oct.*

Nightlife

Most of the serious Anglo-German-Dutch clubbing is in Chersónisos, while the slightly more sedate take to music bars in the villages.

Status, Ag. Paraskeví, Chersónisos. Video projections and party atmosphere, all night.

Camelot, Ag. Paraskeví, Chersónisos. Mock castle theme, big bar, packed with Brits.

Enigma, Ag. Paraskeví, Chersónisos, t 289 702 3634. Plays all the latest Greek hits.

R & B, Mália coast road. DJs from the UK play nothing but R & B; also generous drinks.

Kafekopteíon, Áno Chersónisos, t 289 702 4474. Cool and relaxed music bar housed in a venerable stone building.

Mythos, Koutouloufári, t 289 702 1372. Lovely bar popular with Greeks, far from the sound and the fury of the beach strip.

Mália

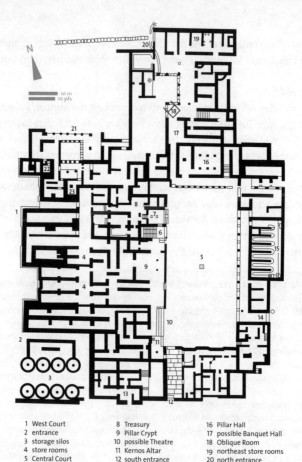

1 West Court
2 entrance
3 storage silos
4 store rooms
5 Central Court
6 Grand Stairway
7 Loggia (opening on to central court)
8 Treasury
9 Pillar Crypt
10 possible Theatre
11 Kernos Altar
12 south entrance
13 Shrine
14 southeast entrance
15 east store rooms
16 Pillar Hall
17 possible Banquet Hall
18 Oblique Room
19 northeast store rooms
20 north entrance
21 Royal Apartments
22 Lustral Basin
23 Archive Room

The entrance to the palace is by way of the **West Court**, crossed by the flagstones of the Processional Way. Eight large round 'silos', once covered with beehive domes, are at the south end of the way, thought to have been grain stores. Studies of Minoan skeletons suggest the system of gathering food in palace centres and redistributing it did their health no favours: Pre-Palatial Minoans, living in villages, ate the fresh food they grew; Old and New Palace Minoans suffered from gum disease, the first Europeans to do so. Fortunately for them, studies also show that they practiced dentistry.

The **Central Court**, re-used from the Old Palace, had porticoed galleries on its north and east ends; in the middle are supports of a hollow altar, or sacrificial pit. A **Grand Stairway** led up into the **West Wing**, where finds suggest the rooms had a ritual role: a raised and carefully paved **Loggia**, where religious ceremonies may have been performed, is near a mysterious round stone in the ground. The treasury, behind it, yielded a beautiful ceremonial sword with rock crystal pommel and a stone axe shaped like a pouncing panther. South of this, in the **Pillar Crypt**, masons' marks (double axes, stars and tridents) are carved in heavy square pillars. The four broad steps here are thought to have been used as a theatre, while in the southwest corner is the unique limestone *kernos*, a round offering table with a deeper hollow in the centre and 34 smaller hollows around the edge. Its similarity to the *kernos* used in Classical times is striking, and it may have been the Minoans who originated the rite of *panispermia*, the symbolic offering of the first fruits from each harvest to the deity.

A long portico, once supported by square stone pillars alternating with round wooden columns, ran along the east side of the Central Court. Mália had no lack of store rooms; narrow ones take up most of the **East Wing** (now protected by a roof), with drainage channels dating from the first palace. North of the Court, the **Pillar Hall** is the largest and most important room of all; the chamber above it, reached by a surviving stair, may have been for banquets. Behind it is another pillar room and the mysterious **Oblique Room**, its orientation suggesting some kind of astronomical or lunar observation. A suite of so-called **Royal Apartments**, with a sunken lustral basin, are in the northwest corner. Many Linear A tablets were found in the **Archive Room**, with the base of a single pillar. Outside the north entrance is an open area which may have been used for bull leaping. A paved road leads north to the so-called **Hypostyle Crypt**, under a barrel-vaulted shelter; no one has the foggiest idea what went on here.

If Mália seems somewhat poor next to Knossos and Phaistos, the Minoan estates found in its outskirts were sumptuous, especially the one northeast of the palace, where the only fresco at Mália was found. In a cemetery by the sea, the **Chrysolakkos** ('gold pit') **tomb** was probably the family vault of Mália's rulers. It was looted over centuries, but French archaeologists found the magnificent twin bee pendant of Mália inside; stylistic similarities suggest that the Aegina Treasure in the British Museum was pillaged from here in antiquity. To the west, part of the Minoan town has been excavated, and protected under a shelter; known as **Quarter M**; its complex network of little cubic dwellings, workshops and ceremonial areas has recently been made accessible for visitors with a series of wooden bridges.

South of Chersónisos: Villages under the Diktean Mountains

Some attractive villages high in the Pediáda region in the western foothills of Mount Díkti are linked by a good road south from Chersónisos. Most tourists don't get further than **Káto Karouzaná**, a designated 'traditional village' for tour parties from the coast. But, hidden away a little further south before Kastélli, signs for 'Paradise Tavern–Byzantine Church', point the way to **Ag. Pandeleímonos**, a fascinating old village under huge plane trees by a spring, built over a Temple to Asklepeios (*the taverna owners will summon the caretaker*). Originally built in AD 450,

Getting Around

Most **buses** from Heráklion to Thrapsanó and villages in the Pediáda leave from Plateía Kíprou, but some run from Pórta Chaníon. There are one or two daily from Chersónisos and Mália, and some from Heráklion to Ierápetra follow the Arkalochóri road.

Eating Out

Kastélli ✉ **70006**
Irida, t 289 103 2023. A pretty café-restaurant in a neoclassical house and garden that makes a very enjoyable lunch stop.
Taverna To Steki. On the north side of Kastélli, a taverna that often hosts music sessions.

A Litany to Dittany

Oregano is a Greek word meaning 'mountain joy', and no variety warms the heart of a Cretan like *origanum ditamnus*, a fragrant small perennial plant of the Labiatae family with distinctive thick hairy leaves, which likes to grow in rock crevices; over the centuries this precious herb, now used in teas or herbal liqueurs, has been behind more than one death, as gatherers took one too many risks to pluck it. For Cretan dittany was attributed uncanny powers by the ancients; when Aeneas was wounded in the Trojan War, Venus rushed to Mount Ida to gather leaves for his cure, and Aristotle wrote how wild goats on Ida, wounded by hunters, could heal themselves by munching on the stuff. It was used to induce and ease labour pains, or in early pregnancy to abort. Dioscorides was the first to mention the tonic effect of Cretan dittany; another Greek name for it, *érotas*, refers to its powers as an aphrodisiac and Viagra-like cure-all for impotence. Cretans recommend tossing dittany leaves in a hot bath if you're feeling low; look for it in shops selling Cretan herbs and spices.

it was said to have 101 doors, but after being ravaged by the Saracens was rebuilt on a more modest scale *c.* 1100, using the stones of old tombs, columns and reliefs. Note the bell made out of a German shell, cut in two. Inside, the nave with very faded frescoes is supported by marble columns from ancient Lyttos, including a striking one made of nothing but Corinthian capitals, stacked like children's blocks.

Kastélli is the largest Pediáda village, named after its long-gone Venetian castle. A short detour west to **Sklaverochóri** has its reward in the 15th-century church of **Eisódia tis Theotókou** (Presentation of the Virgin), with excellent frescoes, forerunners of the Cretan school: a fairy-tale scene of St George and the princess, allegories of the river gods in the Baptism and a Catholic intruder, St Francis, holding a rosary.

Four kilometres east of Kastélli, ancient **Lyttos**, by modern **Xidás**, had close ties to Sparta (some say it was a colony). It was a fierce rival of Knossos after the Doric invasion and remained sufficiently powerful and wealthy to mint its own coins until 220 BC, when Knossos, allied with Gortyn, demolished it. In spite of aid from Sparta, Lyttos never really recovered. The Minoans hog archaeological funds on Crete, so Lyttos is just starting to be investigated, but you can see Hellenistic walls, a theatre and other remains, including a frescoed church built over an early Christian basilica.

With fine local clay, families of potters in **Thrapsanó** (8km west) have made small bowls and large *pithoi* for centuries, using techniques that have scarcely changed in all that time. **Arkalochóri**, to the south, is the scene every Saturday of a big produce and stock market. In 1932, Marinátos and Pláton excavated a sacred cave here and brought forth some exceptional Minoan ritual weapons: the longest prehistoric Greek bronze sword ever found, and gold and bronze axes, one engraved in Linear A, the other with symbols similar to those on the Phaistos Disc – which put paid to notions that the disc was a forgery. Current thinking has it that the sanctuary was dedicated to a warrior deity. The road south rises at **Panagía** for **Embarós**, where Cretan dittany, the island's miracle herb, has been cultivated in recent years. To the south at Mártha, you'll meet the main south coast road between Míres and Ierápetra.

Nomós Lassíthi

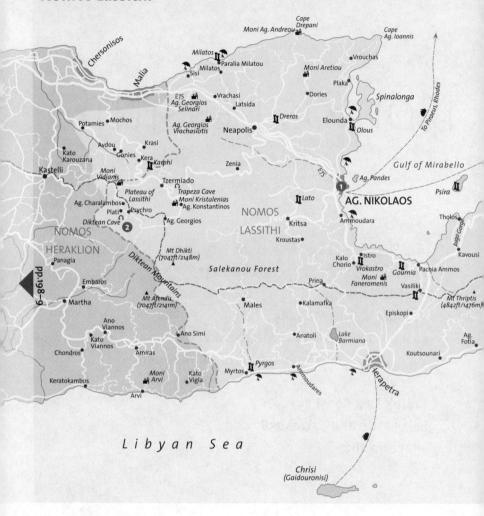

Nomós Lassíthi

Cretan Sea

Libyan Sea

Highlights

1 Ag. Nikólaos, the bustling, stylish little capital on the stunning Gulf of Mirabéllo
2 The great bowl of the mountain plateau of Lassíthi
  and the Diktean Cave, birthplace of Zeus
3 Sandy Vaï, Crete's tropical beach, backed by palm trees rustling in the breeze
4 The Minoan Palace and beach village of Zákros
5 The islet of Koufounísi, the 'Delos of Crete', prized in ancient times for its snails
  and sponges and now an uninhabited desert island

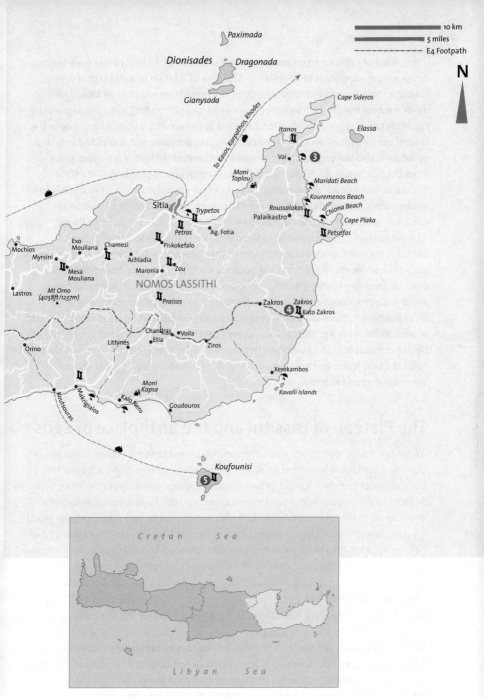

The name of Crete's easternmost prefecture, Lassíthi (ΛΑΣΙΘΙ), comes from the Greek mispronunciation of Venetian *La Sitía*, one of its chief towns. Lassíthi doesn't have the towering peaks that characterize the rest of Crete (although Mount Dhíkti, on its western fringes, isn't exactly a peewee at 7,045ft/2,148m), but it manages to be the most varied quarter of the island, framed to the west by a plateau hanging in the clouds, too cold for olives but planted with apples, potatoes and wheat and irrigated by white-sailed windmills, while the east coast ends at Vaï with a luxuriant, palm-lined tropical beach. Ag. Nikólaos, a fairly new town on the stunning Gulf of Mirabéllo, is the most cosmopolitan of Crete's four capitals; with most of the island's luxury hotels in its environs, this is not the place to come in search of traditional Crete but, as always, you do not have to venture too far from the coast to find it.

Lassíthi was densely populated in Minoan times: if the unplundered palace of Zákros is the most spectacular reminder of their precocious thalassocracy, town sites such as Gourniá, Palaikástro, Vasilikí, Fournoú Korifí and Móchlos have offered vital clues on their day-to-day life. Sitía is one of Crete's most pleasant provincial towns, and if Ierápetra, down on the hot, plastic-coated southeast coast, can come as a disappointment, there are plenty of beaches and two fascinating islets nearby to visit as well. Kritsá, near Ag. Nikólaos, has Crete's best frescoes and its most impressive Dorian remains at Lato. Lassíthians tend to be gentler than other Cretans, and claim to be the best lovers on the island; other Cretans, however, would grant them only superlative potatoes and pigs.

The Plateau of Lassíthi and the Birthplace of Zeus

A steady trail of tour buses makes the winding ascent to the spectacular Plateau of Lassíthi, a high point of Crete both in altitude and atmosphere. To get a feel for the place consider spending a night or two, for it is unique: a green carpet hemmed in on all sides by the Díktean Mountains, snowcapped into April and watered in summer with the aid of white-sailed windmills. A necklace of villages look down into the green bowl, including Psychró, near the uncanny cave where baby Zeus first saw the light of day. Karphí, a remarkable windblasted pinnacle where a band of Minoans took refuge in troubled times, is equally uncanny, and offers the most spectacular views of all.

Best Beaches: Nomós Lassíthi

Almyrós: the best near Ag. Nikólaos, with eucalyptus trees for shade, shallow water, and a play area for kids (*see* p.244).

Sísi (Limáni Beach): popular with families, as kids love to explore the rocks (*see* p.237).

Sitía: on the edge of the town, with fine shingle, a good choice of places for a drink or something to eat, and plenty of space for everyone (*see* p.253).

Vaï: backed by banana plantations and shaded by palm trees, and strongly placed to be the most beautiful beach on the whole island (*see* p.258).

Xerókambos: stretching across several small bays, with fine sand and clear water, and simple tavernas and rooms for rent (*see* p.261).

The Healthiest Shade

Perhaps the best advertisement for the properties of Krási's water is its plane tree, which has thrived on it for the past 2,000 years, give or take a few centuries. This superb specimen measures some 80ft (25m) in circumference and requires 16 people to encompass its girth, although before the embankment was built around the square they say it took 30 people to embrace it; in the 19th century, a café with three tables did business inside the hollow of its trunk.

For all Greeks, but perhaps most of all for old Cretan tree-worshippers, planes are sacred; as they will only grow by fresh springs, they are synonymous with water, and hence with life itself. No village worth its salt would be without at least one in its main square; occasionally, a flowing tap is even embedded in the trunk. According to Hippocrates, the 4th-century BC father of medicine, their shade is the most wholesome (just the opposite of the enervating shade of the fig); the fact that generations of Greeks have spent much of their lives gossiping in *kafeneíos* under plane trees has given rise to the expression *cheréte mou ton plátano*, 'greet the plane tree for me,' or in other words, 'go tell it to the marines.' As proof of Crete's holy status it has the only 29 known evergreen plane trees in the world, most famously at ancient Gortyn (*see* p.213), which proudly engraved the tree on its coins.

Approaches from the West

With your own transport you have a choice of roads up to the plateau. The main route from Heráklion and Chersónisos passes a series of old villages, including **Potamiés**. Just above, the lovely cruciform church of the Panagía, in the abandoned monastery of **Moní Gouverniótissa**, has fine early 14th-century frescoes, including a Pantocrator who stares holes into sinners (pick up the key at the Potamiés *kafeneíon*). Frescoes from the same century decorate the church of Ag. Antónios at **Avdoú**, a pretty place that has lately become one of the centres of alternative tourism on Crete.

If, on the other hand, you take the narrow road that cuts south east of Chersónisos at Stalída, the ascent is far more abrupt. After 8.5km of bird's-eye views over the sea, the village of **Mochós** comes as a pleasant antidote to the coastal cacophony. There are a few places to eat in the main square (**Anonimo** has good *myzíthra*-cheese pies with honey) and some rooms, mostly occupied by Swedish tourists, who know Mochós through their assassinated prime minister Olof Palme, who had a summer residence, Villa Palme, here. South of Mochós the Stalída and Chersónisos roads meet just north of **Krási**, a village famous for its curative spring (*see* above).

Very near Krási, in the village of **Kerá**, the much-rebuilt **Convent of Kardiótissa** may not look much from the outside, but it holds a special place in Cretan hearts. Probably founded in the 1100s, it was visited by the 15th-century Florentine monk Christoforo Buondelmonti, who wrote of the long list of miracles attributed to its icon of the Virgin. In 1498, an Italian merchant and reader of Buondelmonti purloined the icon and, although he had to jettison his whole cargo of wine on the way home as divine punishment, made it to Rome with the image and donated it to the church of San Matteo, where it attracted considerable cult status as the *Madonna della Perpetuo Soccorso*. In 1866 it moved to Sant'Alfonso in Rome, where you can see it to this day.

For the Cretans this is all water under the bridge: they insist that the copy of the icon in their church is the real McCoy, and that it was twice carried off by the Turks to Constantinople but made its way back on its own; the third time the Turks chained it to a column, but it flew back to Crete with column and chain attached. The uprooted column is in the courtyard, while the chain, hanging on the iconostasis, is said to relieve pain miraculously if wrapped around the body. In 1982 the icon was stolen yet again by a gang of delinquents who tried to sell it, but by some new miracle it was found a few days later on a mountain near Heráklion. Cretans were so relieved they ceremoniously walked it back home. In the course of restoration work on the church 14th-century frescoes were discovered; there's a fine portrait of the Byzantine lady who paid for the art, wearing a cloak with a two-headed eagle medallion.

Further along the forbidding grey head of **Mount Karphí** looms up as the road reaches the pass at **Selí Ampeloú**, with the most important concentration of stone windmills on Crete – 24 out of an original 26 are still more or less intact. All were grinding wheat until the 1950s, and three have recently been restored by their owners. After the Seli Ampelou Taverna, the road descends into the Lassíthi plateau.

Villages of the Plateau

Down below, the round emerald plain presents at its best a kind of epiphany; German film director Werner Herzog used it as such, hypnotically, in his film *Signs of Life*. A fertile chequerboard of fields divided by drainage ditches, in a bowl of barren mountains, the plateau was farmed by the Minoans, the Dorians of Lyttos and many others until 1293, when it was such a fierce nest of resistance that the Venetians forced everyone out, demolished villages and churches, set a guard around the passes and persecuted anyone who drew near. Only in 1543, when the Venetians were in a reconciliatory mood, were Greek refugees from the Turkish-occupied Peloponnese allowed to resettle the plateau. To help re-establish its orchards the Venetians built

Getting Around

Bus connections are more frequent from Heráklion than Ag. Nikólaos: there are 2 buses daily direct, one via Chersónisos and one via Mália. From Ag. Nikólaos there are only about two buses each week, usually on Mondays and Thursdays. All buses wind their way up to the plateau, catching most of the villages and ending up at the Diktean Cave.

Festivals

23 April *Panegýri*, Ag. Geórgios.
15 Aug *Panegýri*, Mochós.
29–31 Aug 3-day *Panegýri*, Psychró.
8 Sept Day of the Virgin at the convent of Kardiótissa, Kerá.

Sports and Activities

Kriti Farm, Potamiés, **t** 289 705 1546. A mini-zoo with farm animals and tours by donkey.
ICNA (International Centre of Natural Activities), Avdoú, **t** 289 705 1200. Offers a multitude of options: paragliding, mountain biking, trekking, climbing, caving and more.

Where to Stay and Eat

Avdoú ✉ 75005
Villa Avdoú, **t** 289 705 1606, **f** 289 705 1374, *www.avdou.com* (*expensive*). A 'holistic retreat' and a great cure for stress; modern studios and villas on an organic farm, 20 mins from the beach. Meals are made from homegrown produce, and while there you

10,000 irrigation windmills in 1564, and in the 19th century some 5,500 were rebuilt on iron towers. Most have now been mothballed in favour of the more reliable petrol pump, but some 600 still turn today, and as oil prices mount, others may rejoin them.

Eighteen villages dot the edge of the plateau, not only to keep the best land for farming but also to keep their toes dry; lower down the plateau can get boggy from melted snow. Largest is **Tzermiádo (Τζερμιάδο)** with a population of 1,500, located near a sacred cave and peak sanctuary. A sign points to a path to the first, the **Trápeza Cave** (bring a light), in use since 5000 BC. Long before the first religious shrines were built, Cretans left ivory votive offerings in the mysterious penumbra behind its narrow opening; the Middle Minoans used it for burials. Archaeologists scoff at efforts to change its name to *Cave of Kronos*, to compete with the Diktean Cave trade.

Another more strenuous path (or dirt road part of the way, marked 'Tímios Stavrós') leads up in an hour to the Níssimos plateau and beyond to **Karphí (Καρφί)**, the 'nail', which is a fairly accurate description of the mountain, a weird place that held the loftiest of all Minoan peak sanctuaries (3,800ft/1,160m); views from here stretch not only over the whole plateau, but across the Aegean to the Cyclades on a clear day. Excavated by the affable one-eyed giant John Pendlebury between 1937 and 1939 – his last project before he was killed, fighting alongside the locals in the Battle of Crete – Karphí was the refuge of some 3,500 Minoans, or Eteocretans ('True Cretans'), during the Dorian invasion in 1100 BC. In these inhospitable conditions they built a small town on the Gourniá model and for a hundred years, till about 950 BC, valiantly tried to keep the fires of Minoan civilization burning, before the bleakness and harsh winters got too much for them. Pendlebury found 150 small houses, a temple, chieftain's house or *megaron* with a porch and hearthroom, a tower, barracks and a shrine that contained five of the last known Minoan clay idols of the goddess (*c.* 1050 BC, now in the Heráklion museum), weird, distorted and a yard tall, with a cylinder skirt, detachable feet and long neck, like Alice when she was mistaken for a serpent.

can take on a range of courses, health treatments and other activities.

Tzermiádo and Area ✉ 72052

Argoulias, t 284 402 2194/281 031 0412 (*expensive–moderate*). Six restored traditional houses, with grand views of the plateau and cool even when it's baking outside. Breakfast is included, but self-catering is an option. *Minimum stay three days; open all year.*

Kourites, t 284 402 2194 (*B, inexpensive*). A pleasant, relaxing choice, with 13 comfortable rooms. *Open all year.*

Lassithi, t 284 402 2194 (*E, inexpensive*). Owned by the same family as the Kourites, and with a restaurant. *Open all year.*

Krikri, t 284 402 2170 (*E, inexpensive*). A likeable small hotel with a restaurant. *Open all year.*

Kronio, t 284 402 2375. Long established taverna serving delicious versions of the classics, using local ingredients; try the new potatoes in season. *Open April–early Nov.*

Rhea, Ag. Geórgios, t 284 403 1209 (*E, inexpensive*). Basic budget rooms.

Dias, t 284 403 1207 (*E, inexpensive*). Simple rooms and good food, too.

Psychró ✉ 72052

There are quite a few rooms available in the village to supplement its two simple hotels. The **restaurant** above the shop in the Diktean Cave car park is fine for a simple lunch.

Zeus, t/f 284 403 1284 (*D, inexpensive*). Straightforward rooms. *Open all year.*

Dikteon Andron, t 284 403 1504 (*E, inexpensive*). Just a little more basic. *Open all year.*

If you're on foot, there are tractor paths through the fields, but by car you must follow the road that rims the plateau. Clockwise from Tzermiádo, **Ag. Konstantínos** has the most souvenir shops, while above it the 13th-century **Moní Kristalénias** enjoys a lovely panoramic spot. It has good reliefs and a tragic tale: in 1823, during a baptism ceremony, Egyptian allies of the Turks broke into the monastery, murdered the men and carried off the women and children. One boy taken to Cairo became Ismail Feric Pasha, a minister of war, while his brother, António Kambánis, became a financier of the pan-Cretan Revolt of 1866. Ismail, now a fierce enemy of Crete, led an army up to Lassíthi and burned the monastery and his own village. This wasn't enough to convince Turkish rivals that he was not a crypto-Christian, and later he was poisoned. **Ag. Geórgios**, the next village, is one of the most resolutely old fashioned on the plateau; in a 200-year-old farmhouse is a **Folk Museum** (*open June–Aug daily 10–4*), with everything a Cretan mountain family needed to get by, including a wine-press that doubled as a bed and a fascinating collection of photos of Níkos Kazantzákis.

Psychró and the Diktean Cave

Hail, son of Kronos,
Welcome, greatest Kouros,
Mighty of brightness,
Here now present, leading your spirits,
Come for the year to Dikte
And rejoice in this ode,
Which we strike on the strings, as we
Blend it with the sound of pipes, as we
Chant our song, standing round
this your well-walled altar.
Hymn of the Kouretes to Diktean Zeus

At the southwest end of the plateau, **Psychró** (Ψυχρó) is the base for visiting the **Diktean Cave**, the birthplace of Zeus (*t 284 403 1316; open daily 9–7; adm*). From the car park it's a kilometre up a rocky, stepped path; the locals offer sure-footed donkeys to make the climb, while other guides await at the entrance to hire out lanterns in case you haven't brought a torch of your own. Rubber-soled shoes are equally important; the descent into the gaping maw of the cave can be difficult and slippery.

If you get there early, before the coachloads, the cave is a haunting place, well worthy of myth. Only rediscovered in the 1880s, it contained cult items from Middle Minoan up to Archaic times; its role as the birthplace and hiding place of Zeus from his cannibal father Cronos predates the Idaean Cave's claims, and was confirmed by the discovery in Palaíkastro of the *Hymn of the Kouretes* (the young warriors who danced and banged their shields to drown out the baby's cries). Down in its damp and shadowy bowels the guides point out formations that, if you squint just so, resemble the baby god, his cradle, his cloak and the place where the nannygoat Amaltheia nursed him; to help conceal the birth, Rhea, his mother, spurted her milk into the heavens, creating the Milky Way. Tradition has it that King Minos came up here to receive the law of Zeus every nine years, and that Epimenides the Sage also lived here as a hermit, having strange shamanistic visions.

In nearby **Ag. Charálambos**, the **Gerondomoúri Cave** was used by generation upon generation of ancients as a charnel house, making it one of the island's most important anthropological finds. A comparative study of Minoan bones and skulls with those of over a thousand modern Cretans show that the islanders have physically changed very little, so when you see one of those wasp-waisted teenagers with thick curls, large black eyes and a profile like the *La Parisienne* fresco, you aren't hallucinating. The cigarette invariably dangling from her lips somehow adds to the effect.

North of Ag. Charálambos, Heráklion's Museum of Natural History is currently setting up an exhibit on lammergeyers or bearded vultures (*gypaetus barbatus*) in the pretty **Moní Vidianis** (1854). Bearded vultures, with their 10ft wing spans, are among the largest birds in Europe; Crete has an important colony, with some ten pairs.

The road down from the plateau eastwards to Neápolis (*see* p.239) and Ag. Nikólaos is full of twists and turns, with dramatic views around each bend, where little roadside chapels mark each fatal accident, or miraculous escape from one. Bus drivers sometimes stop for a coffee in **Zénia**, where in the old days a young woman who had hair down to her knees caught the eye of a Turkish captain, who threatened to destroy the village if she would not marry him. At the wedding feast she poured him more wine than he could hold, then took him to bed and lopped off his head. Running to the church, she cut off her famous hair and took the clothes of a soldier and the name Captain Manólis, and, before she was killed in battle, pickled several more Turkish ears (as American Indians used to collect scalps, the Cretans and Turks pickled the ears of their adversaries). Her hair and knife are still on display in the church.

Between Mália and Ag. Nikólaos

East of Mália the new highway cuts inland, avoiding rugged **Cape Ag. Ioánnis**. This is good news for the beach resorts along this coast, which are free of the grind of heavy traffic that bedevils those to the west. **Sísi** (Σίσι) is a chunk of southern California, all pastel architecture, sandy beaches and a cute little port – a turquoise cirque under the cliffs, lined with a palm garden and a cascade of tavernas, bars and pubs serving beans on toast. The main town beach, **Limani**, has interesting rocks to explore and is popular with families; golden-sandy **Boufós Beach** to the east is just as popular.

Next along, **Paralía Milátou** (Παραλία Μιλάτου) offers an unprettified contrast to Sísi: low-key and a bit faded, with fishing boats and a long pebble beach with a few sunbeds and fish tavernas. A few bits of stone just east of the beach recall ancient **Milatos**, one of the most important cities of Homeric Crete. Myth has it that the three brothers Minos, Rhadamanthys and Sarpedon competed for the affections of a beautiful boy. When he chose Sarpedon, his brothers were such poor losers that Sarpedon left Crete for Asia Minor, taking with him the boy and the people of Milatos, who then founded the great city of Miletus. In the *Metamorphoses*, Ovid wrote summing up the decline of Crete and rise of Ionia in the 8th and 7th century BC: 'When Minos was in

Getting Around

There are 2–3 buses daily to Sísi and Paralía Milátou from Heráklion, and 2 a day, Mon–Fri only, from Ag. Nikólaos. All the many buses daily on the Heráklion–Ag. Nikólaos road stop at Neápolis.

Where to Stay and Eat

Sísi ✉ 72400

Kalimera Kriti Hotel & Village Resort, t 284 107 1134, **f** 284 107 1598, *kalimera@compulink.gr* (*A, luxury*). Luxurious hotel on the east side of Sísi with two private beaches, outdoor and indoor pools, tennis courts and very plush rooms. *Open April–Oct.*

Hellenic Palace, t 284 107 1502, **f** 284 107 1238 (*A, expensive*). Modern and comfortable hotel at the west end of Sísi Beach.

Castello Village, t 284 107 1102, **f** 284 107 1462 (*B, expensive*). Modern apartments with a pool, many with lovely seaviews. A good choice for families. *Open April–Oct.*

Zygos Apartments, t 284 107 1279 (*C, moderate*). Smaller, self-catering option with kitchenettes.

Angela Hotel and Apartments, t 284 107 1176, **f** 284 107 1121 (*C, moderate*). The seafront hotel has pool and bar; the apartments, just inland, are more basic.

Camping Sísi, t 284 107 1247. Campsite with pool, near a pretty if somewhat rocky beach.

Mediterraneo. Fine fresh fish on the seafront.

Mama Mia. Nearby, with Italian standards.

Paralía Milátou ✉ 72400

Minos Imperial, t 281 024 2082, **f** 281 024 3757, *www.minosimperial.gr* (*L, luxury*). Opened in 2001, an opulent hotel-bungalow complex, with spacious rooms, suites with private pools, tennis, kids' club and watersports.

Terzákis, t 284 108 1353. Local favourite among all the many fish tavernas.

Taverna Mary Elen. Offers a free carafe of local wine with all fish main meals.

Zephyros. Traditional taverna in the centre of the village, for homemade wine and raki.

Neápolis ✉ 72400

Miliaras, Latsída, 2km west of Neápolis, **t** 284 103 1883. Famous *psistariá* (grill house) serving succulent *souvláki*, chops and baked kid, and delicious salads just plucked from the garden. *Open Mar–Nov, eves only.*

his prime, his very name terrified great nations: but now he was weak and very much afraid of Miletus, the son of Deione and Apollo, for the latter was young and strong.' Up the hill, the old village of **Milátos** proper still has a dusty, forsaken air.

It also has a more recent reason to look forlorn. In 1823, when Hassan Pasha went on a rampage in Lassíthi to dampen hopes sparked by the Greek War of Independence, the **Cave of Milátos** served as a refuge for 3,600 people. Hassan found them, and after two fierce battles the refugees surrendered; the pasha had promised them all safe conduct, but instead massacred the men and children and enslaved the women. The cave is located on the edge of a wild, rocky ravine, 6km from the beach, and a 10-minute walk along a path from the parking area (*bring a torch*). Beyond the bulbous rock that looms above the entrance the main chamber has a low, smoke-blackened ceiling, supported by slender stalagmites. The chapel or *heroön*, built in 1935, contains a glass reliquary full of bones. Today the only residents of the cave are three kinds of bats, and curious little invertebrates indigenous to Crete.

The main coastal highway passes over a ravine, where Cretans often pull over to light a candle by the miraculous icon in **Ag. Geórgios Selinári**, St George of the Moon; the story goes that a monk found the icon, but was refused permission from a Turkish pasha to build a church, and so he did so here in secret, by moonlight. Another, now abandoned monastery, **Ag. Geórgios Vrachasiótis**, is to the south of **Vrachási** (*pick up the key from the priest in Vrachási*) and contains a carved wooden iconostasis that's a marvel of Cretan folk art. Note the relief of the saint and dragon on the 16th-century dedicatory inscription on the belltower. South of Milátos and just north of the highway, **Latsída** has two impressive churches, of Ag. Paraskeví and the Panagía, both with 14th- and 15th-century frescoes.

Neápolis (Νεάπολις) and Ancient Dreros

Immersed in greenery and almond groves, **Neápolis** is the largest town between Heráklion and Ag. Nikólaos. In its former incarnation, *Karés*, it was the birthplace of Pétros Fílagros, in 1340. Raised by Catholics, he became a professor of theology at Bologna and was elected Pope Alexander V in 1409, one of several popes-for-a-year during the Great Schism. Karés predeceased him, though, as the Venetians destroyed it in 1347 after a revolt. The rebuilt village grew into the 'new town', *Neápolis*, capital of Lassíthi until 1905 when Ag. Nikólaos stole its thunder. Many of its churches are from Venetian times, including **Ag. Geórgios** 'the Blood-stained', site of a secret Greek school under the Turkish occupation. In 1770, during the Daskaloyannis rebellion (*see* p.148), Turks raided the church and slaughtered the priest and congregation. In 1827, Cretan rebels got bitter revenge by besieging Neápolis' mosque and burning the Turks inside; when Crete became independent the mosque was replaced by the modern cathedral in the central square. Nearby is a small **museum** (*the museum has been closed for renovation, but is due to reopen soon; t 284 202 8721, normally open Tues–Sun 8.30–3*) with inscriptions from ancient Dreros, a bronze statuette of a bull and statues found in the area. Don't miss Neápolis' lovely, old-fashioned **Kafeneíon Kentron** on the square, in a neoclassical building of 1922.

Ancient **Dreros**, one of the principal cities of Crete in the 8th-6th centuries BC, lies up a narrow winding road north of Neápolis (cross under the New Road and follow signs for Kouroúnes); above a tiny car park, a path leads up through maquis and rocks to a saddle between the two peaks that were once the city's citadels. Amid a jumble of stone walls, steps, inspired by Minoan 'theatrical areas', lead up to a 7th-century BC **agora** where civic and religious meetings were held – the oldest yet found in Greece. Inscriptions found here go back to the late 7th century, and are some of the oldest known in the newfangled alphabetic script the Greeks learned from the Phoenicians. They record laws designed to prevent city oligarchs from running for office too often and gaining power, and their reference to Dreros as a *polis* is our oldest known record of a city-state. Nearby, under a roof, the **Temple to Apollo Delphinios** is from the same period and was one of the earliest temples of stone rather than wood; it yielded the oldest hammered bronze statues found in Greece (now in the Heráklion museum). Pilgrims used to trudge up the long stair from the gorge to pay homage. Today Dreros is a lonely, wild place, with views down to the sea, both to east and west.

Crete's swishiest hotels lie just east at Eloúnda, but the rest of Cape Ag. Ioánnis north of Dreros is lonely, crisscrossed by winding roads linking forgotten hamlets. The most scenic road zigzags up from Nikithaniós to Kastélli and over to Eloúnda (*see* p.245). There are some good icons in the parish church of **Doriés**, near the vaulted stables of an abandoned monastery, and, north of that, the handsome agricultural complex of **Moní Aretíou**, founded by a Venetian nobleman and recently restored.

Ag. Nikólaos (ΑΓ. ΝΙΚΟΛΑΟΣ)

When Agiós Nikólaos was chosen to be capital of Lassíthi in 1905, only 95 people lived in the little amphitheatre of a village, around a lake and a pair of islands on the stunning Gulf of Mirabéllo. In the 1950s its picturesque qualities enticed the first yachties and jet-setters (including a certain Walt Disney), who were charmed by 'Agios', as locals call it. It didn't even have a proper port until 1965. What happened after that is not hard to guess: its resident population multiplied by hundreds, and in the 1970s *Ag-nik*, as Brits renamed it, became the first place on Crete to cross the brashness threshold. But then it evolved again: the pubs and party animals moved on to Chersónisos and Mália, leaving behind a more genteel, more relaxed, more upmarket Agnik, full of jewellery and craft shops and smart bars and restaurants catering to the clientele of the glittering resort hotels around the gulf.

Around Town

Ag. Nikólaos stands on or near the ruins of *Lato Pros Kamara*, the port of ancient Lato, and contemplates the serene islet of **Ag. Pándes**. The chapel of the same name draws pilgrims on 20 June, but at other times you need to go with a cruise party to visit the *kri-kri* goats, the islet's sole inhabitants (who usually hide from visitors in any case). The other main point of contemplation in the town, just a few steps in from the sea and the harbour, is **Lake Voulisméni**, 'bottomless' according to its name, but 210ft (64m) deep according to divers. Believed to be the mouth of an underground river, Voulisméni was often stagnant until 1867, when the local pasha dug a channel to connect it to the sea. It's now completely surrounded by restaurants and cafés, lined up along the waterside or hanging over the cliffs, and plenty of big fat fish call it home, fattened by bread from all the restaurants.

On the seaward side of the lake, behind the tourist office, a small but choice **Folk Art Museum** (*t 284 102 5093; open Sun–Fri 10–4; adm*) has old icons, costumes, embroideries, instruments (including a *toumboúrlo*, a drum often used to accompany the *lýra*) and postage stamps from independent Crete. In the same area, on 28 Oktovríou Street, is the small and informative **Iris Museum** (*t 284 108 2681; open daily 9–1 and 5–8*), which details the plants and flowers found in Crete and their uses in medicine and crafts. Up the hill into town, the lively shopping streets of the city converge on **Plateía Eleftherioú Venizélou**, where locals meet up for coffee or rakí.

The excellent **Archaeological Museum**, at 68 K. Paleológou (*t 284 102 4943; open Tues–Sun 8.30–3; adm*) displays artefacts from Eastern Crete; Neolithic obsidian blades ('still razor-sharp!') and fish hooks, Middle Minoan vases from a shipwreck near Psíra islet, a unique Neolithic phallus-shaped idol from Zákros and the peculiar Early Minoan pinhead 'Goddess of Mýrtos', who could pass for a chicken, her long pipe arms wrapped around a pitcher. Lovely gold jewellery from Móchlos is the oldest Minoan gold yet found. There's a clay staff imprinted with Linear A on four sides and a stone vase in the form of a triton shell engraved with two demons making a libation, both from Mália, and a delicate Late Minoan gold pin, decorated with a bramble design and Linear A inscription. A Late Minoan infant burial in a *tholos* tomb found near Sitía is

Ag. Nikólaos

To Elounda,
Spinalonga,
Ammoudi Beach

Spinalonga

Piraeus, Rhodes & Sitia

Archaeology
Museum

To Heraklion,
Sitia, Ierapetra

Ferry
Terminal

ERITH. STAVROU

SALAMINOS

MILATOU

KORITSAS

S. DAVAKI

PRECIPOSGEORGIOU

PERIKLEOUS

KANDANOLEONDAS

AKTI S. KOUNDOUROU

ETHNIKIS ANTISTASEOS

DOM. THEOTOKOPOULOU

K. PALEOLOGOU

S. KORAKA

Harbour

KORNAROU

KAZANTZAKI

D. SOLOMOU

KAP. FAFOUTI

KONDILAKI

NIKOU PLASTIRA

P

Folk Art
Museum

i

Lake
Voulismeni

Iris
Museum

Bank

AKTI IOSIF KOUNDOUROU

LASTHENI

AKTI THEMISTOKLEOUS

TITOU

NIKOU PLASTIRA

OMIROU

28 OCTOVRIOU

R. KOUNDOUROU

25 MARTIOU

EVANS

PASIFAIS

ARIADNIS

MILOU

SAPOLIDI

TELNINIAS

Post
Office

Telephones

M. SFAKIANAKI

MODATSOU

ALEXOMANOLI

KITRO PLATEIA

AKTI PANGALOU

DIMOKRATIAS

ARKADIOU

GARIL

FILELLINON

DASKALOGIANNI

PLATEIA
ELEFTHERIOU
VENIZELOU

POLITECHNIOU

NIK. FOKA

MODATSOU

MIRABELLOU

MANOUSOGIANI

SOLONOS

TSELEPI

KITRO PLATEIA

Kitro Plateia
Beach

KONTOGIANNI

CHIMARAS

S. VENIZELOU

V. MERARCHIAS

KIPROU

METAMORFOSIS

Ag. Triada
Cathedral

Church of
our Lady

I. KOZYRI

P

Prefecture

To Kritsa,
Ierapetra,
Sitia

PLATEIA
ATLANDITHOS

Hospital

AKTI ATLANTIDOS

Ammos
Beach

P

Bus Station

Marina

To Stadium,
Municipal Beach,
Almyros Beach

N

100 metres
100 yards

displayed exactly as it was found. A Daedalic bust from the 7th century BC looks just like Christopher Columbus, and a unique lamp from Olous has 70 nozzles. In the last room is a 1st-century AD skull of an athlete, from Lato Pros Kamara itself, with a fine set of teeth, a gold burial wreath embedded in the bone of its brow and a silver coin from Polyrenia, needed to pay Charon, the ferryman of the Styx. A plate of knuckle-bones found near the head of a woman may have been used for divination.

Ag. Nikólaos' Beach Selection

Many visitors are surprised to discover that Agnik was asleep when God was handing out beaches. In town there's little shingly **Kitro Plateía**, sheltered and safe for children, named after the cypress wood once exported from here. To the north,

Getting Around

Lane Line, 5 K. Sfakianáki, t 284 102 5249, operates 5 **ferries** a week direct to Piraeus, 5 to Sitía and 3 each week that continue from Sitía to Kárpathos, Rhodes and other islands. The **bus** station (**t** 284 102 2234) is at the south end of S. Venizélou. Buses run frequently to nearby beaches, Heráklion via Mália (every 30mins, 6.15am–8.30pm) and Heráklion airport, and less often to every part of Lassíthi. **Olympic Airways**, 18 N. Plastíra, **t** 284 102 8929. **Port authority**, t 284 102 2312.

Taxis and Car Hire

You can call for a **taxi** on t 284 102 4000 or t 284 102 4100. Ag. Nikólaos offers plenty of places to **hire a car**: try **Sixt**, **t** 284 108 2055, **Budget**, **t** 284 102 2603, **Byron**, **t** 284 102 8480 or **Creta Star**, **t** 284 102 5492.

Tourist Information

Internet access: **Polichoro Peripou**, 25–28 Oktovríou, **t** 284 102 4876. Cybercafé and also a lending library, book and music shop. **Municipal tourist office**, 20 Aktí S. Koundoúrou, **t** 284 102 2357, **f** 284 108 2534. **Tourist police**, 47 Erith. Stavroú, **t** 284 102 6900.

Festivals

Easter Festivities include the burning of an effigy of Judas on a platform in the harbour. **29 May** Ag. Triáda. **15 Aug** Assumption of the Virgin. **6 Dec (St Nicholas' Day)–New Year's Day** cultural events, concerts and art exhibitions.

Shopping

Don't confuse the three streets named after the Koundoúrou family, who were great benefactors of the town. Ag. Nikólaos has some of the best shops on Crete, especially if you're looking for traditional crafts and antiques.

Gold and jewellery shops are clustered above all around R. Koundoúrou and 28 Oktovríou. A general **market** takes place on Wednesdays. **Anna Karteri**, 5 R. Koundoúrou. Wide range of titles in English and books about Crete. **Danielle**, 1 Kondiláki, **t** 284 102 2946. Wide array of handcrafted items, blown glass, ceramics, rugs, lamps and jewellery. **Dia Cheiros**, 2 Metamorfósis, **t** 284 108 2016. Beautiful (if expensive) hand-knotted Cretan rugs and silks, and other weavings from every part of Greece. **Galatia**, 10 R. Koundoúrou, **t** 284 102 2609. Upmarket souvenirs, icluding handmade items using Minoan motifs. **Kera**, Akti S. Koundoúrou, **t** 284 102 2292. Packed full of antiques, textiles, objets d'art. **Kerazoza**, 42 R. Koundoúrou. Puppets, toys and lots of colourful craftworks. **Maria Patsaki**, 2 K. Sfakianáki, **t** 284 102 4619. Traditional textiles from Cretan looms: embroideries, cushion covers, carpets. **Natural Sea Sponge Workshop**, 15 R. Koundoúrou. Selection of sponges, herbs, spices, teas and oils. **Syllogi**, Aktí S. Koundoúrou, **t** 284 102 5570. Stylish shop with Jewellery, oil paintings, antiques, silver and other fine crafts.

Sports and Activities

Ag. Nikolaos Yacht Excursions, **t** 284 102 5041. *lidi@agn.forthnet.gr*. Private motor yacht excursions or fishing trips. **Helicopter Tours of Crete**, **t** 284 108 2493. Amazing but pricey. **Diexodos Adventure Unlimited**, Chavania Beach, **t** 284 102 8098. All sorts of activites; ring them to see what's on offer. **Greg's Watersports**, Municipal Beach, **t** 297 751 1442. Very popular, with banana boats, water skiing, jet skis, paragliding and so on. **Pelagos Diving Centre**, Minos Beach Hotel, **t** 284 102 4376. Diving at all skill levels, including training and beginners' dives.

Aktí S. Koundoúrou follows the waterfront to end at the little beach of **Ammoúdi**; on the next headland is the little stone church that gave the town its name, Ag. Nikólaos, with rare 9th-century BC Geometric frescoes from the Iconoclastic period (*ask for the key at the Minos Palace Hotel*). At the south end of town, near the bus

M/S George, t (mobile) 694 489 5498. A boat that's available for hire for fishing trips round Ag. Nikólaos, with lunch laid on **Nikoleta**, t 284 309 4528. Also a boat for hire: cruises in the gulf to Psira and Móchlos.

Where to Stay

Ag. Nikólaos ✉ 72100

Luxury
St Nicholas Bay, 2km from Ag. Nikólaos, t 284 102 5041, f 284 102 4556, *www.stnicolas.gr* (*L*). A 130-bungalow complex on a peninsula with its own sandy beach, three pools, suites with private pools and jacuzziand every other comfort, including a yacht for trips to nearby beaches. *Open April–Oct.*

Minos Beach, Ammoúdi, t 284 102 2345, f 284 102 2548, *www.mamhotel.gr* (*L*). Built practically in the Minoan era by Agnik standards (1962), but its 132 sumptuous bungalows have been completely renovated to create 'Crete's first art hotel'. Some bungalows directly face the sea, and there's also a fine French restaurant (€60), three bars and a private beach. *Open April–Oct.*

Minos Palace, 2.5km from Ag. Nikólaos, t 284 102 3801, f 284 102 3816, *www.mamidakis.gr* (*L*). Recently renovated resort hotel overlooking the sea in green gardens, with big rooms, steps down to the beach and a seawater pool. *Open April–Oct.*

Candia Park Village, 3.5km north on the Eloúnda road, t 284 102 6811, f 284 102 2367, *www.mamhotel.gr* (*A*). 186 bungalows designed for families, each with two bedrooms and a kitchen. There's a children's play area, large pool, basketball, windsurfing, waterskiing and a small aqua park, and a choice of restaurants. *Open April–Oct.*

Expensive
Hermes, Aktí S. Koundoúrou, t 284 102 8253, f 284 102 8754, *ermis1@ath.forthnet.gr* (*A*).

Large modern rooms on the waterfront, some with great views, plus a pool and links to a diving club. *Open April–Oct.*

Coral, Aktí S. Koundoúrou, t 284 102 8363, f 284 102 8754, *ermis1@ath.forthnet.gr* (*B*). A smart town option, with rooftop pool and terrace. Owned by the same people as the Hermes.

Lato, Ammoúdi Beach, t 284 102 4581, f 284 102 4582 (*C*). Near the bottom of this category, a small, quiet hotel close to the beaches with a pretty pool. *Open April–Oct.*

Melas, 26 S. Koundoúrou, t 284 102 8734 (*C*). Stylish and well-appointed seafront apartments for 2–5 people.

Ormos, Ammoúdi Beach, t 284 102 4094, f 284 102 5394, *www.ormos-crystal.gr* (*B*). Family hotel, with a nice pool and playground; rates plummet off-season. *Open April–Oct.*

Moderate
Panorama, Saroldídi, off Aktí I. Koundoúrou, t 284 102 8890, f 284 102 7268 (*C*). Simple air-conditioned rooms, 50m from the beach, with a roof garden and lovely views over the harbour. Rates include breakfast.

Adonis, Aktí S. Koundoúrou, t 284 105 1525 (*C*). A pleasant guesthouse.

Marilena, 4 Erithou Stavroú, t 284 102 2681, f 284 102 4218 (*C*). Conventional rooms by the seafront, behind the Hotel Hermes.

Inexpensive
The tourist office has a list of over 1,000 rooms to rent in Ag. Nikólaos.

Doxa, 7 Idomeneos, t 284 102 4214, f 284 102 4614 (*C*). A good bet all year round.

Green House, 15 Modátsou, t 284 102 2025 (*E*). Nice cheapie, with little rooms leading out to a small courtyard, overflowing with greenery and a small army of cats.

Perla, 4 Salaminos, t 284 102 3379 (*E*). Pleasant, clean guesthouse in the centre.

Rea, corner of Marathónos and Milátou, t 284 109 0330 (*B*). A good value hotel with a bit of character and excellent sea views.

station, there's a clean but not terribly atmospheric piece of sand simply called **Ámmos**, and a bit further south again, on the other side of the stadium, is the crowded, clean **Municipal Beach** (*a fee is charged for use of facilities*). From there a path leads past little, sandy **Gargardóros Beach** to the bamboo-curtained sands of

Eating Out

Cretan Stars, 18 Akti I. Koundoúrou, t 284 102 5517 (€25). In the stately Koundoúrou family mansion, with beautiful port views and a garden, and serving a versatile mix of Greek, Italian and French cuisine. *Open May–Oct eves only.*

Pelagos, S. Kóraka, just inland from Aktí S. Koundoúrou, t 284 102 5737 (€20). Trendy seafood and a long list of tasty *mezédes* to start with; it's best to book. *Open Mar–Nov.*

Migomis, 20 N. Plastria, t 284 102 4353 (€18). Recently opened, with views of the lake that are lovely in the evening and imaginative Greek cuisine. *Open all year, winter eves only.*

La Strada, 5 N. Plastira, t 284 102 8451 (€18). Italian trattoria that prides itself on its wide ranging and unusual menu; try the herby breads, pizza and wide choice of salads.

Synantysi, Old Heráklion Road, t 284 102 5384. A delightful taverna that's enormously popular with locals for its excellent *mezédes*, including mussels, mushrooms, prawns and squid, and an enticing selection of wines and desserts. *Open eves only.*

Itanos, S. Kíprou, t 284 102 5340. Wide choice of old-fashioned ready dishes (the lamb and spinach in egg-lemon sauce is excellent).

Portes, near Almyrós Beach, t 283 102 8489. Local family-run favourite, with good Greek and Cretan specialities and wine from the barrel. *Closed Sun in winter.*

Trata, M. Sfakianáki. Tuck into dishes such as fish soup, Trata chicken kleftiko and a long list of casserole dishes.

Ofou to Io, t 284 102 4819, Kitro Plateía. A good choice of unusual Greek and Cretan dishes: *tigania* pork with white sauce, *soutzoukakia*, roast lamb stuffed with garlic and cheeses.

To Iroon, 14 Plateía El. Venizélou, t 284 102 5640. Evocative, historic raki bar: ask for a *koustoumáki* (the 'little usual one'), alias raki with *mezédes*.

Dolphini, Ammoúdi Beach. Good local food served by jovial twin waiters.

Grigoris, Stavrós, 200m after the bridge to Almyrós. Exceptionally friendly and good-value taverna.

The Embassy, Kondiláki, t 284 108 3153. A wide variety of reasonably priced vegetarian and fish dishes, as well as English Sunday lunch. *Open until 2am.*

New Kow Loon, 1 Pasifais, t 284 102 3891. The only Chinese in town; good but a bit pricey.

Stavrakakis, Éxo Lakkonía, t 284 102 2478. A 15km drive inland towards Neápolis, the town's favourite traditional *rakadiko*, where the finest raki is served with great Cretan titbits in a very local atmosphere.

Entertainment and Nightlife

After-dark action is not hard to find, concentrated around the lake and port and along 25 Martiou street, locally known as 'Soho'.

Café Ellinikon, Kapetán Kozýri. Excellent rakí, local wine and *mezédes* to start an evening.

Aléxandros, K. Paleológou. A perennially popular roof terrace with background music.

Astrea, 6 Aktí I. Koundoúrou, t 284 102 6937. Very arty cafe bar with a nautical theme.

Roxy, 25 Martiou, t 284 102 2984. Music bar, mainly popular with locals, playing a variety of sounds from Latin to Greek to jazz.

En Plo, 4 Aktí I. Kondoúrou, t 284 102 5831. For cool jazz and reggae.

Lipstick and **Rule Club**, both overlooking the port on Aktí I. Kondoúrou. Two trendy discos churning out techno-electro beats.

Royale, 25 Martiou, t 284 102 6474. Greek music club, popular with 20–30s.

Charlie Chan, Atki St. Kondoúrou, just out of town towards Eloúnda. Trendy bar/club up on a first floor, bathed in kitsch pink neon.

Christina Cinema, corner of Kazantzáki and Ethnikís Antistaseos. Outdoor summer cinema that frequently shows English-language films.

A Cretan Easter Treat: *Kalitsoúnia*

Of all the towns of Crete, Ag. Nikólaos puts on the best show at Easter, and it's also famous for its *kalitsoúnia*, sweet cheese pies, from the Italian '*calzone*', brought here by the Venetians. Outside Crete it's hard to find *myzíthra* cheese, but ricotta is a decent substitute. For the pastry, mix 225ml olive oil, 225ml milk, 900g flour, 110g sugar, and 1 teaspoon of salt dissolved in 45ml of lemon juice. The dough should be soft and smooth. If it's sticky, add a bit more flour. Cover and put to one side.

For the filling, crumble 1kg of *myzíthra* in a bowl, and add 2 well-beaten eggs, 1 tablespoon of cinnamon, 150g sugar and 15g chopped mint. Blend together well, and pre-heat the oven at 150°C. Roll small balls of dough out as thinly as possible and use a glass to cut them into circles around 10cm in diameter. Take a teaspoon of filling, place in the centre of the circle and fold in the edges, leaving a small cheese 'window' in the centre. Arrange on a greased baking sheet, brush with beaten egg, sprinkle on cinnamon and bake for around 20 minutes, until the pastry turns golden brown.

Almyrós, in a lush wetland setting and with watery sports such as jet skis and speed-boat tours. Further on **Ammoúdara**, 2km south again, has golden sand and is a busy resort in its own right, attracting many families. Frequent buses also go to the grey sands of **Chavánia** (4km), in a sheltered bay on the way to Eloúnda, with a snack bar.

Around Ag. Nikólaos

Eloúnda, Olous and Spinalónga

View after view across the sublime Bay of Mirabéllo and its islands unfold along the 12 kilometres north to **Eloúnda** (Ελούντα); below, the rocky coastline is interrupted by pocket-sized coves and private beaches, draped with some of the most glamorous hotels in Greece, the holiday addresses of heads of state, celebrities and the like. If you're not one of them, there are a couple of larger public beaches, too: **Chiona**, near the former salt pans on the way from Ag. Nikólaos, and the sandy municipal beach of Eloúnda in the village itself. If you go up into the little hamlets in the hills, you can still get a feel for the place as it was before it appeared on the international holiday map.

On the south edge of Eloúnda a little bridge crosses an artificial channel first dug by the Venetians in 1204, which separates the promontory of **Spinalónga** from the rest of Crete. The name ('long thorn' in Italian) is how the Venetians pronounced the Greek '*Stin Eloúnda*', and early on the locals adopted the name as well. Along the channel lie the sunken harbour installations of ancient **Olous**, the port of Dreros and goal of the 'sunken city' excursions from Ag. Nikólaos. It's an evocative place, lined with grey and pink stone, a favourite haunt of cranes. The moon goddess Britomartis, inventor of the fishing net, was worshipped here. Her famous wooden cult statue (a *xoanon*) made by Daedalus showed her with a fishtail, and one story has her turning into a fish to escape from the embrace of King Minos. Fish and dolphins also figure in the black, white and brown pebble mosaic floor of the 5th-century **basilica of Olous**, near the channel; one of its walls re-used a stele inscribed with a 2nd-century BC treaty in

Getting Around

Buses run every 30mins between Eloúnda and Ag. Nikólaos, daily 6.30am–11pm. **Caiques to Spinalonga** sail from Eloúnda about every 30mins during the summer, daily from early morning till 4.30pm.

Sports and Activities

Driros Beach Hotel, Eloúnda, t 294 409 2760. A windsurfing centre with small boats for hire.

Where to Stay and Eat

Eloúnda ✉ 72053

Few places in Greece concentrate so many swish resort hotels into a relatively small area.
Elounda Bay Palace, t 284 104 1502, f 284 104 1783, www.eloundabay.gr (L, luxury). A range of rooms and suites and two private beaches, lots of special touches, sports and a fine seafood restaurant. Open April–Oct.
Eloúnda Beach, t 284 104 1412, f 284 104 1373, www.eloundabeach.gr (L, luxury). Rated one of the best resort hotels in the world, incor-porating traditional Cretan architecture and with a beach, cinema, diving, fitness centre, heated pool and two excellent restaurants (see below). Helicopter, sailboat or private island are also available. Open April–Oct.
Elounda Gulf Villas, t 284 022 7132, f 284 022 7811, www.eloundavillas.com (L, luxury). 14 new, very individual villas, around Elounda's most beautiful pool. Each villa has 2–3 bedrooms, jacuzzi, private plunge pool and other luxuries. Open April–Oct.
Peninsula, t 284 104 1903, f 284 104 1889, www.eloundahotels.com (L, luxury). On the headland, with 31 superb suites, indoor and outdoor pools and access to the Porto Elounda's sports facilities. Open all year.
Porto Elounda, t 284 104 1903, f 284 104 1889, www.eloundahotels.com (L, luxury). Less pricey but still very plush, above a small private beach. Choice of comfortable rooms or suites, nearly all overlooking the sea and an 18-hole golf course. Open all year.
Grecotel Elounda Village, t 284 104 1002, f 284 104 1278, www.grecotel.gr (A, luxury–expensive). A mix of rooms, bungalows and villas in a lovely garden, with nice views, pools and a lovely restaurant. Open April–Oct.

Doric dialect between Rhodes and Olous, now in the Ag. Nikólaos museum. **Oxa**, the mountain just behind Olous, supplied the area's pre-tourism wealth in the form of whetstones, from Europe's biggest mine.

Not to be confused with the promontory, the **islet of Spinalónga** (t 281 024 6211; adm) is half an hour by caique from Eloúnda. It was fortified in ancient times by Olous, and its stones were reused in 1579, when the Venetians under Provveditor Lucus Michael made it a stronghold. After the Turkish conquest in 1669 it held out, like the other island forts of Néa Soúda and Gramvoúsa (see pp.120 and 128), as a shelter for refugees and as a base to harass the Turks until 1715, when the Venetians finally handed over the islands to the Ottomans by treaty, transferring any residents to Corfu. In the 19th century, as Crete rose in revolt after revolt, it was the Turks' turn to take refuge on Spinalónga. The Turkish community, over 1,000 people, left in 1904, and then a colony of lepers previously housed near Heráklion were transferred here, so that, until they were rehoused in 1957, Spinalónga could claim the dubious honour of hosting the last leper colony in Europe. Since 1980 the town of Eloúnda has been working on the restoration of the Venetian walls, the poignant little streets, houses, and lepers' church, and has set up a summer café. On the mainland, **Pláka** was the supply centre for the leper colony and now has a tiny laid-back colony of its own, dedicated to rest and relaxation by a pair of shingle beaches. The waters are deep and clear, and the sunsets, when sea and island are soaked in colour, are worth the trip.

Eloúnda Blue Bay, t 284 104 1924, **f** 284 104 1816 (*B, expensive*). A more modest hotel and villa complex with a pool, playground and tennis. *Open April–Oct.*

Akti Olous, near the Olous causeway, **t** 284 104 1270, **f** 284 10 41 425 (*C, expensive*). One of the more popular, less full-on opulent hotels in this area, with a pool and roof garden.

Korfos Beach, t 284 104 1591, **f** 284 104 1034 (*C, moderate*). Pleasant hotel within spitting distance of the beach, and with watersports available, too.

Dionyssos, Eloúnda Beach Hotel, **t** 284 104 1412 (€*100*). One of the top restaurants in the whole of Greece, with maybe the ultimate in contemporary Greek cuisine, featuring rare and forgotten herbs and ingredients researched by chef Giánnis Baxenávis. *Open April–Oct, eves only.*

Blue Lagoon, Eloúnda Beach Hotel, **t** 284 104 1412 (€*80*). Lovely Polynesian restaurant overlooking the sea, serving food from the South Seas and Asian delicacies including great sushi and sushimi. *Open April–Oct, eves only.*

Vritomartis, t 284 104 1325 (€*22*). The oldest taverna in Eloúnda, on an islet in the middle of the port, with well-prepared seafood.

Kalidon, t 284 104 1451 (€*15–20*). Romantically located out on a small pontoon, with international cuisine and a good selection of vegetarian dishes and *mezédes*.

Poulis, t 284 104 1451. Reasonably-priced fish; in contrast to the cats which so often patrol tables in Crete, this restaurant has ducks that will ask you for a scrap of bread.

Marilena, t 284 104 1322 (€*20–25*). Vine-covered garden and Greek and Cypriot dishes.

Katafigio, on the Olous crossroads, **t** 284 104 2003. Former carob-processing factory made into a night club, featuring live Greek music.

Pláka ✉ 72053

Spinalonga Village, t 284 104 1285, *www.greekhotel.com* (*A, luxury–expensive*). The fanciest accommodation here, with stone bungalows built in traditional style, and fine views over the island. Friendly service, good Cretan food in the restaurant and a pool all help to make it excellent for families. *Open April–Oct.*

Kirki, t 284 104 1574 (*D, inexpensive*). A much more basic choice.

Taverna Dolphin. An enjoyable seafront taverna with good fresh seafood.

Above Ag. Nikólaos: Kéra Panagía and Kritsá

Above Ag. Nikólaos, a kilometre before the village of Kritsá, you can examine the most beautiful fresco cycle in Crete at **Kéra Panagía** (*t 284 105 1525; open Mon–Sat 9–3, Sun 9–2; adm*). Set back from a road in an olive grove, it looks like no other church on the island: the three naves with gable roofs that look as if they were stamped from a cookie cutter, training long triangular buttresses, crowned by the simplest of belltowers and a drum-shaped dome, the whole coated with a hundred layers of whitewash. Within, however, the entire wall surface is wonderfully alive with colours and pictures that illustrate the evolution of Byzantine art before the Turks.

The central aisle, dedicated to the Virgin or *Panagía*, dates from the 12th century; in the mid-13th century the first paintings were destroyed and replaced with new ones in the severe, so-called 'archaicizing linear style', characterized by a rhythmic use of lines, especially in draperies, and flat perpectives. Note especially *The Nativity*, *Herod's Banquet* and *Last Supper*, and the patriarchs under the pine trees, clutching to their bosoms platters holding the souls of the Just, while, beneath a damaged *Crucifixion*, in the *Harrowing of Hell* the damned are meekly resigned to their interesting punishments. The four ribs dividing the structure of the dome prevented the painting of the usual figure of the Pantocrator, or Christ in Majesty. Instead, you'll find scenes from the Gospel: *Candlemass*, the *Baptism*, the *Raising of Lazarus* and the *Entry into Jerusalem*, with four angels overhead and prophets and evangelists below. Further down, Saints George and Dimítrios appear as military saints in full gear, while on the northwest pillar look for *St Francis*, with his slightly crossed eyes and Catholic tonsure. It's rare that a western saint earns a place among the Orthodox, but Francis, introduced to Crete by the Venetians, made a considerable impression among the people.

The two side aisles were later additions, painted in a more naturalistic style that came out of Constantinople in the early 14th century. The south aisle is devoted to *St Anne*, an unusual choice in Byzantine art. Even more unusual, many of the scenes are based on apocryphal gospels, perhaps by special request of the donors, whose names are inscribed near the door. A large portrait of Anne, Christ's grandmother, fills the apse, while the frescoes on the walls and in the barrel vaults are characterized by large figures against dark, uncluttered backgrounds, typical of the Macedonian school: the *House of Joachim*, the *Birth of the Virgin*, *Joseph's Sorrow* (for his fiancée's unexpected pregnancy), the *Water of Testing* (Mary is given a pitcher of water to drink to test her purity before marriage) and the *Virgin at the Closed Gate*.

The apse of the north aisle, dedicated to St Anthony, is filled with *Christ Pantocrator*, while the crowded *Last Judgement* covers most of the vaults: female allegories of the earth and sea render up their dead to be weighed on big scales, while the Virgin pleads for mercy. Amid saints on the walls are scenes from the *Life of St Anthony*, and at the end of the row don't miss the portraits of the donors, George Mazezanes (in his white bonnet), his wife and their small daughter, rare pictures of medieval Cretans.

In 1956 Jules Dassin chose the lovely white village of **Kritsá** (Κριτσά) as the location for his film *He Who Must Die*, with Melina Mercouri, and ever since the tourist boom in Ag. Nikólaos its role has been as something of a film set – the Traditional Cretan Village swamped by tourists who are in turn swamped by villagers selling tablecloths, rugs and lace, some more handmade than others. Kritsá is famous for its roll-out-the-barrel Cretan weddings, and although there are too many foreigners around now to get a casual invite as in the past, in August weddings are re-enacted with food and drink for fee-paying 'guests'. There are more churches with 14th-century frescoes: Ag. Konstantínos, Ag. Geórgios and Ag. Ioánnis, just up the Kroústas road.

Ancient Lato

A scenic 3km walk (the path begins near the crossroads) or drive north of Kritsá leads up to Dorian **Lato**, more properly known as *Lato Etera* (*t 284 102 5115; open Tues–Sun 8.30–3*). Its ruins splendidly curl down the saddle between the hills, and offer eagle-eye views over the sea. Named after the goddess Leto (Lato in Dorian Greek), the mother of Apollo and Artemis, the city was founded in the 7th century BC; it flourished through the Classical era and gave birth to Nearchus, Alexander the Great's admiral, before it was eventually abandoned in favour of its port, Lato Pros Kamara (modern Ag. Nikólaos). Archaeologists have picked out some curious Minoan features in the Dorian design: the double **gateway**, the **street of 80 steps** lined with small houses and workshops (one was a dyeworks) and the architecture of its **agora**, with a columnless sanctuary and cistern in the centre. A Doric portico with benches lined the west side; one end of it was converted into a threshing floor by the locals, after French archaeologists excavated the site in the early 1900s.

The wide **steps** that rise from the agora to a **peristyle court** and the **Prytaneion**, where the sacred fire burned day and night, are from the 8th century BC and believed to have been inspired by Minoan 'theatres'; spectators could sit and watch events in the agora below. Monumental towers stood on either side of a narrower stair, leading up to the altar and sacred hearth itself. On the second hill stands the beautifully built, column-less city **temple**, an isolated **altar** and a primitive **theatre** capable of seating a few hundred people. You don't have to wander far to realize that Lato was large and has been only partly excavated; walls stick out helter-skelter everywhere.

A few buses from Kritsá continue up to **Kroústas** (Κρούστας), which is just as pretty but has been spared the tourist hordes. It has some Byzantine frescoed churches and a huge festival for St John's Day (21 June), celebrated with bonfires and dances. A rough road continues to flower-bedecked **Prína**, affording magnificent views and the chance to circle back to Ag. Nikólaos by way of Kaló Chorió (*see* below).

East around the Gulf of Mirabéllo

The stunning coastline that lends Ag. Nikólaos its panache owes its name to a long-gone Genoese fortress of Mirabéllo, 'Beautiful View'. Where sheer precipices aren't crowding the sea, the land around the Gulf of Mirabéllo is immensely fertile, and has been densely populated for some 5,000 years. Frequent buses cover the 10km between Ag. Nikólaos and three sandy beaches at **Kaló Chório** (Καλό Χωριό) and **Ístro** (Ιστρό), lush **Karavostási** beach, quieter **Ag. Panteleímon** with grey sand, named after its little church, and the largest, sandiest and most popular in the area, **Golden Beach**. From Kaló Chorió a path leads to up to **Vrókastro**, a Late Minoan peak sanctuary used as a refuge during the Dorian invasion; a Geometric-era fort stands on the hill.

The main road east continues to the turn-off to 12th-century **Moní Faneroménis**, a dizzying climb but worth it for stupendous views over the gulf. The monastery was built like a fortress into the cliff, sheltering a cave where an icon of the Virgin was found by a shepherd. A nest of resistance against Venetians and Turks, it now has just two monks, one of whom will show you the beautifully frescoed cave church.

Gourniá: 'The Pompeii of Minoan Crete'

East of Ístro the road passes directly below the striking hillside site of **Gourniá** (*t 284 209 4604; open Tues–Sun, 8.30–3*), excavated between 1901 and 1904 by American Harriet Boyd. Boyd was not only the first woman to lead a major dig, but did so under circumstances hard to imagine today: a Classics scholar just out of university, she was in Athens when she heard news of the first big Minoan finds. At once she sailed to Crete, where she met Arthur Evans; the next year, she hired a Cretan foreman and his mother, and the three travelled about eastern Crete on donkeys, looking for a likely place to dig. After a few weeks they had the luck to stumble on the most complete and best-preserved Minoan town of them all.

No one knows its original name; *Gourniá* ('basins') comes from the large number of stone vessels found on the site, many of which are still in place. The town reached its

Getting Around

There are 5 buses daily, Mon–Fri, between Ag. Nikólaos and Sitía, with stops en route (only 3 buses, Sat and Sun).

Tourist Information

Barbarossa Tours, Móchlos, t 284 309 4179. Can reserve a hotel or villa, and have a wealth of information on activities, such as nature walks and off-road motorcycle excursions.

Sports and Activities

Aqualand, t 284 106 1807, *aqualand @agn.forthnet.gr*. Well-organized diving centre for beginners or experienced divers.
Yachting Evolution, t 284 309 4528, *yachtingevolution@sit.forthnet.gr*. Sailing tours to quieter beaches around the gulf.

Where to Stay and Eat

Kaló Chório and Ístro ✉ 72100
Istron Bay, t 284 106 1303, f 284 106 1383, *www.istronbay.com* (L, *luxury*) Fancy but smallish resort hotel built into the hillside, amid fine scenery, with everything a lazy holiday requires, from a children's pool and game rooms to seawater pool and private beach with beach bar. *Open April–Oct.*
Elpida, t 284 106 1403, f 284 106 1481 (C, *expensive–moderate*). On the west side of Kaló

Chório Beach, 500 yards from the sea, with a restaurant and pool and good for families. *Open April–Oct.*

Móchlos and Area ✉ 72057

Aldiana Club, t 284 309 4322, f 284 309 4491. (B, *expensive*). Precludes the need to go anywhere else, with a restaurant, sports, a pool, and nightclub. *Open April–Oct.*
Mochlos Mare, t 284 309 4005 (*moderate*). Four small apartments in a flowery garden, run by the friendly Silignaki family, a few minutes from beaches and the village. *Minimum stay three days; open all year.*
Sofia, t 284 309 4554, f 283 409 4238 (D, *moderate*). Small, pleasant and well run, with air-conditioned rooms with kitchenettes. *Open Mar–Oct.*
Móchlos, t 284 309 4205 (E, *inexpensive*). Similarly priced and close to the beach. *Open all year.*
Ta Kochylia, t 284 309 4432. Taverna with beautiful views of the sea and excellent fish or meat dishes to match. *Open April–Oct.*
Iliovasilema, t 284 309 4777. Café on the water's edge run by an affable Belgian named Yannik; it has the sunsets promised by the name, and good breakfasts.
Natural Taverna, east of Lástros on the Sitía road. All the food (except the fish) comes from their own garden.
Kefalovryssi, Mésa Moulianá, t 284 309 5462. In a pretty setting amid trees, a taverna famous for its authentic ingredients and traditional recipes. *Open all year, but closed Mon–Wed in winter.*

peak c. 1550 BC, when it had a population of approximately 4,000. Narrow, stone-paved lanes meander up and down, densely packed with small houses that originally had a storey or two on top, made of mud brick and tied with timbers, as protection against earthquakes. Tools (potter's wheels, saws, a coppersmith's forge and an oil press) led to the identification of various workshops. At the highest point, a stepped lane leads up to a **palace** (164ft by 121ft/50m by 37m), a mini version of the Knossos model, with storerooms, residential rooms, a lustral basin and light well. Because of its small size, the obligatory rectangular court was located outside the palace; here a stone slab had holes in it for a table where animals were placed for sacrifice (or so archaeologists think). An L-shaped arrangement of steps may be a mini-version of the theatrical areas in the palaces. Just north, the Shrine of the Snake Goddess had its little shelf for Late Minoan cult items, including long, tube-like snake vases. The fact that Boyd found no Linear A tablets here has led to the theory that Gourniá had only limited local authority, handling the traffic of goods across the 'Isthmus of Crete'. In any case, the palace collapsed in an earthquake not long after it was built, only to be reused as workers' housing. The whole was abandoned after a massive fire *c.* 1225 BC.

From Gourniá, it's a short drive down to **Pachiá Ámmos**, a rather woebegone-looking resort village along a sandy beach that corners all the garbage in the Cretan Sea. It stands at the beginning of the Ierápetra road, bisecting the **Isthmus of Crete**, a mere 12km separating the Aegean and Libyan Seas. This was one of the regions first settled by the Minoans: in **Vasilikí**, 5km south, a Pre-Palace Minoan settlement (from 2600–2000 BC) on a low hill (*open Tues–Sun 8.30–3*) yielded in 1906 the first known specimens of what has since been known as 'Vasilikí ware', the Minoans' first distinctive pottery style (*see* p.54). This is one of the few sites where later buildings didn't intrude, and is of special interest for its 'House on the Hilltop', a forerunner of the palaces. Originally two storeys high, it has rectangular rooms connected by long corridors. Some were probably store rooms, others living quarters, and there's a paved courtyard with a rock-cut well or light well. Interior walls were covered in red plaster.

A bit further south, **Episkopí** is worth a stop for its delightful, blue-domed Byzantine church, the see of a Catholic bishop in Venetian times.

Pachiá Ámmos to Sitía: the Cretan Riviera

Pachiá Ámmos is also the crossroads for Sitía, some 47km east down a corniche road that rates among the most scenic on Crete, slithering along the jagged, often precipitous Mirabéllo coast, with the bright lights of Ag. Nikólaos twinkling far below. From **Kavoúsi**, just east of Pachiá Ámmos, you can visit a quiet beach and cafe at **Thólos** and two Late Minoan sites: a settlement and cemetery at **Vrondá**, high on a plateau in the Thriptís Mountains, and **Kástro**, located further up near a fresh spring, with the whole Gulf spread out below. Vrondá, it seems was settled by refugees from Gourniá; when the Dorians invaded, they moved even further up to Kástro and stayed there until the 7th century BC. Next along to the east, **Plátanos** sits on a wonderful belvedere above the gulf, and has a pair of tavernas in which to linger over the sunset.

Móchlos

The earliest Minoan site along the gulf is **Móchlos** (Μόχλος), a charming fishing village with a mild winter climate and a pair of beaches, down, down, down from the main road. The setting is lovely: barren cliffs behind and a small islet of Ag. Nikólaos barely a stone's throw from the shore. This was originally attached to the mainland, giving Minoan Móchlos the advantage of two harbours, one facing east and the other west. It was abandoned after the big disaster of *c.* 1450 BC, and the cemetery of house-like tombs has revealed something of the trade and industry of a proto-urban Minoan town of 300 souls; Móchlos specialized in pots with lid handles in the shape of reclining dogs. Seven intact chamber tombs with clay *larnaxes* were discovered, cut into the cliffs facing the islet. One Late Minoan building on the island is known as 'the House of the Theran Refugees' for its architectural similarities to the top-floor

Looking for Atlantis

And wishing to lead them [the Egyptians] *on to talk about early times, he embarked on an account of the earliest events known here... And a very old priest said to him, 'Oh, Solon, Solon, you Greeks are all children; there's no such thing as an old Greek.'*

Plato, *Timaeus*

As Plato tells it, his friend Critias had heard the story from his grandfather, who had got it from the great Athenian sage Solon himself. Solon in his travels had gone to Egypt, where a priest familiar with ancient records had told him an incredible tale 9,000 years old, of the lost island of Atlantis and how it sank into the sea. Athens had been involved too, in one of that city's most heroic feats. The Egyptian recounted the wonders of Atlantis's great civilization, and how the Atlanteans had grown haughty and degenerate in their latter days and attempted the conquest of all the peoples of the eastern Mediterranean. Athens alone stood against them, and her army won a famous victory – just before earthquakes and floods, sent by the gods to punish the Atlanteans, destroyed the island and the Athenian army, too, in the space of a day.

Plato gives more details on all this in a companion dialogue, the unfinished *Critias*, which has been called the 'first work of science fiction'. It has spawned more crank theories over the last 2,500 years than any book – excepting of course the Bible. And

timbered houses at Akrotíri, on Santoríni; pot sherds from Akrotíri littered the floor on top of a seven-inch layer of volcanic ash. Obviously life went on after the Big Bang.

Yet another Minoan settlement that existed from 3000 BC – and one that likewise continued to exist after the eruption on Santoríni – was on **Psíra**, 2km offshore, where the inhabitants used the pumice that floated ashore to build up the floor of their shrine. The little town was excavated in 1907 by American Richard Seager and, judging by the rich finds, was a prosperous little port, although now it's completely barren. The **House of the Pillar Partitions**, with a bathroom with a sunken tub, plughole and drains, is one of the most elegant in eastern Crete. Psíra is visited on boat trips from Ag. Nikólaos, but you may be able to talk a local in Móchlos into taking you over.

Between Móchlos and Sitía

Returning to the main road above Móchlos, there are more grand views from the lovely village of **Lástros** and **Myrsíni**, a Venetian village with a café ideal for drinking in the view. Visitors are welcome at Myrsíni's pottery and weaving workshops; an art association was founded here in 1920, and there are 14th-century frescoes to see in the church if you can hunt down the key. Further east, in **Mésa Moulianá**, two beehive *tholos* tombs date from the end of the Bronze Age, while in **Éxo Moulianá**, famous for its red wine, the handsome Byzantine church of Ag. Geórgios has frescoes from 1426.

Just before **Chamézi** (Χαμέζι), high above Sitía, a conical hill called **Souvloto Mouri** has a unique oval-shaped Middle Minoan sanctuary, built over earlier Minoan buildings of 2800 BC. One theory has it that it was a coastal lookout post, or even a mini-fortress predating Minoan rule of the waves; others say the older buildings belonged to a farm, and the sanctuary (a number of votive figurines were found here) as soon as scientists started bringing in the facts about the catastrophic eruption of Santoríni, which may have put an end to Minoan civilization, it was only natural someone would make the connection between mythical Atlantis and ancient Crete.

There is no sunken continent in the Atlantic (which probably takes its name from Plato's tale), and if you're looking for Atlantis Crete may have to do. There are some odd hints in the *Critias*. Atlantis' capital was built as a series of concentric rings, alternately land and water, rather like a labyrinth, and at the centre stood a Temple of Atlantis' founder, Poseidon, the god of the sea, along with a sanctuary inhabited by sacred bulls. A pillar stood there, over which one of the bulls was sacrificed 'alternately every fifth and sixth year'. To the Greeks that meant at the end of four- and five-year periods – the nine-year solar cycle encountered in Cretan mythology.

The story of Solon's trip to Egypt is plausible enough, and the Egyptians certainly would have had a memory of Crete in their records, something the Greeks, who had even forgotten how to write in their post-Mycenean Dark Age, did not. Classical Greeks, for all their delight in precision, never seemed to have a very good sense of time. If Solon (or Plato) had misunderstood 9,000 for 900 years, then the date would be remarkably close to the time of the Santoríni eruption. How much of Atlantis came garbled from the Egyptians, and how much was simply invented by Plato – a fellow with quite a lively imagination – will probably never be entirely sorted out.

began as a domestic shrine. The main entrance to the oval house (2200–1550 BC) is on the southeast. A small open courtyard occupied the centre, with a well at the east end, and surrounded by rooms that opened onto it. These days Chamézi is a laid-back place, but can get pretty wild in the *kazaniásma*, or rakí-distilling time, in October. It has a charming **Folklore Museum** by the church, open by request (*ask for Giánni*).

Sitía (ΣΗΤΕΙΑ)

Sunny Sitía has remained more 'Greek' than any other town on Crete's north coast, perhaps because it has a livelihood of its own, devoted to sultanas, olive oil and wine. Its Agricultural Cooperative, with over 8,000 members, plays a major role in keeping up local pride. Especially popular with French visitors, Sitía has a long, sandy beach, but is more pleasant than stunningly beautiful. Its old ring of Byzantine, Genoese and Venetian walls fell to earthquakes and the bombardments of Barbarossa, leaving only a restored Venetian fortress as a souvenir, to close off the west end of the port.

Around the Town

Sitía, with the everyday bustle and gossip of a town of 8,500 souls, the lazy charms of its beach, the pranks of its pet pelicans and general schmoozing along the waterfront is a paradise for lazy visitors. But *la dolce vita* is nothing new here; under the fortress you can see the ruins of a Roman fish tank, where denizens of the deep were kept alive and fresh for the table. The **Archaeological Museum**, incongruously set among garages at the top of Ítanos street (*t 284 302 3917; open Tues–Sun 8.30–3;*

Getting Around

Sitía has a little **airport**, 1km out of town (a taxi into Sitía costs €5). It has flights to Athens 3 times a week, and also to the islands of Kárpathos and Kásos. The **Olympic Airways** office (**t** 284 302 2270) is by the Tourist Office; for **airport information**, call **t** 284 302 4666.

Lane Line ferries (**t** 284 302 5555) run 5 times weekly to Ag. Nikólaos and Piraeus and 3–4 times weekly to Kárpathos, Rhodes and other nearby islands. The **Port Authority** number is **t** 284 302 2310.

The **bus** station (**t** 284 302 2272), is at the south end of the waterfront: there are 5 buses daily to Ag. Nikólaos and Ierápetra (Mon–Fri; only 3 daily, Sat and Sun) and several services each day to Palaíkastro, Zákros and villages around the coast.

Tourist Information

Municipal tourist office, on the marina, **t** 284 302 8300. *Open Mon–Fri only.*
Tourist police, **t** 284 302 4200.

Festivals

24 June *Panegýri*, Piskokéfalo
July–15 Aug Kornária arts festival, Sitía.
Mid-Aug three-day wine and sultana festival.

Where to Stay

Sitía ✉ 72300

Flisvos, 4 K. Karamanlí, **t** 284 303 7135, **f** 284 302 7136 (*C, moderate*). Near the bus station, with sea views and a garden courtyard. Off-street parking is available. *Open all year.*

Apollon, 28 Kapetan Sifi, **t** 284 302 2733, **f** 284 302 2733 (*C, moderate*). Very clean, with air-conditioned rooms. *Open all year.*

Marianna, 67 Misonos, **t** 284 302 2088, **f** 284 302 3929 (*C, moderate*). Charming rooms, and copious buffet breakfasts.

A. Kounelakis Studios, Pétras, **t** 284 302 5273 (*A, moderate*). New, quiet studios with sea views east of Sitía town in Pétras.

Nora, 31 Rouseláki, **t** 284 302 3017 (*D, inexpensive*). Restful budget hotel that's convenient for the ferries. *Open all year.*

adm), has a good little collection of finds from eastern Lassíthi, among them the ivory and gold 'kouros' of Palaíkastro, Minoan *larnaxes*, a wine press and a cache of Linear A tablets from the palace archives at Zákros, a bull-shaped *rhyton* from Móchlos and Daedalic-style votive offerings from the 7th century BC. There are recent finds from Pétras (*see* below), which may be the *Se-to-i-ja* of the Linear B tablets. A small **Folklore Museum** at 33 Kapetan Sifi (*t 284 302 2861; open Wed 5–8, Tues, Thurs, Fri 9–1 and 5–8, Sat 9–1; adm*) has colourful examples of crafts, weavings and embroideries.

Four uninhabited isles (Gianysáda, Paximáda, Paximadáki and Dragonáda) known as the **Dionysádes** lie 18km northeast of Sitía and can be reached by boat, departing from the port every morning at 10am. Mostly rocky, they have sandy coves perfect for a swim in crystal waters; rare Eleonora's falcons often wheel overhead.

Petrás, Trypetós and Ag. Fotía

In ancient times, much of the action in this area was concentrated just east of Sitía. On a low seaside hill at **Petrás**, excavations since 1985 have revealed an important Minoan town, presumably the port of the densely inhabited area from Chamézi to Praisós. Settled in the Pre-Palace period (2600–2000 BC), the town eventually occupied the whole hill and, unlike most Minoan sites, was defended by a cyclopean wall with three sturdy towers until it was abandoned after that fateful day *c.* 1450 BC. Stone-paved streets connected free-standing houses on terraces, with storerooms and workshops on the ground floor. One street led to the top of the hill and the

Archontiko, 16 Kondiláki, **t** 284 302 8172 (*D, inexpensive*). Nice, quiet little hotel on the west side of town. *Open all year.*

Youth Hostel, 4 Theríssou, **t** 284 302 2693. Just east of town and also very pleasant and friendly, with kitchen facilities and a garden.

Eating Out

Sitía is a civilized place, where *mézedes* automatically come with your drink, especially if you join the locals in the rakí bars along El. Venizélou. There's also a clutch of bars near the pelicans' house.

Balkoni, Kazantzaki, **t** 284 302 5084 (*€25*). Great seasonal menu, including delicious Asian dishes, pasta with seafood and roast meats with local vegetables. The old stone building adds to the atmosphere. *Open April–Oct, Tues–Sun for lunch and dinner, Nov–Mar, eves only.*

Zorba's, **t** 284 302 2689 (*€18*). Wonderful location on the water, and if the ready-prepared food can look a bit tired, the seafood, lobster and grilled meats are fresh and delicious.

Sitia Tavern, **t** 284 302 8758. Excellent fresh fish and lobster on Sitiá waterfront, with snails as a free appetiser.

Symposio, 14 K. Karamánli, **t** 284 302 5856. Organic produce goes into a careful selection of Cretan and international dishes. *Open all year.*

To Steki, Papandreou st. Taverna off the main tourist beat, very popular with locals.

Neromylos, Ag. Fótia, **t** 284 302 5576. Located in a former watermill, this is a local favourite for its *mézedes* and grilled meats, to go with a great view over Sitía.

Ianós, 159 El. Venizélou. Music bar playing Latin, jazz, soul and rock, with an internet café upstairs.

Skala, 193 El. Venizélou, **t** 284 302 3010. Cafe during the day that launches into Greek dance music at night.

En Plo, 2 Karamanli, **t** 284 302 3761. Bar with rock, swing and ethnic sounds overlooking the sea; often a good choice to find a party atmosphere.

Hot Summer. Big club on the edge of town with a pool, open well into the early hours.

palace, which covered two terraces on an artificial plateau, surrounded by a retaining wall with a bastion. An east-west corridor leads through a door to the **central court**. Rooms flanking it on the west yielded a libation table and Linear A tablets, and were probably cult places. South of the corridor, another room paved with gypsum slabs has a bench covered with plaster; 12 oblong rooms lie north of the corridor, while at a lower level the storerooms were connected to the court by a monumental plastered staircase. A garden on the west side of the palace separated it from the workshops.

Three km east of Sitía, on the small headland of **Trypetós** ('perforated'), a Hellenistic city, probably ancient *Eteia*, has been excavated since 1987. The sheltered harbour and dockyard, rectangular and hewn out of the rock, gave it its name. The city spread over the rest of the headland on terraces. The southern, landward side was protected by a massive wall, with military installations and houses along its inner side. A 'cult' **hall** has a rectangular hearth and a bench with a fragment containing a *poros* plug, part of a relief or statuette. A U-shaped bench for worshippers surrounded the hearth.

If the town beach at Sitía is too crowded, try the sandy cove of **Ag. Fotía**, 5km to the east. In 1971 a large Pre-Palace **Minoan cemetery** was discovered near the sea (fenced off on a path at the east end of the village), where 250 chamber tombs yielded a fine haul of stone vases, fish hooks and stone axes. The hill above had a large Old Palace building that was mysteriously but peacefully destroyed just after its construction and replaced with a round fort – perhaps part of a coastal warning system, as the oval structure at Chamézi would have been within easy signalling distance.

Inland from Sitía: Minoan Farm Villas and the Last True Cretans

The lonesome plateaux south of Sitía seem lost in another era, and are scattered with minor ancient sites. Most are villas or farms, built *c.* 1550 BC at the end of a Minoan baby boom; between the Pre-Palace and Late Minoan eras (2600–1600 BC), Crete's population is estimated to have multiplied a hundredfold. One such villa is signposted just off the road before **Piskokéfalo**; another, built on several terraces on the hillside and revealed during road construction in the 1950s, is further south just before **Zou**. Yet another Minoan villa was in **Achládia**, 5km west of Piskokéfalo, on a slope overlooking Sitía Bay. The Mycenaeans left their mark in the local necropolis, with an impressive *tholos* tomb of 1300 BC, the best-preserved on Crete.

The *Erotókritos*

Of all the gracious things upon this earth
It is fair words that have the greatest worth,
And he who uses them with charm and guile
Can cozen human eyes to weep or smile.
Erotókritos, 887–90

Sitía is famous for two great men, Myson, one of the ancient Seven Sages of Greece, and Vincénzo Kornáros, died 1677, the otherwise mysterious author of the *Erotókritos*, the island's national epic. First published in Venice in 1713 (a surviving manuscript is from 1710), this 10,000-line romance in verse in Cretan dialect is still memorized and recited today; some shepherds can rattle off thousands of verses at the drop of a hat.

Kornáros took his story from a mediocre medieval French play called *Paris et Vienne*, and re-set it in Byzantine times. It recounts the love between Erotókritos, son of a poor commoner, and Aretousa, daughter of King Heracles of Athens. After serenading Aretousa incognito, Erotókritos is forced to flee Athens after slaying two guards the king sent to ambush him. He boldly returns to win a knightly tournament, but the king still refuses to let the couple marry because of Erotókritos' humble birth, and exiles the hero and then cuts off his daughter's long hair and throws her in prison for refusing to marry the prince of Byzantium. Three years later, Athens is invaded by Vlachs, and all seems lost until Erotókritos reappears on the scene to crush them, unrecognized by all thanks to a magic potion that turned his skin black. The Vlachs' greatest warrior, a giant, challenges him to single combat, and when Erotókritos slays him their army withdraws. Aretousa eventually recognizes her lover in spite of his new colour, although he drinks another magic potion to change it back before they are happily married and he accedes to the throne of Athens.

Interspersed with all the action, Kornáros included enough philosophy to make the *Erotókritos* a rich source for *mantinade* singers – for example, one favourite:

Clouds and mists in
Time disperse;
Great blessings in time
Become a curse.

On the main road south, whitewashed **Maronía** is a pretty place amid emerald terraces. Two km further south the road forks for Néa Praisós and ancient **Praisos**, the stronghold of the Eteocretans – the 'true Cretans' or last Minoans – who took refuge in this remote corner and survived into the 3rd century BC. They co-existed with the Dorians, running an old Minoan shrine of Diktean Zeus at Palaíkastro and keeping up other ancient cults on their three acropoli. By the 2nd century, though, Praisos was competing too openly with Dorian Ierapytna (Ierápetra), and in 146 BC it was overcome. Ironically, this last Minoan town was one of the first to be discovered, in 1884, by the Italian Federico Halbherr, who was mystified by the unfathomable inscriptions in Greek letters, now held to be in the native Minoan language. The Ierapytnans did such a good job of demolishing Praisos that the scenery is the main reason for coming: the foundations of a **temple** can be traced on the first acropolis, but almost nothing remains on the second hill, except a wall and a few remains of houses.

Five km south of Praisos a minor road rises to **Chandrás**, a village in a time warp, and a kilometre from the abandoned medieval village of **Voila** and its 15th-century church. The road east continues to **Zíros**, from where you can go on to Xerókambos beach (*see* p.261). Remains of another long-gone civilization await southwest of Chandrás in **Etiá**, noted for its lovely setting. In the 15th century it was the fief of the Di Mezzo family, who built a fortified palazzo that was the finest Venetian building on Crete, with vaulted ceilings and intricate decoration. Destruction began in 1828, when the Turkish administrators who took it over were besieged by angry locals. It's now under restoration, and the entrance hall and fountain house offer a hint of former grandeur. **Lithínes**, back on the main road, is a charming village with a ruined Venetian tower; the Libyan Sea can just be seen below. If you're continuing south, *see* p.265.

Crete's East Coast

East of Sitía the road continues towards Crete's Land's End at **Cape Síderos**. Some 9km from Ag. Fotía is **Moní Toploú** (*open 9am–1pm and 2–6pm*), one of Crete's wealthiest historic monasteries. Its correct name is *Panagía Akroteriαní*, but Toploú ('cannoned' in Turkish) more aptly evokes this fortress of the faith, on a lonely plateau. The first building was a chapel dating from Nikephóros Phokás' liberation of Crete, dedicated to Ag. Isidóro (hence Cape Síderos). The monastery was founded in the 15th century by the Kornáros family, and rebuilt after its destruction by the buccaneering Knights of Malta, and again after an earthquake in 1612. Square 30ft walls defend Toploú; the gate, which once moved on a wheel, is directly under the *foniás* ('killer'), the hole through which the monks poured rocks and oil on their attackers. Much of Toploú's stone came from ancient Itanos: an inscription from the 2nd century BC embedded in the church façade records the arbitration of Magnesia in a dispute between Itanos and Ierapytna. The campanile is dated 1558. After the barren landscapes and trees stooped by the wind, the lovely courtyard seems like a small oasis.

Toploú has a venerable history as a place of refuge, revolution and resistance, and more than once the brothers have paid for their activities. At the beginning of the

War of Independence in 1821, the Turks captured it and hanged 12 monks over the gate as a lesson to their brothers, although as usual it only made the Cretans mad as hell, and by the end of the war Toploú was theirs again. During the Second World War the abbot was shot by the Germans for operating a radio transmitter for the Resistance. The **museum** (*t 284 306 1226; open Tues–Sun 8.30–3; adm*) houses icons and engravings, including a fine 15th-century *Christ Pantocrator* attributed to Andréas Rítzos and one of the masterpieces of Cretan art, *Great is the Lord* by Ioánnis Kornáros (1770), with 61 lively, intricate scenes illustrating the Orthodox prayer of Megálos Agiasmós.

Palaíkastro (Παλαίκαστρο) and Zákros (Ζάκρος)

Roads to the east coast converge at **Palaíkastro**, a pleasant and popular place to stop over, with fine beaches in easy striking distance. The first edition of Palaíkastro was on route to beautiful **Chiona** beach, at **Roussalakos**: a large, unfortified **Minoan town** on a plain by the sea, inhabited from *c.* 3000 BC until it was destroyed by fire *c.* 1450 BC (*open Tues–Sun 8.30 – 3*). It was a prosperous town with an elaborate drainage system, inhabited by craftsmen and probably under the jurisdiction of Zákros. A main street ran through it, crossed by paved streets (some of which are stepped), dividing the town into nine sectors. Houses along the main street had imposing façades; several had 20 rooms or more on two floors, with open courts supported by columns, antechambers leading into a main room or *megaron*, kitchens, lustral basins, shrines, oil stores, baths and reception halls. One house in Sector C has a luxurious façade and a workshop where Egyptian-style vases were produced. To the northeast are the precinct and altar of a 4th-century BC **Sanctuary to Diktean Zeus** – the one that was maintained by the Eteocretans of Praisos – where the ancient *Hymn of the Kouretes* (*see* p.236) was found engraved on a stone. Later the sanctuary was administered by Itanos, and Zeus was worshipped here from the 8th century BC to the Roman conquest, a time when most locals had moved to the more defensible hill of Kástri.

A rough track south of Palaíkastro leads to **Petsofás**, where a **Minoan peak sanctuary** yielded offerings in the shape of body parts, suggesting the local deity may have had healing powers. North of Palaíkastro, a road leads down to long, sandy **Koureménos Beach**, a favourite for windsurfing (rent boards at the Nathalie Simon club). It has a good fish taverna and a new little harbour, from where boats run to the islets of **Elassa** and **Grandes** offshore. A bit further north, on the road to Vaï, a dirt road signposted **Maridati** leads to an even quieter shingle beach, near another fish taverna.

Vaï (Βάι) and Itanos (Ιτανός)

Palaíkastro is the last bus stop before **Vaï**, its name derived from the Cretan word *váyies*, for palm. Perhaps the island's most beautiful beach, Vaï's silver sands are lined with Europe's only native palms (*phoenix theophrastii*), a species original to Crete. As you approach, signs in the palm forest direct you to a banana plantation to complete the Caribbean ambience, or you can buy a bunch by Vaï's often-gorged car park; the only way to avoid sharing this tropical paradise with thousands of body-bakers is to

Getting Around

There are 4 buses daily from Sitía to Palaíkastro, Mon–Fri (3, Sat and Sun), and 2 daily Mon–Fri to Zákros (one, Sat and Sun).

Sports and Activities

Scuba Diving Club, Vaï, t 284 307 1543. Based on the beach, with full diving facilities.

Where to Stay and Eat

Palaíkastro ✉ 72300

Many people rent rooms, and a **tourist office** in the village (no phone) helps to find them.

Marina Village, t 284 306 1284, f 284 306 1285, *relakis@sit.forthnet.gr* (*C, expensive*). A little resort complex on the beach with its own restaurant, pool and tennis.

Hellas, t 284 306 1240, f 284 306 1340, *www.palaikastro.com/hellashotel* (*C, moderate*). Recently renovated and good value hotel, with a restaurant. *Open all year.*

Thalia, t 284 306 1448, f 284 306 1558 (*D, inexpensive*). Nice budget hotel on a side street, smothered in bougainvillaea. *Open all year.*

Chiona, Chiona Beach, t 284 306 1228. Palaíkastro has some of Crete's best fish and seafood, and at this exceptional taverna superbly fresh fish or lobster are perfectly cooked on the grill. *Open Mar–Oct.*

Kakavia Giorgos Kounelakis, by the sea 2km down a dirt road from Palaíkastro, t 284 306 1227. Famous for its fish soup (ring ahead to order some), fresh fish and oven-baked dishes. *Open all year.*

Zákros and Káto Zákros ✉ 72300

In summer there are a few rooms to let on the road to Káto Zákros, and about 50 beds in rent-rooms by the sea that are in big demand. Nikos Perákis at **Akrogiali** taverna manages a lot of these; also check *www.cretetravel.com.*

Athena, at the end of the beach road, t 284 309 3458 (*inexpensive*). Budget rooms.

Bay View Rent Rooms, 4km from the beach, Káto Zákros, t 284 302 6887, *www.palaikastro. com* (*moderate–inexpensive*). New, tranquil double and triple rooms, overlooking the bay and next to a farm. *Open all year.*

Poseidon, Káto Zákros, t 284 309 3326 (*inexpensive*). Adequate rooms, by the sea.

George, Káto Zákros, t 284 309 3201, *georgevillas@sit.forthnet.gr* (*inexpensive*). Clean, tasteful rooms and a terrace.

Taverna Anesis, on the seafront, t 284 302 6890. Excellent moussaka and spinach pies.

Nikos Platanákis, near the archaeological site, t 284 302 6887. The owner, a gourmet cook, serves delicious specialities including rabbit *stifádo* and grilled fish. *Open April–Oct.*

Xerókambos ✉ 72300

Eolos, t 284 302 6741 (*moderate–inexpensive*). Apartments attached to a mini-market with sea views, by the beach. *Open May–late Oct.*

Villa Petrino, t 284 302 6702 (*inexpensive*). The only accomodation that stays open all year, next to the seasonal **Taverna Kostas**, famous for lamb on the spit (he also does breakfast).

Liviko View, t 284 302 7001 (ask for Katerina Hatzidaki, *inexpensive*). Simple place with a taverna, 300m from the sea.

Kastri, t 284 302 6715. Grilled meat and very fresh fish, overlooking the sea; also rooms.

---

get there at the crack of dawn or star in the next Bounty ad filmed on the beach. There's a decent taverna overlooking the sands, watersports and a scuba diving centre that allows you to explore Vaï's underwater beauty.

Small beaches along Cape Síderos act as crowd overflow tanks and free campsites. The three best lie along the path north of Vaï, including 'deserted city' **Erimoúpoli Beach**, overlooking the islet of Elassa, just below ancient **Itanos**. Inhabited from Early Minoan times (and called *U-ta-no* on Linear B tablets), Itanos minted the first coins on Crete. In 630 BC, according to Herodotus, the Delphic oracle commanded a fisherman from Itanos to found the city of Cyrene in Libya. In later times, after the destruction of Praisos (*see* p.257), the city was a fierce rival of Ierápetra for control of Palaíkastro's temple of Diktean Zeus, leading to the Arbitration of the Magnesians of

132 BC – a decision that went in Itanos' favour, as we know from the inscription at Tóploú. The Ptolemies of Egypt used Itanos as a naval base, and the city exported dyes and glass. Pirates forced it to be abandoned in the 8th century AD, and spoiled a 15th-century attempt at resettlement. Best preserved of the remains are a paleochristian basilica made of stones recycled from earlier temples, and a tower of big black stones.

The Minoan Palace of Zákros

t 284 309 3323; open April–Oct daily 8–7, Nov–Mar daily 8–2.30; adm.

From Palaíkastro a road cuts south through a porphyry-tinted landscape planted with olive groves to the large-ish village of **Zákros**. Here a rich **Minoan villa** from the New Palace era was excavated by the British archaeologist David Hogarth in 1901, with wall paintings, sewers, wine presses and cellars. The villa is a short walk from a dramatic gorge, the stark and beautiful 'Valley of Death', named not because of tourists with broken necks but after its Minoan tombs, cut into the cliffs. On foot it's not too difficult, an 8km walk down the very end of the E4 path to Káto Zákros. Softies can take the new road, chiselled into the cliffs and plied by buses from Sitía.

For decades farmers kept digging up Minoan relics by the sea at Káto Zákros, and it was there that Hogarth next planted his spade, uncovering 12 houses before a torrential downpour forced him to abandon the site – literally a few feet from the prize. This, the **Palace of Zákros**, the fourth-largest and only unplundered palace on Crete, waited until 1961, when Greek archaeologist Níkos Pláton began digging where Hogarth left off. Built in a bay sheltered from the dangerous currents of Cape Síderos, Zákros was built over an older site in the New Palace period (*c.* 1700 BC). The surrounding town was the Minoans' chief port for Egypt and points east, the base of the *Keftiu*, as the Egyptians called them; the importance of trade for Zákros is highlighted by the fact that the valley could never have supplied it with all its needs in food. All collapsed and burned in 1450 BC, and was never rebuilt. Pláton found over 10,000 items here, including large quantities of unworked ivory, which may have been a local speciality, and precious cult items that hint that disaster overwhelmed the residents before they could grab their treasures. The once vital harbour is now under the sea, as Crete's east coast gradually subsides. If you come in winter or early spring, expect puddles.

Zákros, with its 150 rooms, is the smallest of the four major palaces. Entrance to the site is by way of the original harbour road, leading into the northeast court; the covered area south of the road belongs to a large Pre-Palace **foundry**, one of the most important of the period found in the Mediterranean. A corridor leads into the **Central Court**, which preserves an altar base. As usual, sanctuaries and ritual chambers were in the **West Wing**, entered by way of a monolithic portal near the altar. **Store rooms** of *pithoi* are to the northwest, while the **Hall of Ceremonies** extends to the west, with a paved light well and two windows. Traces of frescoes were found here, as well as two fine *rhytons* and bronze saws that may have fallen from the floor above. Wine vessels and cups found in the large room to the south led Pláton to dub it the **Banqueting Hall**. Behind this are the **shrine** and **lustral basin**, perhaps used for ritual purification, and the unlooted **Shrine Treasury**, divided into eight compartments, where Pláton

1	Central Court	19	cistern room
2	Banquet Hall	20	spring
3	Hall of Ceremonies	21	well
4	lustral basin	22	lustral basin
5	shrine	23	altar base
6	archive room of the	24	dye house
	shrine	25	store rooms
7	shrine treasury	26	entrance
8–15	store rooms	27	main road to harbour
16	kitchen-dining room	28	courtyard
17	Queen's apartment	29	workshops
18	King's apartment		

found the rock-crystal vase now in the Heráklion museum. Boxes of Linear A tablets came from the shrine's archive; exposure and damp dissolved the bulk of them into a mass. **Workshops**, one of which was used to make faïence, closed in the south end of the Central Court. In the southeast corner, a **well** with worn steps was used for sacrificial offerings. At the bottom Pláton found a bowl of Minoan olives, perfectly preserved in the water; they tasted good, too, according to the archaeologists.

The east wing of the palace is tentatively identified as the **royal apartments**. The so-called **cistern room** behind them is an enigma: was this plaster-walled basin, 16ft in diameter with a balustrade and steps leading down to the paved floor, a swimming pool, a fish pond or used to float a sacred Egyptian-style ship? Nearby, steps lead into a 'well-fashioned spring', as Pláton called it after Homer's description; it may have been a shrine connected with the spring that fed the cistern. Today, little turtles call it home. At the north end, a large **kitchen** (the only one found in a palace) and possibly a **dining hall** had fragments of original decoration; in the Sitía museum you can see a little barbecue grill discovered here, just right for cooking *souvláki*. In the buildings in the northeast corner of the court, a **lustral basin** (now roofed) was found, along with bits of frescoes showing double axes and horns of consecration.

Only part of the **town** around the palace has so far been excavated. Houses were arranged in blocks, and some had as many as 30 rooms. Some had olive and wine presses; one, discovered by Hogarth, yielded 500 clay seals of imaginary creatures.

A protected archaeological zone, the little fishing hamlet of **Káto Zákros** seems utterly idyllic, with no new buildings or big hotels, or even mobile phone reception; after the daily onslaught of visitors to the palace, you can hear the *flísvos*, the soft whoosh of lapping waves on the shore. The shingle beach is fine for a swim or a snorkel, and if it ever gets crowded, hike over the hill to a far more peaceful strand. Alternatively, if it's really remote soft white sands you have a yen for, head 10km south down the tortuous coast road to **Xerókambos**, in the southeasternmost corner of

Crete (you can also get there on a slightly hair-raising road via Zíros). Xerókambos is minute, with an end-of-the-world feel, set under cave-pocked cliffs, overlooking the tiny **Kavalli islands**; the Minoans had a sanctuary in the mountains above. Ancient salt pans on the beach suggest this may have been the site of the city of Ampelos.

Ierápetra (ΙΕΡΑΠΕΤΡΑ)

By rights **Ierápetra**, southernmost town in Europe, 370km from Africa and with an average annual temperature of 20°C, should be a fascinating place instead of the dull dodoburg it is. Its glories are a grey-sand beach and a plastic-wrapped hinterland – it is Greece's top producer of bananas, pineapples and winter vegetables. It increasingly stays open in winter for snowbirding tourists, but don't expect the Costa del Sol.

The myths say Ierápetra was founded by the mysterious, mist-making *Telchines*, who had dog-heads and flippers for hands. They named it *Kamirós*, the same name they gave to the city they founded on Rhodes. When the Telchines began to foul up Crete's weather with their mists, Zeus sent them packing, and the Dorians, to keep things straight, renamed the town *Ierapytna*. Dorian Ierapytna bullied its way into occupying much of eastern Crete by Hellenistic times, and was contrary enough to hold out against the Romans after they conquered the rest of Crete. Piqued by this resistance, the Romans flattened the city, then rebuilt it in grand style. The Byzantines made it a bishopric, but it was sacked by the Saracens and toppled by an earthquake in 1508.

A Town and an Island

The landmark on Ierápetra's seafront is the 13th-century Venetian **Kastélli**, a small fort later rebuilt by Sammicheli, but with little to see inside (*open 9am–9pm*). It sits above the ancient harbour, once Roman Crete's chief port for Africa, now bobbing with fishing and pleasure craft. Nearby, the domed church of **Aféndi Christós** was built in the 1300s; behind it, in a warren of narrow streets, is a house where Napoleon supposedly spent the night of 26 June 1798, before sailing off to Egypt. There's a little **mosque** with a pretty fountain and a stump of a minaret in the old town, and a few Roman remains. The **Archaeological Museum** (*t 284 102 4943; open Tues–Sat 9–3; adm*), in a former Ottoman school in Plateía Dimarchíou, has the most beautiful things in Ierápetra: a Late Minoan *larnax* from Episkopí, painted with animals and a hunting scene, a charming Roman statue of Demeter (or Persephone) and a black stone stele, bearing a treaty between Ierapytna and Antigonus of Macedonia.

All in all, the best thing to do in Ierápetra is sail away to the golden sands of **Chrisí** (or Gaidouronísi, 'Donkey Island'), an uninhabited islet 13km off in the Libyan Sea. This little paradise, made from the lava of an underwater volcano and ringed by shallow seas, is home to one of Crete's last natural cedar forests, stunted and growing in the dunes. The sea has deposited shells in millions on its north shore; in season temporary tavernas by the beach ward off chances of starvation. Another possible outing, inland this time, is to artificial **Lake Barmiana**, 6km northwest. Dammed to provide water for farms, it's a good place to look for wildflowers in spring and autumn.

Along the Costa Plastica

Sardinia has its Costa Smeralda, Spain its Costa Dorada and France its Côte d'Azur, so it seems only fair that Crete should take the PR bull by the horns and flaunt the assets of its southeasternmost coast: sand and plastic, the latter to force tomatoes to ripen year round so the rest of Greece never has to go without. Just west of Ierápetra, the Costa Plastica is metaphysically dull. The first place that might tempt you to turn in is **Gra Lygiá**, to find relief in the hills, where pretty, rarely visited villages under plane trees such as **Kalamáfka** have a sense of place; the hill just above it is said to be the only spot on Crete where you can see both the Libyan and Cretan Seas. The churches at **Anatolí** and the traditional hill village of **Máles** have important icon collections garnered from abandoned monasteries. Máles isn't far from the **Salekánou Forest** of pine and cypress; if you fancy a day's trek, follow the riverbed down from Máles to **Mýrtos**, after taking in Máles' frescoed church of Panagía Messochorítissa, from 1431.

West of Gra Lygiá there's a beach with a plastic hinterland at **Ammoudáres**. Things were no doubt prettier in the days when early Minoans lived nearby at **Fournoú Korifí** (*now overgrown and fenced in*). In 1968 the British School excavated this Early Minoan

Getting Around

The **bus** station is on Lasthénou, t 284 202 8237: there are frequent services to Sitía (via Makrigialós), Gourniá and Ag. Nikólaos, to Heráklion and to nearby villages.

Boats leave Ierápetra for **Chrisí** at 10.30am, 12.30pm daily in April–Oct, returning at 5pm.

Festivals

July–Aug Kýrvia arts festival, Ierápetra.

Sports and Activities

Scirocco, Mýrtos, t 284 205 1232. Windsurf boards, canoes and other craft for hire.

Where to Stay and Eat

Ierápetra ✉ 72200

Tavernas line the paralía along St Samouil and Kougoumoutzáki, either side of the fort.
Petra Mare, A. Filotheo, t 284 202 3341, f 284 202 3350 (*A, expensive*) Modern and close to town, with a watersports centre.
Astron, 56 M. Kothrí, on the town beach, t 284 202 5114, f 284 202 5917, htastron@otenet.gr (*B, expensive–moderate*). Pleasant and pristine; all rooms have sea views. *Open all year.*

Cretan Villa, 16 Str. Lakérda, t 284 202 8522 (*moderate*). Rooms in an attractive 19th-century house. *Open Mar–Nov.*
Ierapytna, Plateía Ag. Ioánnou Kale, t 284 202 8530 (*D, inexpensive*) Good value rooms.
Coral, 12 E. Nikikatsanváki 12, t 284 202 2846 (*D, inexpensive*). Even cheaper, near the castle, with balconies in all rooms. *Open all year.*
Napoleon, 26 St. Samouil, t 284 202 2410 (€18). Old favourite restaurant for authentic Greek and Cretan food; fresh fish (the owner has his own caique) and snails are specialities.
Portego, 8 Foniadaki, t 284 202 7733. Café, bar and restaurant in a fine old building.
Odio, 18 Lasthenous, t 284 202 7429. Very popular *mezedopolío* and local hangout

Mýrtos ✉ 72200

Esperides, t 284 205 1207, f 284 205 1298 (*C, moderate*). Newish, large hotel.
Mertiza, t 284 205 1208, f 284 205 1036 (*moderate*). Pleasant apartments.

Koutsounári ✉ 72200

Magic Life Club Lyktos and Lyktos Village, t 284 206 1041, f 284 206 1318, www.magiclife.com (*A, luxury*). Queen of the resort hotels on the south coast of Crete: the Club is by the sea, the Village on the hill; both share a lovely beach, pools, restaurants and many extras. *Open April–Oct.*

proto-town of close to 100 rooms, occupied between 2600 and 2100 BC, when it was destroyed by fire and never re-inhabited. Finds here have been vital in reconstructing daily life in the Pre-Palace period; it was located, perhaps for defensive purposes, on a dry hillside, and a first conclusion is that its people must have spent a lot of time fetching water. The small quantity of imported goods such as metal, obsidian blades and stone vases suggest that such valuables were exchanged as doweries or gifts; cereals, grape pips, olive stones and the bones of cattle, goats and sheep confirm that the essentials of the Cretan diet were already established. The oldest known potter's wheel in the Aegean was found here, from 2500 BC. It is estimated the population ranged from 25 to 30 people in five families, suggesting (though this is disputed) that the nuclear family was already the essential unit in Early Minoan times.

Just west (1.7km) another Minoan settlement at **Pýrgos** (*signposted before the bridge, a steep walk up; the site is unfenced*) was excavated by Gerald Cadogan in 1970–82. In a striking setting near the mouth of the Mýrtos river and the valley that supplied its food, the village and its 'country house' stand where the main Minoan route crossed over the Díktean Mountains from Mália. Pýrgos is nearly as old and was

Koutsounári Traditional Cottages and Nakou Village Maisonettes, Ag. Geórgios, above Koutsounári, t 284 206 1291, f 284 206 1292, *nakouvil@otenet.gr* (*A, expensive*).The opposite of Magic Life: 16 rural houses, each self-contained and with a pool; the best are charming stone cottages. *Open April–Oct.*

Camping Koutsounari, 7km east of town, t 284 206 1213. On a mediocre beach, but clean, cheap and has good facilities.

Nikos, t 284 206 1415. Taverna with great Cretan specialities, prepared by a skilled mama. *Open Mar–Oct.*

Mikros Ellinas, t 284 206 1754. On the beach, the place to go if you've a hankering for fish.

Elena Taverna, Férma, t 284 206 1244. Good food in a garden setting overlooking the sea.

Makrigialós ✉ 72300

Ikaros Villas, t/f 284 305 2038, *www.interkriti.net* (*expensive–moderate*). Brand-new studios and apartments in various sizes, with sea views. *Open all year.*

White River Cottages, Áspro Pótamos, above Markigialós Beach, t/f 284 305 1120, *wrc@sit.forthnet.gr* (*expensive–moderate*). The 'White River' was built for olive growers, at the mouth of the Péfki Gorge. Cottages have been restored to create good value alternative accommodation, around a pool. *Open April–Oct.*

Hamlet Cottages, Áspro Pótamos, t 284 305 1434 (*B, moderate*). Tidy rooms, also with a pool, in traditional cottages. *Open April–Nov.*

Aspro Potamos, t 284 305 1694 (*inexpensive*). Ten simple cottages, carefully restored; all electricity comes through solar power, with oil lamps to light at night. *Open all year.*

Porphyra, t 284 305 2189 (€15). Intriguing, creative cusine from a chef who has studied ancient Greek cooking. *Open April–Oct.*

Kalliotzina, Koutsourás Beach, t 284 305 1207. Traditional Cretan cooking, in a very pretty setting. *Open April–Oct.*

Spilia tou Drakou, Kaló Neró Beach, t 284 305 1494 (€18).'The dragon's cave' is a legend for its dishes made with ingredients from the owner's garden and hen house, homemade bread and cheese. Get directions before setting out. *Open all year.*

Nightlife

Daytime Ierápetra may seem docile, but as soon as the sun disappears bars and clubs burst into life. Plateía Eleftherías and Kyrva street are good places to hunt up some fun.

Figaro, 14 Kyrva, t 284 202 3071. Good mix of locals and foreigners, playing Greek and international music.

Pyrsos Club, 21 Kyrva, t 284 202 8332. A castle theme, and Euro-dance and Greek pop.

burned at the same time as Fournoú Korifí, but unlike its neighbour was rebuilt as a villa, which burned down c. 1450 BC. There are cisterns and a tower, and an unusual two-storey tomb with two ossuaries; the remains of 65 people were found here.

Further west, **Mýrtos** is the one village along this coast where you may want to linger: although burned down by the Germans it was rebuilt as it had been, and today has a fine beach and a good deal of charm, with laid-back atmosphere thrown in.

East of Ierápetra

Every year new developments join the tomato tunnels along the Costa Plastica east of Ierápetra. **Koutsounári**, 7km east, is the first nice beach, but sheltered **Ag. Fotía**, 6km further on, is far more attractive. Just east of here, a battered and burned pine forest is slated to become a natural park, the **Dásakis Butterfly Gorge**; true to its name, hosts of red butterflies flit here in late spring. Get there by turning off at Mávros Kólympos; the beginning of the gorge is 13 km up at **Orinó**, and it takes about six hours to walk from top to bottom, ending up at **Koutsourás** beach. The best beach here is at the east end of **Makrigialós**, with sugary fine sand, watersports, tavernas and shallow waters safe for children. A sign from the road directs you to another large **Minoan villa** that burned down around 1450 BC. Excavations have revealed a palace in miniature, with a typical Minoan labyrinthine approach to the entrance.

Every morning in summer, the *Pegasus* makes a day trip from Koutsourás to the island of **Koufounísi** (ancient *Leuke*), where the quiet beaches are sandy and the water perfect for snorkelling (take your own provisions). Inhabited from Minoan times, Leuke owed its prosperity to its rich sponge banks and an abundance of sea snails (*murex brandaris*), whose little bodies were full of the colour used to dye cloth royal purple. Ancient Ierápetra and Itanos fought over it endlessly, as we know from the 'Arbitration of the Magnesians' stele at Toploú. The island was abandoned for good in the 4th century AD; the town, 'Crete's Little Delos', was excavated in the 1970s, and is exceptionally well preserved. Its **theatre** once had 12 rows of seats; the east part of the stage building is still intact, but the rest was looted and destroyed by puritanical Christians; nearby are Roman baths, from the 1st century AD. The town extends south-east of the theatre, and includes an impressive **villa**; the **temple** on the south side of the island was largely cannibalized for the construction of the lighthouse, but near it were two chunks of an enthroned colossal cult statue, more than 12ft high. Later, caves on the west coast were used as chapels by Christians, and some have pictures of saints engraved on the walls and Latin inscriptions (one is dated 1638).

From Makrigialós the main highway heads north to Sitía, while the coast road passes several quiet beaches, including one at **Kaló Néro**, with a 14th-century church of the Panagía with faded frescoes. This is all that survives of once-great **Moní Kápsa**, destroyed by pirates. In the mid-19th century the monastery was rebuilt over the road at the end of a wild ravine, its white walls part of the austere clif. The man behind it, Gerontogiánnis ('Old John'), was a charismatic anchorite who never learned to read and never had any official status in the Orthodox Church, but has been canonized, at least locally, for his defiance of the Turks, faith-healing and occasional posthumous miracle. There's another decent beach and a few tavernas further east, at **Goúdouros**.

Language

Greeks travel so far and wide that even in the most remote places there's usually someone who speaks English, very often with an American or Australian drawl. On the other hand, learning a bit of Greek can make your travels much more enjoyable. Usually spoken with great velocity, Greek isn't very easy to pick up by ear, but, it's always helpful to know at least the alphabet and a few basic words and phrases. Sign language is a big part of Greek life, too: Greekspeak for 'no' is usually a click of the tongue, accompanied by raised eyebrows and a tilt of the head backwards; 'yes' is usually indicated by a forward nod, head tilted to the side.

The Greek Alphabet

Pronunciation		English Equivalent
Α α	álfa	short 'a' as in 'cat'
Β β	víta	v
Γ γ	gámma	guttural g or y sound
Δ δ	délta	always a hard th as in 'though'
Ε ε	épsilon	short 'e' as in 'bet'
Ζ ζ	zíta	z
Η η	íta	long 'e' as in 'bee'
Θ θ	thíta	soft th as in 'thin'
Ι ι	yóta	long 'e' as in 'bee'; sometimes like 'y' in 'yet'
Κ κ	káppa	k
Λ λ	lámtha	l
Μ μ	mi	m
Ν ν	ni	n
Ξ ξ	ksi	'x' as in 'ox'
Ο ο	ómicron	'o' as in 'cot'
Π π	pi	p
Ρ ρ	ro	r

Pronunciation		English Equivalent
Σ σ,ς	sígma	s
Τ τ '	taf	t
Υ υ	ípsilon	long 'e' as in 'bee'
Φ φ	fi	f
Χ χ	chi	ch as in 'loch'
Ψ ψ	psi	ps as in 'stops'
Ω ω	oméga	'o' as in 'cot'

Diphthongs and Consonant Combinations

ΑΙ	αι	short 'e' as in 'bet'
ΕΙ	ει, ΟΙ οι	'i' as in 'machine'
ΟΥ	ου	oo as in 'too'
ΑΥ	αυ	av or af
ΕΥ	ευ	ev or ef
ΗΥ	ηυ	iv or if
ΓΓ	γγ	ng as in 'angry'
ΓΚ	γκ	hard 'g'; ng within word
ΝΤ	ντ	'd'; nd within word
ΜΠ	μπ	'b'; mp within word

Useful Words and Phrases

Yes	né/málista (formal)	Ναί/Μάλιστα
No	óchi	Οχι
I don't know	then kséro	Δέν ξέρω
I don't understand... (Greek)	then katalavéno... (elliniká)	Δέν καταλαβαίνω... (Ελληνικά)
Does someone speak English?	milái kanis angliká?	Μιλάει κανείς αγγλικά?
Go away	fíyete	Φύγετε
Help!	voíthia!	Βοήθεια!
My friend	o fílos moo (m)	Ο φίλος μου
	ee fíli moo (f)	Η φίλη μου
Please	parakaló	Παρακαλώ
Thank you (very much)	evcharistó (pára polí)	Ευχαριστώ (πάρα πολύ)

You're welcome	parakaló	Παρακαλώ
It doesn't matter	thén pirázi	Δεν πειράζει
OK, alright	endaxi	Εντάξει
Of course	vevéos	Βεβαίως
Excuse me, (as in 'sorry')	signómi	Συγγνώμη
Pardon? Or, from waiters, what do you want?	oríste?	Ορίστε?
Be careful!	proséchete!	Προσέχετε!
What is your name?	pos sas léne? (pl & formal)	Πώς σάς λένε?
	pos se léne? (singular)	Πώς σέ λένε?
How are you?	ti kánete? (formal/pl)	Τί κάνεται?
	ti kanis? (singular)	Τί κάνεις?
Hello	yásas, hérete (formal/pl)	Γειάσας, Χέρεται
	yásou (singular)	Γειάσου
Goodbye	yásas, (formal/pl), andío	Γειάσας, Αντίο
	yásou	Γειάσου
Good morning	kaliméra	Καλημέρα
Good evening/good night	kalispéra/kaliníchta	Καλησπέρα/Καληνύχτα
What is that?	ti íne aftó?	Τι είναι αυτό?
What?	ti?	Τί?
Who?	piós? (m), piá? (f)	Ποιός? Ποιά?
Where?	poo?	Που
When?	póte?	Πότε?
Why?	yiatí?	Γιατί?
How?	pos?	Πώς?
I am/You are/He, she, it is	íme/íse/íne	Είμαι/Είσαι/Είναι
We are/You are/They are	ímaste/ísaste/íne	Είμαστε/Είσαστε/Είναι
I am lost	échasa to thrómo	Έχασα το δρόμο
I am hungry/I am thirsty	pinó/thipsó	Πεινώ/Διψώ
I am tired/ill	íme kourasménos/árostos	Είμαι κουρασμένος/άρρωστος
Good/bad/so-so	kaló/kakó/étsi ki étsi	καλό/κακό/έτσι κι έτσι
Fast/big/small	grígora/megálo/mikró	γρήγορα/μεγάλο/μικρό
Hot/cold	zestó/crío	ζεστό/κρύο
Nothing	típota	Τίποτα

Shops, Services, Sightseeing

I would like...	tha íthela...	Θα ήθελα...
Where is...?	poo íne...?	Που είναι...?
How much is it?	póso káni?	Πόσο κάνει?
bakery	foúrnos/artopoleion	φούρνος/Αρτοπωλείον
bank	trápeza	τράπεζα
beach	paralía	παραλία
church	eklisía	εκκλησία
cinema	kinimatográfos	κινηματογράφος
hospital	nosokomío	νοσοκομείο
hotel	xenodochío	ξενοδοχείο
hot water	zestó neró	ζεστό νερό
kiosk	períptero	περίπτερο
money	leftá	λεφτά
museum	moosío	μουσείο
newspaper (foreign)	efimerítha (xéni)	εφημερίδα (ξένη)
pharmacy	farmakío	φαρμακείο
police station	astinomía	αστυνομία

policeman	astifílakas	αστυνομικός
post office	tachithromío	ταχυδρομείο
plug, electrical	príza	πρίζα
plug, bath	tápa	τάπα
restaurant	estiatório	εστιατόριο
sea	thálassa	θάλασσα
shower	doush	ντους
student	fititís	μαθητής, φοιτητής
telephone office	Oté	ΟΤΕ
theatre	théatro	θέατρο
toilet	tooaléta	τουαλέτα

Time

What time is it?	ti óra íne?	Τί ώρα είναι
month/week/day	mína/evthomáda/méra	μήνα/εβδομάδα/μέρα
morning/afternoon/evening	proí/apóyevma/vráthi	πρωί/απόγευμα/βράδυ
yesterday/today/tomorrow	chthés/símera/ávrio	χθές/σήμερα/αύριο
now/later	tóra/metá	τώρα/μετά
it is early/late	íne norís/argá	είναι νωρίς/αργά

Travel Directions

I want to go to ...	thélo na páo ston (m), sti n (f)...	Θέλω να πάω στον, στην...
Where is...?	poo íne ...?	Πού είναι...?
How far is it?	póso makriá íne?	Πόσο μακριά είναι
When will the... come?	póte tha érthi to (n), ee (f), o (m)...?	Πότε θα έρθει το, η, ο...?
When will the... leave?	póte tha fíyi to (n), ee (f), o (m)...?	Πότε θα φύγει το, η, ο...?
From where do I catch...?	apó poo pérno...?	Από πού πέρνω...?
How long does the trip take?	póso keró pérni to taxíthi?	Πόσο καιρό παίρνει το ταξίδι?
the (nearest) town	to horió (to pió kondinó)	Το χωριό (το πιό κοντινό)
here/there/near/far	ethó/ekí/kondá/makriá	εδώ/εκεί/κοντά/μακριά
left/right	aristerá/thexiá	αριστερά/δεξιά
north/south/east/west	vória/nótia/anatoliká/thitiká	βόρεια/νότια/ανατολικά/δ

Driving

Where can I rent ...?	poo boró na nikiáso ...?	Πού μπορώ νά? νοικιάσω ...?
a car	éna aftokínito	ένα αυτοκινητο
a motorbike	éna michanáki	ένα μηχανάκι
a bicycle	éna pothílato	ένα ποδήλατο
Where can I buy petrol?	poo boró n'agorásso venzíni?	Πού μπορώ ν΄αγοράσω βενζίνη?
Where is a garage?	poo íne éna garáz?	Που είναι ένα γκαράζ?
a map	énas chártis	ένας χάρτης
Where is the road to...?	poo íne o thrómos yiá...?	Που είναι ο δρόμος για...?
Where does this road lead?	poo pái aftós o thrómos?	Που πάει αυτός ο δρόμος?
Is the road good?	íne kalós o thrómos?	Είναι καλός ο δρόμος?
EXIT	éxothos (th as in 'the')	ΕΞΟΔΟΣ
ENTRANCE	ísothos (th as in 'the'	ΕΙΣΟΔΟΣ
DANGER	kínthinos (th as in 'the')	ΚΙΝΔΥΝΟΣ
SLOW	argá	ΑΡΓΑ

NO PARKING	*apagorévete ee státhmevsis*	ΑΠΑΓΟΡΕΥΕΤΑΙ Η ΣΤΑΘΜΕΥΣΙΣ
KEEP OUT	*apagorévete ee ísothos*	ΑΠΑΓΟΡΕΥΕΤΑΙ Η ΕΙΣΟΔΟΣ

Numbers

one	*énas (m), mía (f), éna (n)*	ένας, μία, ένα
two	*thío*	δύο
three	*tris (m, f), tría (n)*	τρείς, τρία
four	*téseris (m, f), téssera (n)*	τέσσερεις, τέσσερα
five	*pénde*	πέντε
six	*éxi*	έξι
seven/eight/nine/ten	*eptá/októ/ennéa/théka*	επτά/οκτώ/εννέα/δέκα
eleven/twelve/thirteen	*éntheka/thótheka/thekatría*	έντεκα/δώδεκα/δεκατρία
twenty	*íkosi*	είκοσι
twenty-one	*íkosi éna (m, n) mía (f)*	είκοσι ένα, μία
thirty/forty/fifty/sixty	*triánda/saránda/penínda/ /exínda*	τριάντασαράντα/πενήντα/ εξήντα
seventy/eighty/ninety	*evthomínda/ogthónda/ enenínda*	ευδομήντα/ογδόντα/ ενενήντα
one hundred	*ekató*	εκατό
one thousand	*chília*	χίλια

Months/Days

January	*Ianooários*	Ιανουάριος
February	*Fevrooários*	Φεβρουάριος
March	*Mártios*	Μάρτιος
April	*Aprílios*	Απρίλιος
May	*Máios*	Μάιος
June	*Ioónios*	Ιούνιος
July	*Ioólios*	Ιούλιος
August	*Avgoostos*	Αύγουστος
September	*Septémvrios*	Σεπτέμβριος
October	*Októvrios*	Οκτώβριος
November	*Noémvrios*	Νοέμβριος
December	*Thekémvrios*	Δεκέμβριος
Sunday	*Kiriakí*	Κυριακή
Monday	*Theftéra*	Δευτέρα
Tuesday	*Tríti*	Τρίτη
Wednesday	*Tetárti*	Τετάρτη
Thursday	*Pémpti*	Πέμπτη
Friday	*Paraskeví*	Παρασκευή
Saturday	*Sávato*	Σάββατο

Transport

the airport/aeroplane	*to arothrómio/aropláno*	το αεροδρόμιο/αεροπλάνο
the bus station	*ee stási too leoforíou*	η στάση του λεωφορείου
the railway station/the train	*o stathmós too trénou/to tréno*	ο σταθμός του τρένου/το τρένο
the port/port authority	*to limáni/limenarchío*	το λιμάνι/λιμεναρχείο
the ship	*to plío, to karávi*	το πλοίο, το καράβι
the car	*to aftokínito*	το αυτοκίνητο
a ticket	*éna isitírio*	ένα εισιτήριο

Further Reading

If you can't find these titles at home, the better bookshops in Crete carry many of them.

Beevor, Anthony, *The Battle of Crete and the Resistance* (Penguin, 1992). A concise history.

Butler, Alan, *The Bronze Age Computer Disc* (Foulsham, 1998). A new interpretation of the Phaistos Disc: that it's really a complex astronomical calendar.

Cadogan, Gerald, *Palaces of Minoan Crete* (Barrie & Jenkins, 1976). Good detailed guide.

Castledon, Rodney, *Minoans: Life in Bronze Age Crete* (Routledge, 1994). A good summing-up of the finds, including recent discoveries.

Chadwick, John, *The Decipherment of Linear B* (Cambridge, 1967). How Michael Ventris and Chadwick discovered that the Knossos tablets were in an early form of Greek.

Clark, Alan, *The Fall of Crete* (Cassell Military Paperbacks, 2001). Lively, well written account, with good analysis and anecdotes.

Cox, Anthony, *Still Life in Crete* (Universal, 2001). Crete too has its Peter Mayle: a British ex-journo who sold up and moved to a village near Chaniá with his wife (and dogs).

Detorakis, Theocharis E., *History of Crete* (local edition, 1994). The only book in English to cover the subject in complete depth.

Godfrey, Jonnie and Elizabeth Karslake, *Landscapes of Eastern Crete* and *Landscapes of Western Crete* (Sunflower, 2002). Detailed walking guides.

Hawkes, Jacquetta, *Dawn of the Gods* (Chatto & Windus. 1968). Supports the view that priestesses, not priests, led the Minoans.

Higgins, Reynold, *Minoan and Mycenaean Art* (Thames & Hudson). Fine pictorial survey.

Hopkins, Adam, *Crete, Its Past, Present and People* (Faber & Faber). Excellent introduction to the island and islanders.

Horwitz, Sylvia L., *The Find of a Lifetime: Sir Arthur Evans and the Discovery of Knossos* (Phoenix Press, 2001). Still a great story.

Kazantzákis, Níkos. His Cretan books *Zorba the Greek* and *Freedom or Death* (*Captain Michalis*) are must-reads; *Report to Greco* has vivid scenes of Crete in the 1900s.

Khourdakis, Aristophanes, *Wooden Mary: Folktales from the Island of Crete* (local edition). Cretan fairytales.

Kondylákis, Ioánnis, *Patouchas* (Efstathiadis, 1987). A comic 19th-century 'anthropological' novel about a big oaf in a Cretan village.

Kornáros, Vincenzo, *Erotókritos*, trans. Theodore Stefanides (Merlin Press). Crete's (and Greece's) classic epic poem.

Moss, Stanley W., *Ill Met by Moonlight* (Cassell Military Paperbacks, 1999) Thrilling account of the capture of General Kreipe by one of the leaders of the operation.

Platon, Nikos, *Zákros: the Discovery of a Lost Palace of Ancient Crete* (Scribners. 1971). The story and analysis of his famous find.

Prevelákis, Pandélis, *Tale of a Town* (Doric). Nostalgic story of Réthymnon before the exchange of populations in 1922.

Psilakis, Nikos, *Monasteries and Byzantine Memories of Crete* (Karmanor, 1994). Illustrated guide to the churches and frescoes, packed with fine insights.

Psilakis, Nikos and Maria, *Cretan Cooking* (Karmanor, 2000). With 265 recipes.

Psychoundakis, George, *The Cretan Runner*. A unique, delightful account of the Resistance by an active Cretan participant.

Rackham, Oliver and Jennifer Moody, *The Making of the Cretan Landscape* (Univ. of Manchester, 1997). How Crete got to look the way it does, through geology and human action.

Willetts, R. F., *Everyday Life in Ancient Crete* (Batsford, 1969). Easy-to-read account of life in Minoan times; see too his *Ancient Crete:* (Routledge, 1965) and *Cretan Cults and Festivals* (Barnes and Noble, 1962).

Wilson, Loraine, *The White Mountains of Crete* (Cicerone Press, 2000). The best guide to hiking in the White Mountains.

Wunderlich, H. G., *The Secret of Crete* (Efstathiadis, 1983). Cranky theory that the Minoan palaces were temples of the dead.

Index

Main page references are in **bold**. Page references to maps are in *italics*.

Crete touring atlas

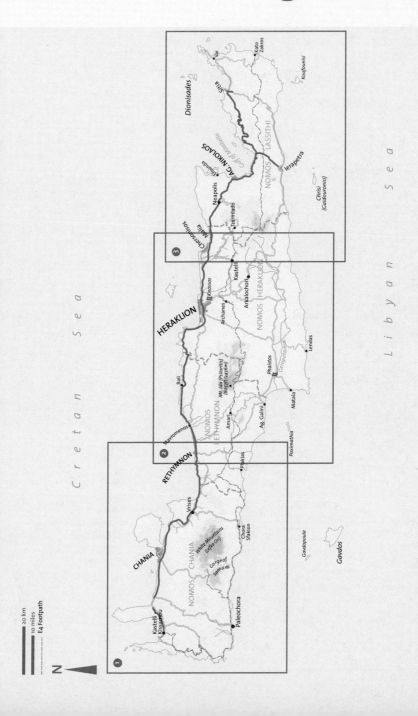

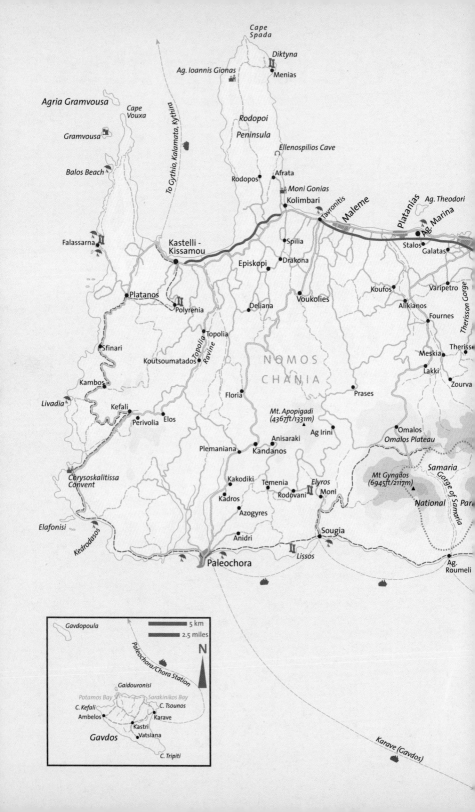

N

C r e t a n   S e a

Katholikon

Stavros

Moni Gouvernetou

Tersanas

Moni Ag. Triada

To Piraeus

*Akrotiri
Peninsula*

CHANIA

+ *Profitis Ilias*

Kourakies

Aroni

Sternes

Marathi

Moni Chryssopigi
Souda

Nea Souda

Mournies

Malaxa

Kalami

*Souda
Bay*

Cape Drapanon

To Piraeus

Megala
Chorafia

Aptera

Plaka

Kokkino Chorio

Kalyves

Almirida

RETHYMNON

Stilos

Gavalochori

Drapanos

Mistria

Samonas

Neo Chorio

Xerosterni

Macheri

Kefalas

Vamos

Fres

Almiros Bay

Vrises

Exopoli

Georgioupolis

Gerani

*NOMOS
CHANIA*

Alikampos

Episkopi

Lake Kournas

Armeni

*White Mountains
(Lefka Ori)*

Kournas

NOMOS

▲ *Mt. Pachnes
(8051ft/2454m)*

Amoudari

Askyfou

Argiroupoli

Lappa

RETHYMNON

Asi Gonia

2

Miriokefala

Kanevos

Koxare

Ag. Ioannis

Asfendos

Kalikratis

Mixorouma

Aradena

Imbros Gorge

Rodakino

Selia

Mirthios

Asomatos

Finix

Anopolis

Koumitades

Plakias

Kourtaliotis Gorge

Loutro

Chora
Sfakion

Lefkogia

Frangokastello

Korakas

Damnoni

Marmara Beach

Ammoudi

*Moni
Preveli*

Palm Beach

Karave (Gavdos)

L i b y a n   S e a

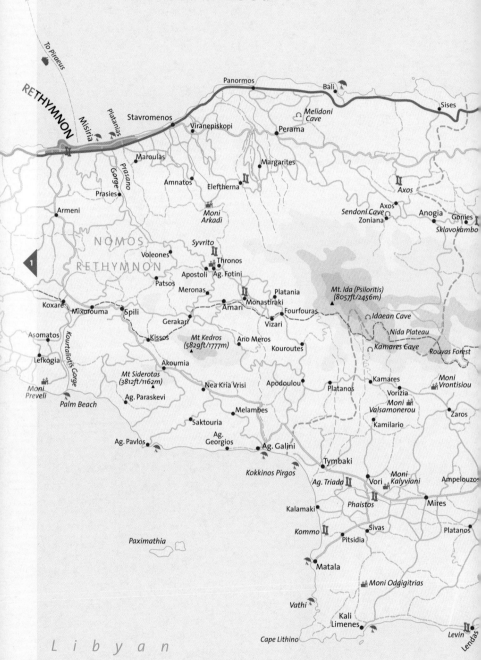

Cretan Sea

Dia

10 km
5 miles
E4 Footpath

N

To Piraeus, Thessaloniki, Cyclades

To Kasos, Karpathos, Rhodes

Cape
Stavros

Ag. Pelagia

Fodele

Savvathiana
Convent

Palaiokastro

Ammoudara

HERAKLION

Amnisos
Vathiano Kambo
Nirou Chani
Kokkini Chani
Gournes

Chersonisos

Skavidaras

Karteros

Cave of Eileithyia

E75

Gouves

Stalida

Mallia

Tylisos

Tylisos

Knossos

Elia

Skotino

Skalani

Potamies

Mochos

Episkopi

Fourni

Avdou

Anemospilia

Myrtia

Kato
Karouzana

Gonies
Kera

Archanes

Peza

Ag Myronas

Moni
Vidianis

Krousonas

Dafnes

Ag Vasilios

Sklaverochori

Kastelli

Lyttos

Profitis Ilias

Vathypetro

Voni

Xidas

Ano Asites

Venerato

Moni Páliani

Choudetsi

Ag. Charalambos
Plati

Ryzenia

Thrapsano

Psychro

Prinias

NOMOS

Diktean Cave

HERAKLION

Arkalochori

3

Ag. Varvara

Metaxochori

Panagia

Gergeri

Embaros

Martha

Ano
Viannos

Ag. Deka

Loures

Priansos

Kato
Viannos

Amiras

Gortyn

Protoria

Philippi

Kato
Kastelliana

Chondros

Geropotamos

Vagonia

Charakas

Pyrgos

Inatos

Keratokambos

Arvi

Loukia

Tsoutsouros

Kapetania

Moni
Koudouma

Libyan Sea

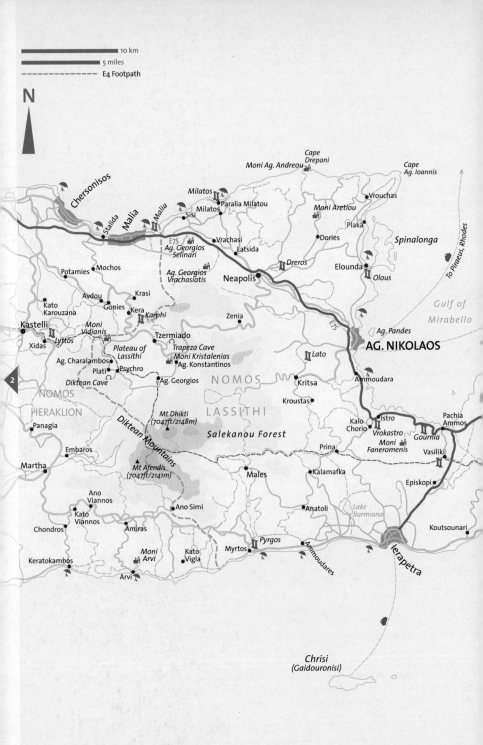

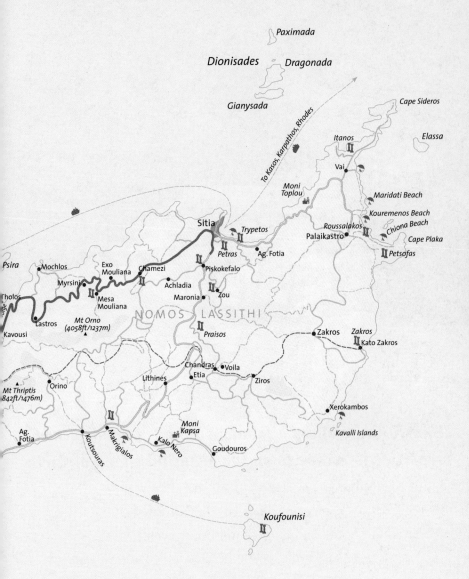

Cretan   Sea

Paximada

Dionisades   *Dragonada*

Cape Sideros

Gianysada

Elassa

Itanos

Vai

To Kasos, Karpathos, Rhodes

Moni Toplou

Maridati Beach

Kouremenos Beach

Chiona Beach

Sitia

Trypetos

Roussalakos

Palaikastro

Cape Plaka

Petras

Ag. Fotia

Petsofas

Psira

Mochlos

Exo Mouliana

Chamezi

Piskokefalo

Myrsini

Achladia

Tholos

Mesa Mouliana

Maronia

Zou

Lastros

Mt Orno (4058ft/1237m)

NOMOS   LASSITHI

Kavousi

Praisos

Zakros

Zakros

Kato Zakros

Chandras

Voila

Mt Thriptis 842ft/1476m

Orino

Lithines

Etia

Ziros

Ag. Fotia

Xerokambos

Moni Kapsa

Goudouros

Kavalli Islands

Koutsouras

Makrigialos

Kalo Nero

Koufounisi

SIMPLY *Crete*

Simply Crete offers a fabulous range of hand-picked properties to escape to on the beautiful island of Crete

Elegant Venetian houses in sleepy hamlets...

...Sophisticated villas with private pools...

...Intimate hotels in historical harbourtowns...

...Simple, rustic houses in seaside villages

To order a brochure, please call our 24-hour brochure line
020 8541 2222
or visit our website www.simplytravel.com